FACING THE MUSIC

by
Harold C. Schonberg

SUMMIT BOOKS
NEW YORK

1   3   5   7   9   10   8   6   4   2

Library of Congress Cataloging in Publication Data

Schonberg, Harold C.
Facing the music.

Includes index.
1. Music—Addresses, essays, lectures. I. Title.
ML60.S382   780   81-470
AACR2
ISBN 0-671-25406-5

Grateful acknowledgment is hereby made to The New York Times Company
for permission to print all of the pieces included in this book, copyright ©
1957, 1959, 1960, 1961, 1962, 1963, 1964, 1965, 1966, 1967, 1968, 1969, 1970,
1971, 1972, 1973, 1974, 1975, 1976, 1977, 1978, 1979, 1980 by The New York
Times Company.

To Helene

Contents

PART III—Composers

PART IV—Contemporary Music

PART V—Opera

PART IX—Miscellany

FACING
THE
MUSIC

Introduction

Wᴴᴱɴ I became a music critic I had worked at the piano almost since babyhood, had gone through the studies that all musicians go through—harmony, counterpoint, theory, even composition and conducting—but my only real talent, such as it was, was listening. I cannot remember ever not listening to music, wrapped in it, living with it and living it, totally responding to it. Virgil Thomson once had some amused, disparaging words to say about musical addicts. I happen to be an addict.

From the beginning I had a freak memory, though only in music. Two or three hearings were enough to place a long composition permanently in my mind. I was born in Washington Heights, on the upper West Side of New York City, on November 29, 1915, and my father, who loved music, had a fairly large collection of Red Seal records. He told me, many years later, that I had memorized all of those records before I could read. I also could identify any of the singers on hearing the record. I was about three years old. The records, curiously, are still in my memory. I vividly remember the disc of Karl Muck and the Boston Symphony in the finale of the Tchaikovsky Fourth and also in an excerpt from one of the Tchaikovsky suites (which I especially loved). I remember crying when I heard the Caruso record of *Vesti la giubba.* (The only other time I remember crying was when I first heard Mozart's G minor Symphony. I must have been eight or nine. Tears rushed to my eyes at the announcement of that wonderful theme.) I remember the

13

Melbas and the Galli-Curcis and the Paderewskis and all the rest.

I also discovered that I had a strange sort of disease. Music was *always* in my head, waking and, apparently, sleeping, and so it is today. It is not always pleasant, this inner, insistent, obsessive counterpoint to daily life. As I type these words, one of the Bach-Busoni chorale-preludes *(Rejoice, Beloved Christians)* is going through my head, triggered by my having, an hour ago, glanced at a new recording of the Bach-Busoni that had just arrived. My wife tells me that she can poke me while I am sleeping. "What are you listening to?" I mumble the name of the piece without waking up. I had trouble in school because of this affliction, and many were the teachers I enraged. They thought I wasn't paying attention. By the time I got to high school I had learned to control myself and look interested in class, even if a Brahms symphony was pounding away in my head.

I never became much of a pianist. Assigned a Beethoven sonata, I would work furiously for a week, extract the essence, and then start reading (or, more exactly stumbling) through the other thirty-one sonatas. I never could play a single one with any accuracy or finish, but by the time I was twelve or thirteen, I was familiar with most of them, and a few years later I had them all in my musical memory, especially when the Schnabel recordings started to come out. With friends, I voraciously read through the chamber-music and symphony literature in four-hand arrangements, automatically memorizing as I went along. What with that, and constant listening to records and the classical-music programs on the radio (and there was an extraordinary amount of live music on the air in the early 1930's), and all the concerts and operas I could get to (my parents let me go to concerts after my twelfth birthday), I knew the standard repertory very well as a youth.

It was all serious music. I disliked jazz then, and still do. The only time in my life I was exposed to jazz was in the army, where it was inescapable. At that, I managed to remain pure, blocking out the sounds that came my way and substituting in my inner ear the *Well-Tempered Clavier* or whatever. I really could do it. In close-order drill, which revolted me even more than K.P. or sentry duty, I would march to the strains of the Chopin E minor Concerto (and very good marching music it is; try it). "Schonberg!" the drill sergeant would roar. "Schonberg! You're bobbing in ranks!" A few years ago, when Bing Crosby died, the deputy managing editor of *The New York Times* asked me to write an appreciation. I told him I couldn't do it; that I had never heard Bing Crosby either in person or on records, and that the only thing I did remember about him were those films with Bob Hope and Dorothy Lamour. The editor refused to believe me, even after I patiently explained that I had spent my life in a certain discipline and that Bing Crosby, undeniably a great man, was outside my discipline. He looked at me as though I had two heads.

As an emergent musician I was helped by my Aunt Alice. She had been a Godowsky pupil and then made a successful career under the name of Alice Frisca for several seasons in the early 1920's. She must have been good. I have inherited her memorabilia, and a second-rater could not have amassed the reviews she got. She got enthusiastic notices in England when she played the Liszt *Hungarian Fantasy* under the baton of Sir Henry Wood, and the French critics were talking about her in terms of Carreño. She gave a successful New York concert at Aeolian Hall, married my mother's brother and never again played in public. Indeed, she hardly ever even touched the piano. She told me that she had started at the age of five, had been practicing seven hours a day from the age of twelve, and that the grind had become distasteful to her. Aunt Alice would play through a piece that was giving me trouble, clarifying the meaning of a phrase or a technical problem. I think I learned more from her than from anybody else.

When I was twelve I resolved to be a music critic. I could always write easily and coherently, and I figured out that to get paid for doing the thing I loved best—listening to music and comparing performances—was the life for me. I had a critical mind from the beginning. A critical mind is constantly asking questions, probing, reading, comparing, trying to work out a rationale. A critical mind also immerses itself totally in its sub-

ject. I had no trouble in school, and I led a fairly normal childhood, but it was music that was a full-time occupation from the
beginning. I read everything about it that I could lay my hands
on, searched out material, tried to formulate a musical esthetic.
It was a call—as much a call as the rabbinate or priesthood.

In Brooklyn College and at the graduate school of New York
University, I took all the music courses and as many English
courses as I could, sitting in at many for which I received no
credit. If I couldn't make it as a critic, I planned to be a great
authority on Elizabethan literature. All of my papers had a musical subject: Browning and music, Shakespeare and music, the
Elizabethan masque, Milton and *Comus*. My master's thesis had
a resounding title: "Elizabethan Song Books: A Study of Their
Musical and Literary Significance." The English Department did
not know how to deal with the musical elements of the thesis,
and the Music Department did not know how to deal with the
literary side. An A-plus was virtually assured in advance.

It was Aunt Alice who got me my first critical job. While I
was in college she sent me to one of her friends, Spencer Driggs,
who ran a monthly magazine named *Musical Advance*. Mr.
Driggs gave me a monthly column, byline and all, and my first
piece came out in 1936. He also wanted me to sell advertising
for his magazine, but the very idea paralyzed me. We settled for
the column. No money was involved in those Depression days,
but I had tickets to concerts, and I had my first forum. I was a
working critic who could rub shoulders with the likes of Olin
Downes, Oscar Thompson, Pitts Sanborn and the other great
ones of the day. Marion Bauer, one of my teachers at New York
University, cheered me on. She was a great lady and an inspiring
teacher, and I became one of her many protégés. I was in her
esthetics and criticism class, and I also studied modern harmony
with her.

Miss Bauer was responsible for my first paid job. The year
after I got my master's degree, she sent me to Peter Hugh Reed,
the editor and publisher of *The American Music Lover*, a
monthly record magazine still in existence as the *American
Record Guide*. Mr. Reed took me on. The magazine was a two-
man operation, and I was assistant editor, record critic, feature

writer, typist, proofreader, makeup man, floor sweeper, and I loved every minute of it.

Mr. Reed ran the magazine from one room in the old Bible House off Astor Place, which he grandly called a suite. The masthead of the magazine listed Paul Girard as business manager. Paul Girard was Peter Hugh Reed. One of the steady contributors to the magazine was Neville d'Esterre. Neville d'Esterre was Peter Hugh Reed. I once asked him how he had come up with such a lovely name. He never answered. In the early 1920's he had toured as an actor in a David Belasco company. Perhaps Neville d'Esterre was one of his roles in a now-forgotten play.

We worked in the messiest office of the Bible House. Once in a while I would make an effort to clean up the litter of papers, records, publicity releases, galley proofs, envelopes, back issues, tear sheets, promotional material, cardboard liners, correspondence. Mr. Reed would get furious. "How can I find anything if you clean things up?" God had intended offices to be messy. The two associate reviewers, Philip L. Miller and Nathan Broder, would come in twice a month or so. Mr. Reed would take us to McSorley's Ale House, and there would be great talk over frankfurters, sauerkraut and beer. Phil Miller at the time was the only man in America who knew as much about vocal records as Mr. Reed. He later became head of the music division of the New York Public Library. Mr. Broder, soon to be one of America's most respected musicologists and a music editor at Norton's, helped out on some editorial work. He would take all copy home after I had worked on it, and send it back with exasperated comments. He was a much less permissive grammarian than I.

Those were the early days of records. Electrical recordings had been introduced only some fifteen years previously. There were only two companies, Victor and Columbia, that brought out large quantities of classical music, though occasionally independents like Musicraft would put out a disc. Every month was then an adventure, because every month brought hitherto unrecorded music by the great interpreters—Furtwängler, Flagstad, Gieseking, Schnabel, the Budapest Quartet, Lehmann, Heifetz. There actually was a time when a Mozart string quartet or a

Wolf song recital or a Mozart opera was coming out on records for the first time. I remember the fuss I kicked up when the Horowitz-Toscanini recording of the Tchaikovsky B flat minor Concerto was released. Why this senseless duplication when there already were versions by Rubinstein and Petri? I also remember nearly putting *The American Music Lover* out of business. I wrote such a violent review about an album—"The Heart of the Piano Concerto," in which Jesús María Sanromá played excerpts from the favorites—that Victor pulled out its advertising. It was the center spread, which paid the printing bill. Mr. Reed was terribly strapped for a while, but he never mentioned it to me.

I think he liked me. I know I adored him.

The war took over four years of my life. All of us knew that America would be drawn in. A year before Pearl Harbor I went to Floyd Bennett Naval Aviation Base to enlist as a flyer. Everything went beautifully at the physical until they threw the Ishihara color charts at me. To my horror, I discovered that I was pastel blind. At least, that is what the doctor told me. I could see primary colors, but certain shades of green and yellow confused me. I asked the doctor what that had to do with flying a plane. "Son," he said, "if you're up there in trouble, and have to take time out to figure which light is amber and which yellow, we don't want you."

The Navy would not have me. I successively got turned down as an aviation cadet by the Army, the Marines and the Coast Guard. I sulked and waited until I was drafted, in January, 1942. One way to get into the air was as a paratrooper, which I became after being commissioned a signal officer at the Fort Monmouth O.C.S. I also was cleared to work on high-level codes and ciphers after arriving in England, where I was a curiosity as one of the early Yanks there. Code work probably saved my life. I was scheduled for the Arnheim jump with the British First Parachute Division, and was pulled out only the night before because I was the only one around who was cleared to handle the incoming coded messages. I remember the first one: "Situation not repeat not good." The British got badly cut up on the jump.

I was one of the first into Paris, there with the first wave. It was one of the great moments in anybody's life, that final sweep from Le Mans and shortly thereafter up the Avenue de la Grande Armée, weeping girls jumping into our jeeps to embrace us.

I ended my army career ignominiously. A complicated airborne operation was being planned by General Brereton, head of the First Allied Airborne Army. (The operation was canceled after the Allies crossed the Rhine.) I was sent to Saint-Avord, near Bourges, to set up communications back to headquarters and to teach the French jumpers in the Premier Régiment des Chasseurs Parachutistes the American system of jumping. On my second jump with them I broke an ankle. There *was* a heavy wind that day. I was not the only casualty. Of the seven hundred or so who jumped, there was one fatality (malfunctioning chute) and about forty injuries. In America when an entire parachute division jumps, there is all but a congressional investigation if there are a half-dozen injuries. I had warned Colonel Faure, commander of the regiment, that there would be trouble because of the wind. I spent V-E day in a hospital in Liverpool, and V-J day on crutches in New York.

After separation from the service in January, 1946, I started to write for *Musical Digest* and *Musical Courier.* On the *Musical Courier,* I inherited the late Leonard Liebling's column, renaming it *Facing the Music,* and am using that title for this book. Irving Kolodin hired me as a music critic for *The New York Sun* in October, 1946. It takes a great deal of luck to break into newspaper criticism. Even then, when there were at least seven dailies, openings did not occur very often. Mr. Kolodin, who had been Oscar Thompson's assistant for many years on the *Sun,* became the critic when Thompson suddenly died. Mr. Kolodin now needed an assistant and took me on after trying me out as a stringer. Even there luck played a part. Arthur Berger, the junior critic of the *Sun,* was moving over to *The Herald Tribune.* Hence the vacancy. Before approaching me, Mr. Kolodin got in touch with Martin Feinstein, who thought about it and finally decided to move into the Hurok organization. Luck.

After working as a music critic for two years, I asked for city-side work in addition to criticism. The *Sun* was agreeable, and for two years I covered everything from City Hall to the Bronx Zoo during the day, and concerts at night.

The reportorial experience was valuable in more ways than I

could know at the time. When the *Sun* was sold to *The World-Telegram* on January 4, 1950, I had to free-lance. Howard Taubman, the music editor of the *Times,* seemed to be interested in me and gave me many assignments for Sunday pieces. He was a brilliant newspaperman and, I believe, the greatest music editor that any American newspaper has ever produced. He had been around for a long time, was news-oriented, had links everywhere, and was always being tipped off to big stories. In a period when no newspaper was very interested in music stories, Taubman was constantly on page one. He liked the idea that I had done so much general assignment reporting. When the venerable music critic Noël Straus became ill, Mr. Taubman recommended to Olin Downes, the head of the department, that I be taken into the music department of the *Times.* Apparently Mr. Downes was dubious. He thought I was too cocky.

But Mr. Downes went along with Mr. Taubman's suggestion, and we became friends of a sort. One of my jobs after I joined the *Times* in 1950 was to take care of Mr. Downes's copy. There never was copy like it. He may have been the only journalist in history to write his reviews in longhand and then correct them on the typewriter. It was a mess, and only one man in the composing room could decipher it. When I worked on Mr. Downes's Sunday pieces, I found it much easier to retype everything and start from there. Mr. Downes could have exasperating work habits. But I admired his real love for music, his enthusiasm, his courtly manners, his gargantuan appetites. He was authentically big, in every way.

Noël Straus had not yet fully retired, and worked at an adjacent desk. He was a fascinating man, over seventy then, a man who lived only for his mind. Mr. Straus had heard everything, studied everything, read everything. He was an expert on Byron, Hopkins, botany, Renaissance art, the voice, the piano, conducting, gastronomy. There seemed to be nothing he did not know. He also was a wit and had a healthy bawdy mind. He could be very funny, in a dry kind of way. Once in a while I could hear some of his conversations on the phone. When it rang, we both would reach for it, and one of us would take the call. But if things sounded promising, I would stay on, especially if it was an information call. We constantly get calls from the public wanting information, as often as not "to settle a bet." Mr. Straus sometimes handled these calls in a unique manner.

Once a lady called asking for the name of Tchaikovsky's patroness. "Sorry," said Mr. Straus. "Our von Meck editor is out for lunch." Even better was the call a man made to settle a bet. I hung on, letting Mr. Straus handle it.

"We are trying to identify a tune," the caller said. "Can you settle the bet?"

"Can you hum or whistle the tune?" asked Mr. Straus.

The man whistled the Dvorak *Humoresque.*

"I congratulate you," said Mr. Straus. "That was the fourth contrapunctus of the fifth polyphonic suite by Heinrich Cornelius von Schmeissmeier, composed in 1672. The interesting thing about it is that it is a canon at the octave. Furthermore . . ." and Mr. Straus went on in this vein for about five minutes.

There was a long pause.

"Would you mind repeating that?" the man asked.

Mr. Straus repeated it.

At the *Times* between 1950 and 1960 I did the usual daily work, nightly reviewing and, after 1955, record reviewing. I became the record editor, in charge of the weekly reviews in the drama section and responsible for the organization of the special record sections. Record reviewing was a hard, thankless job, and its only virtue lay in the fact that record critics get free records. It was a job that seemed to take infinite amounts of time. In the old days at *The American Music Lover* three critics could handle everything. But the 1950's saw the LP disc come of age. Suddenly there were twenty Beethoven Fifths in the Schwann catalogue, twenty-five versions of the Tchaikovsky Violin Concerto, as many of the Schubert *Unfinished,* even five or six complete recordings of the Beethoven quartets. If a record critic took his work seriously, if he was to be of any help to readers who wanted to know what version of this or that to buy, he had to spend hours comparing a dozen or so recordings of the same piece. It got to be a terrible chore. But there were compensations: all kinds of new music to hear, new artists to evaluate, new audio techniques to explore. Record critics ended up with immense working collections. In my apartment there were records on shelves, in closets, under the bed. One by-product was a desperate wife whose dream of beauty and efficiency was buried under an avalanche of records.

Traditionally the low man in a music department gets the least glamorous concerts, and I was no exception. I did know more about the piano and its literature than the other members of the department, and Mr. Taubman was constantly sending me to cover piano recitals. After a while, I think, I was typed by the music world as (a) a frustrated pianist, and (b) a critic who knew only the piano. As a matter of fact, I had spent more time at the Metropolitan Opera—and at the Salmaggi Opera at the Hippodrome, too—than I had in the concert halls when I was growing up. But it may be true that I have more of an emotional affinity to the piano than to the voice, though goodness knows I love singing and do not make many mistakes about vocal quality and technique.

Mr. Downes died in 1955 and Mr. Taubman replaced him. In 1960, after Brooks Atkinson retired as drama critic, Mr. Taubman took over that desk. Turner Catledge, then managing editor of the *Times,* called me into his office. Did I want to replace Mr. Taubman as music critic? What a question.

The *Times* gave me a title: Senior Music Critic. Up to then the chief critic of the *Times,* and any other newspaper, had been known merely as *the* critic. On the *Sun,* Mr. Kolodin had been *the* music critic and I had been an assistant critic. On the *Times,* Mr. Downes and then Mr. Taubman was *the* music critic. I rather liked the title of Senior Music Critic. In 1960 I still looked very young, and people who had been reading me for some twenty years would say, on meeting me, "But you are so *young. . . .*" I would point out that Mr. Downes had been younger than I when he became *the* critic in 1924.

People have strange ideas about the life of the top *Times* critic in so glamorous a city as New York. The popular notion runs something as follows: The critic ambles into the concert hall or opera house in his own good time. He leaves early because of the deadline, and writes his review. Exhausted by this stupendous effort, he has to revive himself with champagne at the Oak

Room, where he bandies words with the great figures of New York's society and intellectual life. At four A.M. he tumbles into bed and sleeps until noon. Then he rises, has a leisurely lunch at the Café des Artistes with Luciano Pavarotti, telling him what went wrong with his last *Rigoletto*. After lunch he drops in to see Vladimir Horowitz, telling him what to play next year; then passes the rest of the afternoon with Zubin Mehta, who humbly asks him how to conduct *Also sprach Zarathustra*; then dines with Anthony Bliss and tells him how to run the Metropolitan Opera; then goes home, has his valet put him into white tie and tails, summons his limousine and is driven to that evening's event.

Maybe it worked that way in the past. One reads the reminiscences of Henry T. Finck or Herman Klein with amazement. They knew everybody, were close friends of artists they regularly reviewed, and were always at parties or dinners attended by the great ones of music.

Today things are different, to a point where many music critics won't even talk to each other, much less become friends with musicians they have to review. There are today, it is true, some critics who actively enter into the musical life of the community.

But not the critics of *The New York Times.*

Naturally we meet many musicians on a professional basis— for interviews, background material, feature pieces, gossip. As newspapermen we have to know what is going on. We cultivate a network of sources and even of Deep Throats. But that is acquaintance, not friendship. Virgil Thomson once said that he could review his own grandmother, and it would make no difference. I was skeptical about that statement then and I remain skeptical now. Can any human be *that* dispassionate? In addition, the musical colony is small and inbred, and it can be vicious. Nobody will ever believe that a *Times* critic can give an impartial review to a friend. Hence as a matter of policy *Times* critics are not supposed to be close to musicians they may be in a position of reviewing. If they are close—and sometimes that is unavoidable—the critic is supposed to disqualify himself. I have been in that position. My late wife went to college with a young man who became a celebrated performer. She did not want to close the door on him, though she did try to keep personal contact to a minimum. In over four decades of professional criticism I have been close to only four musicians, and I won't tell you who they are.

By the same token, no *Times* critic can himself be a performer or composer. No matter how pure he may be, conductors or potentates of the musical establishment will be after him, flattering him, offering him commissions or performances. I saw too much of that on the *Herald Tribune,* where most of the critics were composers, and some of them jockeyed shamelessly to get their music played. Nor is a *Times* critic allowed to write for any publication that would even remotely suggest a conflict of interest. That of course includes writing program or liner notes. It may appear harmless enough, but the critic would then be accepting money from the New York Philharmonic, the Metropolitan Opera or whatever. Some critics write all kinds of program notes; and, considering the salaries many of them receive, it is understandable that they need to augment their income. But it still leaves a bad taste in my mouth.

It is a policy rigidly enforced by me, and it is a policy that angers many musicians. Some years ago I gave an informal lecture (for which, I hasten to add, I did not accept any money) to the Juilliard students. Peter Mennin called me. He said that I was the mystery man of New York music, and that the students and faculty would love to have the chance to size me up and discuss things with me. I accepted. It was a question and answer, no-holds-barred session. Somewhere along the way a boy got up. He had a personal question. Would I answer it? "We hear you do not mix with musicians. What's the matter? Are you too good for us?"

I asked him what instrument he was studying, and with whom.

"Piano, with Beveridge Webster."

"Now *you* answer *me* honestly," I said. "If you knew that Mr. Webster and I were very close friends, would you believe anything I wrote about him?"

That thought obviously had never occurred to him. He brooded about it for a moment.

"No," he reluctantly said.

"And would you believe anything I wrote about another pianist?"

The boy sat down.

In any case, as a junior critic for the *Times* I never could have managed to find the time for a glamorous social life even had I wanted to. Each of the five work days was completely filled up. There were releases to be read, interviews to be held. There may have been a breaking story that had to be taken care of immediately, or an obit to be written, or an advance obit to be prepared, or a press conference to which I had been assigned. There was mail to be answered ("Obviously we were not at the same concert last night . . ."). At home, there were records to be listened to, scores to study, books and magazines to be read, and that took care of days off. I have made an effort to keep up with the literature, and still religiously leaf through European magazines, musicological studies and record reviews. I won't pretend I read everything, but I do go through any article on a subject that interests me.

And in those days there was the Sunday page to worry about. Copy had to be prepared, edited and processed. Pictures had to be located and captions written. Record columns had to be worked up. Layouts had to be made.

Thus—on the *Times*, at any rate—the position of music critic involves as much a journalistic as a musical function. We are highly trained newspapermen who are able to handle any story that comes our way. But, of course, it is the music that comes first, and any *Times* critic has to have impeccable musical credentials. The editors of the *Times*, no matter their degree of cultural sophistication (and a surprisingly large number of them are highly sophisticated indeed), believe that the paper has a responsibility to culture. With the worldwide cultural expansion of the last two decades, cultural space in the *Times* has increased proportionately. Abe Rosenthal, executive editor of the *Times*, may have grumbled when I asked for more help, but he gave it to me, and at the point of this writing the music department of the *Times* has six full-time critics devoted to serious music, a jazz critic, a rock critic and stringers as needed. (A stringer is a non-staff contributor who gets paid for each assignment or Sunday piece.) Arthur Gelb, the deputy managing editor, often cried when I asked for more space, but eventually he always managed to come up with it.

As responsible editors they realize that coverage of the arts demands specially trained writers. Long gone are the days when somebody was picked as a music critic because he happened to be around when one was needed, or because he had taken a music appreciation course in college. They would not think of hiring a music critic without the approval of the head of the department—who, in any case, submits several candidates before one is chosen. The senior music critic has the last word; he is the expert and the editors normally do not challenge his judgment. Through the years, when taking on a new man, I have looked for a combination of musical and journalistic background. The music comes first, of course. We can teach a bright young man a great deal about journalism in a few years. We cannot teach him music; one has to grow up in the art. Music critics, after all, are in effect telling Rudolf Serkin how to play the piano, Zubin Mehta how to conduct, Jon Vickers how to sing; and to do that, one must have a lifetime of background and knowledge to fall back upon. A lot of confidence and a strong ego also help.

My ideas about newspaper criticism are simplistic. I have no highfalutin notions. I work on the assumption that my paper pays me to go to a musical event and write what I think about it. So I go to the concert or opera, return to the office and write what I think about it. This is not much of an oversimplification. I am perfectly aware of the responsibilities of a powerful critic; and, of course, the *Times* critics are ipso facto powerful critics. But as long as a critic retains his integrity, plays no favorites, works out of love for his art, has a passionate conviction and brings to his work a background equivalent to that of the musicians he is reviewing, he can do no more.

I write for no audience, and I express no taste but my own. Basically I write for myself: I have been stimulated, or bored, or excited, or repelled, and I put my feelings down on paper (or, to be exact, on the computer terminals, these days). As much as the composer, as much as the artists who interpret the composer, I am expressing an opinion based on a lifetime of thought. And, almost always, a veteran critic has a much wider fund of experience than the artists, who generally know everything about their own field, not very much outside of it. This may sound arrogant, but arrogance is not confined exclusively to singers, composers or musicologists. Gregor Piatigorsky, at a conference, once listened with fury while performers and their egos were being attacked by a panel of composers. Finally he took the floor. "I know of no composer," he said, "who has written a humble symphony or a sincere sonata." Nor do I. Generally the humble critic, like the humble musician, is the one who has the most to be humble about. If you have strong ideas and fervent beliefs, a certain amount of arrogance is necessarily involved. At least some of us have learned how to express our arrogance in polite, civilized terms.

Young critics tend to enter the field full of grand visions for the betterment of the musical world. They usually are much tougher than the older, more experienced ones. Later all critics come to realize that they are not, after all, going to revolutionize music. As a matter of fact, they learn that what they write is of more importance to themselves than to their readers. A good deal of nonsense has been written about the "power" of the critic. Perhaps the drama critic may have a great deal of power. Not the music critic, though some think they do. (I loathe and despise critics with a power complex: critics who use the job to aggrandize themselves, throw their weight around, try to attract attention to themselves, play favorites or politics.) There is no case in history where a great piece of music or a great performer has been mortally wounded by a negative or stupid review. Critics don't make careers. Artists make careers. A bad review in the *Times* may set a career back for a season or two; a strongly favorable one may help for a season or two. That is about all. There are artists who have received rave reviews in the *Times* and have promptly disappeared. There are artists who have been all but crucified, with no apparent effect on their popularity. For years, as an example, Leonard Bernstein could not get a favorable review in the *Times* or *Herald Tribune*. What difference did an unfavorable review make to him except bruise his ego?

I also find it hard to believe that experienced critics will fail to recognize talent. It is possible to argue about the talent, to question the road it is taking—but talent immediately is apparent. If an artist gets brushed off with a two-paragraph review in the *Times,* the chances are that it is deserved. If an artist gets a half-column negative review, that half-column means that the reviewer is taking the artist very seriously—seriously enough to expend time and effort to make his viewpoint clear.

At best a critic can do nothing more than throw ideas around and make his readers think. Each critic has his strengths and weaknesses, and each follows his particular vision. Right or wrong does not enter into it. Naturally every critic thinks he is "right," just as every musician thinks he is "right," but nobody as yet has been able to define right or wrong. Often I am asked how many mistakes I have made during my career. How can that be answered? My only response is that a judgment can be made about my work fifty years from now. How many major new (or old) creative figures did I miss? Was I right or wrong in not liking the music of Pierre Boulez or Elliott Carter? If, fifty years from now, Boulez and Carter are admired composers, constantly in the repertory, I was wrong. It is the public, not the critic, that eventually determines the fate of a creator. As for judgments on performing artists, we get into a gray area. Most critics and professional musicians are more or less agreed on the basic quality of talent, but it is how the talent is used that creates divisions. Take a conductor like Zubin Mehta. I happen to admire his work, on the whole. Many other critics deplore it, calling him a sensationalist, shallow, interested in effect rather than substance. I see certain strengths in his conducting, others see certain weaknesses. All I can say is that my standards are different from those of the other critics, and what annoys them so much does not bother me at all. "Right"? "Wrong"? I don't know. All I can do is report what my ears and experience tell me.

For there are as many approaches to music criticism as there are critics, just as there are as many approaches to the *Eroica* Symphony as there are conductors. Criticism, like conducting, piano playing, singing, composition or virtually any activity in life, is a function of personality. The critic brings to bear on everything he hears his own background, his own esthetic prejudices, his intuition, his sensitivity (or lack of it), his fallibilities, his assets. Some critics are fascinated with performance practice. Some, especially the younger ones, know relatively little about performance practice but do know a great deal about the techniques of contemporary music. Some approach music as part of the historical continuum. Some approach it impressionistically (these are apt to be the amateur critics) and some objectively. There have been critics who have been bored with music to the point of hating it (which, however, did not seem to affect their critical faculties). Some see music purely as a series of forms expressed in sound. Others see it as a reflection of psyche and soul, as a manifestation of the Divine.

My specialty happens to be performance practice. In a city like New York, with its enormous diversity of music, the position of senior music critic of *The New York Times* can be pretty much what he makes of it. He can ride his hobbies and cater to his own interests as long as certain requirements are maintained. The *Times* is, after all, a newspaper and not a specialized music journal. Certain events are expected to be covered by the leading critic, such as Metropolitan Opera, City Opera and Philharmonic openings, the concerts of superstars, new productions and important premières. I once managed to break the rule—in 1968, when the Metropolitan Opera opened its season with *Adriana Lecouvreur,* bowing to the wishes of Renata Tebaldi. I dislike that opera, and also thought that Rudolf Bing had capitulated to his prima donna. So I looked around to see what else was going on that night, and the only thing so early in the season was a Mozart program in Town Hall, played by young artists. Into Town Hall I marched, and started my review the next morning with "Last night the only good music in New York was played at Town Hall," or something like that. It was a bit childish, I admit, and neither the front office of the Metropolitan Opera nor the editors of the *Times* were particularly amused.

But the *Times* always let me follow my own tastes, and those tastes happen to be oriented in the nineteenth century. Of course I also reviewed a great deal of contemporary and avant-

garde music, and my approach to the avant-garde did not make
me very popular in those circles. Early in my career as senior
music critic I took a strong stand against the international serial
movement, calling it sterile, academic, boring and sure to alienate the public. Naturally I was branded a bourgeois conservative,
and there was a good deal of resentment. Critics are supposed to
encourage the new, not attack it.

But the more I studied and heard the new music, the more
appalled I became, and I saw no reason to be a propagandist for
a kind of music I thought simply hateful. I believed then, as I
believe now, that whatever form or vocabulary a new movement
has, the least one can look for is invention and personality—and
I could find none of that in the dreary exercises of the serial
movement. I watched in amazement as composers from Germany, England, France, America, kept writing much the same
kind of arid, totally dissonant, super-intellectualized music, and
I screamed about it. Nor have I been proved demonstrably
wrong. It may even be that I was right for the wrong reasons, but
the fact remains that during some twenty-five years of serialism
and its derivatives, not a single piece entered the permanent
international repertory. And today composers have all but de-
serted the movement, beating their breasts and crying *mea
culpa,* looking once more to the past and writing a much looser
and more personal kind of music. I take a sort of wry pleasure in
the sight. Perhaps my complaints were justified, after all. I also
find the emergent Neoromanticism much more palatable than
the music of the serialists, and have been able to write about
some of it with real enthusiasm.

It is of course no secret that my critical specialty is in the area
of performance practice, especially nineteenth-century performance practice. It is a useful specialty. A critic on a big-city
daily, after all, spends well over three-quarters of his working
life with the standard repertory. That is what orchestras, opera
companies and most soloists and chamber groups deal with.
Nobody can say much about a Beethoven symphony, but a great
deal can be said about the interpretation and performance of the
work. To make any cogent points about the interpretation of
works of the past, however, a critic must know a great deal
about the performing history of the work.

As a child I realized that performers "did" things to music—sometimes elegantly and convincingly, sometimes outlandishly and stupidly. It puzzled me that pianists could play the same work so differently. The notes and note values were all faithfully observed, the tempos were on the whole similar, the work was *recognizably* the same—and yet there was a vast difference between, say, Harold Bauer, Mischa Levitzki and Josef Hofmann in the same Schumann or Chopin piece. Accents, emphases, chord weightings, inner voices, melodic outlines—each pianist had his own idea of how they should go. It fascinated me, and I grew up constantly comparing performances in the concert halls, in the opera house, on records, trying to figure out why there could be such a complete diversity of approach.

Obviously all of these superior performers were "correct" in their interpretations; they were coherent, convincing and imaginative, no matter how they differed. Thus as a youngster I came to realize that the artist had everything to do with how the music sounded. All that the composer could do was suggest. As most of us today realize, notation is a very inexact science. A composer writes *allegro,* but his ideas of the pace of his *allegro* have to be interpreted by an artist born two hundred years later, and no two artists have exactly the same idea about the original *allegro* marking. Probably the composer never worried about it too much. Composers have been willing to give interpreters a great deal of liberty as long as the intent and feeling of the piece are observed. Slavish adherence to the printed note is a relatively new phenomenon.

Thus anybody engaged in re-creating the bare, mysterious notes and markings of a composer necessarily has to bring his own ideas to them. Notes alone mean nothing, except to the handful of people in the world who have the ability to read and translate into sounds in the inner ear a page of printed music. Notes have to be played, and it is the performer who has to be the intermediary between composer and listener. Music, then, is a reflection, an interpretation, of the mind of the composer expressed through the mind of the performer.

I have spent a good part of my life trying to figure out what "authentic" performance is. It may be that the question is unanswerable, but there are certain guidelines. There is in existence a continuity of performance tradition. There also is the testimony, on old phonograph records, of those hundreds of artists who were born in the nineteenth century and for the most part played, sang and conducted the music of that century. Most people, professionals included, have very little idea of the wealth of material on early records. We can hear Joseph Joachim play Bach and Brahms—Joachim, born in 1831, the greatest Classical violinist of the century, the close friend of Brahms and Clara Schumann. We can hear, also, Pablo de Sarasate playing Bach and his own music—Sarasate, born in 1844, the Romantic, virtuoso counterpart to the severe Joachim. We can hear Vladimir de Pachmann play Chopin, and Chopin was still alive when Pachmann was born in 1848. We can hear the stupendous singers who so excited the world in the last quarter of the century and even before—singers like Patti, Lilli Lehmann, Eames, Melba, de Lucia, Sembrich, Plançon and dozens like them. They were not only close to their period; in much of their repertory they *were* of the period, and they understood certain conventions that composers could not notate, or did not feel it necessary to notate, knowing that all musicians of the day had a common culture.

They were wildly differing personalities, those demigods of the past, but different as they were, they all had certain things in common. They demonstrate an ideal of technique, of color, of tempo, of phrasing, that is a forgotten art today. They also back up Schonberg's Law, which postulates that through the decades there has been a glacial shift in tempos. Musicians today are prevailingly *slower* than they used to be. In recent years we have arrived at the point where slowness and even lethargy seem to be equated with profundity. And that is all wrong. A study of old recordings is one of the most valuable tools in any survey of performance practice, and one largely ignored by students and musicologists.

Most musicians today insist that their primary aim is "to express the wishes of the composer." But every age sees a composer differently. In any case, the farther back in time we get, the less likely is it possible to express the wishes of the composer. Too many things have changed, not the least of which are the instruments themselves, not to mention pitch or problems of ornamentation. A paradox is involved, especially in music up to Beethoven. The closer we try to "express the message of the composer" by playing exactly what he wrote and no more, the farther we may be getting away from his message. I was constantly harping on this point in the early 1960's, trying to break performers away from slavish literalism, and I think I was the first critic to raise the question. I am afraid that I became a bit of a bore on the subject. But it is still my contention that hardly anybody knows much about Romantic performance practice, and even less about Bach performance practice, and I returned to the topic again and again in my Sunday columns. Perhaps it did some good. Musicians at least are aware of the fact that something else besides a strict, literal reproduction of the notes is required.

Sunday columns are a particular problem of the cultural critics of the *Times* or any other big newspaper. In some fifteen hundred words, week after week, we are expected to be philosophers, wits, scholars, entertainers and newspapermen. All of us handle the problem differently. Drama and movie critics usually write a Sunday column on a play or film they already have reviewed, amplifying their original thoughts and bringing new insights to them. That makes life easy for the drama or movie critic. The art critic, who almost never has to write to a nightly deadline, also has a relatively easy time, picking out a major show that interests him and dwelling upon it at great length. He constantly has new material to write about.

The music critic has a harder job. The major part of his task as a critic for a daily newspaper involves well-known music of the past, and it is seldom that any of us can bring fresh insights to the works of the great composers. There is, of course, contemporary music, and all music critics write many columns on new trends. There also is the well-known problem of trying to describe the indescribable. An art or film critic can run photographs of his material. A book or drama critic can print relevant excerpts or supply a précis of the work in question. All the music critic can do in trying to describe tone is fall back on vague, hackneyed words that attempt to give an idea of the way

a piece of music sounds. The learned publications can make a
better stab at it, using technical terminology and printed musical examples. Newspapers are not geared that way; and, in any
case, a music critic who constantly uses abstruse terminology
will not last long in the job. The *Times* lets me get away with
more than most other papers in that respect, but there is a limit.
I still get letters from indignant readers berating me for using
such terrible, incomprehensible words as *cadenza, exposition,
tessitura, serial, tonic-dominant* and the like. "Who do you
think you are writing for?" they want to know.

My way of handling the column was to look ahead and write
about something that was coming up during the week immediately following the Sunday piece. That is called a "news peg,"
and I am a fervent believer in the news peg. I write for a publication that is concerned with the news, and readers want to
know what is happening or going to happen. So I scanned the
programs for the week in question, looking for something that
would give me an interesting topic. It might be the revival of a
little-known opera, or a major work by a minor composer. (I
once wrote an entire column on the Piano Concerto in B flat
minor by Xaver Scharwenka, to the puzzlement and hilarity of
the world at large. Yet nobody lifts an eyebrow when an art
critic writes about the work of a minor Hudson River painter.)
During the height of a season, news pegs were not hard to find.
When the season tapered off, there was the annual article discussing the pros and cons of what the Metropolitan Opera or
New York Philharmonic had accomplished during the previous
six or seven months. When all else failed, there would be a
"think piece," but even there I tried to peg it to something in
the news. I tried not to get into a rut, and almost never did I
have to fall back on rehashing a review. Any critic with ingenuity can find plenty to write about. I must admit, though, that
the Sunday article did become harder and harder for me during
the last two years of the job. I began to feel that I was repeating
myself, that I was too predictable and that I was (as Mr. Downes
used to say) living off my fat. It was an uncomfortable feeling,
one that I never had previously experienced, and it was one of
the factors in my resignation as senior music critic, which took

effect on July 1, 1980. I had warned the paper of my decision the previous year. The *Times* asked me to stay on as cultural correspondent, and I was more than happy to oblige.

The Sunday pieces in this collection appear as originally written though a few of the headlines have been changed. From October, 1960, through July 6, 1980, I have averaged 45 Sunday pieces a year—almost a thousand columns, almost 1.3 million words. Reading these pieces en masse has been not altogether a happy experience for me. I dare say my experience has been as wide as that of most critics, but I do see myself returning to certain concepts again and again. I have attempted to select a wide variety, without too much in the way of repetition; but repetition cannot altogether be avoided, and all one can hope for is the reader's indulgence.

To write those Sunday columns I have been aided by a good memory, a fine working library of books, scores and records, and —when my own facilities fail me—the music library in Lincoln Center. Sometimes I have worked on a Sunday piece weeks in advance, usually when it involved studying a score and listening to recordings of an opera with which I was unfamiliar. More often, I started thinking about a Sunday column only the night before it was due, checking the schedule in search of an idea. Once the idea came, the rest was easy. If my own library did not have enough information, I would trot to Lincoln Center in the morning (or, at least, in those days when the music library was open in the morning), get the information and write the piece in the afternoon.

Today we work on a computer, and the new technology has called for a substantial change in working habits. Most of us like the computer, that remarkably versatile tool. But it has brought certain problems. For one thing, even at the *Times* there were not enough of those gadgets to go around (we are supposed to get more of them soon), which meant a pile-up of hungry-looking critics waiting for a free machine. Some of the more compulsive ones, like me, started getting in very early in the morning to seize a terminal.

It took time to learn how to operate the machine, and there were some missed deadlines on daily reviews as a result. I remember finishing a review just in time for the 11 P.M. deadline, pressing the wrong button and finding myself unable to retrieve the damn thing. We soon learned to write down the directory number, and to make copies both in the directory and on a printout. In the early days I once lost an entire Sunday column because of a power failure (or "outage" in the brave new terminology). We were warned to lock everything into the central computer, paragraph by paragraph. Once the material is so stored, it can be retrieved after an outage. But often, in the heat of composition, I would not take the necessary five seconds or so to break off and lock everything up. So those fifteen hundred words vanished forever.

On nightly deadlines, I found that I averaged about five minutes longer than in the pre-computer days. Five minutes might not sound like much, but when only half an hour is available for a review it can mean the difference between making or missing the edition. But I never missed any. What happened was that the speed of the new process was so fast—about seven minutes from copy editor to pasteup on the actual page—that I really had a good deal of time to play with. Officially the copy deadline was 11 P.M., but I could finish a piece as late as 11:15 and know it would get into the paper.

About that daily deadline. Many musicians bitterly complain that a music critic on a morning paper has to write a reasoned, coherent review in so short a time. Of course *they* can walk out of a concert and immediately analyze it to the last note, in hairsplitting detail and with total recall. It does not enter their minds that a music critic has been trained to do the same thing, only verbalizing directly on the typewriter (or computer). There is no mystery to it. All journalists take deadlines in stride, and most of them actually thrive on it. Some comments about deadlines will be found in the following pages. Suffice it to say that anybody who cannot write a coherent piece in a short time has no business being a music critic on a morning paper.

As a music critic, I have for decades been listening to all kinds of music, some of which I was spectacularly unfit to review. What do I really know about flute playing, or raga, or the harp, or Chinese music, or any number of things that I, like any other music critic, occasionally had to face? We all grope with the mysteries as best we can. My own rationalization, when faced with an instrument or a kind of music with which I am unfamiliar, is that a musical line is a musical line on any instrument, and at least we can respond to the artistry of the performer or the content of the music, treading warily as we go along. It is a problem; but it is, fortunately, a problem that I largely have been able to avoid since 1960, when I became senior music critic. After years of being assigned concerts, now I was in a position to select only those that interested me, and no longer had to worry about the exotic odds and ends that necessarily had me bluffing or writing desperately obfuscated prose. And in the Sunday pieces, of course, I wrote only about things I knew something about. With the whole world of music to draw from, there never was a lack of subject matter. The following cross-section will, if nothing else, give an idea of the variety of material that the leading critic of a great metropolitan daily has at his disposal. The Sunday pieces, by and large, have been a joy, a relief from the daily grind, a chance to ruminate, do battle, enjoy oneself; and one can only say with old Robert Burton:

> *When I go musing all alone,*
> *Thinking of divers things fore-known,*
> *When I build castles in the air,*
> *Void of sorrow and void of fear,*
> *Pleasing my self with phantasms sweet,*
> *Methinks the time runs very fleet.*

PART
I
Criticism

Containing a pleasant invective against poets, pipers, players, jesters and such like Caterpillars of a Commonwealth.

—STEPHEN GOSSON

On September 4, 1960, I wrote my first Sunday article as senior music critic of The New York Times. I spent some time thinking about it. Among other things, Howard Taubman in an adjoining column was writing his first piece as drama critic, and I did not want to be upstaged. My views on criticism as represented in this article did not change much in the ensuing two decades. Indeed, when I came to write my valedictory article, I found myself repeating ideas in this first one. But I had not looked at it for twenty years.

On the whole, I tried to stay away from Sunday pieces about criticism, and I doubt if I wrote more than a dozen during my tenure. For some reason I found this kind of piece too personal. I felt I was blowing my own horn, and I always felt uncomfortable introducing myself into the column. Perhaps this was part of growing up on the Sun and the Times, where the first person singular was generally frowned upon. In my early days at the Times critics were not allowed to use it. Olin Downes was a master at the editorial "we." He rolled it out with organ-like sonorities: "We had never heard such a magisterial performance of..." Not until Clive Barnes came to the Times as dance critic did the first person singular appear in reviews. He never could understand my reluctance to use it. "A review is a personal expression," he would tell me. It still appeared too ego-centered for me, and I have seldom used it in daily reviews. But I occasionally did in Sunday pieces when the subject directly involved me, as it did in the following piece.

A Search for Truth

M_AX_ BEERBOHM once wrote an article on why he was not fit to be a drama critic. Bernard Shaw wrote many articles clearly explaining why he was a better music critic than anybody else. Both of these great men were indulging in *jeux d'esprit*, knowing very well that the only difference between them and the public —the slight matter of genius, taste and literary ability aside— was that they had a forum, and anybody with a forum is automatically a senator. Rank has its privileges, and among them is the privilege of astonishing the bourgeoisie.

But it is not essential to have a forum to be a critic. All of us are critics and have been speaking prose all our lives, even if only a few of us get paid for the honor of adding to the gaiety of nations with our printed observations. Every time we pass judgment on a movie we have seen, a book we have read, a meal we have eaten, a girl we have kissed, a painting we have studied, we are observing a critical function.

Criticism is an indispensable function of any reasoning human being. It occurs at the very moment of birth, when we open our mouths in protest and critical commentary and start yelling. Some of us never stop. Criticism is an attitude toward the world, and art is only one of its provinces.

Basically, criticism is nothing more than the ability to verbalize about the meaning and worth of any specific object, whether it be a new symphony, the quality of a singer's voice, the latest automobile from Detroit, or a bill passed by the Congress. The more knowledge one has about the subject, the better one's position to attempt the verbalization; and the clearer the verbalization, the better the criticism.

Fortunately it does not take genius to appreciate genius. Thank goodness for that, else very few of us would be in a position to listen to music intelligently, much less write about it. But it does take constant thought, application and study to appreciate well.

A knowledge of technique and terminology is only part of the answer. Some of the finest musicians have made the worst critics. What is more important is identification with the performers' or composers' aims. A knowledge of technique comes from the brain. Identification comes from the heart, or spirit, or soul, or what have you. Brain and heart must work in tandem in any critical (i.e., appreciative) capacity, just as they have to work in tandem in any creative capacity. The prime purpose of criticism is to point out what is valid and permanent in any creative contribution of mankind. No critic can do that unless he has something permanent and valid upon which to base his judgments.

Complicating the matter is that none of the basic terms has ever been defined, despite the efforts of thinkers from Socrates to I. A. Richards. Truth, beauty, music itself—what are they? If anybody has come across an all-embracing definition of music I would love to see it; and please don't send in the bromide about music's being a rhythmical alternation of tones. It just doesn't work.

But we keep on thinking there is such a thing as beauty, and we know there is such a thing as music and we all (to adapt a line of E. B. White's) are on the dog-track of life, chasing the mechanical rabbit called truth and barking loudly as we go, but never quite catching up with it. The ultimate truth must always evade us, for we are finite beings in an infinite universe.

Yet all is not entirely shrouded in mystery. Music, like the other arts, does have a discipline, and much of this is mensurable. The composer makes a ground plan and sets notes on paper. Within certain leeways, these notes and his directions about them must be observed. There are several ways of playing a piece correctly, but there are millions of ways of playing it incorrectly. Thus, criticism can be a catalogue of vices as well as of virtues.

That is why so many professional musicians dislike critics. The feeling stems from the universal reaction pointed out a few hundred years ago by Chaucer's Wife of Bath: "I hate him that my vices telleth me, and so do mo, God woot! of us than I." Of all living creatures, public performers are, by necessity, the most egomaniacal. Being such, they actively resent criticism. They are the ones who have raised the heartrending cry about "constructive" versus "destructive" criticism.

What the professional means is that if a critic tells him he's glorious, sublime and the greatest musician since David, the critic is constructive. If he tells him, politely, that he has the musical instincts of a two-year-old playing with a rattle, he is destructive.

But the hard fact remains that many well-meaning but mediocre musicians have deluded themselves into believing that they are important artists. Ordinarily no great harm is done; there is no Gresham's law in music, and bad musicians will not drive out the good. In any case, no age has had a monopoly on bad musicians, just as no age has had a monopoly on genius. And, generally, the mediocre musician, provided he sticks to it, has always been able to make a career, helped by ill-informed or too-lenient critics. Music criticism, far from being too stern, is these days more lenient than it ever has been.

Yet is it "destructive" criticism to point out at the very beginning that an aspiring artist is manifestly unfit for the concert stage? Is it "destructive" to call a piece of music a piece of trash when it is a piece of trash? Must mediocrity always be sent away with a pat on the head and a bit of candy as a consolation prize? In art is there any room for evasions and half truths? Must the moos of the sacred cows invariably be accepted as golden sounds?

These are questions that every critic must answer for himself. If he is honest, he will admit the inevitability of error and he will do his best to make amends for his frailties. But if he deserves to be called a professional critic he must also be motivated by much the same ideal that motivates the creator. A concomitant is that he will have spent just as much time with the mysteries of the craft as has the creator himself. Music, or any of the arts, is not a part-time endeavor. It is a way of life, in which the fortunate ones never become jaded. It is a constant, day-and-night association with tones strung together to make some sort of meaning.

It develops to the point, as it does with any professional, where listening becomes almost reflexive as well as intellectualized. This does not mean that the professional—composer and performer as well as critic—cannot respond emotionally to a beautifully turned phrase, or to the beauty of a Mozart melody or a Schubert modulation. But the professional always listens on two levels.

One level is that of sheer, sensuous enjoyment, in which the sounds and the logic of the composer are followed. Beneath that level, the professional's busy little mind is in a frenzy, asking all kinds of questions. He ends substituting himself for the performer.

Listening becomes the purest of empathic experiences. You, the listener, are on stage with the artist. You have made with him that long, long walk from the wings. You know his strengths and his weaknesses, where he is nervous and where he is confident. By the time the opening group is half through, you have a very good idea of how the last half of the program is going to sound. Musicality and intelligence reveal themselves instantly, and so does their lack. By the same token, it should not take much more than five minutes to establish an artist's technical fitness.

Listening to music on such a professional level is not an innocent experience. It can be savage in its intensity, cruel in its understanding, arrogant in its superiority. But it is the only way a professional can listen. If it has its defects, it also has its virtues. If the pains are intensified, so are the pleasures. And when a great artist is engaged on a great piece of music, the pleasure can be blinding. That, after all, is what performer, critic and public live for in music: those rare and wonderful moments when man transcends man.

Sept. 4, 1960

Musicians find it hard to believe that a critic can write a reasoned, coherent review in as little as half an hour. But I found it surprising that the editors of Opera News, *supposedly a professional operation, would raise that old nonsense once again, and I had to answer them.*

Enough "Constructive Criticism" Already

CRITICISM IS in the news. The December 17th issue of *Opera News* has an editorial bewailing the fact that music critics are not living up to their responsibilities. And last weekend saw a symposium named The Current State of Criticism in the Performing Arts. It was sponsored by the National Endowment for the Arts and brought together critics of music, drama, films and art. This symposium ended up as all such symposia do, with various critics hotly defending a point of view, trying to pass as universal truths the results of their own experience and attitude toward life. (This writer was no exception.) It proved, if nothing else, that the egos of critics flourish as luxuriantly as the egos of artists.

One point that inevitably came up in the symposium, as it came up in the *Opera News* editorial, was the deadline problem. The weekly and quarterly critics expressed dismay at the very idea of writing a review in an hour or so under deadline pressure, and tended as a group to discount newspaper criticism.

There seems to be a prevalent notion that the longer it takes to write a review (or any piece of prose) the better it necessarily must be. That is nonsense. Style comes tumbling out every whichway. Some writers are naturally fast and some are slow; and it would be a perverse reader who preferred a bad slow writer to a good fast writer.

If a writer does happen to be fast, and if he is a mature professional, his work is not going to be materially different no matter how much time he has. The fast writer would type much the same review if he had a full month to think it over, except that in music criticism the later review might not be as good. Music is an art that exists in time, and time has a habit of receding. Once a musical performance has ended, it has disappeared forever. That is why some music critics can operate only when the sound of a performance is still hot in the ear. A day later the sound is that much more removed in time, and hence that much harder to recapture. One result is that the review then comes out lacking the immediacy and urgency that a first-hand response can give.

The implication of those who demand that critics take more time is that reviewing is otherwise a matter of snap judgments. That too is nonsense. Any qualified critic is bringing ten, twenty, thirty or more years of experience to bear on a particular performance. He walks out of most musical events knowing perfectly well what has gone on, and he is not going to change his mind overnight.

Nor is there anything in the least "oppressive" (that is *Opera News*'s word) about the necessity of meeting a deadline. A review is formulated in the concert hall or the opera house, not at the typewriter. It is at the actual performance that impressions are sifted and conclusions made, and what remains is the process of putting thoughts coherently together on paper: not so hard, mysterious or onerous a task as *Opera News* seems to think.

In new or avant-garde music, of course, problems arrive. But those are problems that have to be solved more or less on the spot. Previous exposure to new music naturally helps. That is why some critics try to get a score in advance, and that is why they would love to attend rehearsals if they have the time. (The job of critic on a great metropolitan daily involves a great deal of desk work.) *Opera News*, which is published by the Metropolitan Opera Guild and is a house organ for the Metropolitan Opera, comes up with a suggestion that will raise hollow laughter from the New York critics. The critics, says *Opera News*, should insist on attending dress rehearsals from start to finish.

But what are we supposed to use at the Metropolitan Opera? A bomb? An order from the Supreme Court? The critics have been invited to one dress rehearsal, that of *Antony and Cleopatra*. From that point the Metropolitan Opera, in its infinite wisdom, has closed its doors to the press. Perhaps its attitude is understandable. A house that has run up an appalling deficit, that seems to be having all kinds of troubles with its machinery, that has had a disastrous reception in the international press, is probably not too anxious to have reporters on the premises.

Back to the *Opera News* editorial. It starts with a peculiar bit of reasoning: (1) The critic of *The New York Times* greatly praised *Die Frau ohne Schatten*. (2) Therefore, tickets for the Metropolitan's production are hard to come by. (3) It is true that every Metropolitan Opera performance since the season opened has been sold out. (4) It is also true that productions lauded in the press will be more quickly sold out. (5) Thus the responsibility of the press has never been greater. (6) There are those who feel that critics can be compelled to live up to this responsibility. Weird logic.

And this "responsibility" is never defined. What is this responsibility? Is it to sell tickets? Is it to make the sold-out doubly sold-out? Some of us have thought, in our innocence, that it was the job of a music critic to attend performances and write what he thinks about them, on the basis of whatever background, sensitivity and judgment he happens to possess. The critic is merely passing an informed point of view. His is a subjective statement, backed by whatever hard fact can be brought to bear. It is a statement that may not necessarily be right or necessarily wrong. It is opinion, supported (one hopes) by a passionate belief in a set of standards to which artists and even impresarios must aspire. It presents ideas and concepts; and the public has to be taught to read them as ideas and concepts rather than holy writ; to accept or reject, not to believe blindly.

The *Opera News* editorial brings back those two tired, bleating words: "constructive criticism." Constructive criticism, the refuge of the Nice Nellies and Rollos who do not want to rock the boat, or say derogatory words about anybody, but who want pat-on-the-back criticism with perhaps an occasional slap on the wrist. But not a hard slap, mind you. They are the ones who want to prescribe aspirin when the disease is galloping consumption. They simply cannot get it through their heads that a strong review can, under certain circumstances, be infinitely more constructive than a weak one; that for large and immovable objects heavy ammunition is needed. Nor can they get it through their heads that a critic can be motivated by passion for an art he loves, so that he will lash furiously out at anything he thinks cheapens or degrades the art.

And, finally, *Opera News* quotes Rudolf Bing on his novel plans for the future. "When I do leave the Metropolitan, I plan to wage a war to force music critics, critics of opera, to be licensed." The picture is not without charm. One can visualize a jury of Rudolf Bings and a Bingian judge passing on the qualifications of a cringing critic. " 'Let us both go to law: *I* will prosecute *you.* —Come, I'll take no denial; we must have a trial: For really this morning I've nothing to do. . . . I'll be judge, I'll be jury, said cunning old Fury; 'I'll try the whole cause and condemn you to death.' " Although it does seem that Mr. Bing, in view of the current season, is scarcely in a position to make proposals for licensing music critics. Who knows but that somebody conceivably, just conceivably, might propose working up a set of qualifications for licensing opera impresarios and general managers.

DEC. 18, 1966

Very often letters from readers prompt Sunday pieces, of which the following is an example. Every Times *critic gets a good deal of mail, generally of a derogatory nature. The parents of a young artist who is roughly handled get relatives and friends to write furious diatribes, thoughtfully sending copies to the publisher and managing editor. Publishers and managing editors are used to this, and they are also used to important people who try to get critics fired. Unless there is an instance of proved malfeas-*

ance on the part of the critic, the Times *always backs up its writers, though once in a while worried editors would pop into my office wondering if a complaint about me or a junior critic was justified. The matter generally stopped there. It is true that the* Times *has discharged three drama critics in my time, but that had nothing to do with pressures from the public. For reasons of its own—justified or unjustified—the* Times *decided that those men were not doing the kind of job expected from a* Times *critic.*

Why a Critic Follows the Score

THE LETTERS one gets. On my desk for some months has been reposing a furious diatribe about the review of a pianist I wrote about in February. The writer was mad. Also scatological. Also ungrammatical. Also unoriginal ("we were not at the same concert": I wish I had a dollar for every time a letter came in with those immortal words). Also anonymous.

He did raise a few points worth discussion, however, including my frequent habit of bringing scores and the sheet music to concerts. "If you didn't have your nose buried in the Beethoven sonata scores, you might have been able to get involved with the playing and have had time . . . to enjoy the beauty of his playing. If you are silly enough to take the printed page as the gospel truth and if you are not at this stage of your career familiar with the Beethoven sonatas then perhaps retirement is to be considered?"

That remark about taking the printed page as gospel really hurt. As far as I know, I was the first critic anywhere, in books and articles, to inveigh against the deadening, stultifying literalism that in my opinion was afflicting performances everywhere. Year after year I was patiently, and sometimes not so patiently, pointing out that that music was more than an architectural plan; that notation was an inexact science; that it was the artist's job to reflect his own personality as well as that of the composer. I screamed and carried on, pointing out that literalism was fake musicianship; that composers themselves, especially the nineteenth-century composers, expected performers to take liberties in phrase and tempo and even, occasionally, with the text.

I believed then, as I believe now, that surprisingly little is known about Romantic performance practice—and it is still nineteenth-century music that forms the bulwark of the repertory. Artists know that they have to "do" something in this music, but they do not exactly know what has to be done. The result is mannerism instead of style. Or literalism instead of spontaneity.

Only in recent years has there been a re-examination of Romanticism, and now musicians are beginning to come around, as well as critics and anonymous letter-writers. As one who in a way started the whole thing, I am rather pleased—and amused —to find my words fifteen years back parroted almost verbatim as though they were brand new. But to be accused of the very thing I have fought against? Go soak your head.

About this business of bringing scores to concerts: It is not to check up on the artists. Rather it is to *see* as well as hear what they do. I dare say I know the literature as well as my furious anonymist. But even in pieces that we have memorized at the keyboard, how many without the music in front of us remember every dotted eighth note, every tempo indication, every expression marking? The point of bringing the music is to look at what has come down to us, and then see exactly what the artist does with it.

For every artist, even the literalist, "does" things to music. Listen to twenty different recordings of the *Waldstein* and you are necessarily going to get twenty slightly—or in some cases not so slightly—different views of the sonata. It may be hard to tell the literalists apart, but when the score is before you, differences do spring to life.

Score reading, except for certain modern works, is not that difficult, especially when the piece in question is one that you know. An experienced score reader does not have his nose perpetually in the score. He turns pages more or less automatically, knowing exactly where the musician is going to be at any given point. He may not even look at the pages. But when something a bit unusual happens, there is the score to verify the point.

When something unusual does happen, I jot it down. My scores are full of little notations about the habits and ideas of musicians: an effective luftpause that Bernstein may have inserted into a Mahler symphony; a fermata that Bjoerling employed in a particular aria; a curious way of taking a phrase by this musician; a harmonic change by that; a reorchestration, an unexpected change in tempo, an accelerando—whatever the artist "does" that is away from the printed mathematics of the score. All are noted down, with the names of the perpetrators. Perhaps in future years scholars might have an interesting time going through my score collection.

And I have the habit of timing performances. I do it automatically, pressing the plunger of my wrist watch. Timings are interesting. I find it intriguing that on one occasion Isaac Stern played the Brahms Violin Concerto in 38 minutes, 15 seconds; and the next time around, 32 minutes, 27 seconds. Different conductor, different hall, different acoustics, and Stern felt differently about the concerto that day. Interesting. Proving nothing at all, but interesting. I find it interesting that Toscanini, reputedly a "fast" conductor, was slower than Rossi in the *Falstaff* recording. I find it interesting that certain artists are invariably outside the orthodox tempo parameters.

Most interesting of all, some twenty-five years of timings in my scores lead to the conclusion that there is a sort of glacial shift in the contemporary understanding of tempo. Teachers tell us time and again that because of the speed of our modern age, tempos also have speeded up. Older musicians, they say, were representatives of a calmer, more relaxed age and were nowhere near as rushed as we are. But the timings on my scores suggest otherwise. Far from being faster, we seem to be much slower than our forebears were. Perhaps it has been the crazy, skewed idea of "musicianship" operating in our time, but whatever the reason, timings today are slower than they were a generation ago.

And that is why I take scores to concerts. Not to see how closely musicians adhere to the score, but to see how they depart from it. Musicians without ideas are not very stimulating musicians. When a musician has ideas, I like to jot them down as part of a permanent record that otherwise would instantly vanish as soon as the piece was over. Performance is such an evanescent art. A painter fixes a conception forever with the tip of his brush; the writer is there for eternity; the poor performing artist's ideas in the concert hall are a brilliant bubble that explodes upon the instant. (Yes, he can make records, but those are so different from what happens when stage and audience interact in a live performance.)

Dare I also say that some musicians can be so dull that following the score is an antidote against going to sleep? There also are scores and scores. Does a conductor use a corrupt version of a Haydn symphony or is he educated enough to encompass the latest findings? What Bruckner edition is he using? And so on. Bringing scores to concerts can answer many questions. I won't apologize to my angry friend. On the contrary. One remark, though, I shall keep in mind, and try to turn pages more quietly. Scores in large format and old, crackly paper are not easy to manage.

SEPT. 18, 1977

With this article I made way for Donal Henahan, my successor. In it, I am afraid, are many of the ideas, sometimes expressed in much the same words, that I had been promulgating through the years. At least I have been consistent. I did not consciously crib from earlier pieces, no more than T.R.B. of The New Republic *does when he writes about the parliamentary system or overpopulation or ecology. He has kept hammering away on some favorite subjects, and so have I. Nobody ever changes. As we grow older we merely become an intensification of what we originally were. My ideas about music and criticism happened to be formed very early along, and I spent the greater part of my active career trying to develop certain concepts that had fascinated and preoccupied me from the beginning. I think the same is true of any critic who has enjoyed any kind of tenure. It is true in the music criticism of even so brilliant a stylist and creative a mind as George Bernard Shaw.*

A Critic Reflects on Forty-four Years in the Business

IT WAS twenty years ago that I became proprietor of this column and was officially licensed to dispense wit, wisdom and panaceas over its counter. It was thirty years ago that I came to *The New York Times*. It was forty-four years ago that I became a music critic. That was on a long-departed magazine named *Musical Advance.* I had a monthly column, a byline, and could rub shoulders with the likes of Olin Downes, Noel Straus, Lawrence Gilman, Oscar Thompson, Pitts Sanborn, Irving Kolodin, Louis Biancolli, Robert Bagar and Jerome Bohm and a half-dozen others I could mention, none of whom knew I was alive. I peered at them from a respectful distance, the new boy in class.

Now the time has come for a change. Well over a year ago I warned the *Times* that when I became sixty-five, in November of this year, I wanted to resign as senior music critic. A new point of view, I felt, was needed, a fresh look at composers, repertory, performers, the philosophy of music. I had done it for forty-four years. Now it should be somebody else's turn.

And so from Donal Henahan, effective next week, will come the wise words on this page, the calls to arms, the contumely, the occasional pratfalls. His will be a different mind, a different approach, and thus there may well be a change in emphasis from the notable leniency, kindness, elevated prose, generosity and world view with which this column and the position of senior music critic of *The New York Times* have been conducted. Mr. Henahan may become realized as the George Bernard Shaw of American music critics, or maybe the Sam Breakstone, forever demanding perfection. Whatever he does do, it is now his baby.

But before flags are run up worldwide to celebrate my departure, hold! I am not leaving. The *Times*, bless its corporate little soul, has asked me to stay on as cultural correspondent, an all-embracing title that will permit me to poke around here and there, perhaps as often as not on this page.

Funny thing, criticism. It is often despised, and with good reason, considering some of its practitioners. Yet criticism is a necessary part of the human condition, and it has always been with us. Nor have critics changed very much during the course of the centuries. The best ones always have been naggers, didacts, drawing universal laws from their own fallibilities. George Bernard Shaw, in his valedictory as drama critic in 1898, was only half kidding when he wrote that his reputation had been built up fast and solid "on an impregnable basis of dogmatic reiteration." But that is what critics with any passion or conviction do. They hammer at certain things again and again, determined to set matters right, sublimely convinced of their own unique, shining capability.

Some critics profess to work according to a set of immutable esthetic and technical laws. They are only fooling themselves. There are no immutable laws. There is only the critic himself: his background, his taste and intuition, his ideals, his literary ability. If style is the man, so is criticism, and his criticism always ends up a reflection of what he is. In many respects criticism is solipsistic. I have never met any critic in any field (and that includes myself) who did not operate according to principles he had solidified when very young; and, as I say above, we tend to draw universal rules from our own experience. But the older one gets, the more chimerical the whole idea becomes. Criticism turns out to be nothing—*nothing*—more than the verbalization of one's responses to the object being criticized.

Of course it is to be hoped that the critic beings to the object much the same mental processes that the creator had experienced in forging it from the resources of his own imagination. That means the critic has to have gone through equivalent studies and development. But at the end it all comes down to what the critic thinks, and his thought is necessarily a reflection of his own personality. Critical egos being what they are, we all feel that our response is right and that the response of others (unless they agree with us) is wrong. Like the character in *How to Succeed in Business,* we believe in ourselves.

But that does not necessarily make us "right" or "wrong," and in any case right or wrong has surprisingly little to do with criticism. Criticism rather has to do with concept, with idea, with an effort to pass the creative processes of somebody else's thought through a critical filter and thus throw light on the work or the performance in question. It is a critic's job to make his readers think, and beyond that there is little he can do. For the great creators of mankind always have operated independently of criticism, and a work of art eventually finds its own place in the hierarchy. Similarly, in the long run, the public also operates independently of criticism, eventually putting its seal of approval on a work or dismissing it contemptuously. A critic can scream and yowl, prod and push, help a little or hurt a little, soothe or bruise. But his at best is a short-term effort, and he learns eventually to hitch himself to the musical Pegasus and enjoy the ride.

And what a ride it has been during my four-plus decades! What convulsive changes there have been! Musical life before World War II was quiet and respectable, dead between the ears. In those days there was a seven-month season, during which opera houses, orchestras and recitalists played much the same limited repertory year in and year out. (Those who complain about the limitations of the repertory today, often justifiably so, should have been living at that hour. It was impossible.) At the end of April there was no more music in the concert halls until the following October. Who could stand the heat of concert halls during the hot months in those pre-airconditioned days? There was plenty of outdoors music around the country. But there was only one important summer festival, given by the Boston Symphony in Tanglewood. Today, of course, the season never stops; and every hamlet in the United States seems to have its own music festival. A local chamber of commerce would feel naked without one.

Today's audiences are infinitely more sophisticated, and for that we can thank the LP disc, which was introduced in 1948 and appears to me to be the single most important musical development of our time. Within two decades after 1948 virtually the entire repertory was on records—a repertory that extended from early Renaissance to the latest concoction of John Cage or Pierre Boulez. The music lover had a whole world free to explore, and many did. Before the war it was possible for a record critic to have heard every disc in the catalogues. I know; I was one. There were, after all, only two major record companies and a handful of tiny independents that sporadically issued one or two records a year. The glorious spate after 1948, with hundreds of record companies getting into the act, swept even the most devoted and dedicated listener head over tea kettle. Nobody could keep up with it. All of a sudden there was a quantum jump in musical knowledge all over the world.

There even came a wide variety of new music, suddenly available for a public that stubbornly refused to touch it. I am not going to dwell much here on the postwar avant-garde years. The subject bores me. Composers think that critics are put on earth only to praise their music and make propaganda for it. That is the "duty" of the critic. He has to drop everything to bow before somebody who has the ability to put notes on paper. Some critics, afraid of being considered reactionary, swung along, nice little pooches rewarded by pats on the head (and, often, secret contempt). Those were the "good" critics, the ones alive to the responsibilities of their profession.

But it so happened that I thought the serial-dominated music after the war was a hideously misbegotten creature sired by Caliban out of Hecate, and I had no hesitation saying so. Nor has it been proved that I was all wrong. Certain it is that the decades of serialism did nothing but alienate the public, creating a chasm between composer and audience. Composers today write differently and think differently, and suddenly seem interested in writing music that actually means something to their listeners.

At least it was a wild period. What polemics and agitation! Today things are much calmer. Torpid, even. Nothing much seems to be happening, and composers are searching for a style. One of the elements of the new style, inconceivable to those revolutionaries who a short time ago were preaching a complete break from the past, is a return to older music. The past has become fashionable; everybody looks for roots. A new Romanticism is in the air, and the next decade will see a much looser, more personal kind of music.

Equally cataclysmic have been the societal changes in music over the last four decades. Music has become Big Business. Nobody has assembled definitive statistics, but it seems that cultural events in America draw a much bigger audience and are responsible for a much greater investment in real estate and financing than all sports events rolled together.

That would have made our prewar ancestors dissolve in astonishment. Orchestras on a fifty-two-week contract! Cultural centers all over the country! Money for the arts coming from federal, state and local governments! Industry and foundations, rather than individual philanthropists, pitching in to support culture! Summer festivals as a proliferating way of life! An opera explosion, with groups all over the country giving thousands of performances a year, and the Metropolitan Opera confident enough to embark on a one hundred million dollar endowment fund drive! A chamber music explosion, with that most intimate of musical expressions becoming a heavy growth industry!

Naturally it's not all roses. Inflation today is hurting all cultural organizations, and many of them have been forced to retrench. There is worry about elitism in some quarters, populism in others. There is concern about the possible politicization of art through the National Endowment in Washington. There is a feeling, prevalent in much intellectual thought, that the big cultural centers are acting as supermarkets, selling a popular, highly advertised product rather than taking the lead and trying to raise the level of its community. There are worries that this country simply cannot absorb the number of eager, talented young musicians processed annually from the schools and conservatories. There is the competition syndrome, which is anathema to many informed musicians (more fancy supermarket packaging).

But when one compares the current state of American culture in general, and music in particular, with what was the norm in the 1930's, one has to stand up and cheer. For where culture then was a phenomenon restricted, by and large, to the big cities and a few university towns, today it is taken seriously by millions and millions of Americans, from the head of state down. Even if some of this is only lip service, the fact remains that never in its history has the United States paid so much attention to the arts.

Change there has been; but change is not always for the better. In some areas there has been a retrogression. The 1930's were the last decade of consistently phenomenal singing, especially in the Wagner repertory. With Leider, Flagstad, Traubel, Branzell, Telva, Lehmann, Melchior, Schorr and List at their height, a quality of performance was provided that the present age cannot begin to duplicate, and there is no indication that any Wagner singers are coming along remotely comparable to their great predecessors. Nor has contemporary piano playing been able to match the genius—in the Romantic school, anyway—of Hofmann, Rachmaninoff, Lhévinne, Moiseiwitsch, Friedman and Novaes. Standards of performance today are at a uniformly high level, but there are so few peaks! How many conductors today have the passion and charisma of Toscanini, Furtwängler, Stokowski, Koussevitzky, Beecham, Monteux, Klemperer, Kleiber, Szell? How many violinists can electrify the way Heifetz did, or tear you apart the way Kreisler did?

Of course every period has its own performing styles, and today's style does not favor the strong personalities of yesterday's masters. We seem to prefer a quieter, more homogenous product. We have the mistaken idea that Romanticism in performance means excess liberty. This is a subject on which I have been writing for decades. The study of performance practice has been one of my passions; and what's the use of having a forum if you can't use it to bore your readers? My contention is that the Romantic style, far from being anarchistic or egocentric, is aristocratic, highly controlled and, if anything, classic—and I have any number of old recordings to prove it. The amusing thing is that young artists today take unmentionable, idiotic liberties in rubato and tempo, with the crazy idea that this is "Romantic" style.

But enough, before I start one of my hysterical lectures. None of us, you see, ever really changes. Obviously, as long as I am around, George Bernard Shaw's Doctrine of Dogmatic Reiteration will live on.

JULY 6, 1980

PART II

Performance Practice

An old custom is sacred, when it is a bad one.
—HECTOR BERLIOZ

In one of my earliest pieces, in 1937 in Musical Advance, I wrote about the stagnation of the repertory. Things changed after World War II and the advent of the LP disc. These days musicians are, on the whole, much more adventurous in their programming than were the pre-war crop. But in 1960, when this piece was written, the repertory was still relatively static, and in some respects it still is. The 1979–80 season in New York, for instance, was The Winter of the Carnaval. At least thirty pianists, many of them internationally famous artists, decided to come to town with that popular Schumann piece. Each decade, also, has its fashions, which younger musicians tend slavishly to follow. The piano music of Schubert was rediscovered after the war, and programs of the last three sonatas became a commonplace. Every young pianist wanted to show what a deep thinker he was. The new symphonic hero was Mahler (he still is), and conductors promenaded Mahler across the musical scene like ducks in a shooting gallery. The big showpiece for piano turned out to be Ravel's Gaspard de la Nuit. Surprisingly few instrumentalists show much imagination in their programs. An exception is an artist like Maurizio Pollini, who often plays avant-garde music.

Mention is made below of Haydn's 104 symphonies. Recent scholarship has raised that number, but in 1960 the received figure was 104.

Artistic Suicide

ALL OVER the world, at this very instant, recitalists are putting the finishing touches to their oncoming programs. Very soon, they will be facing us. In a month, the season will be well under way.

Those recitalists may not know it, but programs seem to run in cycles. Somewhere along the line, there is a sort of mystic intervention that makes an awful lot of musicians turn up with the same work during the course of a season. The winter of 1950–51, it may be remembered, was the Winter of Prokofiev's Seventh Sonata. Pianists from France, pianists from Austria and Germany, pianists from England, Mexico and America, all simultaneously decided that their lives would be an empty mockery if they did not immediately program the Seventh.

A year or so later, it was The Winter of the *Etudes symphoniques.* Not long ago, it was The Winter of the Franck Violin Sonata. It seemed impossible to attend a violin recital and not hear it. The Winter of the Brahms First will be remembered with shudders. The Brahms First is a noble work, but, when every conductor tromped in and out of town with it, one had an irresistible urge to scream in protest.

There is only one explanation for these winters of discontent. Toward the close of any particular season, when musicians are thinking of what they will do next year, there stirs a little man. This little man is a native of Erewhon, which, as everybody knows, is bounded on the north by Poictesme, on the south by Laputa, on the east by Ruritania and on the west by the seacoast of Bohemia. He has purple hair, red eyes, blue wings and is the natural son of Mrs. Harris out of Harvey.

On the well-known moment between midnight and twelve P.M. on the thirty-first of February, he comes out. He flies in all directions at once, whispering in musicians' ears. He is the one who really invented subliminal advertising. "The *Appassionata,*" he insinuates. "The *Appassionata.* The *Appassionata.* The *Appassionata.* The *Appassionata.*" Musicians all over the globe stir uneasily and get the message. Sure enough, like sheep, they come to town the next season with Beethoven's *Appassionata.*

No other explanation can account for the phenomenon. But recitalists, especially young ones, would do well to fight all implanted suggestions.

For program-making is a serious matter, and a career can well depend on it. One of the myths that has been implanted for generations is that a program must follow a chronological course. Thus, the majority of recitalists dutifully begin with the early Italians and work their way to the twentieth century.

In most cases, the overall results are doomed to failure. No artist who ever lived has been master of all styles. Even a genius like Rachmaninoff sounded rather silly on those rare occasions he played Mozart or Debussy. And yet, year after year, march the divisions of hopefuls with programs that encompass a capsule history of music.

Thus, we get the spectacle of an ardent young violinist, obviously of a temperament that would tear down the hall in Paganini, scraping away at unaccompanied Bach. Or the converse: a young man who would be only too happy to play unaccompanied Bach to the best of his considerable ability along those lines, but who feels it his duty to play Paganini miserably.

Why in the name of artistic suicide do these things so often happen? Simply because tradition, that dried-up and unimaginative old spinster, has so decreed.

It is high time that artists realized they should program only the things that they feel they can play, not the things they think they should play. If an artist has a Romantic temperament, he should avoid Scarlatti or unaccompanied Bach, and confine himself to Chopin, Schumann, Liszt, Brahms. If his allegiance is to the moderns, or with Hindemith, Prokofiev and Schoenberg; out with everything else.

But then enters, draped in black, the figure of the wise man. How, he asks in his infinite wisdom, can an artist be judged until he plays Mozart and Beethoven? *They* are the ultimate test, and not until then can the artist be given a pass to the pantheon. So says the wise man.

But this argument, though it has been parroted for years, is nonsense, and dangerous nonsense at that. Is it not good enough that an artist does a particular segment of the repertory with flair? Is not a fine Ravel interpretation preferable to a second-rate Beethoven one? Should not an artist be given credit for what he can do, rather than insults for what he does not even attempt to do? What smug superiority it is to set up standards by which a butterfly must be compared to an Elgin marble!

And, indeed, the very basic idea of the wise man is open to argument. For an artist can be judged very well without measuring the arc of his genuflection to the Classic gods. For one thing, much more can be learned about a pianist's technical qualifications from the few seconds of Chopin's First Etude than from an entire Beethoven sonata. As for musicianship, if the wise man does not think it requires style, taste and culture to play the C major Etude—or the Tchaikovsky Violin Concerto, for that matter—he had better go back to school. Of course, the Chopin Etude demands a different kind of musicianship from that required in Mozart or Beethoven. Naturally. But how many times do we have to be told that apples and roast beef cannot be compared; that a Herrick quatrain is worth as much, in its way, as a Milton ode?

All recitalists, then, should forget all about old lady tradition and concentrate on what they do well. As for any given program, it still takes taste and knowledge to construct a good one. And here the instrumentalists and conductors should show much more initiative than they have been showing.

Conductors, especially, are impossible. Of Haydn's 104 symphonies, only a dozen or so are in the active repertory. We get the same things over and over again. Yet there are the wonderful No. 39 in G minor and No. 49 in F minor, or the remarkable No. 80 in D minor, to mention but three seldom-heard ones. Why don't we hear them? The answer can be expressed in one three-syllable word: laziness. Laziness and nothing more.

The same applies to violinists who keep on returning with the Franck Sonata rather than the Fauré A major or E minor; to pianists who think the world is palpitating for the nth performance of the *Waldstein* (while the great Op. 101 languishes in relative obscurity); to singers who do the *Lucia* Mad Scene with piano accompaniment, rather than program Schubert's *Hirt auf dem Felsen.*

Recitalists and conductors should try to get out of the rut of program-making. The public should complain until they do. There are, fortunately, a few musicians who do take their art seriously and try to assemble programs that break out of the straitjacket of tradition. But there are not too many of them. The New York public can rest assured that it will hear the *Kreutzer* Sonata and the Bach Chaconne at least thirty times this year. And next year. And the year after that.

SEPT. 11, 1960

It was this article, written in 1961, that made musicologists and some of my colleagues regard me as hopelessly bourgeois, romantic and completely out of touch with Baroque research. Now, twenty years later, I stubbornly stick to my original position. In 1961 not too much work had been done on Bach performance practice, and the educated musician tended to accept the conclusion of musicologists as holy writ (no matter to what extent musicologists were innocent of the realities of music-making, which so many of them still are). Things have changed. Today there is a realization that every creative figure, especially the highly pragmatic J. S. Bach, worked on much looser premises than the specialists of 1961 would begin to concede. The musicologists had set up "rules," but twenty years later it can be seen that those rules were rigid and often unmusical. At the Thomas Dunn performance of the B minor Mass in question, everything in me shrieked that it was all wrong. The conducting was careful, yes; honest, yes—but dry, unimaginative, basically insensitive. There are, of course, many basic practices that have to be observed in Baroque or Classic performances. But some of those who were so proud of their musicological "accuracy" tended to forget that the composers were red-blooded men writing red-blooded music. A blazing line, a beautifully shaped phrase, an insight into the Affekt of the score—these are much more important than a correct appoggiatura. Young critics today are hypnotized by form, by the architecture of music. But where composers from Bach on have written, or spoken about, or have been quoted on the meaning of their music, its emotional content, I have not encountered from them (except from certain contemporary composers) one word about the form and structure of their music. When Mozart writes to his father about the key structure of Die Entführung aus dem Serail, *he is not discussing form. He is explaining the emotional meaning of the passages.*

Performing Bach En Masse

PROBLEMS OF performance in Baroque music are ever with us. Not long ago, in Carnegie Hall, Thomas Dunn conducted Bach's B minor Mass with a chorus of twenty, an orchestra not much larger, a harpsichord continuo and the usual soloists. The idea was to approximate conditions in Bach's own day. But what resulted, I thought, was an example of misplaced scholarship in which the most majestic choral work ever written sounded tiny; in which the exultant shout of the Gloria and the thundering basses of the Sanctus emerged through the wrong end of the telescope, making mouselike little sounds. Could this have been Bach's apocalyptic vision? I thought not, and said as much.

Whereupon the letters began to come in. A fat lot *you* know about Bach, the letters said. Many of the letters quoted an extract from Bach's memorandum written on August 23, 1730, to the Town Council of Leipzig. It is a long memorandum with an equally long title: "Short but Most Necessary Draft for a Well-Appointed Church Music; with Certain Modest Reflections on the Decline of the Same." The pertinent extract, quoted by most of the correspondents, is as follows:

> In order that the choruses of church pieces may be performed as is fitting, the vocalists must in turn be divided into 2 sorts, namely, concertists [soloists] and ripienists [chorus singers].

The concertists are ordinarily 4 in number; sometimes also 5, 6, 7, even 8; that is, if one wishes to perform music for two choirs.

The ripienists, too, must be at least 8, namely, two
for each part.

Every musical choir should contain at least 3 sopranos, 3 altos, 3 tenors, and as many basses, so that
even if one happens to fall ill (as very often happens,
particularly at this time of year, as the prescriptions
written by the school physician for the apothecary
must show) at least a double-chorus motet may be
sung. (N.B. Though it would be still better if the classes
were such that one could have 4 singers on each part
and thus could perform every chorus with 16 persons.)

Thus wrote Bach himself, and it should settle the problem.
But it doesn't, because of certain attendant circumstances; and
those who take the above extract as holy writ without studying
the memorandum in full are only deceiving themselves.

For Bach set forth his specifications not as the ideal but as a
practical way of working with what he had at his disposal.
Which was not much. As Bach stated elsewhere in the memorandum, the vocalists in Leipzig were made up of the pupils of
the Thomas-Schule, of which Bach was the head. Now, at the
time he wrote to the Town Council, he had fifty-five students
at his disposal.

These 55 [he wrote] are divided into 4 choirs, for the
4 Churches in which they must perform partly con-
certed music with instruments, partly motets, and
partly chorales. In the 3 Churches, St. Thomas's, St.
Nicholas's, and the New Church, the pupils must all be
musical. [That is, they should know how to read music
fluently.] The Peters-Kirche receives the remainder,
namely those who do not understand music and can
just barely sing a chorale.

Whereupon, at the end of the memorandum, Bach indicates the musical worth of his singers. He lists them by name, and ends up with a curt: "17 usable, 20 not yet usable, and 17 unfit." (The grand total is fifty-four, not the fifty-five he had previously mentioned, but no matter.)

All of which means that Bach's vocal forces were small not by choice but by necessity. Indeed, as the memorandum is read, it is quite obvious that Bach would have jumped at the chance to triple or quadruple his forces. The key words are "at least." He wants "at least" twelve singers in a choir. He demands "at least" eighteen persons, and preferably twenty, for the instrumental forces. The ripienists must be "at least" eight. "At least" does not mean "at most" in any language. What Bach was saying to the Town Council, in short, was something like this: "You miserable penny-pinchers expect good church music with no singers. How about coming across and giving me something to work with?" In his own dry words, "A well-appointed church music requires vocalists and instrumentalists."

The memorandum further displays Bach's difficulties in Leipzig. He complains that the chorus is not as willing as it used to be, for the slight stipendum that it used to receive had been withdrawn. He complains even more bitterly that the string quartet in the orchestra had to be played by students, thus depriving the chorus of four badly needed singers. (In a chorus of twelve, deprivation of four does indeed make a sizable difference.)

And, Bach continues, "Thus far only the Sunday music has been touched upon. But if I should mention the music of the Holy Days (on which days I must supply both the principal Churches with music), the deficiency of indispensable players will show even more clearly, particularly since I must give up to the other choir all those pupils who play one instrument or another and must get along altogether without their help."

The conclusion seems clear enough. Those who read Bach's words about a chorus of sixteen, and take them literally, are missing the whole point of the memorandum, which is a desperate plea for more singers and a bigger orchestra. How big? That we do not know. It is safe enough to say that Bach would not have wanted a monster chorus of a size that would have blurred the contrapuntal lines of the Kyrie of the B minor Mass. It is also safe to say that in the orchestra he would have done considerable doublings, with a far greater complement of oboes and bassoons than we would use today. He also would have used a small organ instead of a harpsichord, though on this point scholars are still arguing.

As far as the B minor Mass itself goes, too, is there not such a thing as internal evidence? Regardless of what Bach actually used, because he had to, large forces appear implicit in the nature of the writing. "Large," of course, is a relative term, but the great moments of the B minor Mass (and the *Saint Matthew* Passion and other equivalent works) surely demand a volume of tone grander than the pipings and squeakings of a chorus of eight, or twelve, or even twenty. Bach must have had an enormous (for his day) sound in his inner ear when he penned those sublime notes. Or else internal evidence means nothing.

These days we are too prone to let the findings of scholarship dominate the actual meaning and essence of music. The scholarly mind does tend to deify minutiae. (I once took a graduate course in Chaucer. All the Ph.D. applicants knew everything about the various head-links and end-links of *The Canterbury Tales*, about Harley 1758 and the two Caxton editions. But I never did run across one who had read the *Tales* all the way through.) Composers, or any creative figures, have a disconcerting habit of thinking differently from the scholars. And what the great composers thought is just as important as what they did.

Nov. 5, 1961

About fifteen years later I returned to the same topic, but this time it was a discussion of Bach and the organ. My viewpoint had not changed. Bach played without color and virility is not Bach but rather a false twentieth-century idea about him.

But Would Bach Play It Like This?

THE CONCERT that Anthony Newman gave the other week succeeded, if nothing else, in raising all kinds of questions about Bach performance practice on harpsichord and organ. Newman, who may be one of the idols of the younger generation—at least Philharmonic Hall was sold out, and the audience was overwhelmingly youthful—played such popular pieces as the *Passacaglia*, the *Great* Fantasy and Fugue in G minor, and the Preludes and Fugues in B minor and D major. In all respects his performances were thoroughly "modern." But were they Bachian?

They were modern in that all the notes were there, accurately set forth. Newman is a fine technician, and that applies to his pedal technique; his flying feet acted as though they had eyes in heel and toe. Also modern was Newman's determination to keep himself out of the music. His was a super-objective succession of performances in which the main object—indeed, the only object—was a faithful translation of the notes. Tempos were fast. Rhythms were metronomic. Ritards and other expressive devices were scrupulously avoided. The only liberty that Newman granted himself was a prolongation of the final notes in a piece perhaps a little longer than necessary. The result was a Bach—to these ears, at least—devoid of grandeur, of quality, of color, of flexibility. It was what Sol Babitz, the musicologist, has called "sewing-machine Bach."

But could Bach himself have played his organ music in a manner so devoid of personality?

Let's look at some facts. We know for a fact that Bach himself was a vigorous, red-blooded, cantankerous, stubborn man, certainly not the kind of eunuch that Newman's performances might have suggested. With all that, he was anything but a pedant. His daring organ modulations disturbed the worshippers at his church in Arnstadt, and his mind worked in anything but conventional ways. Forkel, his first biographer (1802), reports that Bach allowed his pupils great liberties. "He let them dare whatever they would and could. . . . As he himself attempted everything possible in this respect, he liked to see his scholars do the same."

Forkel's statement is not merely the recollection of a man writing fifty-two years after Bach's death. In Bach's own day there were many who were amazed by Bach's vigor and freedom. His obituary notice testifies to the point: "How strange, how new, how expressive, how beautiful were his ideas at improvising." The key words here are, of course, "strange . . . new . . . expressive . . . beautiful." A musician named Constantin Bellermann, who heard Bach play, attests to the fact that when Bach was seated at the organ console, the results could be thunderously exciting. Trying out an organ in Cassel, Bach "ran over the pedals with this same facility, as if his feet had wings, making the organ resound with such fullness, and so penetrate the ears of those present like a thunderbolt, that Frederick, the legitimate hereditary Prince of Cassel, admired him with such astonishment that he drew a ring with a precious stone from his finger and gave it to Bach as soon as the sound had died away." Bellermann wonders what would have happened had Bach used his hands as well.

Bach was greatly interested in sonority. Carl Philipp Emanuel Bach wrote of his father that the first thing he would do in trying an organ was test its volume. "Above all I must know whether the organ has good lungs." To find out, Bach would "draw out every speaking stop and play in the fullest and richest possible texture. At this the organ builders would often grow quite pale with fright."

Not much is known about Bach's registrations, but the evidence is clear that he used a great deal of unusual color. Forkel again: "To all this was added the peculiar manner in which he combined the different stops of the organ with each other, or his mode of registration. It was so uncommon that many organ builders and organists were frightened when they saw him draw the stops. They believed that such a combination of stops could never sound well, but were much surprised when they afterwards perceived that the organ sounded best just so, and had now something peculiar and uncommon, which never could be produced by their mode of registration."

But however Bach registered, whatever volume and bigness he strove for, he never lost sight of the expression. For this we have the words of one of his pupils, Johann Gotthilf Ziegler, in 1746. Bach, said Ziegler, urged him not to play offhand or by rote, but according to the *Affekt* of the words of the chorale—that is, according to the sensibility and expression of the matter at hand.

It was in 1753, only three years after Bach's death, that his son, C. P. E. Bach, published the first part of his essay on how to play keyboard instruments. Bach's son, trained by his father, provides an invaluable insight into Bachian performance practice. He makes it clear, for instance, that good playing is much more than skillful technique. Indeed, C. P. E. Bach casts scorn on those "who astound us with their prowess without ever touching our sensibilities." He wants, as J. S. Bach undoubtedly did (where else did C. P. E. get his training), the performer to immerse himself emotionally and even physically into the music. "In languishing sad passages the performer must languish and grow sad. Thus will the expression of the piece be more clearly perceived by the audience. . . . Similarly, in lively, joyous passages, the executant must again put himself into the appropriate mood. And so, constantly varying the passions, he will barely quiet one before he rouses another."

Good performance was never rigid or metronomic. "Passages in a piece in the major mode which are repeated in the minor may be broadened somewhat on their repetition in order to heighten the effect. On entering a fermata expressive of languidness, tenderness, or sadness, it is customary to broaden slightly." And then there is the use of rubato, about which C. P. E. Bach goes into with great detail. Rubato is the delicate art of varying the rhythm without distorting the basic meter, and C. P. E. is quite specific on the subject. "When the execution is such that one hand seems to play against the bar and the other strictly with it, it may be said that the performer is doing everything that can be required of him." (It is interesting that Chopin said almost the same thing about rubato.)

Carl Philipp Emanuel Bach also adds that most keyboard works contain rubato passages.

In view of all this, there is no reason to approach Bach in the dry, unemotional way so many contemporary musicians do. It is true Bach was not a romantic, and nobody would want romantic dynamics and expressions applied to his music. But it is also true that Bach's great music shrieks for a big, emotional approach—confined, to be sure, within what is known of the way he himself played his music. It seems altogether clear that Bach's big structures are not encased in granite. Sections have to be set off by a delicate use of ritards. Organ mixtures have to have color and sonority. Rhythms have to be flexible. Above all, the *Affekt,* the emotional meaning of the music, has to be brought out. In real life Bach was a vigorous and even violent man, and it is clear that he made music in a red-blooded manner. Present-day interpreters should do no less.

AUG. 26, 1973

The 1960's were still an anti-Romantic period, and virtuosity was held in disdain by everybody except the public. Even such supreme instrumentalists as Jascha Heifetz and Vladimir Horowitz were getting bad reviews from the intellectual writers as early as the late 1930's. Ignored in the polemics was the obvious fact that no artist can be a great performer without a technique fully up to the demands of the music he has elected to play. Technique comes first, and then it is up to the artist to determine exactly what to do with his technique. Some flaunt it ("Is Rockefeller ashamed of his millions?" Moriz Rosenthal once rhetorically asked.) Some keep it in subservience. The

Liszts and Clara Schumanns are still very much with us. But, unfortunately, a musician may have the greatest ideas since the invention of the printed note, and none of them does him any good if he does not have the fingers, lungs, lips to put those ideas into effect. When I wrote this defense of virtuosity, some of my colleagues' worst suspicions about my superficiality were confirmed. One of them took me aside and gave me a lecture on musical probity. I thought I had made it clear in the article that virtuosity was only a tool, though the most important one of any musician. Obviously I was fighting a few generations of ingrained prejudice. Today, when even Liszt operatic paraphrases have returned and are being taken seriously by the intellectuals, there does seem to be a more general acceptance of virtuosity as a legitimate part of music.

About Virtuosity

WHEN NICOLAI GEDDA, a few weeks back, threw back his head, opened his mouth wide and came out with the big, big D in *I Puritani*, the audience recoiled in amazement and then came back with a roaring ovation. No tribute was more deserved. The big, big D may not bulk large in the esthetic scheme of things, but as a manifestation of vocal virtuosity it was electrifying.

There are those, though, who sneer at virtuosity. It was ever thus. Ernest Newman once wrote an essay in which he compared the virtuous with the virtuosos. Clara Schumann, Joseph Joachim and the others of that school were the virtuous. To them music was a holy temple, not to be disturbed or smeared by excesses of virtuoso display. Technique was a means to an end, nothing more, and the artist was a humble envoy at the feet of the composer. How Clara Schumann, that purest of musicians, detested the virtuosos!

And how the virtuosos detested Clara! "If you want to hear how Schumann's music should *not* be played," Liszt once said, "listen to dear Clara." Liszt, of course, was the archetype of the nineteenth-century virtuoso, and during the century his school was dominant. To the Liszts, Sarasates, Wieniawskis, Pattis and Ole Bulls of those years, the performer was more important than the music. Lip service was paid to the composer, but when the chips were down the performer had no hesitation in making alterations here and there to show off *his* instrumental or vocal genius.

Today the ideas of Clara Schumann have taken over, and virtuosity has become almost a dirty word. So dirty, indeed, that it is about time somebody sprang to the defense of virtuosity. For the line between the virtuous and the virtuoso is not all that clear. In certain kinds of music—the bel canto operas, the Paganini caprices, the Liszt rhapsodies—virtuosity is the very raison d'être. In other kinds of music, virtuosity is alien to the entire concept. But—and this is a very big but—a virtuoso equipment is needed to play nearly all music.

Perhaps some definitions are in order. Technique is the ability to reproduce the notes as the composer wrote them. Virtuosity is the showing off of technique. In certain music of extreme difficulty, technique and virtuosity are almost allied. Beethoven's *Grosse Fuge* or the A minor Quartet, or Bartók's Fourth Quartet, need four instrumentalists of power-house caliber. The music itself may be among the most abstract, antivirtuoso expressions of the human mind, but it cannot be played well by any but supreme technicians who also have virtuoso instincts. The same goes for the Chopin études, the Brahms intermezzos, Bach's *Well-Tempered Clavier* and, come to think of it, the Mozart piano concertos. The same goes for *Fidelio*, Wagner's *Ring* and the Mendelssohn Violin Concerto.

Naturally the artistic results are up to the taste and musicianship of the performer. All of us have heard impossibly bad performances of Mozart and Bach from great technicians who had no idea of the music. (Equally bad performances, incidentally, can result just as much from inhibition as from virtuosity.) There is, of course, such a thing as misapplied virtuosity, such a thing as lack of style and scholarship. But that is not the argument. The argument is that the music cannot be expressed at all if the performer does not have the complete physical means to express it freely; and the better the physical means, the better the chances for a good performance.

As for virtuosity as such, there is nothing wrong with it, given the time and place. And so we get back to Gedda's big, big D, Joan Sutherland's interpolations in *Ah, non giunge*, Vladimir Horowitz's octaves in the Liszt Sixth Rhapsody and Zino Francescatti's finger work in Paganini. All of these are examples of musical tightrope-walking, and music would be considerably the poorer without them.

For they illustrate a reflex, a daring, a coordination and training that may be purely empathic in their result but that nevertheless have a value, even an esthetic value, of their own. The performers are doing impossible things with ease, and we identify with them. There is a build-up to incredible tension, and then release. The phenomenon, of course, is not confined to music. The ballerina successfully finishing the thirty-two fouettés, Unus standing on one finger, a 3:56 miler—all of these are tributes to the triumph of will over flesh, to a certain kind of dedication that has driven their bodies in an attempt to achieve things nobody else has achieved.

Are they worth achieving in the first place? Of course! They are not adding to human wisdom but they are decidedly adding to human enjoyment. We all must have our cakes and ale. And in music it is surprising how many composers have written with the virtuoso specifically in mind. Not technique: sheer, unadulterated, blazing virtuosity, without which the music is preposterous. One need do no more than think back to earlier this season, when Donizetti's *Maria di Rohan* and Rossini's *William Tell* were presented with singers who could not begin to handle the music. The results were appalling. Rossini and Bellini demanded high-soaring eagles, and we got ostriches. The very meaning of the music was dissipated.

Even the purest musicians recognized the value of virtuosity. There was Mozart, writing to his father about two of his piano concertos: "I regard them both," he noted with satisfaction, "as concertos which are bound to make the performer perspire." There was Beethoven, swarming all over the piano in his improvisations. There were Handel and Scarlatti, trying to outdo each other on the clavier. Great virtuosos have special gifts, know they have them and are not reluctant to put them on display.

It should be emphasized that virtuosity on its highest level does not mean merely loud and fast. The great virtuoso, as contrasted to the slam-bang exhibitionist, knows how to husband his resources. He uses his special gifts to achieve a certain end, and unleashes his powers only when they have to be unleashed. No conspicuous waste for him. When the heavy guns swing into place, they are aimed at a target worthy of the ammunition expended. Musical history does show, after all, that the greatest virtuosos have generally also been the greatest interpreters; and just because a performer can play the blazes out of Liszt does not necessarily mean he is lost in Opus 109.

APRIL 28, 1963

The subject broached in this article is discussed today much more heatedly by musicians and musicologists than it was in 1963. There was a surprising ignorance about the traditions in Mozart playing—an ignorance shared by all of us at the time. For ideas that were then accepted as "true," laid down by the best scholars of the period, have—shall we say—turned out to be highly debatable. The then-accepted "rules" of Mozart playing and conducting were rigid. Today we realize that the "rules" were in constant flux even in Mozart's own day. There are still so many unexplored areas. I am convinced, for example, that the bass underpinning of Mozart's piano music is completely misunderstood. Most pianists play the concertos as though they have only a right hand, and they entirely miss the color of the pieces. I think I was right in asking for more freedom in performance, coupled to a study of the conventions of Mozart's day. A great deal of work has been done on the subject since 1963. And yet conservatories continue to turn out their brilliant kids who have next to no idea of the history of performance practice. How could they? Their teachers, whom they respect and often revere, are generally of a generation in which such matters were unknown.

A Matter of "Authenticity"

THIS IS a bit belated, but it will serve as an admirable text for a sermon now that a new music season is upon us. It also will be a paradoxical text: one that will plead for the necessity of authenticity while performing older music, and will at the same time point out that authenticity is impossible.

It started with the Mozart series conducted early this summer by Erich Leinsdorf and the Boston Symphony at Tanglewood. This writer wondered whether it was necessary to have as many strings as the conductor used. He also queried some of the points of scholarship in the performances—trills going every which way, and so on.

Whereupon letters started to come in. They boiled down, most of them, to a series of simple questions: what makes *you* so sure that you know the answers? Were you alive in Mozart's time? Do you own any of Mozart's recordings? Have you the faintest idea of Mozart's tempos and dynamics? *Can* you have the faintest idea of Mozart's tempos and dynamics? Smart guy.

And, in many respects, those questioners had a point. For today it is literally impossible to achieve authenticity in performances of Mozart, Haydn and Beethoven (much less Bach and the other Baroque composers; but let's save Bach for a future time). If by authenticity we mean a literal translation of the notes as Mozart would have heard them, it is impossible because too many traditions have been lost and too many factors have physically changed.

One of the changed factors, for instance, is pitch. Today's pitch is A-440 (though many orchestras, especially American ones, go above that in a quest for brilliance). In Mozart's day, pitch was about a half tone lower. Those high F's in the "Queen of the Night" aria were E's in Mozart's ear. Were he to hear a performance today of his G minor Symphony, Mozart would scream in agony. For he, with possibly the most perfect ear of anybody who ever lived, would be hearing his symphony a half-tone sharp, and the aural disturbance would be intolerable to him.

Not only pitch, but the actual instruments have changed. Woodwinds today are keyed quite differently. Horns sound different. Even violin sound today is different, thanks to the introduction of the chin rest and wire strings. The chin rest, which Louis Spohr is said to have made fashionable early in the nineteenth century, makes it possible for violinists to use a much faster, wider vibrato—a vibrato completely unknown in Mozart's time.

These are physical differences, and any sensitive conductor or solo performer who plays Mozart should be aware of them. Not that anything can be done about these physical factors. No violinist today is going to put aside the chin rest, nor is a horn player going to return to a valveless instrument.

But there are other factors about which nearly all conductors today display a blissful ignorance. These even extend to textual matters. Several years ago, H. C. Robbins Landon, in *The Symphonies of Haydn*, carefully collated all modern editions against original manuscripts or first editions. He came up with some real shockers, pointing out error after error in the modern editions. How many conductors have taken the trouble to collate their scores against the Robbins Landon corrections?

Or take the size of present-day orchestras playing Mozart and Haydn. Now, it would be a mistake to think that those two composers liked small orchestras. Mozart was carried away with big groups, and there were a few in Europe at the time, notably the Mannheim orchestra, that almost approximated symphonic groups of today. But the balances were different. Mozart's orchestra increased wind instruments in relation to strings. Writing home to his father on one occasion, he chortled with joy over the large number of strings in an orchestra he had conducted, "and bassoons doubled, of course." Hardly a living conductor cares anything about studying the problems of balance in the Mozart orchestra according to Mozart's own practice.

Nor does he concern himself much with ornamentation. Ornamentation in Mozart's time was a less complicated subject than it was in Bach's. Yet Mozart ornamentation is integral to the music. Do trills start on the main note (as is almost the universal custom today) or the upper (as they almost universally did in Mozart's day)? One hears Mozart performances in which the soloist trills one way, the orchestra another in the same phrase; and not only that, but in any given phrase, conductors today will let their string section do what it wants, the result being some violinists trilling one way, other violinists doing it quite differently at the same time.

And what about differences of national style in early music? This is a subject about which nearly all performing musicians know nothing. There is a marked difference between an eighteenth-century French, and an eighteenth-century Italian or German score. Each nationality developed its own peculiarities in rhythm, dynamics, phrase and ornamentation. Those interested can get a brief summary of those differences in Thurston Dart's valuable little book, *The Interpretation of Music,* recently published by Harper in its Colophon paperback series.

There are other problems facing a present-day musician who wants to present "authentic" performances of old music. A major one is the matter of the performer, in the orchestra and out. In Mozart's time (and indeed up to the First World War) the performer was king, and was allotted a much greater role than he is today.

The irony is that today's search for "authenticity," and its consequent concentration on fidelity to the printed note, completely neglect the fact that in previous days the printed note was merely a rough guide, not a sacred writing. Performers in those days were expected to embellish on the printed note. That showed their "taste." This even extended into the Romantic period, and the autobiographies of Louis Spohr and Ignaz Moscheles give ample testimony to the freedom expected of the performer. Mozart bragged that he never played his concertos twice the same way; he introduced all kinds of variants, embellishments and cadenzas. The notes of any composer up to Beethoven were not intended to be literally translated. And in singing, the performer threw everything overboard. Often the results were unrecognizable, even to the composer.

So where do we stand today? Authenticity being impossible, does that mean anarchy must rule? Not necessarily. Granted the difficulty of the problem, there still remain a few avenues of approach. If we cannot match the original style, we still can approximate it. We can approach the spirit of the music, if not the letter.

That means that musicians today should make a much more stringent study of old styles (a subject, by and large, ignored in conservatories). It means that conductors must realize that the Mozart and Haydn symphonies are lean and sinewy works in which every note is balanced against every other note, every tonal relationship against another. Swamping the winds with thick violin sound is simply not good Mozart-Haydn style. That much, at least, conductors can realize.

All musicians should study the harmonic and emotional significance of the appoggiatura in classic music—a most important subject that too many performers are not even aware of. And musicologists should, instead of poking fun at the illiteracy of many of today's musicians, get together and provide a workable book of performance practices in old music, a book in which everything is carefully spelled out and documented. One of the byproducts of such a book will be a demonstration that performers will have more leeway, not less. But it will be a controlled leeway based on a firm stylistic knowledge, and not the Romantic anarchy that prevails today.

Oct. 6, 1963

I got a lot of letters on this one. Apparently in 1966 my plea for more freedom in performance was so novel as to be actually shocking. Purity and purism do not automatically mean correctness, and even the purest text can be misleading. Once a friend of mine, a skillful amateur pianist, decided to work on Haydn's F minor Variations. He mentioned this to his teacher —a world-famous pianist of notable integrity and dedication —and mentioned that he had just purchased the Schirmer edition of the Haydn. The teacher was outraged. "That is a corrupt edition!" My friend was ordered to get the Henle edition and also was given, as a present, a copy of Haydn's autograph. The Henle edition, as scrupulous as ever, faithfully reproduces the autograph. But what the teacher did not know was that the first English edition of the F minor Variations, published while Haydn was alive, is much closer to the Schirmer edition than to the Henle or to the autograph. The English edition has "Romantic" slur lines in the bass of the first measure, indicating that Haydn wanted the bass countermelody of F–E natural–F against the melodic line on top. The "corrupt" Schirmer edition follows the first edition. So what price purism?

Of Purists and Purity

VLADIMIR HOROWITZ's piano recital, three Sundays ago, represented a kind of interpretive freedom that has all but vanished. In my review I wrote something to the effect that purists probably would not like his approach. Whereupon came a letter from a reader in Boston. Am I correct, he wanted to know, in taking it that you use the term "purist" as a sneer word?

Maybe yes, maybe no. Yes when the concept of purism is unsupported by real stylistic knowledge. No when the exponent of purism has enough imagination to realize that what is behind the notes is just as important as what is in the notes, and perhaps more so.

It is a complicated problem. The aim of any good musician is to reproduce the ideas of the composer as closely as possible.

But reproduction of the ideas involves a set of intangibles as well as direct translation of the printed note. For example, every age has a set of conventions in musical performance. Many of these conventions could not be notated, for musical notation is at best an inexact and even frustrating science; or those conventions were not notated because the composer took it for granted that any performer automatically would do certain things.

Thus in a Mozart piano concerto there were conventions that today are largely ignored. A pianist today, in the name of purism, plays every note as written. If he is especially conscientious, he goes back to the original score, following exactly every one of Mozart's dynamic, rhythmic and textual instructions. He is pure, all right. He also is dead wrong.

Mozart himself, and we have this in his own words, never played his concertos twice the same way. In the name of "taste," he ornamented, embroidered, inserted cadenzas, changed things. This was especially true of slow movements. Mozart would have played legato passages "as smooth as oil." But when slur marks for legato were not present, he would have used a détaché kind of finger stroke. Legato in Mozart's day was only a special effect, like the vibrato on the violin. But today all pianists use constant legato, just as all violinists use a continuous vibrato. Stylistically this is dreadful, when applied to classic music. But that does not stop even the purist from using it.

What is more, Mozart would have employed all kinds of rubato effects. Again we have this on his own authority, and on the authority of many good musicians of his day. But a pianist these days who dared use a pronounced rubato in Mozart would be derided, and the critics would gleefully jump all over him. Yet such a pianist would be in reality closer to Mozart style than one who employs a direct, unvarying metric. Which is the purist?

There is also the matter of ritards. Purists today tend to frown on any kind of slowing-up within a composition, unless the composer specifically indicates a ritard. But there is a great deal of evidence to show that in Beethoven's day a tremendous amount of metrical freedom was allowed. Schindler and Czerny, both pupils of Beethoven, tell us that ritards are to be used to set off the appearance of the second subject in sonata-form exposition. Indeed, Schindler's analysis of how Beethoven wanted his Second Symphony played is an eye opener. In one short section of the slow movement there are about eight tempo changes—slight ritards and accelerandos.

And when we come to Romantic performance practice, which hardly anybody today understands, we arrive at a kind of freedom that, by present standards, is breathtaking. Purists are apt to be literalists, and that is exactly the wrong way to approach Romantic music, for the Romantics had a most cavalier attitude toward the printed note. Liszt himself gave Alexander Siloti permission to change the ending of one of his pieces. The Romantics went in for extremes of dynamics and expressive devices that would be considered vulgar today. Yet if we are so pure, and are so anxious to get close to the composer's intentions, we should by all means make a study of Romantic performance practice and bring back those devices. For that is how the composer expected his music to be played. And hardly anybody today does it.

The point is that purists tend to resort only to the printed note, without a proper knowledge of the devices that go to make up correct style. In short, the trouble with purists is that they are not purists. They are imposing on earlier music the esthetic and emotional standards of their own age, with as much success as an elderly grade-school teacher trying to be Lillian Russell. Unless we are able to unblock ourselves, to rid ourselves of the notion that the printed note is the only secure thing on which to lean, we are going to be pedants, not interpreters.

Of course in any case the ideal of complete stylistic identification is a chimera. It is, quite literally, impossible to play earlier music as the composer heard it. Pitch and instruments themselves have changed too much. But what we can do is try to capture, as closely as possible, the spirit in which a work was conceived. This involves a careful study—in which an interpreter's own musical instincts come to the fore—wherein an area is staked out between pedanticism and eccentricity. Self-expression unsupported by a good deal of musicological fact is no good at all. But neither is musicological fact unsupported by self-expression.

When it comes to musicological fact, though, interpreters today are not going to learn much from the musicologists about Romantic performance practice. Musicologists in the last generation have done an immense amount of work in the period before the nineteenth century, and virtually nothing after that. We are in their debt for the instructions they have given us about Mozart and his predecessors. But most of the active musical repertory comes after the eighteenth century, and musicologists seem to regard Romanticism with the distaste of a teetotaler confronted by a bottle of Lafite 1953. They don't (to chant an old refrain that has appeared so often in this column) know what they are missing.

MAY 8, 1966

I was happy to receive the Neumann book discussed below. Published in 1979, it backed up in extraordinary detail the conclusions I had independently reached more by intuition than by the application of a knowledge as vast as that of Frederick Neumann. Mr. Neumann, a scrappy man who relishes a good fight, took on the entire musicological establishment in this imposing book. As these lines are being written, the full returns are not yet in, but reviews in learned publications suggest that the book is going to change many ideas hitherto regarded as sacrosanct.

On Trills and Other Ornaments

MUSICOLOGY is no less mutable than any of the other artistic or scientific disciplines. Bits of knowledge are added to bits of knowledge and the result, when put together, often overturns received opinion. A recent hefty publication with an equally hefty title, *Ornamentation in Baroque and Post-Baroque Music, With Special Emphasis on J. S. Bach,* by Frederick Neumann (Princeton University Press), is not only the definitive book on the subject to date. It will also make many scholars and musicians revise some of their pet ideas.

For decades musicologists have been working on performance practice in pre-Romantic music, from Beethoven back to the Middle Ages, and the topic of ornamentation occupies a highly prominent position in any study of the subject. It is not a "dead" matter of interest only to scholars. Rather it involves any musician and, by extension, music lover. All pre-Beethoven music was ornamented, and, generally speaking, the farther back in time the music is, the more it was ornamented—with trills, grace notes, mordents, appoggiaturas, acciaccaturas, accents, interpolated cadenzas, diminutions and the whole battery of embellishments that performing musicians brought to their art. To perform old music with any degree of style or sophistication, the musician must have a comprehensive knowledge of correct ornamentation and the conventions that the performers and composers of the time brought to the music.

This information has been supplied for well nigh a century by musicologists, beginning with such pioneers as Edward Dannreuther and Arnold Dolmetsch. Working on the principles laid down by those two—and other—men, scholars have by now thoroughly investigated the problems. Many of us thought that the "rules" were pretty much codified in recent years. We are all very sophisticated now. We have been taught that it is improper in classical music to begin a trill on the main note. We have immersed ourselves in the proper way to play a *Vorschlag*, a mordent, a *Nachschlag*, a *coulé*, a *Schneller*, a *Doppeltcadence*. We think we know something about *notes inégales*.

What's more, we have been applying strict rules to the old music we have been playing. Musicians rush to Donington, to Dart, or whatever the source, to look up the meaning of a musical symbol, and they then treat the execution of the symbol as an eternal law, to be applied under all conditions in any set of circumstances.

Now comes Mr. Neumann, who has spent a decade reading everything ever written on the subject, and he has come to the conclusion that much of what we have been told simply does not apply. Previous scholars may or may not be right in their interpretation of any individual symbol, but their findings simply cannot be raised into a set of universal rules. For, according to Mr. Neumann, there was no such thing as common seventeenth- or eighteenth-century practice. Nor did composers expect their interpreters to stick slavishly to a set of rules. Taste, imagination and insight were much more important. Composers expected performers to ornament their music, but they wanted it done with style and musicianship.

Mr. Neumann makes the point, which this column has been yammering at for years, that music is no more than a set of admittedly inefficient notations on a printed page, waiting to come to life through the efforts of the performer. He cites great composers and theorists of the eighteenth century who kept pointing out, as Couperin did, that "Just as there is a great distance between grammar and rhetorical delivery, there is an infinitely greater distance between musical notation and artistic performance." Thus, Mr. Neumann concludes, "literalness in performance is not a virtue but a vice which grows in proportion to the age of the music. This is true even of the most solidly structural elements. The implications of this fact are raised to the second power with regard to ornaments that are predestined by their very nature for improvisatory flexibility."

Tables of ornaments supplied by composers, even such great composers as Couperin and Bach, are "thrice removed" from the reality of desirable execution, Mr. Neumann says. Those are merely "the abstract nature of any general model," which in reality "has countless concrete embodiments that differ with one another through innumerable variations of countless elements." In Bach's day a performer knew what was the conceptual essence and what was not. "There was little danger that he might mistake the model for a pattern to be reproduced mechanically." But many modern researchers have made the mistake of taking the models of ornament tables "as strict norms, as dies from which they must cast ever-identical coins."

The point that is basic to Mr. Neumann's study is that the

ornament does not dictate the musical logic. Rather, the musical logic dictates the ornament. Take the problem of the trill.
Almost every treatise of the eighteenth century specifically said
that the trill must start on the upper note. Does that make it a
universal rule? Not so, says Mr. Neumann. That "rule" will
have to be substantially revised. For one thing, he points out
many examples of main-note trills. Indeed, he believes that the
habit of starting the trill on the upper note came late to Germany, and that the main-note trill "was by far the most commonly used design from Froberger and Kerll to Reinken,
Murschauser and Buxtehude."

What about Bach and the trill? Well, says Mr. Neumann, the
current doctrine that confines the Bach trill to the upper note
"becomes highly suspect. Here too it is unrealistic to assume
that Bach, in an environment offering the richness of a wide
choice, would have confined himself to the poverty of a single
design that is utterly inadequate to meet the needs of his infinitely varied musical contexts."

There are technical reasons, among others, why the concept
of the upper-tone trill must be approached with caution, not to
say suspicion. One reason advanced for the use of the upper
partial in the trill is the glint of welcome dissonance it can give
to the musical texture. But, Mr. Neumann warns, if the upper-
note trill is slavishly followed, what can result is not the welcome dissonance. Instead there can be parallel fifths and
octaves, the worst sin in Baroque and Classical harmony; and
he provides several gruesome examples of parallels resulting
from starting the trill from above.

In any case, Mr. Neumann does not believe in the harmonic
reason for the Bach trill. It is wrong to think that all of Bach's
trills are "harmonic" ornaments. Quite the reverse is true.
"Probably the great majority of Bach's trills are of the 'melodic'
category that intensifies linearity without affecting harmony. It
is a misbelief that all of Bach's trills have to start with the upper
note. That Bach's trills frequently started on the main note
is made probable through a powerful and long-standing Italo-
German tradition (still fully operative in Buxtehude) and upheld
by much musical evidence."

Nor does this apply only to Bach. "For many composers, among them Vivaldi, Domenico Scarlatti, Handel and probably all other masters of their generation, the main-note design was most likely the basic trill form."

At the end of his book, Mr. Neumann offers some advice to the present-day musician. It is his conclusion that too many complex issues are involved for "simplistic" rules to cover the contingencies; that a valid and convincing performance must be "an act of artistry, not a historical demonstration"; that there is no such thing as a "definitive" performance; that the execution of ornaments in early music was much freer than generally assumed. Mr. Neumann may or may not be right in all of his findings and conclusions, and for a long time to come musicologists are going to pick over his book, taking exception to this or that. But his central thesis will be a corrective to the rigidity imposed on performance practice by too many musicologists of the last generation. Now it remains for an expert of Mr. Neumann's stature to do an equivalent book on nineteenth-century performance practice, a field that has been researched hardly at all. It is confidently assumed that since most music in the repertory stems from the nineteenth-century, everybody knows all about it. The assumption could not be wronger.

JUNE 3, 1979

Since this piece was written I have dug out some evidence supporting my view that repeats are not to be slavishly observed, just because they are there. In the October, 1966 Music and Letters, *Nicholas Temperley took a look at Sir George Smart's timings between 1819 and 1843. Smart was the conductor of the Philharmonic Society in London, and his own timings in standard works of Beethoven, Mozart and Haydn indicate that they were very close to today's timings without repeats. Smart's scribblings on the programs specifically tell us that repeats were often omitted, and that seems to have been the practice of the day. François-Antoine Habeneck, the great French specialist in Beethoven in the 1830's, did not, according to Berlioz, take the repeats. Dvorak was irritated when the repeat in his Sixth Symphony was observed, and the manuscript score in Prague has the repeat crossed out with the written remark: "Once and for all, without the repeat." There is every indication that composers often left repeats optional, from Frescobaldi (who says as much in the introduction to one of his organ books) to the late Romantics.*

Modern Literalism and Repeats

Here's a complicated and a dull subject, but an important one: the problem of repeats. A repeat in music is a note-for-note restatement of a portion of a composition, directed by the composer. In standard sonata form, for example, the exposition is almost always supposed to be repeated. In Bach movements, especially those in binary form, repeat signs ask the performer to replay each section. And so on.

In our own time, most repeat signs except those in small units, such as in minuets and scherzos, have been generally ignored. That is, they have been ignored by performers up to the last decade. Nowadays, with the almost maniacal determination of performers to reproduce the printed note exactly as the composer left it, all repeat signs are being observed. Sometimes this results in hearing a piece of music as if for the first time. Take Schubert's pretty little Sonata in A (Op. 120). As the older pianists presented it, the sonata was a charming *morceau.* Clifford Curzon's timing was typical: 15 minutes, 36 seconds. But last fall Ashkenazy played the same sonata, and his timing was 22 minutes, 5 seconds. Same sonata; and still pretty, though no longer little. Ashkenazy took all of the repeats.

Serkin in 1956 played the Schumann *Etudes symphoniques* in 17 minutes, 23 seconds. In 1963 he took all of the repeats, extending the work to 22 minutes, 14 seconds. Not long ago, Sawallisch conducted the Vienna Philharmonic in Mozart's *Jupiter* Symphony. His timing was 24 minutes, 50 seconds. When Leinsdorf conducted it a few years ago, he took all the repeats, and we had a *Jupiter* running 37 minutes, 58 seconds.

As a matter of fact, tempos in general seem to be broadening out. Today's musicians, in an effort to get away from anything that might be construed as "virtuosity"—a dirty word—tend to take fast sections slower than they used to be taken. That, plus the new concept of observing every repeat (especially in Classic and such early Romantic works as the Schubert sonatas), can give the music the aspect of being seen through one of those freak lengthening mirrors.

Little has been written on the subject of repeats, and whether or not they should be taken. Those who say yes claim that the composer knew what he was doing; that there is an architectural reason for the repeats, and they should be observed. Those who say no point out that most repeats, especially those in the Romantic period, were a matter of pure convention; that the composers wrote them in out of sheer habit.

Not only musicologists have avoided the problem. Early manuals on music have very little to say about repeats. Of one thing we are certain, though. Any performer today who takes a repeat in any slow movement of Bach, and plays it exactly the same way the second time around, is all wrong. He may be right in observing the repeat; but he is missing its whole point in not ornamenting and embellishing it. That was the essential point: for the performer to demonstrate his "taste" and skill by adding his own ideas to those of the composer.

In his new book on musical form, Wallace Berry touches on the problem. He indicates that repeats may be regarded, in many cases, as a survival of an earlier practice; and then "their relevance to mature single-movement sonata form becomes questionable." One reason often advanced for repeats is to impress the themes of the exposition on the listener's mind; but this,

Berry suggests, "is of doubtful validity and fails to take into account the evolution of single-movement sonata form from binary antecedents."

Very few musicians of an older generation bothered much with repeats. Perhaps they were right; perhaps they were closer to the tradition than we are. And there is one precedent that can be cited. In his biography of Beethoven, Anton Schindler has a long section discussing the way Beethoven himself played two of his piano sonatas. He writes, about the G major (Op. 14, No. 1): "Those who truly enter into the spirit of this fine movement will find it advisable not to repeat the first part." He gives as his reason: "The gratification of the listener will be unquestionably increased, while it may be possibly diminished by the frequent repetition of the same phrases." Now, Carl Czerny studied with Beethoven; and both Liszt and Leschetizky studied with Czerny; and between them, Liszt and Leschetizky turned out most of the greatest pianists of the century. Might it be that in not observing the repeats they were working much closer to Beethoven's own performance practice than those determined and dogged pianists and conductors today who insist on repeating everything?

It is hard to avoid the suspicion that today's musicians are so doing because of slavish imitation. Is there really a structural necessity for taking all repeats? I am inclined to doubt it. Obviously certain repeats should be observed, and Eric Blom points out some examples in his article on repeats in Grove's Dictionary. He cites several Beethoven sonatas in which a special point is missed if the pianist goes right through. What Blom does is plead for some common sense.

"In modern performing practice," he writes, "it is by no means imperative that a composer's demand for a repeat should be obeyed, but each instance of it deserves to be considered on its merits, and treated as the performer thinks fit."

This makes sense. It makes more sense than slavishly deciding in advance to observe all repeats. And if the performer is one of those conscientious but uninspired players, the results can be excruciating. Instead of a performance being dull, it is twice as dull. A great imaginative artist can get away with it, but great imaginative artists are always rare. What all others end up with is the letter but not the spirit of music. Today, overwhelmingly, the letter is considered more important than the spirit. And that is terribly wrong.

It all comes down to the phenomenon noted many times in this column. Our age has developed a school of musical literalists in which application occupies a higher place than inspiration. They try to get themselves out of the music, striving for a sort of superobjectivity. But in so doing they miss an important part of the mystery of the recreative process. For all interpretation should be—and was, until very recent times—the refraction of a creator's thought through the prism of the performer's mind. If the performer refuses to have a mind, that is his privilege, but you can't expect much vitality in interpretation to result.

MARCH 20, 1966

The complaint voiced in this article remains with us almost as much today, though there are signs that change is coming. Musicologists are just beginning to turn their attention to the last century, and there even is a scholarly publication concerned with Romantic music (though that, like most musicological publications, is predominantly archival and analytical, with very little concern about performance practice). It has remained true that musicologists, who can be as arrogant as the next musician, continue to poke fun at the performing artist and music critic. They have the Ph.D., which puts them into an exalted class. But their ideas about Romantic performance practice are as vague as those of the musicians they deride. I think, however, that the next decade will be seeing a much larger amount of work on the subject. It is the coming field.

Romanticism and
the Modern Mind

WHEN ARTURO BENEDETTI MICHELANGELI played the *Emperor* Concerto with the New York Philharmonic a few weeks ago, it was clear that an unusual pianist was at work. But how unusual was not to be revealed until his solo concert in Carnegie Hall. It was there that the originality displayed in his concerto performance veered directly into eccentricity; and quite a few pianists in the audience walked out mumbling to themselves. Indeed, some left at intermission. Most professionals hated the concert. Michelangeli's playing ran counter to some of their most sacred precepts. But the man has a remarkable projection, something on the order of a Richter, and he seemed to hypnotize the nonprofessionals in the audience.

I myself was quite disturbed by the recital. Nothing in the *Emperor* had prepared me for the willful approach Michelangeli brought to Beethoven (the C minor Sonata, Op. 111) and Chopin (the B flat minor Scherzo). In retrospect, it is easy to see that any experienced listener might have guessed. The soloist playing a concerto is necessarily held in restraint by conductor and orchestra. Tempos and rhythms are established, and the soloist has to work within a certain framework. At a concert he is on his own. Michelangeli's originality in the *Emperor*, even within the framework, should have suggested that his solo concert would undoubtedly be a most unconventional affair.

So it was. Michelangeli can do anything at the piano; he is an extraordinary technician, a master of color effects and obviously an intellectual. But his musical ideas are, by most current standards, weird. He illustrates a kind of Romanticism that went out of vogue as far back as the turn of this century. At least, many of his devices are Romantic: the lingering on notes, the slowdown to introduce new musical material, the long ritards, the unconventional phrasings, the all-too-obvious stresses, as subtle as a slam in the face.

But, and this is what bothers me, I am not convinced that as Michelangeli plays he is representative of true Romanticism. Indeed, I do not think he has the faintest idea about Romanticism. The great Romantic instrumentalists of our day—and here I am thinking of men like Kreisler, Hofmann, Rachmaninoff, Gabrilowitsch, men whose training was in the nineteenth century—did take all kinds of liberty with the music. No matter how many liberties they took, however, there was in their playing a unified element, a consecutive sweep from beginning to end; and this involved an emotional as well as architectural sweep.

In Michelangeli's playing there was no consecutive sweep. Lines were constantly being broken, and both the C minor Sonata and the B flat minor Scherzo came out as a collection of details. The piano itself, and certain pianistic devices, appeared more important than the consecutive flow of the music.

Now, I—of all people—have no objection to any artist taking considerable leeway. Indeed, it is to be welcomed in this era of instrumental conformity, where the playing of one artist is like the playing of any other artist. But I object strenuously to the kind of musical approach that distorts line, meter and meaning. The secret of Romanticism is freedom (which means leeway in expression even to the point of slight textual changes) coupled to the kind of mind that has the ability to link phrase to phrase, section to section, movement to movement. Most young pianists today have the latter to the detriment of the former. Michelangeli has the former but not the latter.

He really is a modern pianist who tries to be Romantic, but he simply does not feel Romanticism. All of his Romantic devices sound arbitrarily superimposed, and, as such, forced and artificial. With his phenomenal ability, and with his almost eerie power of projection, Michelangeli is going to continue to excite audiences everywhere he plays; but he is also going to misrepresent certain kinds of music if he continues to play as he did in Carnegie Hall the other week.

The subject of Romanticism and the modern mind is a complicated one. Most of our active musical literature is Romantic and post-Romantic, and it seems to be an article of faith that musicians understand this kind of music, but are less equipped to handle Classic and Baroque. As a matter of fact, the reverse is true. Thanks to a generation of concentrated musicological research from Mozart back to the early Renaissance, young musicians today seem to have a much better idea about pre-Romantic music than about music from 1830 to 1900, which means the bulk of the repertory.

I mean that quite seriously. Just as any educated musician today knows a good deal about performance practice in Mozart's time, almost none knows anything about performance practice in Liszt's. For one thing, next to nothing has been written about it. Most musicological research concerns itself with early music. For another, up to now most musicians in the West have been brought up in an antiromantic era, and the traditions of Romanticism have all but vanished.

Most young musicians do not even know how to read the notes of a Romantic piece. A composer like Schumann, for instance, took great pains to indicate inner-voice relationships, carefully marking the phrases, notating the flags of individual notes so that they stand out clearly. He did not do this for fun, it has a harmonic and polyphonic meaning. But no young musician even notices them when he plays the *Carnaval* or *Kinderscenen*, just as he fails to bring out stepwise bass notes, a convention universally practiced by the Romantic pianists and expected by the Romantic composers.

Of course even in its own day Romanticism had its excrescences and exaggerations. There are bad artists in every generation. But one of the crying needs of present-day musicology and present-day interpretation is a thorough study of performance practices of the nineteenth century. Nobody is going to expect any musician to accept, slavishly, the fruits of whatever research turns up, no more than any musician is expected to follow slavishly the fruits of present-day Bach research. Any musician must read, study, experiment and make up his own mind. He can do that with the enormous wealth of material currently available about performance practices in the eighteenth century. But about the nineteenth there is nothing at all.

FEB. 6, 1966

*Not only forgotten nineteenth-century performance practice
but also forgotten nineteenth-century music has constantly interested me, and that has made me something of an oddball in
intellectual musical circles. But I failed to see why some idiotic
Baroque note-spinning should be taken seriously while the
much more interesting (all right: interesting to me) music of
the pre-Romantics and Romantics should be allowed to be despised. How can the music of Chopin be understood without
some knowledge of Hummel, Field, Dussek, Moscheles and
Kalkbrenner? I found some of that music of real merit, and had
no hesitation inflicting my tastes on my readers. If art critics
could write long pieces about minor Barbizon and Hudson
River painters, and be generally applauded, if literary critics
could write infinitely boring studies about long-forgotten nineteenth-century novelists and poets, I felt that I had the right to
indulge in some of my enthusiasms. And I did.*

*The Metropolitan Opera Festival at Newport lasted only one
summer, to be replaced by the Newport Music Festival which,
for years, unearthed forgotten nineteenth-century music for all
instrumental combinations. More recently the festival has oriented itself toward more standard programs, though it still has
some unusual odds and ends in it.*

Then Miss Bingley Sat
at the Pianoforte

IT IS an evening at Netherfield House, and Mr. Darcy is writing
a letter to his sister. He is being pestered by the doting Miss
Bingley. "Tell your sister," she says, "I am delighted to hear of
her improvement on the harp." Presently he appeals to Miss
Bingley and Elizabeth Bennet for the indulgence of some music.
Miss Bingley, anxious to show off, seats herself at the pianoforte.
Mrs. Hurst sings. Elizabeth turns over some music that lies on
the instrument.

Jane Austen does not tell us what kind of music was there.

One likely candidate could well have been the Trio for Cello, Harp and Piano by François Adrien Boieldieu. Why not? The piece probably was composed around the time *Pride and Prejudice* was published, in 1813. It was scored for a very popular combination of instruments. It contained surefire material, being a potpourri of themes from Mozart operas. It was brilliant without being too hard for amateurs.

What brings all this to mind is the fact that this Boieldieu piece was played by three musicians of the Metropolitan Opera the other week at Newport; and, listening to it, all I could think about was Jane Austen. Several Sundays ago, writing about the Metropolitan Opera Festival at Newport, I ventured the guess that the peripheral events—the lectures, the chamber-music concerts and taped operas—would be of more importance than the "big" things of the festival, namely, the evening operas in concert form. We can always hear *Otello* or *Aïda*. But things like the Boieldieu have not been given a public performance for a hundred years or so, and probably will not be heard for another hundred, if ever—not unless a remarkable shift in repertory takes place.

What the eager musicians of the Metropolitan did at Newport was to ransack libraries and collections for forgotten music of the nineteenth century. The idea was to present chamber concerts and connoisseur concerts of music that had a bearing on opera. That explains the presence of the Boieldieu. He was an important operatic composer at the turn of the nineteenth century, and this piece served a double purpose: to illustrate a non-operatic piece by an opera composer (the festival also presented chamber music by Donizetti, Verdi, Ponchielli and others) and also to illustrate his ideas about Mozart.

Boieldieu's work appeared on a program entitled "Salon Music of Opera Composers." It was a genre drawing-room piece illustrative of an enormous quantity of printed music up to about 1850. There actually was a time in history when there was no television, no radio, no phonograph, no player piano, no cinema. And, some hundred and fifty years ago, concerts were few and far between. So people had music at home. If you were an Esterházy, you had the means to keep a full orchestra and engage a

Haydn to compose for it and conduct. If you were part of an upper middle class family, you had a piano, most likely a harp, and you listened to your daughters and their friends sing and play.

And what did they sing and play? Songs, ballads, and above all arrangements from opera. When spectacularly successful works like Meyerbeer's *Huguenots* or Auber's *Masaniello* had their premières in Paris, everybody wanted to sample the music. Not everybody could get to Paris, but publishers could and did arrange the music of *Huguenots* and *Masaniello* for every conceivable combination that could be played by amateurs—for solo piano, piano duet, violin and piano, flute and piano, violin solo, trio, harp solo, harp and piano, harp and violin, flute, harp and piano, and so on.

Composers like Franz Hünten and Henri Herz made fortunes transcribing this kind of material for the palpitating young ladies of Europe. Piano solos were especially successful, and they ranged from simple melodies to the fiendish transcriptions by Liszt and Thalberg for the supervirtuosos. As often as not, all titles were published in French. That was fashionable: *Variations brillantes et grande fantaisie sur des airs de l'opéra 'Leicester, ou Le Château de Kenilworth,' de D. F. Auber, composé par J. Rosenhain.*

As the century progressed, opera transcriptions began to fall from favor, but that did not in the least stop the production of salon music. Some composers, like Moritz Moszkowski, concentrated on graceful piano pieces for the home (and these pieces also were taken up by every virtuoso of the period). Other composers wrote drawing-room chamber music. On one Newport program were Gounod's *Hymn to St. Cecilia*, for violin, piano and organ; and the Saint-Saëns Serenade for Violin, Viola, Piano and Organ. Not every house in Europe had an organ, but many had harmoniums (those small pump organs that used to be part of so many American parlors at the turn of the century), and at the concert a harmonium instead of organ was used.

Both the Gounod and Saint-Saëns pieces had much in common: sweetness verging on the saccharine, rich harmonies, a deliberate (some might say cynical) attempt to woo. But at the same time, both pieces had an extraordinary amount of period charm, like a Corot painting. Corot has come back into favor, and it is not impossible that such musical equivalents as these Gounod and Saint-Saëns works might also make the turn. Saint-Saëns especially. He was a really important composer, and in some respects the first of the neoclassicists. One of these days I will write a piece about him.

There was a Trio for piano, violin and cello by Michael Balfe, who got on the Newport program because he was primarily an opera composer. Today he is forgotten. His most famous work, *The Bohemian Girl*, seems to be out of the repertory, and his disrepute is such that the Schwann long-playing record catalogue does not have a single entry under his name. This A major Trio turned out to be a very respectable work. Balfe clearly had been influenced by middle-period Beethoven, and the first movement of the trio is built on a theme not unlike the one that opens Beethoven's C minor Violin Sonata. The piano writing is vigorous and idiomatic, and the first-violin part of virtuoso difficulty.

Listening to this fascinating work and, indeed, to the music on all the other programs, one was again struck by the realization of how much music of the nineteenth century remains unexplored. In unearthing some of this material, the Metropolitan Opera Festival not only came up with unexpected riches, but established itself as—of all things—a protagonist of the Romantic revival in a field of music outside opera. Perhaps it was an example of serendipity. But many of us are thankful.

SEPT. 3, 1967

Not much has changed since this article was written. Conservatories all over the world continue to produce expertly trained instrumentalists and singers who seem to be turned by the same lathe. *So few have any personality, imagination, flair, audience rapport. It is a cause for concern. Artists today do not even seem to like their audience. Many years ago I wrote a Sunday piece on their behavior. They look intently at the conductor, at the orchestra, at the ceiling—everywhere but at the audience, except when acknowledging applause. They seem to want to be anonymous. Artists used to have an aura. It had nothing to do with show business. They represented something. The only thing most of today's artists represent is gray uniformity.*

All Those Smart Kids, Where Is Their Individuality?

Can there be such a thing as too much musicianship? Or, to put it another way, misapplied musicianship? I was thinking of this, while browsing through the new Juilliard the other week, and also while talking to some of the Manhattan School of Music officials. I was looking at those smart Juilliard kids, all bursting with genius, all eager to set the world on fire when they come out: these smart kids who can do everything, who pride themselves on their expertise, who have the arrogance of youth and talent.

And who have a tendency to look alike, sound alike and think alike.

The conservatories are at fault, and they have been at fault for many years now. Any sensitive musician going around the world has noted the same thing. The conservatories, from Moscow and Leningrad to Juilliard, Curtis and Indiana, are producing a standardized product (I am speaking of young performers, not composers). The really talented youngsters are being groomed for the big time and, specifically, international competitions. They come out with spectacular techniques, with a good deal of integrity and respect for the composer, with a big repertory. Then they compete. Many hop from competition to competition, knowing well in advance what jurors like: clarity, undeviating rhythm, easy technique, "musicianship." I put the word musicianship in quotes, because, as often as not, it is a false kind of musicianship—a musicianship that sees the tree and not the forest, that takes care of the detail but ignores the big picture; a musicianship that is tied to the printed note rather than to the emotional meaning of a piece.

Conservatory teachers will deny this. They unanimously say that they always try to bring out the individuality of a student. But they as well as their pupils are slaves of this age, and it is an age that is, on the whole, objective. The fact remains that there is a dreadful uniformity today, and also an appalling lack of knowledge about the culture and performance traditions of the past. For this there are many reasons. One can cite the post-Schnabel, post-Toscanini, post-Stravinsky emphasis on adherence to the printed note (not that they themselves always obeyed their own rules). One can cite something much earthier —the heavy work loads carried by the students. They have to practice their heads off, take a full academic schedule, play in the conservatory orchestra or sing in the opera workshop. That does not leave much time for reading, or even listening. It is surprising how narrow the interests of most students are. They are slaves to their instrument or their voice and have little time for anything else.

That is why it is so important for conservatories to insist that students immerse themselves in other kinds of music, and to see to it that they are exposed to different kinds of esthetic philosophies and performance standards. For instance, there is a smug assumption that technique today is better than it ever was, that all the better kids from the conservatories can play circles around the equivalents of a past generation. This is nonsense. There are no pianists coming up today with the equipment of a young Rachmaninoff, Lhévinne, Hofmann or Horowitz. Violin technique has not gone beyond Heifetz, Elman or (judging from his records) Sarasate. We won't even talk about singing. All one has to do is listen to a record of Caruso, Slezak, Melchior, Abendroth, Melba or Galvany to see what has vanished from the earth.

But how many kids know those records? How many conservatories, as a matter of fact, have good record collections of the great performers of the past? (Or, having them, know how to use them?) Yet one would think it should be mandatory for students to be exposed to the work of the great musicians of the past. Perhaps they might even get an idea or two.

And they should be exposed to scholars who know the history of performance practice, which most teachers do not. Too many teachers, conditioned to twentieth-century ideas, teach Bach and other Baroque music exactly the wrong way. This leads to what musicologist Sol Babitz calls "sewing-machine Bach." It so happens that the performers through Mozart's time, and well into the nineteenth century, had immense leeway. The printed note was only a general guide, and the performer was expected to take it from there. The City University of New York is currently having a series devoted to performance practice problems, and in his inaugural lecture Robert Donington pointed out that Bach and the others actually preferred to leave as much as possible to the performer. That is why Baroque music has so few expression marks. The composer trusted the performer to play according to the dictates of his own skill, taste and imagination.

Donington also quoted Johann Mattheson's famous list. Mattheson was a major composer and a friend of Handel, and he wrote, in 1713, that everything could be portrayed in music: "love, jealousy, hatred, gentleness, impatience, lust, indifference, fear, vengeance, fortitude, timidity, magnanimity, horror, dignity, baseness, splendor, indigence, pride, humility, joy, laughter, weeping, mirth, pain, happiness, despair, storm, tranquillity, even heaven and earth, sea and hell—together with all the actions in which men participate." Students should be made to memorize this passage. It could be a corrective against the dry, metrically exact, objective manner in which so much Bach is played.

The point is that few conservatory students anywhere in the world are made acquainted with this kind of material. It is not that they have to take it on faith. Even scholars disagree, as the delighted audience noted a few Fridays ago at one of the City University lectures, when the peppery Sol Babitz and the urbane

Robert Donington all but came to blows over a disputed reading of an eighteenth-century source. But students have to learn some of the prerogatives of being an artist-performer, and they also have to learn that a good deal of the approach taught to them in the conservatories must be unlearned. This is especially true of performance practice in Romantic music, but I already have had my say about that.

It should be a truism that you can't understand the present unless you understand the past. Conservatory training today is concentrated too much on the present, and one result is that graduates come out knowing next to nothing about certain practices in music of the past that were taken for granted only fifty years ago. There are people who know a great deal about these matters, and conservatories should consult them. There also is on records a sweep of performance practice from the middle 1850's, and even before. When you listen to Pachmann playing Chopin, you are listening to the playing of a man who was born while Chopin was still alive. Whether or not you like his playing, he represents the living tradition of the period from mid-century on, just as those singers on records who sang under the batons of Seidl and Richter and other Wagner-trained conductors presumably knew something more about the nineteenth-century literature than singers do today. And yet conservatories keep on functioning as though this material does not exist!

Oct. 19, 1969

The young Daniel Barenboim was one of the few conductors of his generation with the instinct to vary a piece of music, getting delicate shifts into rhythm and phrase. His inspiration was admittedly Wilhelm Furtwängler, and many critics could not stand his work, accusing him of being a bad copy of his master. I found him convincing and refreshingly original.

In quoting Anton Schindler on Beethoven, I am perfectly aware of the low repute in which Schindler is held by musicologists. Schindler has been found inaccurate in many of his dates and facts. But that does not necessarily invalidate his remarks on Beethoven's style. Nor did anything that Schindler wrote in respect to performance practice contradict other contemporary reports.

Yes, the Artist Can Disagree with the Composer

LET'S TALK about rhythm, the heart and soul and lungs and legs of music. It is rhythm that sets off a piece of music and propels it to its end. It is rhythm that, properly handled, lends interest to a musical line. But it is amazing how many musicians have so little feel for rhythm. This is especially true of conductors. Either they establish a rhythmic pattern at the beginning and relentlessly pursue it, one-two-three-four, one-two-three-four, or they try to vary it by breaking up the pulse, and then there is chaos. Only a handful have the secret of maintaining the basic pulse and making delicate variations within it.

The basic pulse is the meter, and that is indestructible. Meter must be maintained. If a piece of music is in threes, or fours, or sixes, there must be a constant feeling of threes, fours or sixes. But while meter is unalterable, many things can rhythmically be done within the meter. There can be slight adjustments, changes in tempo, accents. Only the finest musicians have this secret, this ability to modify rhythm without changing the basic meter.

These rhythmic modifications have to be made. Notation is at best an inexact science, and in addition there are certain conventions that composers expected. The conventions go back to Bach and undoubtedly before. Man is not a metronome, and the greater the musical mind, the more liberties—within the meaning of the meter, of course—he allows himself. Not long ago it was universally believed that a musician who played Bach was not allowed to tinker with the rhythm. But a minimum amount of research would have made it clear that Bach was always tinkering with the rhythm. His pupils described how Bach, playing or conducting his own music, was greatly concerned with the *Affekt*—the emotional and expressive meaning of a piece. If we can be sure of one thing, it is that Bach would have played his music with great freedom and equal color.

Similarly Mozart, who was always writing about rubato. Similarly Beethoven, if Anton Schindler is to be believed. Schindler was a pupil of Beethoven's, and wrote a book that contains a few bar-by-bar descriptions of how Beethoven played two of his sonatas and conducted the Second Symphony. The other week, Daniel Barenboim conducted the Philadelphia Orchestra in the Beethoven Second, and I was struck by the manner in which Barenboim closely approximated what Schindler has written. I do not know if the young conductor has read Schindler, but his delicate rhythmic and tempo modifications in the slow movement were exactly in line with Schindler's strictures.

Schindler isolated measures 55 through 75 of the slow movement. At measure 56 he calls for a *poco accelerando*—a slight speeding-up. At measure 59, in the last half of the bar, he indicated a *poco lento*, a delicate slowing-down. This continues through the first half of the following measure, after which the original tempo of the movement is resumed. (The entire passage, if done with subtlety as Schindler describes it, makes musical sense and adds a lovely, piquant quality to the flow of the music.) At measure 63, Schindler wants another *poco accelerando*, up to the last half of measure 68, where the initial tempo comes back. At measure 71, *crescendo and accelerando*. At the beginning of measure 75, *poco allegretto*.

Schindler warns that these devices must be handled with taste and discretion. He himself hated the exhibitionistic conducting that was coming in with the Romantics. But he wanted Beethoven's music to be performed with expressivity, "with little breaks in the tempo" to provide interest, contrast and tension. The secret, of course, is to integrate these devices within the pulse in a natural-sounding manner. A sensitive musician, such as Barenboim, can do it. Others are stiff and uncomfortable when they try it.

Another thing that impressed me about Barenboim was his avoidance of accented upbeats. He always gave the feeling of pulse, and he never threw the meter askew even when he was beating through the measure. Accented upbeats drive me out of my mind. They are hard to describe in words, but let's try. Say a piece of music is in common (four-four) time, and there is a sequence of three rests and a quarter note, followed by a bar with four quarter notes. A careless or rhythmically sloppy musician will come down heavily on the first of those five notes, accenting the last note in the bar with rests, rather than the first note in the following bar. What we then hear is a grouping of five—"ONE-two-three-four-five"—rather than "... and-ONE-two-three-four." It is as if an actor were to declaim: "TO be or not to BE, that is the quesTION." The entire meter goes cockeyed.

Probably this matter of rhythmic inflection cannot be taught. Some musicians are born with rhythm, and they seem to be able to take all kinds of liberties without distortion. Wilhelm Furtwängler was one; Josef Hofmann and Sergei Rachmaninoff were two pianists who never made a rhythmic mistake; neither did Toscanini, the interpretive and rhythmic antithesis to Furtwängler. Toscanini had the reputation of being absolutely literal, but he wasn't. No musician can be. Man, as I say, is not a metronome, and Toscanini, so much stricter than Furtwängler, nevertheless was constantly adding tension to his line with subtle rhythmic variations and tempo modifications.

The trouble today—and here I come back to the topic with which I bore everybody within sight—is a lack of knowledge of the traditions of performance practice. Musicians have been trained too much toward literalism and not enough toward meaning. They have been so cowed by professors who insist that they play exactly what is written, and no more, that they lose sight of the expressive qualities of music, and especially of Romantic music. In an effort to correct Romantic excesses—and there always have been musicians who are vulgar and exhibitionistic—they now lean so far in the opposite direction that their interpretations are all but sterile.

They do not realize that composers always expected an artist to give his own idea about the music. A score is merely a guide, not Revealed Truth; and while it presents the notes that the composer wants played, it can do no more than suggest how the relationships within those notes can be brought together. That is up to the artist; and while the artist may be the servant of the composer, he is also his own man. He can even disagree with the composer; and, more often than not the composer will go along with him.

Coenraad Bos, the accompanist, used to tell the story of himself and the *Vier ernste Gesänge* of Brahms. When the music was published, Bos thought there were some awkward figurations, and he changed them. At one performance he looked into the audience and saw Brahms. Bos was paralyzed with fright, but it was too late to change his modifications. At the end of the concert Brahms came back in great spirits. "Marvelous!" he boomed. Far from being angry, he thanked Bos for his intelligent realization of a difficult technical problem.

DEC. 13, 1970

The eternal problem of style was discussed by Charles Rosen in the recordings supplement of the March 19, 1972 Sunday Times. Mr. Rosen, pianist, scholar and intellectual, put forward a case for a middle road. But I thought he was a bit slipshod in his presentation, and there also were some statements that ran counter to my pet beliefs. So I hastened to reply.

Two Critics, Two Opinions— But a Bit of Common Ground

INTELLIGENT MUSICIANS have always concerned themselves with style and the history of performance practice. Obviously a pianist is not going to play a Mozart sonata with the same agogics and dynamics with which he approaches a Liszt rhapsody or a Brahms intermezzo. But what is there in the Mozart style that makes it Mozartean? What makes Brahms Brahmsian as contrasted to Lisztian? The question of style is of special urgency today, because there does seem to be a growing interest in Romantic music, and very few musicians understand or feel Romanticism. As this column has been insisting for over ten years, musicians today know less about the Romantic style than they do the Classic, despite the fact that it is an article of faith that since most of the repertory is Romantic or post-Romantic, everybody knows about it.

Last week the pianist Charles Rosen raised the issue in the recordings pages of this newspaper. In a lengthy article, he pointed out some of the problems facing a present-day musician who plays music of the past. He indicated that there really was no such thing as "right" or "wrong," and he set up what he regards as today's polar approaches: the innovationist versus the conservationist. The innovationist, Rosen says, "abolishes the past by treating the music as if it had been written today." The conservationist, too, "paradoxically abolishes the past by wiping out everything since the music was written." Rosen calls for a compromise between the demands of the innovationist and conservationist.

But in the course of his argument, Rosen makes some statements that should be examined a little closer. Let's start at the beginning of his article, and his discussion of Debussy. He points out, correctly, that the old, Gieseking way of playing Debussy's piano music featured "wonderful tone control, with the rhythmic contours slightly blurred under a delicate wash of pedal." Today, musicians approach Debussy differently, looking for more clarity and rhythmic differentiation. Which is the more authentic? "The question," says Rosen, "is unanswerable."

But is it unanswerable? Debussy is on record as stating that he wanted to create a piano music "without hammers." He wanted the fingers to "penetrate into the notes." He experimented with novel pedal effects, calling it a "breathing pedal." He himself played the piano that way. So reliable an observer as the composer Alfredo Casella described Debussy as playing so that "one had the impression he was actually playing on the strings of the instrument, without the mechanical aid of keys and hammers. He used the pedals as nobody else ever did."

Is clearer testimony needed? What on earth does a composer have to do to make his wishes clear? On Debussy's own words, and Casella's evidence, Gieseking's approach was right and the approach of the newer school wrong. Rosen cites Debussy's own playing as evidence. "The only recording of Debussy at the piano is unspeakable in rhythm, pedal and phrasing." I do wish that Rosen had been a little more specific.

First of all, Debussy made more than one recording. He made four, in Paris, in 1904, with Mary Garden—three of the *Ariettes oubliées* and the Tower Scene from *Pelléas.* He also made eight piano rolls for Welte-Mignon, but those are completely untrustworthy, as all Welte-Mignon rolls are. If Rosen is citing a Welte roll as evidence, he should have said so. Pianists cannot be judged on piano rolls; the rhythms are stiff and the pedalings often superimposed. Tempos also are unreliable.

Records are infinitely more trustworthy than piano rolls. My copies of the four Debussy records are, unfortunately, in anything but mint condition, and the piano sound is faint. But more than enough comes through to show Debussy's playing as supple and elegant, and I can find no trace of the "unspeakable" rhythm and phrasing that Rosen finds so objectionable. There are a couple of romanticisms in the playing. Here and there Debussy holds on to a note for the sake of rubato. But on the whole the playing is, if anything, cool and classic.

Taste in style, Mr. Rosen says, swings back and forth. That it does. "Artur Rubinstein's rich, passionate sweeping line is no closer to the 'real' Chopin—and no farther away—than the cooler, more elegant manner of pianists like Josef Hofmann, my teacher Moriz Rosenthal, Ignaz Friedman and others. . . ." (To call the heroic, mercurial, fantastic, inconsistent Friedman a cool and elegant pianist is like calling Niagara Falls a tricklet. Has Rosen heard, say, Friedman's recordings of the *Revolutionary* Etude and double-note Etude in C, or *La Campanella*, or the A flat Nocturne of Op. 55?) Well, the "real" Chopin *is* impossible to pin down. But that does not mean anarchy, or every man his own Chopinist.

For there was something in common in the way the great Chopinists played, though they may have been as dissimilar as De Pachmann and Rachmaninoff, or Artur Rubinstein and Hofmann, for that matter. All had an aristocratic line, all had a gorgeous tone, all had a delicate rubato, and above all there was a melting legato in which tone was linked to tone. The greatest Chopin players of my experience—pianists such as Hofmann, Friedman, Gabrilowitsch, Lhévinne, Rachmaninoff—were very aristocratic, controlled artists. Their performances had none of the eccentricities and leeway commonly thought of as "Romantic." That is how I remember them, and my memory is backed up by their recordings.

Of course, all of those artists took "liberties," in that they recognized certain unnotated conventions that were part of the period and are now generally ignored. Very few, however, took liberties to the point of changing harmonies or melodic notes. The liberties were in dynamics, metrical shifts (especially ritards) and inner voices (not really liberties, for Romantic composers carefully notated those inner voices, and it is not their fault if present-day pianists choose to ignore the instructions).

How much liberty to take? Rosen cites Liszt playing a Chopin mazurka with so many liberties that Chopin himself, to teach his friend a lesson, went to the piano and played it correctly. (It was not a mazurka, incidentally. It was a nocturne, and the story, told by Josef Nowakowski, is to be found in the Karasowski biography of Chopin.) Liszt was notably free toward other men's music, and the story rings true. Which does not mean that no liberties were allowed. Rosen quotes the famous Rossini story about hearing one of his arias "performed with the added ornaments some musicologists now tell us are essential." Rossini asked the singer: "Lovely, my dear, who wrote it?" A very nice story, except that Rosen does not tell it completely. The singer was Adelina Patti, the aria *Una voce poco fà,* and the composer himself was at the piano. Patti overembellished, and Rossini was furious. But he later told Saint-Saëns that it was the *excess,* not the fact of ornamentation itself, that had made him angry. "I wrote those arias to be embellished by the singer," he told Saint-Saëns.

Surely Mr. Rosen is not trying to tell us that it is wrong to embellish the Rossini arias. Every major music library in the world has manuscripts of the cadenzas of great singers—singers of Rossini's own day and shortly afterward—that were sung in the bel canto operas, and in the Verdi operas for that matter. I am not saying that present-day singers should follow suit. I am merely saying as a matter of historical fact that all singers at one time added embellishments not written by the composer. Whether or not present-day singers should follow suit is something else. But if it is historical "accuracy" you are after, you had better start embellishing. If you are a good artist, you will embellish with taste. If you are vulgar, you will sound vulgar. That is how it always was, and probably always will be.

With one element of Rosen's discussion there can be no argument. Obviously it is impossible to duplicate the conditions under which certain music of the past was created. Instruments, pitch, conventions, tempos—all have changed. One secret of the great performer is that he can vitalize music by virtue of a more secure feeling for relationships than less gifted musicians have, and that has little to do with "period." Anyway, talk about "going back," or "historical approach," or "text," especially in relation to Romantic music, leaves me part bored, part irritated, part amused. I have heard pianists who, in the name of "historical accuracy," use so insane a rubato, so exaggerated a rhythmic distortion, that the music is torn apart. An excess of freedom in Romantic performance can be as bothersome as tightness. And so Rosen and I finally come together. A compromise is necessary. But what are the specifics of that compromise? And there, alas, Rosen and I will probably break apart immediately.

MARCH 26, 1972

Toward the middle of the 1970's, musicians suddenly seemed to become aware of the new (to them) areas of the Romantic period, and works that had been all but universally derided ten years previously started to return to the repertory. The Friedman and Kalichstein-Ashkenazy series gave me still another springboard for a dive into my favorite topic.

The Search for Romanticism

ROMANTICISM HAS been in the air for a few years, and all of a sudden it's fashionable. How does one know? Because managers are climbing on the bandwagon. They are using the term as a come-on label. When Joseph Kalichstein and Vladimir Ashkenazy play at the Lexington Avenue "Y" tomorrow night, it is billed as a concert in Kalichstein's "Romantic Piano Festival." The other week, when Erick Friedman started his two-concert series of violin concertos in Carnegie Hall, his public relations people were making a big thing out of this "Romantic festival."

But it isn't a Romantic festival, not as the term should properly be used. When Kalichstein and Ashkenazy, tomorrow night, play four-hand pieces by Mozart and Schubert, that has as much to do with the Romantic revival as a single dollar bill has to do with the Gross National Product. It is not a "Romantic" gesture for Friedman to play Brahms, Sibelius and other repertory violin concertos. There has been only one Romantic festival in New York this year, and that was at Hunter College, where Raymond

Lewenthal, a musician who really knows what the Romantic revival is about, held forth.

Lewenthal and his supporting musicians looked around and came up with rarities that had seldom if ever been played in New York. When Lewenthal, cadaverous, tall and saturnine, came out wearing black, and a black silk topper decorated with a mourning band, and led a procession of four singers and four desperately squealing oboists in Alkan's *Funeral March for a Parrot, that* was the Romantic revival. It was not only fun; it brought forth a wondrous, tongue-in-cheek example of proto-Satie composition. When Lewenthal resurrected music by Reinecke, Thalberg, Liszt and some wildly forgotten composers, *that* was the Romantic revival.

You can't go around programming repertory items and calling it the Romantic revival. The closest Friedman came to that in his series was through concertos by Wieniawski and Vieux-temps, both of which are pretty well known. Had he showed some initiative and come up with, say, the Joachim *Hungarian* Concerto, or the once-popular Goldmark, or the Spohr Ninth, or anything outside the repertory, he might have had some legitimate claim. Not this way, though. And Kalichstein's series misuses the concept of "Romantic piano festival" all the way down the line.

Most musicians are just feeling their way when it comes to Romanticism. There are very few specialists around, which may sound like a curious thing to say when the overwhelming bulk of the active repertory is Romantic. Nevertheless it is true. Until the past few years, very few instrumentalists looked outside the standard composers; their repertory was as adventurous as the path of a windshield wiper.

Not only instrumentalists. Musicologists virtually ignored the nineteenth-century Romantics, and by and large they still do. Musicologists were in the forefront of the Baroque revival 25 years ago, and they have done brilliant work in the study of performance practice from Beethoven backward. But it has remained not for musicologists but for practical musicians like Lewenthal and Frank Cooper in Indianapolis to take a really close look at the minor Romantics. Thanks to them, and to Glen

Sauls and John Stranack of the Newport Music Festival, and thanks to Robert Commagere of Genesis Records and Gregor Benko of the International Piano Archives, the Romantic revival was started.

To some musicians there still is something vaguely disreputable about the Romantic revival. If you are a specialist in Gesualdo, or some obscure Baroque figure like Zelenka, everybody nods understandingly and pats you on the back. You are a scholar, your work comes out in the approved publications, and your papers have more footnotes than text. But if you specialize in Gottschalk, say, or the piano music of Moszkowski, or what the Scharwenka brothers meant to late nineteenth-century Romanticism, you are an object of suspicion. You cannot be *serious*, really. I mean . . . *Gottschalk*, for God's sake.

Slowly, however, the minor Romantics like Gottschalk are beginning—just beginning—to receive recognition from the intellectuals. There is a great deal that can be learned from these minor figures. Once in a while, as with Gottschalk's national music, two generations ahead of its day (his Latin-American pieces were not to be duplicated until World War I and Milhaud's *Saudades do Brasil,* only the Milhaud pieces are not as good as Gottschalk's), the music itself has a great deal to offer. The minor figures set the big ones into better perspective. These minor figures, too, often have a surprising degree of individuality—much more so than their corresponding brethren of the Baroque period.

Another aspect of the revival is of extreme value, and it has to do with performance practice. Thanks to a combination of factors, many of the traditions of Romantic performance practice have been forgotten. The result has, in some cases, been sheer desperation. Sensitive young artists know that there is something in the music—in its rubato, its agogics, its structure, its concept of sound—that the notes on the printed page cannot reveal. So they flail around, indulging in wild exaggerations under the impression that this is "Romantic" playing. Or they retreat into the equally wrong practice of strict literalism.

What they have to learn, and what the Romantic revival may help them learn, is that Romantic performance practice as measured by its greatest exponents is a controlled, aristocratic, even classic style. In the piano playing of Hofmann, Rachmaninoff, Lhévinne and other giants of the period, the legendary "Romanticisms" are almost always confined to ritard effects that bridge contrasting sections, and to inner voices that are brought out because the composer has clearly indicated that he wants them brought out. In the violin playing of Sarasate (which can be studied on records), the rhythms are regular, the line is poised and there is none of the tugging and hauling that so many youngsters conceive of as Romantic style.

Thus if nothing else, the Romantic revival can help young musicians play their Chopin, Schumann, Brahms and—yes— late Beethoven in a much more authentic manner than they do at present. Rehearing music of the nineteenth century in performances that approximate the practices of the time may come as a shock to some of the old-maid musicians and critics who have dominated ideas about performance up to now. It's high time they were shook up.

MARCH 21, 1976

PART III
Composers

Thank God, I compose well enough to be able utterly to despise the judgment of critics.

—HUGO WOLF

Articles about composers, great and minor, occupied a large part of my Sunday output. The following article was written toward the beginning of the Mahler revival. It is true that there is much in his work that disturbs me, but one would have to be deaf not to feel the fascinating mind behind his music, and the unusual imagination that went into some of the writing. Mahler today has become the great symphonic idol, the musical spokesman for a generation, and his music has swept the symphonies of Tchaikovsky and even of Brahms somewhat aside. I have felt that Mahler is generally admired for the wrong reasons. The patent Beethoven-like sublimity of his symphonies annoys me, and it was that aspect to which I addressed myself here.

The Beethoven chord at the beginning of the last movement of the Ninth Symphony, to which I refer, is usually analyzed as a D minor chord with the B flat triad acting as an appoggiatura that resolves into the tonic. But it is a very long-held appoggiatura, and I like to think of it as a bitonal chord.

Mahler's Mystic Ninth

BEETHOVEN AND Bruckner, Beethoven and Mahler. Earlier in the season Herbert von Karajan and William Steinberg gave us Bruckner, and only a few weeks ago Josef Krips conducted the Ninth Symphony of Beethoven. This week Georg Solti turns his attention, with the New York Philharmonic, to the Mahler Fourth. And a complete design is formed. The Beethoven Ninth

121

is the peak of an equilateral triangle, with Bruckner and Mahler, at the two points on the base, looking up at it.

Beethoven's Ninth was to the nineteenth century what Stravinsky's *Sacre du Printemps* was to the early twentieth. It was so big, so unorthodox, so full of new ideas and workmanship, so packed with intensity, that it put its imprint, consciously or unconsciously, on all composers who followed. The Ninth, too, was not only a symphony, it was an ethical testament, what with its call to universal brotherhood expressed in the choral finale. Thus the late Romantics, who gloried in reading extramusical things into music, found it doubly irresistible. The Ninth was the musical and ethical ideal toward which all subsequent music had to approach and the standard against which all symphonic music was to be measured.

No two composers pursued this ideal more than did Bruckner and Mahler. In recent years the tendency has been to poke fun at the Bruckner-Mahler coupling. We are told that they were not the Siamese twins of music; that intellectually and emotionally they were opposed personalities; that really their music has very little in common. But, really, are they that far apart? They were contemporaries, they both wrote tremendously extended symphonic works, they both pursued a vision. And, above all, they both were the spiritual grandchildren of the Beethoven of the Ninth Symphony.

In Bruckner's case, the Ninth-fixation consisted of an unconscious repetition of technical and melodic devices used in the Beethoven D minor. How many of Bruckner's symphonies start with a tremolo in the low strings, as does the Ninth, and then go on to melodic material derived from the common triad again as does the Ninth! How many slow movements of Bruckner echo the soaring violin passages of the Beethoven adagio! How many chordal juxtapositions resemble the monster chord (B flat major against D minor—perhaps the first polytonal chord in history, almost a hundred years ahead of the famous F sharp against C major chord in Stravinsky's *Petruchka*) that opens Beethoven's last movement!

Much the same, too, can be said of the Mahler symphonies. This is all the more strange in that Mahler was such a different man from Bruckner. The latter was simple, devout and in many respects a childlike human being. Mahler was morbid, highly intellectual, an obsessive neurotic (these are not my words but those of the psychoanalyst Theodor Reik) who had consulted Freud, and a man who all his life was psychically tortured. A great man, a fascinating man and, I believe, a supremely greater composer than Bruckner: but both had much the same vision, and both tried to achieve it to the depths of their soul.

The Beethoven Ninth could well have been the symbol of Mahler's music. Reik, whose book, *The Haunting Melody,* is a fascinating exploration of Mahler's creative processes, believes that Mahler had "an unconscious or rather repressed ambitious wish to compete with Beethoven and his Ninth Symphony." Mahler also was frightened at the implication of finishing a Ninth Symphony. Had not Schubert, Bruckner, Beethoven himself, died before finishing a Tenth? When Mahler did get to work on a Ninth Symphony, and finished it, he crossed out the number and published it as *Das Lied von der Erde.* Then, when composing his next symphony, he told his wife: "Actually it is, of course, the Tenth, because *Das Lied von der Erde* was really the Ninth." And, when it was near completion, he said: "Now the danger is past."

As a matter of fact, it was not past. He died a few months after finishing the work that was published as his Ninth Symphony.

The more one hears and studies the symphonies of Bruckner and Mahler, the more one becomes aware of the incessant subconscious plagiarism from Beethoven's D minor. At the same time, the more one becomes aware of the many points of similarity in the symphonies of the two later composers. Their *adagio* movements are frequently conceived in much the same spirit. It is amazing, too, how much Austrian folk-like music of a laendler nature impregnates Bruckner and Mahler. The laendler is a rustic dance in three-quarter rhythm that was the precursor of the waltz.

Where the two symphonists diverge is in intellectual force. Here the estimate must necessarily be personal. Most listeners feel that Mahler is at his most profound in his slow movements, or in massive architectural creations like the choral finale of the

Resurrection Symphony. But these, to me, are closest to the Beethoven Ninth and are precisely the weakest, most derivative examples of Mahler's output. The ghost of Beethoven is not only too close; it has seized the pen. Mahler, to me, is at his greatest when he can break away from his Beethoven fixation. The "Burlesque" movement of Mahler's Ninth Symphony, for example, impresses me as a colossal concept: infinitely daring, looking to the future rather than to the past, terrifying in its sardonic message.

It is in movements like this that Mahler is a prophet, not in those so terribly earnest, basically wishy-washy and sentimental slow movements, where he was carefully planting his own footsteps into the marks that Beethoven's feet had trod. Fortunately, in every single one of the Mahler symphonies occur moments where he shucks off his fixation and takes off into areas where no composer has ever been. That is why Mahler's symphonies are fascinating, and why they are so superior to the Bruckner symphonies. Bruckner had a much more conventional, commonplace mind, and he was never able to fly straight into the sun. Mahler at his best did so, right into the empyrean.

Of course he was a complicated man, and complicated men write complicated music. Most people make some kind of peace with themselves and the universe. Mahler never did. What is the meaning of life? Is there reward or punishment in the beyond? *Is* there a beyond? Whence do we come? Where do we go? Mahler always was asking Why? Why? Why? Bruno Walter thinks that each of Mahler's symphonies was a new attempt at an answer to the questions eternally plaguing the composer's mind. These questions were at once banal (because they are questions that all mankind has asked) and piercingly profound (because nobody has ever answered them). They were also obsessive (because most people early in life arrive at some kind of solution and thereafter do not trouble themselves with the kind of incessant questioning that marked Mahler's entire life).

Did he, at the very end, perhaps realize that he had been following a musical god false to him? It was not Beethoven of whom he thought on his deathbed. He lay in a coma, under oxygen, with one finger conducting an imaginary orchestra.

Eyewitnesses say that a smile was on his lips. "Mozart darling, Mozart darling," Mahler murmured twice, and then he died.

JAN. 7, 1962

Since this piece was written, there have been the two Faubion Bowers books on Scriabin and a number of scholarly studies. In 1965 Scriabin was not played very much. But Vladimir Horowitz, who plays Scriabin inimitably, began programming some of the late pieces after his return to the concert stage in 1965, and where Horowitz goes, others follow. Today Scriabin's late sonatas are a concert-hall staple. It is the early music— those charming preludes and etudes—that is neglected. A pity. In the early 1970's there was a flurry of Scriabin's orchestral works. That seems to be over. Another pity.

Scriabin: That Marvelous, Sensuous Mystic

WE DON'T get much Scriabin any more, even if, a few weeks ago, Lorin Maazel led the New York Philharmonic through the *Poem of Ecstasy.* Not only is the composer out of favor, but there seems to be active resentment when his music is played. Let a pianist present a group of early Scriabin preludes and etudes, and critics will go out of their way to condemn the music as nothing but diluted Chopin. Let one of the late piano pieces be programmed, and the musical intelligentsia is up in arms, inveighing against Scriabin's diffuseness, vagueness and fake philosophy.

Thus it is with some diffidence that I set my piping treble

against the great roars of his detractors. I happen to adore his music, all of it. It is true that there is a strong Chopin element in his early piano pieces. But there is not more Chopin than Scriabin; and those graceful, melodic, aristocratic, perfectly proportioned piano pieces, up to about the Fourth Sonata, belong in every pianist's repertory.

The really significant contribution of Alexander Scriabin, however, comes with the later works, and to understand those it is necessary to know something about the man. He was born in 1872, died fifty years ago this month in Moscow at the early age of forty-three, was an important touring pianist, and, in the words of Gerald Abraham, was an "amoral little mystic." It was that mystical element that colored all of his later music. Scriabin passed from Wagner's prose writings to Nietzsche and then to a vague form of the theosophism so popular in Russian circles around the turn of the century.

Was Scriabin a religious fanatic? Was he a little mad? He conceived his last and greatest work to be what he called a "Mystery." This involved the end of the world and the emergence of a new race of men. Signaling the end of the world was a performance of the Mystery, in which music, dance, poetry, colors, perfume would be combined. At the climax of the music, the walls of the universe would cave in. "I shall not die," said Scriabin. "I shall suffocate in ecstasy after the Mystery." He thought of himself as the true Messiah, and wanted his Mystery to be performed in a temple in India, hemispherical in shape. He even purchased a sun helmet, a Sanskrit grammar, and had inquiries made about the site for his Mystery.

As he got involved with these schemes, his music constantly changed shape. But it is a change that goes along a straight line, from the Fifth Piano Sonata through the symphonic poems. There have been no major studies of Scriabin's music in English, and one can only guess how much his religious and mystical ideas dictated his musical forms. At much the same time, for example, Arnold Schoenberg was working toward what was to develop into a method of composition with twelve tones. But where Schoenberg always worked according to musical concepts, Scriabin seems to have been governed by outside factors.

Yet there is something strangely parallel between the music of Schoenberg and that of the late (after 1908) Scriabin. And there is no indication that either was influenced by the other. But both started to break away from the triadic harmony of traditional music, to investigate a musical harmony built on fourths instead of thirds. Scriabin evolved what has come to be known as the "mystic chord"—C, F sharp, B flat, E, A, D. This chord, in fourths, is the basis on which all of Scriabin's later music is erected. In addition, Scriabin's music became increasingly dissonant. He discarded key signatures, teetered on the brink of sheer atonality, and his music is a black mass of accidentals, fearsome-looking chords, all but unplayable pianistic figurations.

It is this quartal dissonance that helps make so much of Scriabin's music so amazingly modern. A generation ago it was inexplicable. Since then, the world has become used to the harmonies of Schoenberg and his school, harmonies that have become the basic vocabulary of the avant-garde. Nobody is going to say that Scriabin's music is going to be confused with Schoenberg's. But there are areas in both composers that are tangential. A work like Scriabin's Tenth Sonata, with its strange trillings, its quartal harmonies, its disjunct melodic line, its dissonance and complete disregard for the conventional amenities, is surprisingly close to some of Schoenberg's piano pieces.

Technical considerations aside, there are some aspects that link the strange late works of Scriabin with his simple and direct early ones. To the very end his harmonies, no matter how complicated and dissonant they became, have a certain sensuous quality. Music by itself cannot be erotic, but some composers have more of a feeling for rich harmonic combinations than have others. Scriabin had this more than almost any composer in history. For want of a better term it is called sensuous. There also is a certain kind of melody characteristic of Scriabin, and those big, sweeping gestures of the *Poem of Ecstasy* or *Prometheus* are little but expansions of such works as the *Poème* in F sharp.

In his earlier works there sometimes is a nationalistic quality in Scriabin. Later that was to disappear (or, if it remains, it is exceptionally well hidden). He is not considered one of the Russian nationalists, though he did influence several of them. His Piano Concerto of 1894 leads right into Rachmaninoff; and Stravinsky, when he came to compose the *Firebird,* had not only Rimsky-Korsakoff in his blood, but also sections of the *Poem of Ecstasy.* In his day, Scriabin was taken very seriously.

Richard Anthony Leonard, in his *History of Russian Music,* suggests a parallel between Scriabin and William Blake. Both were mystics, both were activated by a personal vision, both produced works of art that can only be explained in terms of religious eccentricity, and both invented their own symbolism. Thus neither can be approached superficially. Their work has to be studied, and an understanding of what they were trying to do involves what they were and what they did as well as what they created.

At bottom, of course, everything settles down to the value of what they created. In Blake's case, posterity has decided the issue. Scriabin, on the other hand, has been largely ignored outside of Russia, and there does not seem to be any indication of a revival or a reappraisal. This grieves those of us who consider Scriabin one of the most original, fascinating, enigmatic, revolutionary—and, yes, rewarding—composers of the century.

APRIL 11, 1961

I was wrong in one thing about the Ives Fourth Symphony. Within two years a pair of recorded performances followed the Stokowski recording. Ives was riding high in the 1965–1970 period. Today the furor has died down, though a handful of his works remains securely in the repertory. The United States has produced only two really nationalistic composers—Louis Moreau Gottschalk and Charles Ives. Aaron Copland? That cowboy from Brooklyn is much too sophisticated.

Ives: Complex and Yet Simple

Last week we were talking about Charles Ives and his strange mixture—his ferocious modernism, used basically to evoke the spirit of an American past. Since then his Fourth Symphony has come and gone. Leopold Stokowski conducted the world premiere last Monday. But that does not mean the sounds are forever vanished. Stokowski and the American Symphony Orchestra are going to record the score. It most likely will be the only available recording for years to come. For no pickup orchestra is going to be recording this work, and the chances are that no established symphony will, either. Not unless the forces involved do what the American Symphony Orchestra did—get outside funds for plenty of additional rehearsals.

Stokowski and his players had to take each measure apart. They went through the symphony phrase by phrase. They had to. Take the second movement, which starts with some woodwinds and percussion in six-eight meter, clarinets in five-eight, bassoons in seven-four, pianos in two-four, violins in four-four. I mean, you don't just sit down and *read* this stuff.

It turned out that the effort was worth all the trouble. Through the fearsome complexities, through the tonal walls of dissonance and chaos, through the polyrhythms, came something essentially quite simple and even endearing. The Fourth Symphony is a nationalistic work that is constantly quoting musical fragments of a past America. These fragments may be disguised, but their use lends to the symphony a certain flavor unique in American music—or in any music, for that matter.

Ives, who died in 1954 (but who stopped composing in 1928), was quite voluble about his nationalism. Nationalism, he once wrote, should not strain for effect. All that is necessary is that the composer's interest, spirit and character sympathize with, or intuitively coincide with, that of the subject. "Whatever excellence an artist sees in life, a community, in a people, or in any valuable object or experience, if sincerely and intuitively reflected in his work," then that work and he himself are a reflected part of that excellence.

Instinctively a man of the soil, a man who had great respect and even veneration for the nineteenth-century basics—the land, nature, simple religion, the family unit—Ives equally instinctively shrank from sophisticated or glossy music. He said that Debussy would have been a better composer "if he had hoed corn or sold newspapers for a living, for in this way he might have gained a deeper vitality and a truer theme to sing at night and of a Sunday." Provincial? Of course; and unabashedly so. Similarly, Ives had nothing but contempt for Richard Strauss. To Ives, Strauss was always medieval, as against Beethoven's modernism. All Strauss did was to capitalize a talent rather than search for "the inner, invisible activity of truth."

The point about Ives is that he was always searching for that truth. He was not interested in pretty sounds ("My God! What has sound got to do with music!") and he was impatient with the limitations of men and instruments ("Is it the composers' fault that man has only ten fingers?"). He looked forward to the time "in some century to come, when the school children will whistle popular tunes in quarter tones, when the diatonic scale will be as obsolete as the pentatonic is now."

He was not a professional avant-gardist, though, just as he was not—never!—an academician. He was a Yankee skeptic, one who weighed this and that. He was fascinated with quarter tones, for instance. His father had experimented with them long before they ever became talked about. But "quarter tones or no quarter tones, why tonality as such should be thrown out for good, I can't see. Why it should be always present, I can't see. It all depends, it seems to me, a good deal—as clothes depend on the thermometer—on what one is trying to do."

Naturally the fact that Ives, the successful insurance man, was also a part-time composer had a great deal to do with the way his music sounded. He had started composing in 1884, and not until 1927 was an orchestral work of his publicly performed. Very few took his music seriously. Those who did thought twice about struggling with orchestral scores of such complexity: those masses of tone, those wild dissonances, those bitonalities, those impossible rhythms. Goodness knows that many composers of the time—Bartók, Schoenberg, Berg—composed music extremely difficult to perform. But their music is almost child's play compared to Ives's.

Many have speculated that had Ives received performances, had he come up against the necessities for a more practical approach, had he had more actual experience in scoring and in musical organization, he would have written a different kind of music. Perhaps; and this writer once thought so. Now he is less sure. Ives was not the kind of man to be budged. From the beginning he deliberately set out to compose a different kind of music. He could not have been less interested in the academic approach—in sonata form, in conservatory fugue and theory. He was out to express something different. He wanted to hew something out of American rock, make something grow out of American earth, reach into the essentials of the American character. That could not be done as Brahms did it, or Debussy, or anybody else. It had to be done without recourse to the old rules, and a new kind of music had to be created.

No. Had Ives been a smoother composer, a more graceful one, a more melodious one, well and good—but he would not have been Charles Ives. He himself had something to say along that line. "Some fiddler," he wrote, "was once honest or brave enough, or perhaps ignorant enough, to say that Beethoven didn't know how to write for the violin. That, maybe, is one of the many reasons Beethoven is not a Vieuxtemps. Another man says Beethoven's piano sonatas are not pianistic. With a little effort, perhaps, Beethoven could have become a Thalberg."

Ives did not draw the moral, but the inference is clear. Had he smoothed out his rugged, uncompromising, individual approach, had he been a "practical" orchestrator, had he worn a sonata suit, a contrapuntal necktie and a diatonic shirt, he might have become a Paine. Or even a MacDowell.

MAY 2, 1961

There were many other things I could have said in this article had I had the space. Debussy derided Grieg, but I could have cited Grieg's G minor String Quartet and the influence it had on Debussy's String Quartet in the same key. (I once picked up the Grieg quartet on the car radio, and it took me a minute or so to realize it was not Debussy.) I could have gone into more detail about the Grieg songs. Are there many more beautiful ones in the late Romantic repertory than To a Water Lily? *There has not been much of a Grieg renaissance, though some of his music has been creeping back, and a few critics recently have written excited articles about their rediscovery of the Norwegian master. The Romantic revival I predicted in the last paragraph of this article has come to pass, and several specialized record companies have indeed been feverishly searching out the music of Hummel, Gade, Kalkbrenner and Moszkowski (not yet Leybach or Volkmann, though). The revival took less than the twenty years I predicted. But Grieg has not been a prominent part of it.*

Grieg: Once Popular, Now Faded

SEVERAL WEEKS ago a pianist put the Grieg Ballade on her New York recital program. Almost to a man the critics rose in wrath, condemning the piece, and by implication the taste of the woman who programmed it. A few days later, when the Norwegian Festival Orchestra came to town, Grieg's Piano Concerto in A minor was (naturally) on the program. It was with quite a shock that many of us who were present suddenly realized that it had been a long time since this once-popular concerto turned up at a serious concert. At summer concerts and pop programs, the Grieg A minor and *Peer Gynt* are still around; but seldom in Philharmonic Hall or Carnegie Hall. Pianists no longer play the *Lyric Pieces,* singers avoid *Haugtussa* and the other songs. Yes, Edvard Grieg is definitely out of fashion.

In his own time, Grieg (1843–1907) was one of the most popular composers of the century. He rode on a wave of nationalism, the same kind of nationalism that produced the equally
popular Dvorak. But whereas Dvorak composed operas and symphonies, Grieg was primarily a miniaturist, and he fell almost as
rapidly as he had risen. Debussy scornfully referred to his music
as bonbons wrapped in snow, or filled with snow (I forget the
exact phrase), and he did not mean it as a compliment. Soon no
creative mind would take Grieg seriously. His once piquant harmonies, which had titillated three generations of music lovers,
suddenly were accused of being cloying, oversweet. The new
generation looked upon Grieg with the same condescension
with which they gazed upon the portraits in great-grandfather's
family album.

Grieg, in short, was as out of fashion as the stovepipe and
velveteen jackets of the day. Along with the music of Liszt and
Mendelssohn, both of whom also were swamped by the anti-
romanticism of the post-World War I period, Grieg's contribution was dismissed with a careless wave of the hand. In recent
years, though, Liszt and Mendelssohn have made a comeback.
Liszt especially. A truer perspective than the old one shows that
in many respects he was—even more than Wagner—the spiritual father of the twentieth century. And Mendelssohn's music
is today appreciated for the perfectly balanced thing it was. But
Grieg yet languishes.

Perhaps the time has come for a reassessment. Nobody can
put up a case for Grieg as one of the immortals. But he was one
of the band of minor composers—Borodin, Fauré, Smetana and
the others of that category—who did bring something new to
music; and what Grieg had to say he said gracefully and prettily,
with considerable style and with a compositional technique perfectly suited to his content. His music certainly does not deserve
the scorn with which it is so often received these days.

Take the G minor Ballade, a piece that I happen to admire. It
starts with a slow, almost Franckian series of highly chromatic
chords, not in the least nationalistic, and proceeds to a series of
variations. Not until the glittering fourth variation, with its cadence using the raised sixth (typical of Norwegian folk music),

does the nationalistic element appear. Throughout the work the writing is in beautiful taste, virtuosic without being showy. The influence here is Schumann, to whom the German-trained Grieg owed so much, but it is not a slavish imitation. Quite the contrary. The G minor Ballade is an honest piece of music, melodically inventive and miles above the cheap type of salon writing prevalent at the time.

But it is not an easy piece to bring to life these days, for the tradition it represents is gone. Pianists like Percy Grainger or Leopold Godowsky (who recorded it in the 1920's; and it is a shame that this extraordinary performance by one of the greatest pianists in history has not been made available on LP) could bring freedom and an authentic feeling to it, but pianists today are apt to play it literally, destroying its spontaneity, not knowing when to relax a tempo, when to use rubato, how to bring out the inner voices. Composers on a supreme level can survive almost any manner of performance, but lesser composers are peculiarly vulnerable to their interpreters.

And so most people today know Grieg only by *Peer Gynt*, the Concerto and a couple of Norwegian Dances. There is much more to him than that. One of his collections of nationalistic dances, called *Slatter*, is bleak and unprettified, strangely close to what Bartok was to do with his piano transcriptions of Hungarian folk melodies. Many of the *Lyric Pieces* are certainly as good as some of Mendelssohn's *Songs Without Words*, and better than most. The G minor Quartet and the three Violin Sonatas are beautifully laid out, appealing in content, grateful to play and to hear. And the Grieg songs are of extreme beauty. He was one of the really distinguished song composers of the century, and in the *Haugtussa* cycle, or such individual songs as *A Swan*, he hit perfection in a small package.

He never struck very deep, and there is no passion in his music. Like his contemporary Fauré, with whom his music has so much in common, Grieg represents charm and grace, elegance and style (though it must be admitted that Fauré was much the subtler of the two). And, again, like Fauré, he is not a composer with whom one wants to have a steady affair. For that we turn to the universal men, to the Mozarts, Bachs, Bethovens. But that does not mean the music of so skillful a composer should be cast into the garbage heap. Grieg still has a good deal to offer, bonbons and all.

One of these days his music is going to be rediscovered, much as the last two decades have seen the rediscovery of dozens of Baroque composers whose names until recently were known only to specialists. We still are in the midst of the Baroque revival, especially on records. Not a month goes by but that there are discs upon discs containing the scores of such worthies as Albinoni, Fasch, Corelli, Locatelli, Froberger, Telemann and names even more mysterious. Some of this music is good, but much of it is sheer Kapellmeister doodling, phrase following dull phrase in predictable patterns. At present there is no sign of an equivalent Romantic revival, in which record companies will feverishly search out the music of Hummel, Gade, Kalkbrenner, Moszkowski, Leybach, Volkmann, Scharwenka and Henselt. For that we'll have to wait another twenty years or so. But when this Romantic revival does occur, Grieg and his music will occupy a prominent place. And deservedly so.

MARCH 27, 1966

I probably have written more about Mozart than about any other composer. The man as well as his music fascinates me. I have never adhered to the doctrine, so fashionable today in certain circles, that the music of a composer stands alone; that it is necessary only to analyze the work, everything else being supererogatory. To my way of thinking, it is impossible to understand any music without knowing a good deal about the man who composed it. Mozart needs a great deal of scholarly and biographical work. It is amazing that this most popular of composers has not had a definitive modern biography of the kind Jacques Barzun has brought to Berlioz, Maynard Solomon to Beethoven or H.C. Robbins Landon to Haydn. The best source for an understanding of Mozart still is the three-column collection of letters translated by Emily Anderson.

Mozart et Père:
Is an Analysis Needed?

LAST WEEK, in connection with the Mozart festival currently in progress in Philharmonic Hall, I had a few words to say about various views of Mozart in the generations following his death. It now occurs to me that I left unexplored one view that is of great interest and importance: the reaction of Mozart's father, Leopold, to his supremely gifted son.

Leopold was a fine musician and the author of an important book on violin playing. He was a solid bourgeois citizen with great common sense but little imagination; and he also had a great respect for money, social standing and what today we would call job security. He immediately recognized the gifts of his son and, it should be added, of his daughter, Nannerl, five years Wolfgang's senior, who also was a prodigy, though not in his class. When Wolfgang was six years old, his father started making concert tours with him. These continued, off and on, for some years. Finally, when Wolfgang was twenty-one, he and his mother set out on a tour that took him through Germany and to Paris. (She died in Paris.) All during this time, there was a constant interchange of letters between father and son.

Never was there a time when Leopold doubted in the least the musical gifts of his son. But, much to his grief, he discovered that as the boy grew older he seemed ill equipped to meet life on equal terms—at least, according to Leopold's views about life. Leopold was sober, thrifty, industrious. Wolfgang was easy-going, gregarious, and, to put it bluntly, a soft touch. There was something of Polonius in Leopold, and he constantly was bombarding his son with sage advice. Respect money. Do not trust strangers. Never go out walking at night. Plan ahead. Cultivate the right people. Act with dignity.

But just as Leopold was a Polonius, Wolfgang had a bit of Micawber in him. Everything was going to turn out all right. Tomorrow. "Little by little my circumstances will improve." What a trial Wolfgang turned out to be! He wasted money, frittered away his talents, was lazy, cultivated the wrong people. Above all, Wolfgang was naive. He never did learn to assess another person's character. Time and time again, Leopold writes to his son warning him about his tendency to like everybody. "All men are villains! The older you will become and the more you associate with people, the more you will realize this sad truth." He begs Wolfgang not to be so easily swayed by flattery.

But Wolfgang goes his merry way. He probably is afraid of his father. Certainly his letters often are evasive. Everything will be all right soon. Yes, he has lost money. No, he has not made any decent contacts. In vain does Leopold tell his son that "flattering words, praises and cries of 'Bravissimo' pay neither postmasters nor landlords. So as soon as you find there is no money to be made, you should try to get away at once." Occasionally Leopold loses his temper, especially when Wolfgang writes vague letters full of pious moralizings. "Blast your oracular utterances and all the rest!" Leopold does not want to know what his son thinks of life. He wants to know whether a good job is coming up, and where those gold ducats disappeared to.

He also worries that Wolfgang's loose social habits will make him an object of ridicule. Especially, keep away from musicians. They are low in the social order, and it does not pay to be too friendly with them. That includes composers as important as Gluck, Piccini and Grétry. To them, be polite and nothing more. "You can always be perfectly natural with people of high rank, but with everybody else please behave like an Englishman. You must not be so open with everyone!" Poor Wolfgang probably flinched when he got a letter from his father. Nag, nag, nag; all well-meaning, but no less irritating for that—especially as Wolfgang knew the admonitions were deserved. That made them all the harder to take.

Leopold had no hesitation assessing his son's character. Wolfgang would open a letter and read things like: "You have a little too much pride and self-love; and secondly you immediately make yourself too cheap and open your heart to everyone; in short, wishing to be unconstrained and natural, you fall into the other extreme of being too unreserved." Leopold points out that Wolfgang demands appreciation and sulks when he does not get it. Thus he is open to flattery and flatterers who "in order to bend you to their selfish purposes, praise you to the skies." Leopold says he is telling Wolfgang all this for his own good; and, indeed, it is true that Leopold's letter of February 23, 1778, sounds like a genuine *cri de coeur:* "The purpose of all my remarks is to make you into an honorable man. Millions have not received the tremendous favor which God has bestowed upon you. What a responsibility! And what a shame if such a great genius were to founder! . . ."

Later, in 1782, Leopold objectively described his son to Baroness von Waldstein in Vienna. By this time Wolfgang had completely gone his own way. Among other things, he had just about broken his father's heart by marrying Constanze Weber, and he had relatively little to do with his father after that (though correspondence continued and they exchanged visits). Leopold gave up and suffered in Salzburg. He was not at his son's wedding. The Baroness had thrown a party for the newlyweds, and Leopold wrote her a letter of thanks. It also contains a frank estimate of Wolfgang's character, plus a good deal of bitterness.

Wolfgang (writes Leopold to the Baroness) has "an outstanding fault, which is, that he is far too patient or rather easygoing, too indolent, perhaps even too proud, in short, that he has the sum total of all those traits which render a man inactive; on the other hand, he is too impatient, too hasty and will not bide his time. Two opposing elements rule his nature, I mean, there is either too much or too little, never the golden mean. If he is not actually in want, then he is immediately satisfied and becomes indolent and lazy. If he has to bestir himself, then he realizes his worth and wants to make his fortune at once."

Leopold knew his son. He also did not know his son. The two were emotionally too far apart for any real contact. Leopold could see nothing but the flaws in Wolfgang's character. He failed to realize how high-strung Wolfgang was, how badly he needed encouragement rather than homilies. It also is unfortunately true that Wolfgang had character flaws that messed up his whole life. But many of those flaws can probably be traced to the unnatural childhood imposed upon him by his father. And so the two, father and son, tortured each other for years, establishing a classic love-hate relationship. Only a musically trained psychiatrist could untangle it; and, of course, it would at best be informed guesswork. But the attempt should be made if, as said last week, Mozart is to be brought into the twentieth century.

AUG. 6, 1967

When Gary Graffman played the E flat Piano Concerto by Mozart's son, it occurred to me that I knew virtually nothing about him. Obviously some research was in order, and this Sunday piece resulted.

Mozart's Son—Perhaps That Name Was Too Much for Him

WOLFGANG AMADEUS MOZART had two sons. Neither married, and the line stopped with them. Karl Thomas Mozart (1784–1858) became an Austrian government official. He probably had musical talent; he studied piano with the great Dussek and was supposed to have been very skillful. But he neither appeared in public nor composed anything for his instrument. It was Franz Xaver Wolfgang Mozart (1791–1844), who was about five months old when his famous father died, who did become a professional musician. And Franz Xaver Wolfgang is currently in the news, in that Gary Graffman has been playing his Piano

Concerto in E flat (Op. 25) and will bring it to New York for the first time on August 19 at the Mostly Mozart Festival.

Talk about unknown composers! Who has ever heard a note of the music of the younger Mozart? Back in 1940, Karl Geiringer, the eminent musicologist, read a long paper on Wolfgang Amadeus Jr. (so Franz Xaver was called during most of his life), but nobody was prompted to seek out any of his music despite Geiringer's endorsement: ". . . Faintly melancholy . . . peculiar and subtle charm . . . certainly deserves revival. . . ." Thus Geiringer. But poor W. A. Jr. has left as much impression on our age as he did on his. He lived quietly and he died quietly, a retiring, inoffensive man of little force and no self-confidence who bore the mighty name of Mozart.

There are a few lithographs of him. He was a little man, almost as short as his father. The face that looks at us is refined, melancholy, not very strong. We do not know enough about his life and mental processes to attempt much of a psychiatric profile. But certain things about his character are known, thanks to the diaries of Vincent and Mary Novello.

Vincent Novello was a musician active in London in the early years of the nineteenth century. A composer, choirmaster and organist, he also founded the famous publishing house that bore his name. Vincent had a sheer fixation on Mozart, "the Shakespeare of music." In 1829, he and his wife Mary went to Salzburg to present a sum of money to Mozart's sister—a sum raised by admirers of the composer. Vincent also was gathering materials for a biography of Mozart, though he never did get around to writing it. While in Salzburg, the Novellos had the good fortune to become acquainted with Mozart's widow, and also with W. A. Jr., who had come from the Polish city of Lvov (or Lemberg, as it was then called).

The younger Mozart was teaching in Lvov at that time. Certainly his musical credentials were impeccable enough. He had studied with Hummel, Salieri, Albrechtsberger, Streicher, Neukomm—the best musicians of the day. As early as age thirteen, he was playing the piano in public. Already he was a composer; his Op. 1 had been published when he was eleven. At seventeen, he went off to Poland, taking a job with a nobleman. Later he broke away from teaching the children of noblemen and set himself up as pianist, composer and teacher in general.

He was a shy, retiring boy who developed into a shy, retiring man. Perhaps the name of his father was too much for him to bear. Of course this is the obvious thing to say, but there is much evidence for it. He simply could not thrust himself forward, to the disgust of his ambitious mother. It was not that he was lazy. From all accounts he was a good pianist, and lazy boys do not develop into good pianists. But even when he was sixteen he lacked assertion and had to be pushed. "Although he gets help on all sides," his mother wrote to her other son in 1807, "he does almost nothing unless he is forced."

The Novellos could see that the shadow of the father dominated the son. In Salzburg young Mozart spoke enthusiastically about his father's music and even played some of it. "He said there had been many fine musicians in the world, but he might be allowed to say but one Mozart." In the meantime, Constanze Mozart von Nissen had not changed her mind about her younger son. She told Novello that she regretted that her son was "of so lazy a character." And she told Vincent that her son "wanted courage." Constanze was a tough old biddy. Poor W. A. Jr., full of self-deprecation, told Vincent that he thought he might have done something if he had met with encouragement—"but now too late." Sad.

Yet it was not only Constanze who looked upon W. A. Jr. with a pair of realistic and exasperated eyes. The piano manufacturer Johann Andreas Streicher told Vincent that "Young Mozart was of an inert nature but possessed great genius." From Streicher comes a charming story about the boy. At young Mozart's debut in 1804, Streicher asked him to give an improvisation. Mozart protested that he could not do it "and even broke into tears." Streicher insisted and gave the boy as a theme the minuet from *Don Giovanni*. Finally W. A. Jr. sat down "and blew out the candles to show he was playing entirely without any notes to assist him and performed the most masterly and charming variations upon the theme that had been given to him so unexpectedly, to the astonishment and delight of all who had heard him."

Streicher later urged the young man to write a symphony. "But Mozart, who always appeared to underrate his talent and feared that whatever he produced would be compared with what his father had done, and of course to his own disadvantage, had not the courage to follow Streicher's advice." And in 1829 W. A. Jr. told Mary Novello that "so much is expected of him from the circumstance of his name that it has become a burden to him."

Thus it does seem clear that the younger Mozart spent his life under the domination of a father he never knew and could not have remembered. Could that have been one reason why he exiled himself to Lvov? There he faded away. As a young man, W. A. Jr. had a certain distinguished quality, according to the painter J. P. Lyser. But Lyser met him again in 1834 and was shocked: "The figure appeared shrunken, the eyes dull and with an expression of profound melancholy; the forehead was bald, and the back of the head alone covered with sparse fine grayish hair."

Toward the end of his life, W. A. Jr. went to Vienna. But even after his death in Carlsbad he could not escape his father, as witness the inscription on his tombstone: "W. A. Mozart, musician and composer, born July 26, 1791, died July 29, 1844, son of the great Mozart, resembling the father in appearance and the nobility of his soul. May the name of his father be his epitaph, as his veneration for him was the essence of his life."

What about W. A. Jr. as a composer? Judging from the E flat Piano Concerto, which was first played by him in 1818, he had plenty of talent and even some originality. The first movement evokes Mozart strongly. But the composer also knew his Beethoven. The slow movement has some pre-Romantic figurations. In the salonlike last movement, one hears fashionable composers of the day—Weber, Hummel, Moscheles. W.A. Jr. was, in short, an eclectic. If, however, he could play the last movement in tempo as written, he was a decent enough virtuoso. There is some very effective writing here. The E flat Concerto is, on the whole, a well-written and attractive work. The son of Mozart had nothing to be ashamed of in this well-crafted piece. But the son of Mozart must also have known where this concerto stood in relation to his father's concertos—and that was the tragedy of his life.

MARCH 17, 1974

Thanks to Agi Jambor, I received the material for a Sunday piece that I can safely describe as somewhat unusual. I wondered if the Times *would print it. After I sent it up to Seymour Peck, at that time the editor of the Sunday Drama Section (so Arts and Leisure was then known), I waited anxiously for a comment. Nothing. The piece duly appeared, as written, and then I waited anxiously for condemning letters. Nothing. Maybe nobody ever read it.*

How Koczwara Came to a Grievous End at Miss Hill's House

THIS IS a family newspaper, and certain matters need be approached only with the greatest of delicacy. Especially is this true when the writer happens to be so unworldly and innocent a person as the conductor of this column. He lives surrounded by books, immersed in music, floating embryo-like in his quiet world, altogether inexperienced in the ways of man. Thus it was with Sir Robert Burton, who in his *Anatomy of Melancholy* (Part III, Sec. II, Mem. II, Subs. IV, in the chapter entitled "Artificial Allurements") listed certain sexual habits before abandoning the field in fright. "But what," he wrote, "have I to do with this?"

Yet we all desire to know the truth, and duty compels me to bring to public attention a bit of musico-sexual history that has been forgotten for almost 200 years. It concerns the composer Franz Koczwara (or Kotzwara, or Kotzwarra, as his name was variously spelled in those free and easy orthographic days).

Several weeks ago I wrote about Koczwara when the Newport Music Festival brought to life his *Battle of Prague,* for solo piano, with violin, cello and drums ad lib. Koczwara (c. 1730–1791) was born in Prague and settled in London in the 1780's. He played the viola in theaters, and suddenly became famous when he composed his battle piece. Arthur Loesser, in his great book, *Men, Women and Pianos,* has a great deal to say about Koczwara and his masterwork. The music he describes as having all the proper battle appurtenances—marches, bugle calls, the word of command, the hail of bullets, cannon shots, an attack with swords, cries of the wounded. All these were captioned in the music, so that no dullard would miss the point.

The Battle of Prague was published around 1790 and, says Loesser, "became a phenomenal success and spread like a petty plague that seemed unabatable through the decades. We will not hesitate to state that among the English and their cultural dependents, it remained for more than half a century the best-known, most played long piece of pianoforte music on both sides of the Atlantic; there are persistent references to it in nineteenth-century literature, from the novels of Thackeray and Mark Twain down to cartoons in Punch." One of the earliest exponents of *The Battle of Prague,* says Loesser, was a Miss Hoffmann, who in 1792 played it at the Assembly Rooms in Turnham Green. Miss Hoffmann was six years old. She was accompanied on the drums by her brother, "an artist who had attained the discreet age of three and a half."

But Koczwara, concluded Loesser, "was not permitted to enjoy even this early harvest of glory. He had already achieved another perpetration—not a musical deed, but one that later critics might have thought a subtly appropriate companion to *The Battle of Prague:* on September 2, 1791, he had gone to Vine Street, St. Martin's, and there hanged himself in a whore house."

Early editions of Grove's Dictionary of Music and Musicians

merely state that he hanged himself in a house of ill fame. Later editions add that the death was under mysterious circumstances. The current (1955) edition of Grove's has a footnote:

> That he did not hang himself, as is generally said, appears from the title of a book found by Dr. Alfred Loewenberg in a catalogue: *Modern Propensities:* or, an Essay on the Art of Strangling, etc. Illustrated with several Anecdotes. With Memoirs of Susannah Hill, and A Summary of Her Trial at the Old-Bailey, on Friday, Sept. 16, 1791, On the Charge of Hanging Francis Kotzwarra, At her Lodgings in Vine Street, on September 2.

On my desk is a photocopy of *Modern Propensities*. It was sent to me by the pianist and harpsichordist, Agi Jambor, who read the review of the Newport performance and thought I might be interested. Interested? The pamphlet is fascinating, and if nothing else clears up the mysterious circumstances of Koczwara's death. He did not hang himself, nor was he murdered. On the other hand he did hang himself, or had himself hanged.

The pamphlet has a rather long essay before getting down to Susannah Hill and the Old Bailey. It also has a remarkable woodcut, showing Miss Hill attaching a rope to the composer's neck. She is smiling happily. He is smiling happily, too. He is sitting on a pallet, with a glass of liquor in his right hand. With his left hand he is doing something regrettable. On the floor in front of him is something that looks like a flagellant's whip. But what have I to do with this?

Modern Propensities starts on a moral tone, regretting that the "objects of corporeal gratification" have remained "exactly such as they were in the beginning of time." Animal and vegetable life, says the pamphlet, are fixed to certain propensities from which they cannot swerve or release themselves. Sex is the dominating force. (The author of the pamphlet refers to sex as "the conjunctive means by which the species is perpetuated.") And as sex is an "ecstatic enjoyment," mankind has experimented with aids to "enlarge and enrapture the practice." The pamphlet describes several such devices. And it is one such device that bears directly on the death of Franz Koczwara.

It seems that some of the London sports believed that a touch of hanging was a great aid to certain lagging functions. For, as medical men of the day attested, "Every thing which produced irritation in the lungs and thorax, produced also titulation in the generative organs: that the blood by such means being impeded in its regular velocity, rushed to the center, and there formed, by sudden and compulsive operations, a redundancy of those vivifying secretions which animate and invigorate the machinery . . ."

Apparently this made great logic to those whose tastes ran toward experimentation, and there was something of a rush to try it out. There were dangers. The Reverend Parson Manacle, who doted on the practice, tried it once too often and expired in the process.

Which brings us to Susannah Hill. She was born in Somerset, was seduced under promise of marriage, and went to London and into business for herself. On September 2nd she was visited by a man she had never seen before. He came to terms with her and drank copiously of brandy and water. Then he and Miss Hill went into the back room. His tastes, according to the testimony, were rather peculiar. Then he demanded to be hanged for five minutes. Hanging, he said, would raise his passions. Miss Hill shrugged, went out to purchase a rope, and strung him up for five minutes. When Miss Hill cut him down, he fell to the ground. She ran to a neighbor for help, and a surgeon came, attempting to bleed the deceased. It was too late. Thus died Franz Koczwara.

At the Old Bailey, Judge Gould heard the case, and after the testimony was released, he immediately dismissed Miss Hill. She returned to 5 Vine Street, presumably never again to follow the practices of Parson Manacle. The "unfortunate—if not lamented" Koczwara lived on through his *Battle of Prague,* a work that for some fifty years far exceeded the Beethoven sonatas and Chopin études in popularity. But none of the sweet young ladies who strummed the battle piece, with expression, knew anything about the life and death of Franz Koczwara, which, under the circumstances, was just as well.

AUG. 30, 1967

Whether or not he was the greatest of all American composers —and I believe he was—Charles Ives certainly had the most fascinating and unconventional mind of all of them. I received the Concord *Sonata and other Ives material from Mrs. Lucille Gale Knapp after my review of the Ives Fourth Symphony appeared. Not until I leafed through the* Concord, *a few weeks later, did I realize what a treasure I had. I notified John Kirkpatrick of the find. Mr. Kirkpatrick, who gave the world première of the sonata in the 1930's, has done much biographical and archival work on Ives, and he was especially excited because the notations on the flyleaves were the first part of a longer essay of which Yale University had the remainder. Mr. Kirkpatrick and I spent a long afternoon with Ives's handwriting and arrived—we think—at an accurate transcript. It was published in the* Charles E. Ives Memos, *a valuable Ives source book edited by Mr. Kirkpatrick.*

Ives: Compulsiveness, Complexity, Dissonance and Power

I HAVE BEEN looking through the score of the Ives *Three Places in New England* which Pierre Boulez and the New York Philharmonic programmed last week. Part of the fun in reading any music by Ives is in the written commentary he so often supplied. There will be homely explanations, or quasi-poetic explanations, or polemic explanations. Thus on page 8 of the orchestral score (in the Birchard edition) there is an asterisk at Section D, and at the bottom of the page, the following: "From here on, though with animation, still slowly and rather evenly. Any holding back and variation should be of a cursory kind. Often when a mass of men march up hill, there is an unconscious slowing up. The drum seems to follow the feet, rather than the feet the drum."

A few years ago, through the kindness of Mrs. Lucille Gale Knapp of Mount Kisco, I came into possession of a copy of the first edition of Ives's *Concord* Sonata. Scribbled on all of the flyleaves, in Ives's characteristically illegible handwriting, is part of an essay about his harmonic and musical theories. The music itself is full of Ives's corrections and emendations, many of which were incorporated into the Arrow Edition of 1947. But there is even an extra bonus. Scattered throughout the pages are little comments, scrawled in pencil, that Ives had to make about the piece. Some are provocative, some are funny. Perhaps they were intended for Lawrence Gilman, from whose library the volume came. Gilman, for many years music critic of *The New York Herald Tribune*, was one of the first influential writers to take up the Ives cause.

Sometimes the marginalia are as much stream-of-consciousness as anything else. Ives always jotted down, furiously, the first thing that came into his head, and there is a kind of intellectual shorthand that one must follow. He wrote very fast, letters colliding with other letters. Only Beethoven had worse handwriting.

Anyway, in this edition of the *Concord*, Ives starts right out, on the verso of page 1. "And Emerson had more 'grit and dagger' than some nice Harvard Profs I think! and Billy Phelps agrees with this." There are scribbled-in tempo indications, with metronome marks, and exhortations to the player. Wrong notes are corrected. Figurations are made easier to read. There is constant admonition that the pianist must "go by position not time value of notes." At the top of page 10: "For instance, here all the 7 notes in diatonic scale and two others (on 5) are sounding together when meas. gets here. Thus in this way the written notes show what the ear hears and not what the eyes see. In other words, if this chord tune was put in half notes as Rollo says it is proper to—it wouldn't, for the sounds you [?hear], and therefore wrong." (I have added some punctuation to Ives's scrawl.) Rollo is Ives's general term for those "nice" and polite listeners with academic musical minds. Thus, at the beginning of page 21, the first page of the *Hawthorne* movement, "Don't try to please the ladies, Rollo! Line her out! And not the same nice way every time, Rollo!"

There are programmatic hints. Under the first measure of *Hawthorne*: "Or in the early morning—start pianissimo—if you feel that way." The dynamic that Ives has penciled at the beginning is "mezzo-forte or mezzo-piano." (The Arrow edition has piano.) Page 22, last line, beginning of treble clef in the left hand: "May be played by assistant pianist—in the dark—or off the street." Ives's mind could run in curious channels. On page 25 is the famous passage where the pianist presses down on a strip of board 14¾ inches long. Ives has made the pencil notation: "As distant bells." And, again, "Distant bells over the graveyard as heard by the ghosts." Once again, on the bottom of the page: "To sound as distant bells—better for another piano (away) or bells 'off stage.' " As for the wooden strip: "This is not playing with a club—as Mr. Rollo says—when you hit a nice key on the piano (keyboard!) you hit a long board or stick which hits the hammer, which makes a nice tone." At the bottom of the last line of music on this page is a fermata, over which Ives has written: "This is a kind of protest or moan, and may be heard as a sort of question: 'What's all this?' "

On page 26 is an instance of Ives's harmonic theories. There is a C sharp which, a few notes later, emerges as a D flat. Of this enharmonic change: "Those C sharps and D flats are not the same nice notes. They have different meanings—like it or not!" Bottom of page 33, measure before the end: "These are very hard to play fast enough (good place for side line player to be). Hit [the D sharp] hard and brave as soon as possible!" Ives did not care if ten pairs of hands were put to use, as long as the effect he

wanted could come through. On page 44: "It is more important
. . . to keep the horse going hard than to always play the exact
notes." And, at the bottom of page 45, with its fierce dissonances, comes a walloping exhortation: "Never mind the lily-
ladybird ears! Be a Man! Don't be afraid to harm the thumb.
Soak the black keys Hard." This passage continues for several
pages. Ives keeps begging the pianist: "Hard at it! Don't let it
sound pretty and nice." Or, "Help the soft ears walk out!"

In the third movement, *The Alcotts,* Ives has specified all
kinds of echo effects that are notated but not explained in the
Arrow Edition. The vibrating F sharp is explained as "Just a
partial moan from one of his daughters!" There are little programmatic touches. Under the first staff on page 57, Ives has
written: "I play it quite fast, and old 'Bronson' [Alcott] getting
somewhat excited and 'talkin' loud.'" At the very end of the
Alcott movement, Ives has pencilled in another echo F sharp:
"Sometimes I'd play this echo note *pppp* but probably better
not." The F sharp does not appear in the Arrow Edition.

There is some amusing byplay in the last movement, "Thoreau." On pages 62 and 63 is a series of kinetic explanations:
"Faster—he gets after somebody or something. . . . He quiets
down again. . . . He gets going high again. . . . He sits down again
and listens to nature. . . . Something begins to stir him again."
"He," of course, refers to Thoreau. Later on there is more of this,
including Thoreau's listening to the Concord bells.

None of this is program music, no more than Beethoven's
Pastoral Symphony is program music. Everything that Ives
wrote is evocation rather than description, and all these pencilled notations in the *Concord* are no more than guides to feeling. The more I hear the music of Charles Ives, the more it
impresses me as a musical evocation of the American past, or,
more specifically, a New England past—a past that Ives identified with so closely. It is an evocation of village bands and village greens that his music evokes, a past that encompasses
Emerson and the transcendentalists, the Civil War, the church
and folkways, the aspirations and dreams of an America that
was quieter and so much more rural than the America that Ives
lived through as an old man. The tough-minded Ives was in his

way a sentimentalist. But he expressed his vision in music of unprecedented convulsiveness, complexity, dissonance and power; and, as we all know, with an amazing series of technical departures that anticipated virtually every musical experiment of the decades ahead. That is what makes his music so eternally fascinating—this evocation of the past expressed in music of the future.

MARCH 30, 1969

The Boulez retrospective of Liszt was a fine idea that did not succeed, thanks to the conductor's inability to understand or feel the Lisztian rhetoric. More than any composer I know, Liszt is vulnerable to his interpreters. A convincing performance of his music demands a peculiar combination of extroversion and introversion, rhetoric and aristocracy, brilliance and intimacy. It takes a special kind of mind. At the turn of the century the Liszt style was part of every musician's background, but the traditions soon disappeared, only a handful of Liszt works survived, and his very name became a synonym for all that is vulgar in music. But I have always considered Franz Liszt to be one of the seminal forces of the nineteenth century. It pleases me that in recent years Liszt has made a strong comeback, and is now—even if grudgingly—beginning to be accepted as the force of nature he was.

Liszt: A Seminal Force of Romanticism

YOU CAN'T keep a secret in New York. When a famous conductor goes to the music library and starts looking through scores by a given composer, one of the page boys, who may also be a Juilliard student, tells his friends, and they tell other friends, and within a week everybody in the field knows about it. Or the Philharmonic assigns certain repertory to certain soloists, and it is supposed to be a secret, but no musician has as yet been born with tape permanently over his mouth.

And so, for the last few months, everybody knew that Pierre Boulez was going to concentrate on Franz Liszt and Alban Berg during his first season as musical director of the New York Philharmonic. The press conference held last Wednesday surprised very few newspapermen. Only the details remained to be filled in: who would conduct what, and what were the actual dates?

It was, of course, expected that Boulez, the great protagonist of twentieth-century music, would select one of his heroes of the Second Viennese School. The Alban Berg retrospect (so the Philharmonic calls it) will not only present a cross section of Berg's music, it will present virtually everything. Berg published very little, putting the major part of his creative effort into his two operas—*Wozzeck* and the unfinished *Lulu*. Symphonic suites from both operas will be programmed, and also the Violin Concerto (Berg's only work in that form), the Three Orchestral Pieces (Berg's only work for full orchestra), the *Kammerkonzert*, the concert aria *Der Wein* and his two sets of songs with orchestra. That leaves very little of Berg's music unrepresented. What is there left? The Piano Sonata, the String Quartet, the Four Pieces for Clarinet, and some songs. There remains the *Lyric Suite* for string quartet, and Boulez will conduct that in a version for string orchestra made by the composer in 1929.

None of this music is unfamiliar. Berg's music has been recorded substantially complete, and is thus available to anybody who wants to explore it. In addition, *Wozzeck* has become all but a repertory piece, and the unprecedented interest in the music of Schoenberg and his pupils that sprang up after World War II has caused Berg to figure prominently on programs.

But Liszt! That is a different story. It is surprising to find such an avowed antiromantic as Pierre Boulez interested in Liszt, the most romantic of all the Romantics. One would have thought the lamb would eat the wolf, the Cardinal would get married,

Wall Street would rebound, America would make peace with Hanoi, before Boulez would lie in the same bed with Franz Liszt.

In recent years, however, there has been the beginnings of a reconsideration of Liszt, and Boulez probably has been discovering, through a study of the scores, that old Franz was a mighty creative figure, that he was more prophetic than some of the current idols, notably Gustav Mahler. For without Liszt, music would probably not have developed the way it did.

Liszt, of course, has always suffered from a bad reputation. He has been considered a poseur, a vulgarian, a composer without taste or integrity, a showman interested only in meretricious effect. And all of that is present in some of his music. The trouble is that he has been considered in black and white. He was so overwhelming a figure that his faults have been stressed out of all proportion, coming to a climax in an all but insane book by Ernest Newman. In *The Man Liszt* Newman could see no good in him at all, and that unlovely muckraking job has been accepted as gospel in some quarters.

Consider Franz Liszt. He was the greatest pianist of his day and most likely the greatest of all time. As a musician he had everything—a perfect ear, the ability to hear a long and complicated piece of music and immediately play it back as written. He was probably the greatest sight-reader who ever lived. Poorly educated, he pulled himself up and ended a thoroughly literate man. Incredibly good looking as a young man, his amours were the talk of Europe. Later in life he befriended all struggling composers who crossed his path. He also turned out most of the great pianists of the latter half of the century.

He was a complicated man, pulled by religion in one direction, the flesh in another. And his music is equally complicated. More than any of the early Romantics, he broke free of previous influences. Mendelssohn basically was a Classicist. Schumann and Chopin made passing gestures at the sonata form of Beethoven and Mozart. Liszt almost never worked in sonata form. He worked out his own rules. His larger forms were generally cyclic in nature (César Franck in the 1840's was also working along this line, but it was Liszt who popularized it), featured by transformation of thematic material. Often an entire work, as in the

B minor Sonata, would be evolved from a cell at the beginning. In this there is a direct link from Liszt to serial composition.

Harmonically the man was a raving genius. He was experimenting with chordal combinations that carried the seeds of atonality long before Wagner. As one outstanding instance, the opening chords of Wagner's *Tristan und Isolde* have been hailed as the break from standard tonality. Their harmonic vagueness leads to a suspension of a tonal home base as it was then understood. But those chords were not written by Wagner. They were written long before *Tristan und Isolde*, and can be found note for note in a Liszt song of 1845 named *Ich möchte hingehn*. (I say, "note for note," and that is substantially true, even if one note is a D natural instead of a D sharp.) Wagner was always stealing harmonic ideas from his father-in-law, and admitted as much. There is the story of Liszt and Wagner sitting in a box as the curtain goes up on *Tristan*. Says Wagner, "That's your chord, papa." Says Liszt, "At least now it will be heard."

It was Liszt who invented the symphonic poem. Without Liszt, the career of Richard Strauss would have taken a different turn. It was Liszt who experimented with a kind of psychological song (and those songs are so little heard!) that directly anticipates Hugo Wolf. It was Liszt who invented a kind of piano technique without which the *Jeux d'eau* of Ravel would be inconceivable. It was only Liszt who could write the strange works of his last period—works that he never attempted to have published, works bare and lean, works that strongly suggest the impressionism of Debussy and the dissonances of Bartók.

Yes, his music could be bombastic, but it threw a mighty shadow over the century; and even that bombast, that rhetoric, was an important part of the Romantic upheaval. Liszt admirers —and by now you will have reached the conclusion that I am one—rather enjoy that rhetoric. If nothing else, it is supported by the harmonies of one of the most inventive minds music has produced, and it is a much more subtle harmony than Liszt's bad reputation would indicate. No wonder it came as an explosion in its time (not that I want to underrate the harmonic genius of Chopin, just as explosive in its way). Impartially considered, Liszt was one of the three seminal forces of Romanticism (Chopin and Schumann were the others), and his mind was much more daring and imaginative than that of the infinitely more eclectic Wagner. Wagner's immense position in music is based on a different set of factors. But it should never be forgotten that Wagner never started to compose really great music until he had been exposed to Liszt the man and Liszt the composer.

And so the Philharmonic, for the first time in its history, is taking a thorough look at Liszt. We shall be hearing some of the infrequently encountered symphonic poems and the even more infrequently encountered choral works, together with music that is familiar. It will indeed be a retrospect, and all one can say, in addition to offering thanks, is that it's about time.

Jan. 31, 1971

More than any American composer, Aaron Copland represented the period in which I grew up. Stravinsky and his Neoclassicism, true, had attracted a generation of Americans, but it was Copland who was their idol. It is hard to think of a serious American composer of the period who was not under Copland's influence, one way or the other. Music was to take a different turn after World War II, and the new composers worshipped at different shrines, but even then the genial, intelligent Aaron Copland served as the symbol of a dedicated musician who always was the spokesman, interpreter and champion of new talent.

Copland: He Wanted to Reach Us

THE AARON COPLAND 70th birthday observances continue, and on Tuesday the Metropolitan Museum will show some of the films for which he wrote the music. The entire American musical colony has been anxious to pay homage to Copland, as well it might.

Whether or not he is the dean of American composers (Virgil Thomson is a few years older), there can be no doubt that in Aaron Copland an entire period is symbolized. He is the American composer who caught the imagination of a wide public. And, aside from his talent as a composer, Copland has for some fifty years been the spokesman for American music. As organizer, teacher, propagandist, critic, lecturer and expositor, he has been by far the most voluble, articulate and respected American musician of his time. In the early 1920's he began to spread his wings, and ever since then fledglings have crept under them for comfort and protection. If Copland has ever pushed any of them into the cold, there is no record of it.

It was in the 1930's and early 1940's that he was at his height. Consider the 1930's. Here was Copland, the head of what amounted to an American school (one or two composers might dispute this statement), and on the other side there was the Establishment. Very little new music was heard in the concert halls. The New York Philharmonic, dominated by Toscanini, could not have been less interested. Stokowski in Philadelphia was programming some sensational stuff, but his biggest splashes came from the better-publicized modernists, such as Stravinsky (with *Le Sacre du Printemps*, still a novelty) and the Schoenberg of *Gurrelieder*. Stokowski conducted very little of the new American music, though he did present Copland's *Dance Symphony* in 1931. In Boston, Serge Koussevitzky was more hospitable. He was the one conductor with a strong interest in Copland's music, and Boston was the one place in America where Copland could count on getting his latest works played.

In the concert halls, the new American music seldom was heard. Instrumentalists, by and large, were still trained in the Romantic tradition, and a piece such as Copland's Piano Variations caused them infinite trouble. Fingers did not go where they were *supposed* to go. And it was a music that the public did not like (nor does it even today). It was too dissonant, too stripped down, too unmelodic, too defiantly purged of Romanticism.

But it was these same Piano Variations that fascinated the younger generation of American composers. No composer anywhere in the world had written music like this. In this piece of music there may have been hints of Stravinsky's rhythmic innovations, and even hints of Viennese dodecaphonism. Basically, though, it owed little to anybody. That special treatment of the piano, those unorthodox leaps, that logical organization, those idiosyncratic harmonies—all these were things that hypnotized the new wave of American composers. They all knew that writing music in this manner was no easy way to make a success with public and publishers. But they also realized that it was authentic music, powerful and individual music, "American" music.

Copland himself recorded the Piano Variations. In those days, it was one of his few recordings. Very little contemporary music was available on records in the 1930's. Composers then really had trouble. Much of Copland's time was spent organizing concerts. He worked closely with the International Society for Contemporary Music and with the League of Composers. The New School was a haven in those days. Nor were Copland's activities confined to the United States. He preached the cause of American music in England and the Continent. More than any one man, he was responsible for bringing the work of the new American school to international attention.

It is interesting to speculate what would have happened had not Copland changed musical styles. As a composer of jagged abstract works, he had the complete respect of the musical community—but while his name was known to the general public, his music by and large was not. Copland fretted about this, and was a big enough man to suggest that perhaps the fault was not entirely with the public. It was senseless, he said, for composers to continue working in a vacuum. And so, starting about 1935, he began to write a different kind of music.

In hindsight, it is not *that* different. Copland had evolved a personal style, with a certain kind of harmony, rhythm and texture that were, well, Coplandish. In shifting to a more popular kind of writing, all he did was use a type of nationalistic melody superimposed over the essential Copland textures. (This is an oversimplification; but *Appalachian Spring* is recognizably from the same hand that wrote the Piano Variations. The famous "esthetic shift" of Copland is more a change of emphasis than a change in esthetic.)

What Copland did in the works that made him popular—especially *El Salón México, Billy the Kid, Rodeo, Appalachian Spring* and the *Lincoln Portrait*—was to show that "modernism" and popular appeal are not necessarily incompatible. These scores had appealing melody and catchy rhythms, and a general air of sophistication, but they were also undeniably modern—modern in the sharp dissonances, modern in orchestration—the work of a composer who knew every contemporary trend, yet who could put them into a package that still had individuality and integrity. There was nothing at all eclectic-sounding in the Copland nationalistic scores, for his own personality and musical profile were too strong.

Virgil Thomson had previously hinted at this kind of writing in a handful of scores, but it was Copland who popularized it. His music had a bite that the blander music of Thomson lacked. (Anyway, Thomson's specialty was the sung word, and in his songs and operas his music achieved more success than Copland's entries into that area.) For two decades American music was full of Copland disciples trying to write as the Master did. Very few of them made it. Up to World War II, the American school was still headed by Copland, Harris, Thomson, Piston, Schuman and Barber. Of the last-named five, only Barber might be considered in any way Copland-influenced, and that minimally.

But American music from 1925 to 1945 had many promising oncomers, and most of those were in one way or another under Copland's wing. Israel Citkowitz, Paul Bowles, Leonard Bernstein, Leo Smit, Harold Shapero, Robert Palmer, Lukas Foss, David Diamond, Marc Blitzstein, Arthur Berger, Irving Fine, Alexei Haieff—these were some of the Copland epigones. Some are now dead, some have stopped composing. Copland himself does not compose much any more. There are theories. Leonard Bernstein, in the November, 1970, issue of *High Fidelity* magazine, suggests that Copland stopped because his music was no longer fashionable (that is, fashionable with the new generation of composers). But can that be the reason? Copland himself later indicated that Bernstein was just talking for Lenny.

Admittedly, however, it might be hard for a man who for so long had been the leader of American music to find himself considered an anachronism. Copland did attempt some serial scores, without much success. It is hard to imagine so fertile a mind running dry, though that has happened in the history of music. And, whether or not fashionable with the post-serialists, Copland remains the most popular and the most played of serious American composers. He would not, as Elgar did with his Third Symphony, tear up a work with the petulant observation that nobody wanted it. A great number of people would most definitely want it. So Copland's attitude remains a mystery. But his position in the history of American music is no mystery.

Feb. 28, 1971

When Joshua Rifkin recorded his first disc of Joplin rags in 1970, I wrote a long and enthusiastic piece about it. Normally I would have passed the record by, but some years previously, in Seattle, I had run into William Bolcom, who was one of the original Joplin revivalists. Remembering his enthusiasm, I put on the Rifkin record and found it enchanting. Two years later, when Treemonisha *had its world première in Atlanta, I wrote another Joplin piece—and could not resist getting John Powell's letter into it.*

Scott Joplin: A Real Composer with Something to Offer

SCOTT JOPLIN is in the news again. The Joplin renaissance started about two years ago with the recording by Joshua Rifkin of a group of Joplin's piano rags. Suddenly everybody woke up to the fact that Joplin was a real composer with something to offer. Those bittersweet rags, with their syncopations and evocative turn-of-the-century melodies, and with their astonishingly imaginative harmonies, and with their recreation of a period in American life, and as the work of a black composer—all this added up to a phenomenon that was greeted with admiration and delight. In short order came more ragtime recordings, including a disc of Joplin himself in some pianola rolls he had cut in 1916. There were Joplin concerts, and the pianist Alan Mandel has been touring Europe with a Joplin group on his program.

Now there have been two more major contributions to the ever-swelling Joplin renaissance. From the New York Public Library come the two imposing volumes of *The Collected Works of Scott Joplin*—all the piano rags in Vol. I, and all the vocal music (including the opera *Treemonisha*) in Vol. II. Vera Brodsky Lawrence was the editor in this first publication of the library's projected Americana Collection Music Series. And from Morehouse College in Atlanta has come the world première of the Joplin opera. *Treemonisha* was given two staged performances on Jan. 28 and 29 at the Memorial Arts Center in Atlanta.

Ragtime started to disappear during World War I. It was replaced by jazz. But during its great days, from the publication of Joplin's *Maple Leaf Rag* in 1899 until Joplin's death in 1917, ragtime not only swept America. It swept the world. Rudi Blesh, in his introduction to *The Collected Works*, has something to say about ragtime overseas. In France they called it *le temps du chiffon*. In Vienna, ragtime was played on coffee-house zithers. In Scotland, pipers skirled the *Maple Leaf Rag*. The Sousa Band enjoyed great success with ragtime when it toured Europe. Debussy used ragtime in his *Golliwogg's Cakewalk* and *General Lavine—Eccentric*. Brahms, just before his death, was thinking of writing ragtime.

It turned up in the most unexpected sources. When I wrote an article about Joplin in this column some time ago, I received from a nice reader a copy of a letter that the American pianist-composer John Powell had written from Vienna in 1902. Powell at that time was studying with Theodor Leschetizky, the teacher from whose classes had come such great pianists as Paderewski, Schnabel, Szalit, Friedman, Horszowski and many others. One night at Leschetizky's home there was a dinner party. Powell, relaxed, was talking with Paula Szalit.

"Then," he writes, "came one of the greatest shocks of my life. Everybody asked the Prof. to play again. He seated himself at the piano and Murphy brought him a great file of sheet music and put a piece before the Prof. upon the piano. I heaved a sigh of contentment and settled myself in my chair, closed my eyes and awaited the strains of Beethoven or Chopin. Suddenly I started up. Pandemonium had broken loose. Everybody had crowded around the Prof. singing and shouting at the tops of their voices and dancing like maniacs. When the clamor subsided a little I managed to distinguish the strains of *The Honeysuckle and the Bee*. I almost fainted. *Smoky Moses, Rastus, My Coal Black Lady*, and a mass of others followed in quick succession. When I recovered from my first shock of surprise I joined in the merriment. When the file of music was exhausted he improvised a charming Negro dance that was, however, far more Hungarian than Negro. The party broke up at 4:30. . . ."

It is pleasant to think of the stout, bearded, dignified Prof. banging out *Rastus* and other rags. What he would not have played was any part of *Treemonisha*. Nobody knew it, and that was the despair of the latter part of Joplin's life. Previously he had composed a ragtime opera, *A Guest of Honor.* A 1903 copy-right exists, but the music was never published and has disap-peared. (It was not the first opera by an American black composer. Harry Lawrence Freeman's *The Martyr* had been pro-duced in Denver in 1893.) Joplin then turned to an opera that would express the ideals of his race—the concept that through education the black man would liberate himself.

He worked on it for some years. Nobody would publish it, much less stage the work. In 1911 Joplin, at his own expense, issued a vocal score. He also orchestrated the opera, but those orchestrations have been lost. In 1915 Joplin arranged for a run-through in Harlem, with singers grouped around a piano. *Tree-monisha* was a flop. Two years later Joplin was dead.

In *Treemonisha* Joplin was torn two ways. He wanted to write a "real" opera, and that meant harmonies used by "real" com-posers. *Treemonisha* is not a ragtime opera. Joplin tried to write arias in Metropolitan Opera style, and he used a harmony con-sisting of Late Romantic altered chords. He also wrote his own libretto, and it is pretty bad. Treemonisha discovers that she is not really the daughter of Monisha and Ned. "I am greatly sur-prised to know that you are not my mother," she sings. "We are all surprised," responds the chorus. The language of the libretto is on that level.

But if *Treemonisha* is accepted as the period piece it is, the score is full of delights. Joplin, no matter how hard he tried to be "operatic" in the European sense, could not evade his back-ground. And his background was Afro-American—the world of folk tunes and spirituals, of ragtime and syncopation, of sad melody and revival-meeting outbursts, even of barber-shop quar-tets and popular ballads. All of this plays a part in *Treemonisha.* It is a folk opera, a genuine folk opera, and it breathes a quality that could have come from nowhere but turn-of-the-century America as seen through the eyes of a minority member.

Thus the opera is greater than the sum of its parts. And when Joplin started to write the kind of music that was close to him, *Treemonisha* is enchanting. The spiritual-like ending of the sec-ond act, *Aunt Dinah Has Blowed de Horn,* is one of the great curtains of American musical theater. It hits the listener like an

explosion—exultant, swinging, wonderfully spiced harmonically. This is the real thing. And so is the ending of the opera, *A
Real Slow Drag*. This differs a little from the *Dinah* number,
because it starts out in a minor key, and is unusual in that the
melodic key note is on the second degree of the scale, which
lends a haunting feeling of irresolution to the tune. But after the
introduction in minor comes the big F major chorus, *Marching
Onward*, and this is every bit as good as the *Dinah* chorus. The
audience that heard this at the première just about went out of
its mind.

There are other things. Monisha's long (too long; it has to be
cut) solo, *The Sacred Tree*, is sweet and simple, with a flowing
line. The choral passages of *Good Advice*, starting with *O yes,
ah feel lak I've been redeemed*, are extraordinarily moving. This
is the very essence of the Negro spiritual. There is a good deal of
dance in *Treemonisha*, including a divertissement when bears
come out of the forest and frolic, growling "Oo-ar," and it has a
touching naiveté. The barber-shop quartet, *We Will Rest
Awhile*, was received with glee by the Atlanta audience. Other
sections of *Treemonisha* are harder to take, though one can sympathize with what Joplin was trying to do. In any case, there is
more than enough in *Treemonisha* to show that its composer
spoke in a unique voice. At the sessions of Afro-American music
in Atlanta, at Morehouse College, everybody was referring to
Scott Joplin as a genius. Well, there are varieties of genius; and
in his modest way Joplin was one.

FEB. 13, 1972

*The 1960–80 period saw the revival of many Rossini operas in
New York, and I dutifully wrote Sunday columns about them
as they appeared. But nothing gave me more delight than the*
Péchés de Vieillesse, *and the Scotto recital gave me a chance to*

discuss these exquisite, effervescent miniatures in more detail than I could have done in a review.

Even Rossini's "Sins" Aren't Serious

WHEN ROSSINI died, in 1868, all of the obituary notices—and for this great man there were obituary notices from St. Petersburg to San Francisco—pursued much the same line. What a loss to mankind that Rossini had not written an opera since *William Tell* in 1829! True, the *Stabat Mater* had been written during Rossini's retirement after the première of *William Tell.* A few writers even knew of the existence of the *Petite Messe Solennelle.* Otherwise there was nothing. Or so they said.

But there was something, as Renata Scotto so imaginatively demonstrated at her Carnegie Hall concert a week ago Monday. She devoted an entire evening to Rossini; and, apart from a pair of opera arias, concentrated on the solo songs and duets found in the collection that Rossini called *Péchés de Vieillesse,* or "Sins of Old Age." Scotto was not exactly exploring unknown territory, for singers do look into the *Péchés* every now and then. But a whole evening of them was a daring enterprise—and it worked. For the music is so varied, so pretty, so witty, so sophisticated, that there was no feeling of dullness or repetition. Scotto even called upon three other singers to share the fun, and there were duets for soprano and mezzo, soprano and tenor, even tenor and bass.

Rossini, after all, was one of the important composers of history. And during his "retirement" he did much more than create *tournedos Rossini* and experiment with spaghetti recipes. Sharp, intelligent, he looked around him and missed nothing. The new chromatic harmony of Chopin and Liszt, the Berlioz kind of Romanticism, the Wagner concept of music theater—all passed before him, and all were studied. Certain it is that his later music, such as the *Petite Messe Solennelle* or many of the

Péchés, are much more sophisticated harmonically than any of the music in his famous operas; and, indeed, many of the *Péchés* anticipate Satie, especially in such titles as *Les Hors d'Oeuvres,* or *Mon Prélude hygiénique du Matin,* or *Valse Torturée,* or *Valse Antidansante.* The more one looks into this body of music, the more one admires it. Some of the piano solos are as lovely and charming as any of the songs and ensemble numbers.

Rossini himself made light of these little pieces. He composed them for two reasons: he could no more stop composing than he could stop breathing; and he needed material for his famous *Samedi soirs,* those Saturday entertainments at his home in which the greatest artists rushed to participate. Not long before he died, Rossini was asked why he had stopped composing for the theater after 1829. "Quiet!" he said. "Don't talk to me about that. Moreover, I compose constantly. Do you see that cabinet full of music? All of it has been written since *William Tell.* But I don't publish anything, and I compose them because I cannot help myself." His wife put all of these little compositions into the cabinet that Rossini referred to. Many are still unpublished.

It seems that Rossini was not joking when he said that he did not want these pieces published. He was remarkably secretive about them. Among his "house" pianists were Camille Saint-Saëns and Louis Diémer, and Diémer many years later left some reminiscences about Rossini and his *Péchés.* Rossini called himself "a pianist of the fourth class," meaning a rather weak technician, and composed his piano pieces accordingly. But seldom could he be lured to the keyboard. Diémer took care of that.

"The Maestro," he wrote, "asked me to play his new compositions for him, and I gladly accepted. Thus I became the habitual pianist of his weekly soirées, interpreting his manuscripts each Saturday. I had to study them at his house because he did not want to entrust them to anyone. After two or three times" —that is, after he had read through a manuscript two or three times—"I succeeded in committing to memory the pieces to be played during the evening. He had composed many, including a most diverting parody of Offenbach's music, to be played with one finger; a tarantella in which one heard the passing of a parade; . . . certain preludes, *Profound Sleep with Startled Awak-*

ening; and finally a series of little pieces that he called *Les Petits Riens*, to which he gave such curious titles as *The Hors d'Oeuvres, The Anchovies, The Radishes, A Caress for My Wife*, etc.''

It was considered a great honor to be invited to one of the Rossini Saturday evening musicales. But creature comfort was not one of the pleasures of the occasion. As a Viennese newspaperman complained, "Rossini's residence is very far from being large enough to accommodate the number of persons invited. The heat was something indescribable. . . . Now and then a servant with refreshments worms through the gasping crowd, but it is an odd fact that only a very few persons (and those mostly strangers) take anything worth mentioning. The lady of the house, it is said, does not like their doing so. About the present Madame Rossini I have nothing further to tell than that she is rich, and was once beautiful.''

It was there that many of the *Péchés* were first heard. Rossini did not take them seriously. He took nothing seriously, including his own operas. Serious-minded musicians were irritated by Rossini's constant banter. He was always joking, especially about his own compositions; but as often as not he had his tongue in his cheek and he was famous for his rapier wit. He made people uncomfortable; when he joked about his own music, there was a suspicion that he also was having a secret little laugh at the person with whom he was talking.

There always was a streak of irony about him, as in his remark to a young lady standing between him and the Duke of Wellington. "Madame," said Rossini, "how happy you should be, to find yourself placed between the two greatest men in Europe." This story made the rounds and was cited as an example of Rossini's conceit. On the contrary; he was poking fun at the pompous Wellington.

There must be close to 200 of the *Péchés de Vieillesse.* The title comes from five bound volumes—Nos. IV to VIII—in which the composer refers to this collection of 56 semi-comic pieces for the piano. "I dedicate these sins of old age to the pianists of the fourth class, to which I have the honor to belong." In all there are fourteen volumes of manuscripts: songs in Italian and French, duets, even an album *"pour piano, violon, violon-cello, harmonium et cor."* Wouldn't it be one of the supreme ironies if, in years to come, these *morceaux* are taken more seriously as works of art than the majority of Rossini's operas? It would be an irony that would have amused Rossini more than anybody else.

MARCH 27, 1973

Somewhere around 1950, Ricardo Odnoposoff, a well-known violinist of the day, played some of Reger's solo violin sonatas, and those graceful miniatures had nothing in common with what I had considered to be the essence of Max Reger. I started looking at his music, have been interested in it ever since, and have gone out of my way to hear it. Reger still has a terrible reputation in musical circles, but he also has some devoted admirers, among whom Rudolf Serkin is the most devoted of all. When Serkin returned to Europe in the fall of 1980, after a long absence, it was with the Bach variations of Reger.

Max Reger: Better Than His Notices

RUDOLF SERKIN on Tuesday will play in Carnegie Hall, as a labor of love, the *Variations and Fugue on a Theme of Bach* by Max Reger. I have the music before me as I write. Universal Edition, taken over from Bote and Bock. Forty-three of the densest-looking pages of notation this side of Sorabji. Often a Brahmsian look to the writing, though the sound is not Brahmsian. Consistent chordal writing of the kind that takes a big, strong hand to grasp. Complicated figurations. A monster of a piece, and very seldom played in public these days. Among the big international virtuosos, has anybody played it in recent years except Serkin and Gina Bachauer?

Serkin came to the *Variations and Fugue* through Arnold Schoenberg. It is well known that Schoenberg had respect and admiration for Reger. There is a letter from Schoenberg to Alexander Zemlinsky, dated Oct. 26, 1922, discussing repertory. "Reger," wrote Schoenberg, "must in my view be done often; 1, because he has written a lot; 2, because he is already dead and people are still not clear about him. (I consider him a genius.)" Scattered throughout Schoenberg's writings are references to Reger that make it clear that Schoenberg put him on as high a plane as Mahler and Richard Strauss.

When Serkin was about sixteen years old—this would be around 1919—he studied with Schoenberg, and the composer had quite a few things to tell the young pianist about Reger. Schoenberg said that of all contemporary composers Reger had been closest to leaving tonality. "One step further and he would be with me." Reger himself also felt an affinity. Once he told the violinist Adolf Busch that of all modern composers he felt closest to Schoenberg. The two composers were, of course, to take different directions. But at the beginning they did have much in common. They were born within a year of each other —Reger in 1873, Schoenberg in 1874. Their early music was in a highly chromatic texture stemming from Wagner. Reger stuck to that and Schoenberg eventually moved on to his "emancipation of the dissonance" and then dodecaphonism. But in their early years both were traditionalists.

Reger died in 1916, and Serkin never met him. They did have a date. Serkin had worked up Reger's Piano Concerto (imagine that, from a boy of thirteen!) and was supposed to play it for the composer in Vienna, but that was not to be. Later, Serkin was to be the great exponent of Reger. About ten years ago, the pianist devoted a season to the Reger Piano Concerto and also recorded it. And during the summer months at Marlboro the hills of Vermont are filled with the sounds of Reger's chamber music, which Serkin considers the most important aspect of Reger as a composer.

It is a riddle to Serkin why Reger has dropped out of the repertory so completely. Very few musicians look at his music, and the younger critics despise it. To them, Reger is equated with everything bad, overblown and vulgar in late Romanticism. Reger also has the reputation of writing nothing but monster works—those long orchestral variations on one theme or another, followed by a colossal fugue. But, as Serkin points out, Reger did not always write big. Serkin cites such works as the *Tagebuch* for piano, or the "songs, so beautiful," or the tiny sonatas for unaccompanied violin. Why, he wants to know, don't conductors look at the Reger Sinfonietta, or Serenade, or Symphonic Prologue?

As for the *Variations and Fugue on a Theme of Bach*, Serkin expresses nothing but admiration for it. "I love it and have played it since I was sixteen," he says. "I loved it from the beginning. Most people think it is complicated. I think it is simple. The music is emotionally direct. It may be on a theme of Bach, but there are no real Bachian elements in it. The music is a series of variations like fantasies. Often Reger goes off on his own, with hardly any reference to the Bach theme. The ending of the fugue has three elements juxtaposed. It looks thick but it really isn't."

In this work there is a kind of chromaticism that goes beyond Franck or even *Verklärte Nacht*. There also is a kind of dissonance that may remind listeners of the fact that Reger was considered a modernist in his day. But present-day listeners ignore the dissonance, and young intellectuals are apt to be bothered by the ultra-rich chromaticism. They find it cloying, with as much backbone as a marshmallow. But how much of Reger's music have they heard? Very little is in the repertory. The point is that Reger should not be judged purely on his grandiose works, such as the *Mozart* Variations for orchestra (which, incidentally, I myself happen to like; but everybody knows *my* tastes).

Reger himself thought of his music as a continuation of the German tradition. He claimed that his music was written in the spirit of Bach and Beethoven. "I can say with good conscience," he wrote in 1914, "that of all living composers I am probably the one who is closest in touch with the great masters of our rich past." The music of his own day composed by epigones of Wagner and Strauss he called "perverted rubbish." Big, stout, stub-born, Reger loved a good fight, and during his career was always getting into scraps with critics and fellow musicians.

Footnote to history: One of the famous stories about Reger has him writing to a critic: "I am sitting in the smallest room of my house. Your review is before me. Shortly it will be behind me." Several years ago I used the story in this column, wondering all the while whether it was really true or not. So many wonderful stories about musicians turn out to be apocryphal. Several weeks later I received a letter from a Mrs. Frieda Weiler in Dallas:

"I am an old lady—89—and a musician," wrote Mrs. Weiler. "Reger was a good friend of my late husband and mine. When he gave a concert in Kassel where we lived, he spent many hours mostly till late in the night after it in our house. . . . When Reger first came into our house, I was amazed, he filled the whole space of the door. . . . The anecdote you wrote is a true story. The addressee was: Professor Karg-Ehlert (who by the way dedicated to me his 'Haidebilder'). He confirmed that he had received the card." Karg-Ehlert (1877–1933) or Elert, as it is more usually spelled, was a pianist-organist-composer-teacher who still lives today by virtue of a spectacular series of organ works, many of which have remained in the repertory. Apparently he also did some music criticism. And apparently he got Max Reger very, very angry.

Dec. 2, 1973

Not long after this piece appeared, two biographies of Percy Grainger were published, and they tell us a great deal that previously had been hinted at by people who had known the popular pianist-composer. It turns out that he was a racist and had some rather spectacular sexual hangups. He also was an interesting musician and one of the true originals. If his was a minor creative talent, when judged alongside the great ones, he nevertheless did write some music that has never disappeared from the repertory. I should have written something about Grainger the pianist in this article. His playing was unusually lucid and breezy. He left many records as testimony. One of my favorites is the Bach-Liszt A minor Prelude and Fugue. I have never heard the fugue played with such verve and clarity.

No One's Laughing at Percy Grainger Anymore

LAST WEEK, at the McMillin Theater, there was a concert devoted to the music of Percy Grainger. *Percy Grainger!* The very idea of a Grainger concert would have evoked howls of laughter twenty years ago. Grainger in those days was primarily regarded as a pianist. He also was the purveyor of such pretty tunes as *Country Gardens* (his most famous piece), *Shepherd's Hey* and *Molly on the Shore.* Kitsch, in short.

But if the intellectuals refused to take him seriously as a creative figure, concertgoers thronged to his concerts. He was a remarkable pianist—big, breezy, uninhibited, ultra-romantic. This tall, remarkably handsome man with the aquiline profile and figure of an athlete, also was good copy. Grainger was one of the eccentrics of music. Often he would don a knapsack and hike from concert to concert. When he married Ella Viola Ström, he took over the entire Hollywood Bowl and invited his friends plus, in effect, the entire city of Los Angeles. The highlight of the affair was his bridal present, *To a Nordic Princess*, a composition he himself naturally conducted.

His musical credentials were impeccable. He had come out of Australia, where he was born on July 8, 1882. In Germany he studied with James Kwast and Ferruccio Busoni, then started concertizing and composing. Grieg was very interested in the young Australian, and a great friendship resulted after they met in 1906. "If I had his technique," Grieg said, "my conception of the nature of piano playing would have been exactly the same." Grieg taught Grainger his A minor Concerto, and for the rest of his life Grainger was the "official" interpreter of that popular piece.

Before settling in the United States in 1914 (Grainger became a citizen) he had his headquarters in England and was an active member of the emergent British musical nationalists. Like Bartók in Hungary, Grainger went around the countryside with a gramophone—locating and recording folk music, transcribing it, using the material as a basis for his own music. He was part of a group that included Gustav Holst, Ralph Vaughan Williams, Carl Dolmetsch, Cecil Sharp and Philip Heseltine.

He took folk music with utmost seriousness, and never considered it primitive or unformed. "Believing as I do," he once wrote, "that music is always perfect amongst all races, at all times and in all places, I cannot admit any conception of musical progress that sees music passing gradually from worse to better, and which therefore belittles primitive music or the earliest traceable beginnings of art music." Quite the contrary. Grainger believed that the best music should aspire to the spirit of folk music. Most music, he stated, was held back by "highly artificial and rule-clad forms." Folk music, on the other hand, showed much greater freedom and irregularity—a condition towards which art music should aspire.

The influence of folk music can be traced in nearly all of Grainger's music. There are the obvious derivations, of course, his direct translations for piano, or voices, or whatever, of folk music. But the folk presence breathes through Grainger's abstract works and, especially, in his so-called "free music."

"In this music," Grainger explained, referring to his free music, "melody is as free to roam thru tonal space as a painter is free to draw & paint free lines, free curves, create free shapes. ...In FREE MUSIC the various tone-strands (melodic lines) may each have their own rhythmic pulse (or not), if they like;

but one tone-strand is not enslaved to the other (as in current music) by rhythmic same-beatedness. In FREE music there are no scales. . . . In FREE MUSIC harmony will consist of free combinations (when desired) of all free intervals—not merely concordant or discordant combinations of set intervals (as in current music), but free combinations of all the intervals (but in a gliding state not needfully in an anchored state) between the present intervals . . ."

This is a statement that Ives or Varèse would have applauded. Grainger was composing unusual music at the turn of the century. But he was marked forever by *Country Gardens*, which is not representative of his over 600 works. Grainger was not taken seriously as a composer. When he died, in White Plains on Feb. 20, 1961, nobody would have given him much chance of making it as a creative figure.

But he was not forgotten, as it turned out. In 1966 Benjamin Britten put his enormous prestige behind Grainger's work. In an Aldeburgh Festival program he presented an entire evening of Grainger. "Grainger is my master," he said. Several years later Britten, Peter Pears and others collaborated in a disk of Grainger's music, and that attracted much attention. It might be worthwhile mentioning that Grainger himself had a long career in the record studios—from around 1910 to the late 1930's. He played a good deal of his own music, in addition to standard keyboard classics by Liszt, Schumann, Chopin and others. Some of the interpretations are eccentric. All are pianistically dazzling.

Thanks to Britten, and to a Grainger festival in London in 1970, Grainger suddenly became respectable. Only last year a significant piece of Grainger scholarship was issued—Music Monograph 2, published by the Department of Music of the University of Western Australia. It was *A Complete Catalogue of the Works of Percy Grainger*, edited by Teresa Balough.

Obviously nobody is going to be in a great rush to come out with a Grainger *Gesamtausgabe*. One works on the premise that Grainger was a minor composer who composed his share of salon fluff. But his period pieces do have great charm—yes, even the famous (or infamous) *Blithe Bells*, which gussies up Bach's great melody, *Sheep May Safely Graze.* In many respects Grainger was a child of his time.

But in certain prophetic pieces he was ahead of his time. Some of the Busoni theorizing might have rubbed off on young Grainger; and there was the influence of the British Folk Music Society figures. But whatever the reason, Grainger did compose some music that, in its freedom, alertness, daring (for its time) and real verve, is much more interesting than a good deal of the more ambitious and pretentious music of the day.

And there was that defiant iconoclasm that extended even to the instructions to the performer. No Italian for Percy Aldridge Grainger. None of those *molto adagio* and *più crescendo* markings. When you want the performer to arpeggiate a chord, you write: "violently wrenched." When you want the melody emphasized, you write: "The top notes louder and sharper than the rest." When you want a big climax you write: "louden lots." And when you really want the pressure to be applied, you write "louden hugely."

APRIL 25, 1976

Bright young pianists these days are more and more turning to the fortepiano for the music of Haydn, Mozart and Beethoven. There is even beginning to be a fearsome kind of purity that extends into the music of later composers. Some specialists now tell us that the music of Schumann should be played only on an instrument of Schumann's day; that Liszt sounds better on an 1850 Erard than on the modern concert grand, and so on. Right now it is the fortepiano that is attracting most attention. Coming years will be seeing an even greater use of the instrument in concert and for recordings. Those who hear the Beethoven sonatas for the first time on a fortepiano are in for a shock. The music sounds very different.

Did Beethoven Ever Find a Piano That Made Him Happy?

SEVERAL MONTHS ago this column discussed early pianos and their role in the music of Haydn, Mozart and Beethoven. It is a problem very much on the minds of literate musicians today. For those three composers wrote piano music for an instrument that was a long way from today's modern concert grand. They heard a different sound in their ears; they were accustomed to a different kind of piano action; and they wrote accordingly. Thus no piano today, unless it is a replica of the "fortepiano"—the instrument used before the Romantics came along—can give a true idea of piano music through Beethoven.

Beethoven's piano music poses special problems. Mozart and Haydn had accommodated themselves to the early instruments. But Beethoven, the first of the modern virtuosos, was notoriously unhappy with the instruments then in vogue. He was constantly looking for a bigger, more sonorous sound; for an extension of the keyboard itself (early instruments had only five octaves or so), for more subtle pedalling devices. Therefore the question was raised here: under those circumstances, might not the modern piano be a superior vehicle for Beethoven's keyboard music than the more slender instruments of his own day? Would it be misapplied scholarship to play Beethoven sonatas on the Viennese instruments he so cordially hated?

The article evoked many letters, notably from Owen Jander of the Wellesley College music department, Malcolm Bilson of the Cornell University music department, and the pianist Paul Badura-Skoda. Bilson is a pianist who, like Badura-Skoda, has not only given public performances of Haydn, Mozart and Beethoven on early nineteenth-century pianos but has also made recordings of their music on them. All three correspondents maintain very strongly that Beethoven's music is best served by the Viennese pianos of his own day, citing William S. Newman's researches as support.

In the Fall, 1970 issue of the *Journal of the American Musicological Society,* Newman wrote a long article that has become famous in musicological circles. Newman, a brilliant scholar, looked at every available scrap of material pertaining to Beethoven and his pianos, and came up with a heretical notion. Up to then it had been an article of faith that Beethoven preferred the English type of action over the Viennese. (The English action was heavier and more sonorous; the Viennese lighter and more flexible.) Not so, wrote Newman. In his closely-reasoned article he concluded that "Beethoven did not swing over to the English pianos but maintained his allegiance to the Viennese makes." Most present-day specialists in performance practice—Jander, Bilson and Badura-Skoda among them—believe Newman has proved his point.

But has he? A very careful reading of the Newman article suggests only that Beethoven disliked *all* the pianos of his day. For, as one follows Beethoven's lifelong dissatisfaction with the instrument, it becomes apparent that he was looking for things that no manufacturer at the time could supply. He had to work with what was available to him, but he cried and he raged and he kept demanding improvements. Newman admits as much. And if it is true, as Newman states, that "Beethoven started with and never abandoned his allegiance to the gentler, more subtle, pliable tone of the Viennese pianos, especially in Streicher's newer instruments," could the reason merely be that the unhappy composer had no options?

Newman is skeptical about Beethoven's much-discussed attachment to the big instrument that the London firm of Broadwood sent him in 1818. Most scholars of the past have maintained that this was the instrument of Beethoven's dreams. But, says Newman, the piano presented "innumerable action problems from the start." (That may have been inevitable. Any instrument would suffer the way things were carted in those pre-railroad days.) In any case, Newman continues, "The Broadwood came too near the end of Beethoven's piano production, its range was too limited, its action may have seemed too heavy, and Beethoven was too deaf by then for the piano to have any meaning for him apart from the honor of international recognition."

But does not Newman at the end of his article weaken his case by admitting that the piano as an instrument never seemed to come up to Beethoven's desires? It was getting there, but Beethoven never lived to see it. Jander points out that in Beethoven's lifetime the piano had developed from a five-octave instrument to a six-octave instrument and finally to "a six-and-a-half-octave monster that will accommodate the final sonatas. . . . In this remarkable evolution 'the Viennese instrument' more than doubles its physical weight."

In short, the piano was fast heading toward the instrument that we know today, and no doubt Beethoven would have rejoiced had he had an 1860 instrument at his disposal.

The fact remains, of course, that Beethoven did not write for that later instrument. Pianists today still have to tussle with the problems inherent in the music he did compose, and its relation to the instrument he actually used. The octave glissandos in the *Waldstein* Sonata can be managed on a Viennese piano but not on today's monsters. On Beethoven's own piano the permanently held pedal in the D minor Sonata can make a wonderful effect, but not today. Many of the chordal weightings are resilient on a Streicher piano of 1805 but soggy on a modern instrument. And so on.

Even within Beethoven's own pianos there was considerable variation. Badura-Skoda reports that he once played two consecutive performances of the Fourth Concerto, one on his (Badura-Skoda's) own 1817 Broadwood, the other on his 1824 Graf. "The Viennese-type pianos," he writes, "offer another advantage over the English pianos of that period, preceding the invention of the double-escapement introduced by Erard in 1821, which marked the turning-point in the development. The Viennese-type had a far more sensitive action, which allowed a wider dynamic range. Needless to say, it is not the actual loudness but the dynamic range which produces the impression of power and expressiveness."

All pianists who have experimented with Beethoven's music on the fortepiano find that they can achieve certain effects not otherwise obtainable. Bilson writes that he never could follow Czerny's instructions about the D minor Sonata. (Carl Czerny was a Beethoven pupil who had a good deal to say about the way

Beethoven played his own music.) "I tried as hard as I could, but could never quite get convinced that this was feasible; in my mind's ear it sounded wonderful, but on the Steinway pianos we had on hand at the University of Illinois where I was teaching at the time, it did not seem realizable. On the fortepiano it is just as natural as it could be; in short I found the instrument on which what I heard with my inner ear could be realized."

And Jander on the finale of the *Moonlight* Sonata. He could not see how the fortepiano could ever handle that "firespitting finale." But then he tried it out and was overcome. "That finale as performed, say, by Rudolf Serkin, on a modern grand with its massive metal frame and its heavy felt hammers, is a thrilling, thunderous experience, to be sure. On the five-octave instrument that was known to Beethoven in Vienna in 1802, when he wrote that sonata (and at that point I don't think Beethoven had ever seen or heard a six-octave instrument), that *Moonlight* finale is an absolute *blitz*. This is a hair-raising, searing experience."

It may be that the economics and entrenched habits of the musical world will keep fortepiano concerts to a minimum. But that is for the time being. More and more pianists are entering the field; more and more universities and music schools are looking into the use of "authentic" instruments toward more "authentic" performances. That applies to all instruments, not only the fortepiano. In a few years we may have a well-trained, enthusiastic crop of specialists, all eager to make converts to the True Religion. The cause of musical truth will then be that much further advanced.

MAY 22, 1977

Any piece with the universal appeal of The Stars and Stripes Forever *has to be taken seriously. When Eugene Ormandy brought the Philadelphia Orchestra to China in 1973, with pro-grams of Beethoven, Mozart, Roy Harris and the like, the only work that meant anything to Chinese audiences was the Sousa march. There seems to be no society, no race, that does not respond to* The Stars and Stripes Forever *and, only to a slightly less degree, to the other great Sousa marches. The man was, and has remained, an American symbol, and he has far out-lived nearly all of his "classical" musical contemporaries. We don't hear much music by Paine, Chadwick, Parker, Griffes or MacDowell, but John Philip Sousa is ever with us.*

Sousa, Father of the Big Brass Band

TOMORROW NIGHT will see a concert by Sousa's Band in Carnegie Hall. Well, not exactly Sousa's Band. But the young players of the Yale University Band will be wearing uniforms copied from those worn by Sousa's players. Keith Brion, the conductor, will be wearing a white wig and mustache, will be wielding an actual baton used by the great bandmaster, and will be attempting to copy Sousa's beat and mannerisms. The program will be a replica of an actual Sousa program, cut down somewhat from its original three-hour length. And, inevitably, *The Stars and Stripes Forever* will end the program. It should be great fun.

In recent years the nostalgia craze has revived forgotten Broadway musicals, Scott Joplin, genre painting and the player piano. Why not John Philip Sousa? He was by far the most popular American musician of his day—the best-known, one of the best showmen, the composer of operettas (of which *El Capitan* has been enjoying a modest revival) and, of course, the greatest marches ever written by an American or, for that matter, by anybody else. There are those who will say, not cracking a smile, that *The Stars and Stripes Forever* is the greatest piece of music ever written by an American composer.

That spine-tingling march came to him almost in a vision. As he tells the story in his pleasant, chatty autobiography, *Marching Along,* he was on board ship to America. As the vessel got under way, Sousa began to think of certain problems that awaited him on his return to New York. "Suddenly I began to sense the rhythmic beat of a band playing within my brain. It kept on ceaselessly playing, playing, playing. Throughout the whole tense voyage, that imaginary band continued to unfold the same themes, echoing and reechoing the most distinct melody. I did not transfer a note of that music to paper while I was on the steamer, but when we reached shore, I set down the measures that my brain had been playing for me, and not a note of it has ever been changed." Later, Sousa set his own words to his most famous composition. Sample:

> Let the eagle shriek from lofty peak
> The never-ending watchword of our land;
> Let summer breeze waft through the trees
> The echo of our chorus grand.
> Sing out for liberty and light,
> Sing out for freedom and the right.
> Sing out for Union and its might,
> O patriotic sons.
> Other nations may deem their flags the best
> And cheer them with fervid elation,
> But the flag of the North and South and West
> Is the flag of flags, the flag of Freedom's nation.

In our sophisticated age it is hard to remember the importance of band music in the American scheme of things. Question: What is America's oldest musical organization with a continuous record of activity? Answer: The United States Marine Band, founded in 1798. Compared to that, the New York Philharmonic, which came into existence in 1842, is a Johnny-come-lately. Throughout the United States, until a relatively short time ago, there was not a city without its bandstand in the park, at which audiences would gather to hear the kind of music they loved. It is a tradition almost extinct today, though a few bands do carry on the tradition. On a nice summer night people would cheer the *William Tell* Overture, or a favorite son playing cornet solos, or the minister's daughter bashfully singing a few of her "numbers." There would be a potpourri of patriotic songs, a series of marches, the *Anvil Chorus*, popular tunes of the day.

In Washington, the Marine Band was kept on the run. It was the President's personal organization, and it supplied music for all occasions. The band would greet visiting dignitaries. It would play at state dinners. It gave weekly concerts on the White House grounds, weekly concerts at the White House itself, Thursday concerts at the Barracks, Wednesday concerts at the Capitol. President Harrison gave permission for national tours, and the Marine Band under Sousa's direction rapidly became America's most popular musical group.

When Sousa took over the band in 1880 it was a pretty sloppy group. John Philip Sousa (1854–1932) was actually born in Washington, D.C. His father was Portuguese, his mother German. (In later years there were persistent rumors that the name "Sousa" was made up by the famous bandmaster to get the letters "U.S.A." into his name. Not true.) The boy was something of a musical prodigy, developed into a fine violinist, and seemed to be able to learn any instrument easily. At thirteen he became an apprentice in the Marine Band. A few years later he was all over the country, as violinist and conductor of orchestras in various touring shows. He met his wife in a road company of *Pinafore*. His father had connections, and talked the commander of the Marine Corps into engaging young Sousa to reorganize the band completely.

Sousa had a job on his hands. At Marine Corps pay, not many good musicians could be secured. Not at a top salary of thirty-eight dollars a month, descending to thirteen dollars for the lower ranks. Sousa was permitted to make all kinds of administrative and musical changes (though the salaries remained the same). He was a fine musician and a conductor with a sharp ear. Slowly he whipped the band into shape. His ideal was to get players only of solo caliber, and while he never could do that until he formed his own band in 1892, he did make the Marine Band one of the best military groups in the world.

In his day there were thousands of bands in the country, but when he put together his own group it immediately became the best. It also made Sousa rich and famous. He had a genius for composing marches that became a permanent part of the American culture. *Washington Post, El Capitan, The Thunderer, Semper Fidelis, High School Cadets, United States Field Artillery.* In all there are 136 marches, plus successful operettas (he once had four running simultaneously), plus songs. He was a busy man. He also took time out to write a few novels, and very bad they are. He was a crack shot, owned and rode his own stable of show horses, played enthusiastically poor golf and had a good time out of life, crisscrossing the country, taking the band on four European tours and one around the world.

He and his band were among the earliest recording groups. Unfortunately, the great days of Sousa's Band coincided with the acoustic period of recording. Acoustic records may have been kind to the human voice, but they simply could not handle large groups. For the early—1900–10—recordings, how many players could Sousa have grouped around the horn? A dozen at most? Still, those primitive records give us an idea of his tempos, and also of the precision he demanded from his men. Later there were a few electrical recordings, post-1925, which show Sousa's Band under better conditions. His records sold in the millions.

Naturally he was a voluble spokesman for his kind of music. He was well aware of the hostility of what he called "affronted musicians" when he arranged Wagner and other untouchables for band. Sousa called this "artistic snobbery." But, as he pointed out, he was introducing *Parsifal* excerpts to audiences ten years before it had its American première at the Metropolitan Opera. To Sousa, a good tune was a good tune whatever its provenance, and he would equate *Turkey in the Straw* with any melody created by the great composers, even if "for musical highbrows I suppose, the thing is déclassé." He played down nationalism in music; a good melody no longer belonged to any single country but was the property of the world.

He was an entertainer and proud of it. Entertainment, he said, was of more real value than technical education. He would not take over a symphony orchestra if one were to be offered to him; he could reach more people, touch more people, musically educate more people, and certainly entertain more people, with his band. Sousa was in so many ways an archetypal figure of his times. He represented the young, emergent America, with its jingoism, its confidence, its lustiness, its growing appetites, its populism, its parochial tastes, its generosity, its tendency to see things in black and white, its faith in an expanding future. And, above all, its assumption that God had touched the land with the tip of His little finger.

APRIL 2, 1978

Just after the war, in 1947, I wrote a long article about Gottschalk for Musical Digest, *and have been writing steadily about him ever since. I even contemplated a biography, but Robert Offergeld, who had been working on Gottschalk for years, was ahead of me. During my years on the* Times *I must have written at least a half-dozen pieces on Gottschalk. To me he was the first true American nationalist as well as a brilliant pianist and a stylish author (his* Notes of a Pianist *is an amusing, literate account of the America and South America of his time). I find his music standing up remarkably well: it has character, personality and originality. For its day it is remarkably sophisticated. No wonder it took Europe by storm in the 1850–80 period. Gottschalk was a pioneer, and his music is an important part of the American legacy.*

Gottschalk and His Monster Concert

EUGENE LIST is at it again. On the evening of May 2 he will be the guide through a "monster concert" in Carnegie Hall devoted mostly to the music of Louis Moreau Gottschalk. It will be the 150th anniversary, almost to the day, of the American composer's birth; he was born in New Orleans on May 8, 1829, and died in Rio de Janeiro on Dec. 19, 1869, at the age of forty. It is fitting that Mr. List be the one to put this program together. In 1956 he recorded, for Vanguard, the first-ever LP disk devoted to Gottschalk, thus focusing attention on a fascinating composer known at that time only to a few specialists. Since then, Gottschalk has returned to the national consciousness. He is played in concert, there has been a spate of Gottschalk recordings, and the glamorous Louis Moreau is beginning to come into his own as America's first true nationalist composer.

Off and on, Mr. List has been giving monster concerts for 10 years. The idea stems from Gottschalk himself. In the musically innocent days around the Civil War period, touring musicians felt it necessary to amuse as well as educate their audiences. They played variations on "Yankee Doodle." They gave barn-yard imitations on various instruments. Gottschalk's contribution was the monster concert. He would round up as many pianos as could fit on a stage, arrange well-known music for ten or more pianos played by twenty or more pianists, and bring the rafters down with the *William Tell* Overture or one of his own nationalistic pieces. Audiences loved it.

Thus the stage of Carnegie Hall on May 2 will house ten concert grands. On them will be played such pieces as Gottschalk's arrangement of the *William Tell* Overture and of Weber's *Oberon* Overture (ten pianos, twenty pianists). There will be duets, vocal music and solos. A few other composers, each of whom had some relationship with Gottschalk, also will be played. Mr. List has found several piano works by Stephen Foster, Gottschalk's almost exact contemporary. He also has programmed a few works by Ernest Guiraud. Guiraud (1837–92) was, like Gottschalk, born in New Orleans and, again like Gottschalk, went off to study music in Paris. Guiraud is remembered today mostly as the man who wrote the recitatives for Bizet's *Carmen* and as the musician who completed Offenbach's *Tales of Hoffmann*. He was an important man in his day, and another of his claims to fame is the fact that he was Debussy's theory teacher. Guiraud and Gottschalk were friends.

From all over the country pupils of Mr. List are coming to participate in the monster concert. One hopes that Mr. List will not run into the trouble that Gottschalk experienced in San Francisco in 1865.

As Gottschalk himself tells the story in his *Notes of a Pianist,* that wonderfully literate and urbane diary, he had arranged the March from *Tannhäuser* for fourteen pianos. "On the eve of the concert," Gottschalk writes, "one of my pianists fell sick. What was I to do? Put off the concert? Never! A warmed-up dinner is never worth anything. . . . Announce only thirteen pianos? Another error, still more dangerous. The public wants to hear fourteen pianos, and if you give it one less it will think itself robbed. . . . The difficulty was becoming insurmountable. San Francisco, although filled with all the corruption and with all the plagues arising from civilization, then possessed but thirteen first-class pianoforte players."

Gottschalk was in a quandary. The proprietor of the hall came to his rescue. His son, he said, was an amateur pianist "of the first class," who played Liszt, Thalberg and Gottschalk without difficulty. The *Tannhäuser* piece, Gottschalk was assured, would be child's play for the young man. Gottschalk was suspicious. "But the father spoke of him with such assurance that I accepted his son's assistance (God protect you, O artists, from the fathers of amateurs, from the sons themselves, and from the fathers of female singers!)."

So Gottschalk and the young man met for a practice session. The amateur loftily told Gottschalk that a rehearsal was unnecessary. He could play the fantasies of Liszt. All very well, Gottschalk tactfully said, but for ensemble playing there were such things as tempo and coordination. He gave the tempo and insisted that the amateur play. Down sat the young man "and, like all amateurs, after having executed a noisy flourish, attacked with boldness and innocence" the music. After two measures Gottschalk knew the worst. The boy was hopeless. "My position became horrible. To refuse his assistance—the assistance of the first amateur in San Francisco! elegant and rich . . . It was impossible." Gottschalk started to brood. Should he cancel?

It was Gottschalk's piano tuner who saved the day. The object was to prevent the amateur from being heard. The tuner simply removed the interior mechanism from the vertical piano, leaving the keyboard intact. The evening came. The amateur demanded a location in full view of the audience. Gottschalk was happy to oblige, and had the crippled piano moved to the appropriate spot.

"One, two, three—we begin. It goes on marvelously. In the middle of the piece I looked at my amateur; he was superb; he was sweating great drops; he was throwing his eyes carelessly on the audience and performing with miraculous ease the passages apparently the most difficult. His friends were in raptures."

The march ended to great applause. A repetition was demanded. Before it could start again, the amateur decided to play a little chromatic scale on his own. "I see him now! The stupor that was imprinted on his countenance was inexpressible. He began his scale again. Nothing. The piano was mute." He tried to get Gottschalk's attention and was ignored. Gottschalk hastily started the encore. "My young man, to save appearances before the audience, made the pantomime of his passages, but his countenance, which I saw from below, was worth painting; it was a mixture of discouragement and spite. The fury with which he struck the poor instrument, which could do nothing, was very funny."

Gottschalk ended his story with a moral: "Beware of amateurs."

It was in San Francisco that Gottschalk got into the trouble that sent him fleeing to South America, where he remained until his death four years later. He had been accused of corrupting the morals of a girl, and a tremendous storm was kicked up. Those were the days of lynch law in California, and Gottschalk made it to the boat just in time. It was a big, nationwide scandal —Gottschalk had been a matinee idol—and the affair made all the papers in America. Everybody knew he was a notorious womanizer and was prepared to believe the worst about him. His name was dragged through the mud.

Last year some material about this unhappy episode was discovered by Lawrence Glover, a descendant of the family through

Gottschalk's youngest sister, Blanche. Mr. Glover inherited a treasure trove of Gottschalk papers, photographs, music and memorabilia. Among the papers were drafts of a letter in which Gottschalk presented his side of the case. He called the charges against him a lie—"a villainous, rascally, infamous falsehood from beginning to end."

According to Gottschalk, he was merely accompanying a friend, Charles Legay, who had made a date with a young lady in Oakland, across the bay from San Francisco. Legay wanted Gottschalk along because his lady was bringing one of her friends. Gottschalk arrived at the Oakland ferry, found it and Legay gone, and hired his own boat for the trip to Oakland. There he did run into Legay, and they set forth on their adventure.

The girls showed up, late at night, having slipped out of their rooms at the Oakland Female Seminary. Gottschalk claims that he did not want to have anything to do with the girl that Legay's friend had brought along. He recognized her; she was a notorious flirt. Nor was she, Gottschalk insisted, a minor. "The young lady is at least twenty years old."

Gottschalk says that he broke away and returned to his hotel, leaving Legay with the girls. When the girls returned to the seminary they were caught trying to get into their rooms, and they told everything. "To make a long story short," Gottschalk writes, "a paper next morning published the news of a most villainous crime perpetrated by a celebrated *strolling* pianist and appealing to the most violent passions of the people in a language well calculated to rouse the ire of the community."

In real anguish Gottschalk writes an *apologia pro vita sua*. "I have friends who care for me, but their number is insignificant if compared to that of my enemies. Is there any man who attracts public attention without creating enmity? Is not the fact of doing something better than most others a sufficient reason to be disliked by that immense portion of humankind who cannot tolerate superiority? Think also of the relish for scandalmongers! You might for years say that Gottschalk paid all his father's debts, supported his family since he was twenty years old, brought up and gave a splendid education to four sisters and two brothers, has given money to every poor young artist he found on his way, has done no harm to anyone, willingly, has never written about a brother artist but to praise his talent, you might say that and ten thousand times more and be convinced that it will be kept in religious secrecy; but publish tomorrow that G. has committed the most unheard of brigandage, and it will spread like wild fire all over the land, no one (perhaps a few friends excepted) doubting the truth of the facts and many adding''

That is where the letter stops. The last page or pages are missing. Anyway, that is Gottschalk's side of the story. For the rest of his life he was in exile. He spent six months in Peru, a year in Chile, two years in Argentina and Uruguay, and his last seven months in Brazil. As a pianist and as an aristocrat with impeccable manners, he was one of the most famous men in South America.

In 1869 the scandal had died down, and Gottschalk was being beseeched to return to the United States. Max Strakosch wanted to manage concert tours for him. There was talk of a National Conservatory of Music in New York, to be headed by Gottschalk. It was not to be. While organizing one of his monster concerts in Rio de Janeiro, the overworked Gottschalk fell ill and died of a ruptured appendix. By that time the German-dominated school of academic American composers was beginning to take charge, and Gottschalk and his music went into rapid decline. Composers should write symphonies, sonatas and fugues. It has remained for our generation to realize the genius of this innovative, sophisticated citizen of the world from New Orleans.

APRIL 22, 1979

PART IV

Contemporary Music

To build systems is only to invite dizziness; permanence belongs only to what has been well said.
— ALFRED KERR

It was this article that convinced many musicians that I was hopelessly reactionary. I don't think I am (though probably no reactionary thinks he is one). I had been listening to serial music for ten years and had come to the conclusion noted below. Were I writing it today, there would be some changes. At least one of the Stravinsky pieces—the Symphony in Three Movements—which was seldom heard in 1961 is now programmed with fair regularity. I also overrated Gunther Schuller, who composes prolifically but has added very little to the active repertory. Otherwise I stand on the position I took against the serial movement; and I honestly believe that pieces like this and the ensuing ones helped maintain some sanity during the period when the international avant-garde was doing such a superb public-relations job on itself.

An End in Itself

THE NEW YORK PHILHARMONIC's performance, a short time ago, of Pierre Boulez's second *Improvisation on Mallarmé* highlighted the fact that music is currently in a transitional period. What a difference there is between the composers in the decades after the First World War and those after the second! The period from 1920 to 1940 saw the flowering of such disparate figures as Stravinsky, Bartók, Berg, Webern, Prokofiev, Poulenc, Copland, Vaughan Williams and Hindemith, to mention a few of the more prominent names that come immediately to mind. But the period from 1945 to 1961: what has it produced? Not many would claim that Dallapiccola, Orff, Stockhausen,

191

Menotti, Britten, Boulez or Cage have the stature of their immediate predecessors.

Most composers today are looking for a language. Traditionalists like Britten and Menotti are getting fewer and fewer. The period is dominated by the twelve-tone school, with the electronic composers (Stockhausen) and the Dadaists (Cage) exerting quite a bit of force. But the twelve-tone school is no longer the school of Schoenberg and Webern. It is a school that wants to extend serial technique into areas outside of pure tone; into areas encompassing rhythm, duration and even the mathematics of chance. More than ever before—and this goes for the other arts, too—it is an age of avant-gardism, in which established values have so been pulverized that there exist few criteria to determine the artistic validity of the new music.

The trend is toward greater and greater complexity, and in this Boulez is a true child of his age. His Second Piano Sonata, which was introduced to America about a dozen years ago by David Tudor, is one of the most fearsomely complex pianistic layouts that ever turned an instrumentalist's hair gray. Boulez, born in 1925, happens to be a thoroughly literate musician who studied under Messiaen and Leibowitz. He was one of the postwar Young Turks who became hypnotized by serial technique, and for a decade or so he was the most vociferous spokesman for the new school in Europe. "Any composer," he has written, "who has not felt—I do not say understand, but felt—the necessity of the twelve-tone language is SUPERFLUOUS. For everything he writes will fall short of the necessities of his time."

It is that phrase, "the necessities of his time," which motivates Boulez and most other composers of the avant-garde. The trouble is that neither they nor anybody else can define what the necessities are. And what they, in their restless intellect, are doing is superimposing a sociological or ideological theory over the natural processes of composing music. Many of them, hopping from one style to another, are not hypocrites (we are speaking of the sincere musicians rather than of the opportunists and phonies who jump on every new bandwagon). They are merely confused. Lacking the profound self-confidence and inner strength of the great creators, they desperately wheel this way and that, trying to combine into a viable form the influences that beat down on them.

As a result, none of them really has gained a foothold in the active repertory. It is hard to think of any twelve-tone work that is a repertory piece. A concomitant result is that there is an international style of composition that is virtually devoid of individuality. Hardly anybody writes neoclassic music any more. Nationalism, except for the work of a few Russians, is about gone. Hindemith means nothing to the avant-gardists, nor does Prokofiev, or even Bartók. (There are exceptions, of course. Carl Orff has carved out a little empire for himself, and a composer like Gunther Schuller is attempting an interesting fusion of jazz and dodecaphony.) But, by and large, the work of an American avant-gardist has little to differentiate it from the work of an English or French or Italian one. And most of it sounds what it is: the conformity of avant-gardism which has developed its own academism. And pure academism, whether the product of the academy or of the avant-garde, is always pulverizingly dull.

It is rather interesting, too, that very little music of the advanced serial type reaches the large public, though it is by far the most voluminously composed by the musicians of the post-World War II generation. Even when a composer so universally respected as Stravinsky writes in the idiom (*Threni*, sections of *Agon, Movements for Piano and Orchestra*) the music is dutifully presented—once. As a matter of fact, it is amazing how little of Stravinsky's music after the *Symphony of Psalms* and *Oedipus* has entered the active orchestral repertory. How long has it been since you heard an orchestra in the Symphony in Three Movements? The Symphony in C? The Symphonies of Wind Instruments? *Orpheus? Scènes de Ballet?* And if Stravinsky, with his enormous reputation, cannot attract much response from conductors and public in his non-serial music, much less his more "advanced" serial works, the work of the young experimentalists has that much less chance to enter the repertory.

One of the troubles with much of the new school is that it makes a virtue of complexity and intellectualism. The intellectual act of juggling a tone row seems to be the end in itself; and its only helpful by-product seems to be the chance it gives other composers to write long, learned and technical articles about it. Complexity, of course, can yield great music when there is imagination and feeling behind it, as witness Bach's *Art of Fugue* and the last five Beethoven quartets. And it seems to be a fact that the twelve-tone avant-gardists respond, among all the composers of the past, most to Bach and Beethoven. For those two are among the most intellectual of composers. But they were more than technicians. Whereas today, technique seems to come first.

Composers will be coming along—tomorrow, the day after tomorrow—who will synthesize the age, just as Wagner synthesized the efforts of the men who preceded him. Transition does not mean death; and while we may be in a transitional period, there certainly is enough activity around to make it perpetually exciting and interesting. There is a lot of bad music in every age, and there is no reason why this one should be an exception.

Only it seems that there is less great music being created at the moment than in any comparable period. The main reason is the determination of the creators to aim for a degree of extreme complexity that loses touch with reality, and even with artistic validity. Many of them write honestly and mean well. But there is the Elizabethan proverb about the man who went to bed thinking that he had God Almighty by the little finger, and woke up to find that he had the Devil by the big toe.

MARCH 26, 1961

Year after year I kept returning to the subject. The point I was trying to make in this article—that Schoenberg and his school were a dead end—did not increase my popularity among composers. Yet I looked around and could find no avant-garde com-

poser who had any kind of public acceptance. Composers kept on talking about the cultural lag. I kept on insisting that a cultural lag could not last forever; and that if a piece like Pierrot Lunaire, *say, had not found a wide public in fifty years, perhaps it was the music's fault and not necessarily the public's.*

Where Are the Young Composers?

On the one hand, the statistics show a rich, glowing picture. We are assured that never before has there been such an interest in music in America. More people are attending concerts than ever before; more recordings are being purchased; cultural centers are popping up like crocuses in the spring. And all of this appears to be true. But, as always, there is another hand. So, on the other hand, in at least one aspect of our creative life there is gloom.

Over the holidays we were talking, at different times, to two American composers, both of them highly respected, both of them middle-generation (around fifty years old), both of them also active as teachers. After the knives were sheathed, we got into the problem of the young composer. Gloom settled down. "There are a lot of them," said Composer A, "but where are they?" Said Composer B, "If I had to name an outstanding compositional talent in America among the younger generation, I would be stopped cold. I know there's a lot of writing going on, but nothing seems to be happening."

These were not idle remarks carelessly thrown off. Both of these men are propagandists for American music and are desperately looking for talent. So are the music publishers. "We had plenty to go on in the nineteen thirties," says the director of publications of a major American firm, "Copland, Barber, Piston, Schuman, Harris, those were the Big Five. Then there were Riegger, Sessions, Moore, Thomson. Kids like Shapero, Carter,

Berger, Dello Joio and Haieff were coming up. It wasn't so much a question of liking or not liking their music. The point is that they were discussed. People were talking about them."

And, all are agreed, there is nowhere near so much comparable discussion today. The Big Five, most observers thought at the time, were the start of an American school. They were the pioneers, and the youngsters would follow. But for some reason, the youngsters didn't. Contemporary composition in America —and this is true for much European composition outside of the Soviet bloc countries—has not focused itself, and in recent years seems to be dribbling itself away chasing fad after fad.

There probably is an imposing set of reasons. One might be the presence of so many major European composers permanently in America after the late nineteen thirties. Instead of pollinating, they tended to dilute. Instead of opening up new vistas, they tended to form schools around themselves. Schoenberg and Krenek were the leading twelve-tone specialists, and they sent forth disciples. Hindemith had his school of American composers, and so did Milhaud. They were very strong influences, and their students ended up writing like Schoenberg, Hindemith and Milhaud instead of like themselves.

Up to only the last five years or so, an aggressive type of dissonant modernism was very much the style, whether Schoenbergian dodecaphonism or Milhaudian polytonality. The twelve-tone school was by far the most important, and as time goes on, it seems more and more certain that it was a withering influence. Schoenberg, Berg and Webern had much to contribute themselves, as creative figures, but perhaps they were a dead end rather than a new path. Twelve-tone technique nevertheless reached into virtually every corner of contemporary composition, finally enwrapping such recalcitrants as Stravinsky and Copland. Any kind of romantic writing was hooted down, and academic figures like Howard Hanson or Douglas Moore were accepted only on sufferance—and never by the intellectuals.

Right now there are indications that Romanticism is on its way back. Certainly operas like Moore's *Wings of the Dove*, Ward's *The Crucible* and Giannini's *The Harvest*, all of which were heard for the first time this season, would not have had a chance of being staged ten years ago. They are conservative operas by conservative—i.e., post-Romantic, vintage 1890—composers. There also are indications that the twelve-tone hold, especially the Webern craze, has spent its force.

But in the meantime it is hard to think of a young American composer who has a strong, individual style. At the moment the young American composer is confused. He lies in a very fluctuating magnetic field, and is tugged this way, that way. John Cage and his aleatoric music still exert a pull. Electronic music is the very latest fad. The twelve-tone school is by no means dead. A Bartókian type of dissonance can be noticed in such young composers as Leon Kirchner. On the whole, young American composers today are writing in the eclectic, cosmopolitan style. Much of it is anonymous-sounding, and very little has vitality or personality behind it.

It can, of course, be said that at any time there always have been various influences around a young composer. But in any generation there have been a few who have ruggedly gone on their own way and—more important—captured the public imagination. A composer is no good unless he has a public, and the great rebels of music have always had their following from the beginning. Also their detractors, but that is part of the fun. The followers howl, the detractors yowl, and a great fuss is kicked up. If the composer has what it takes, he comes through. If not, he is forgotten. But while the fuss is going on, he is always in the public eye.

For some reason, there is little of that excitement today—not even in professional circles. For about sixty years now, the public seems to have made up its mind that it does not like extreme dissonance. If truth be told, many performers who have made big reputations as specialists in modern music also hate the stuff, and have said as much to this writer. They perform it because they are gifted along that direction, or because they feel it is their duty, or because it is the only way for them to keep busy, but many of them do not like it.

As a result, the overwhelming majority of today's avant-garde music is greeted with a huge ho-hum not only by the public but also by many professionals. There must be an answer. There has to be an answer. Perhaps the public is correct in refusing to accept sectarian music—music written as the offshoot of a school and not of a personality. Perhaps we need a trend toward simplicity. Perhaps faddism has to be stamped out. Perhaps we need more melody and fewer retrograde inversions. The final perhaps is that a couple of geniuses have to come along, demagnetize themselves and fuse everything into a powerful, personal expression. Whatever the answer, there seems to be nobody coming up in America strong enough to do the job.

JAN. 14, 1962

This article was written in response to the outpouring of mail that the Jan. 14, 1962 piece (see above) evoked. Looking back, after twenty years, I don't think that any composer active in 1962 was "a really strong American composer." Who were the ones featured so prominently in Perspectives of New Music, *the house organ of the American avant-garde during the 1960's? Milton Babbitt, Elliott Carter (the Big Two at the time), Seymour Shifrin, Lukas Foss, Charles Wuorinen, Donald Martino, Billy Jim Layton, George Perle, Arthur Berger, John M. Perkins, George Rochberg, Ralph Shapey, J.K. Randall, Lejaren Hiller, Andrew Imbrie, Mel Powell, Harvey Sollberger and George Crumb, to take a quick glance through its pages. Many professionals would rate Carter as a major composer. I do not. I have suspicion about a composer who at the age of 71 (at the point of writing) has not been able to attract a public. I would apply the same argument to Roger Sessions and his music. The muchtalked-about Babbitt seems to have been more an influence as pedagogue and guru than as a potent creative figure. Crumb seems to be the only one whose music has any kind of circulation. Most of the others are names known only to specialists. And so, despite the contumely, I do not think I was wrong.*

The Failures of Contemporary Composition—Again

A FEW WEEKS ago this column went out looking for a really strong young American composer and could not find one. Then the mail started coming in, the gist being that this writer was (as Ella Logan once sang in *Finian's Rainbow*) "a rotter/and a lotta/dirty names." Most of the mail was written by composers. It seemed to be the product of a conditioned reflex, like the angry buzzing of a warrior bee when an enemy approaches the hive.

The general idea of all the mail was that a composer puts notes to paper, and hence is the sacred guardian of a mystique deserving of respect and support; and the more complicated the manner in which he puts notes to paper, the more he should be supported. But that, really, was not what I was writing about. It was the philosophy and esthetic of so much contemporary composition that bothered me. Dissonance, or twelve-tone music, or advanced serial technique has nothing to do with it. Nor does Romanticism, for that matter. A strong Romantic renaissance is in the making, but I find the derivations of Moore and Ward as unpalatable (and more so) as the experiments of Cage and Stockhausen.

Dissonance is a term that does not mean much any more. Bartók's middle period contains as much dissonance as anything to be heard today. So does a piece like Ives' *Housatonic at Stockbridge.* The point is, to what expressive value is dissonance put? Dissonance for the sake of dissonance is as esthetically empty as consonance for the sake of consonance. And it is a fact that nearly all the great composers in history have been called dissonant in their own day. That goes as much for Mozart and Beethoven as it does for Chopin and Schumann, Mahler and Stravinsky and Bartók.

But never before in history have we had such a concentration on paper music. Paper music (or "eye music") is the kind that looks beautiful on paper and can be subject to the most fascinating analyses. The trouble is that in actual performance the mind will not take in the carefully plotted relationships that the composer has written down. Intellectually we may know that the last movement of a specific work is a retrograde of the first: that is, it is the same, only played backwards. But the ear will not take it in, even if the eye and the mind will. Twelve-tone music is great for compositional tricks like this. Only too often the trick is passed off as a substitute for the real thing.

This is the grammar of music, not music. We all know that yesterday's revolutions are today's platitudes, and every avant-garde phenomenon ends up bound in its own type of academism. In any case, every age has a dual esthetic—the esthetic that is, and the esthetic that is to be. Here is where the cultural lag comes into operation. Most of the public—and this has always been true—adheres to the esthetic that is. In our day, it is the mainstream of music extending, roughly, to the beginning of World War I. The esthetic that is to be will be the language of the dodecaphonists, the electronic music composers and even Dada, but all assimilated into a common and comprehensible (to the general public) language.

And it is only wishful thinking to maintain that because a work is new it must, ipso facto, be supported. In any age the overwhelming mass of creative effort is second-rate. Our age is no different. Up to now, what with musical figures like Bartók, Vaughan Williams, Prokofiev, Stravinsky, Poulenc, Hindemith and Schoenberg, to mention a few names that come instantly to mind, we have not done badly at all. But below the big figures is the struggling mass of composers with the technique to express themselves, but without the genius to make their message memorable.

Most of the correspondents who were angry about the conclusions I drew seem to think that it is the duty of a critic to pat everybody on the back. This is known as "encouraging talent," and is supposed to be "constructive." I call it coddling. Indiscriminate praise has been the bane of the generation. So many critics are afraid of being called reactionary, and are so lacking in confidence of their own abilities, that they have indulged in a positive orgy of back-slapping, making obeisances in the direction of anything that happens to be à la mode. That goes as much for critics in the other arts as it does for music critics.

The one comfort is that no critic can alter the course of a positive forward movement. A good review never put an artist or composer permanently on the map, and a bad review never broke him. It is by a body of work, not by an individual performance, that the composer will live or die. All a mistake in critical judgment does, in the long run, is make a fool of the critic —a contingency the good ones are gladly prepared to accept. If not—if he thinks that his words are supported by scripture and Blackstone—he should be held to the ground while small pins are inserted in him to let the hot air out.

Thus good music will flourish with or without the help of a critic, and the big men—the geniuses—will go their own way. There is no such thing as a misunderstood genius; it is a contradiction in terms. Van Gogh is perhaps the only great creative figure who did not attract a devoted following in his own day. Even Schubert, whose importance was not fully realized at the time, was recognized at his death as the greatest song composer in Germany, as his obituary notices will demonstrate; and his impact was such that the young Robert Schumann, on learning of Schubert's death, wept all night.

History also points out that the big figures of a period are not necessarily the lasting ones. Spohr, Moscheles, Heller, Boieldieu, Kalkbrenner, Hummel: so fantastically successful a hundred or so years ago! And forgotten so soon afterward! But they were followers, not leaders. The great men almost immediately put their mark on the age, and if they live long enough (Schubert, after all, died at 31) their impact is shattering. They literally alter the course of music. Stravinsky and Schoenberg, in our century, certainly did.

But, as I wrote, there seems nobody among the young composers in America strong enough to make that kind of impact. (It is hard to believe that if there were a composer of such power his work would be unknown.) Technicians we have all over the place. The owner of a bright, inner flame of the kind that pro-

duced a Charles Ives—that is missing. Avant-garde conformity
spreads over most of our creative ambience, and that is the
close-order drill to which so many of our young composers seem
to be marching, led by a couple of very vociferous sergeants.

FEB. 11, 1962

*There was much anguished talk about the future of the sym-
phony orchestra in the 1960's, much of it supplied by composers
whose work was not being played by symphony orchestras. I
wrote several pieces on the subject, ridiculing the idea that the
symphony orchestra was dead or dying. That idiotic talk has
long disappeared, but it was symptomatic of the times.*

The Future of
the Symphony

LEONARD BERNSTEIN'S observations and meditations on the
present state of the symphony and the symphony orchestra,
elsewhere on this page, were originally scheduled to appear here
at the end of last month. The newspaper strike took care of that.
Now his piece runs just after the end of his first series of appearances with the New York Philharmonic. It is a fascinating piece
and deserves running. It also deserves comment, not in any dis-
putatious manner but with a seriousness equal to the seriousness with which he has approached the subject. For he raises
problems that are being discussed by musicians all over the
Western world today.

Mr. Bernstein's attitude is one of doubt and, as he puts it,
"Hamlet-like torture." Are symphonies a thing of the past?

What will become of the symphony orchestra? Is tonality dead forever? To none of these questions has he a ready answer. He reflects the liberal mind, which sees all sides of every question; and his problems are complicated by the fact that his own instincts are conservative: conservative that is, in relation to the avant-garde music that is so publicized and talked about today.

The revolutionaries of the avant-garde have no such doubts. All revolutionaries, almost by definition, have one-track minds. They are propped by their faith, propelled down their one-way track by the bubbling intensity of their motivation, and they ruthlessly run down anything in their way. The thing they despise most of all is the liberal mind, and when the revolution comes, the liberal is the first to go. Revolutionaries want passive obedience, not doubt and the questions that liberals are constantly raising. In the cold war preceding the revolution, the liberal is always branded as a conservative by the revolutionary, a fact noted quite a few years ago by George Bernard Shaw.

Today's musical revolution, "the present crisis in composition," as Mr. Bernstein puts it, involves the complete breakup of tonality and the development of new forms that have nothing in common with forms of the past. It took hold around the end of World War II, and basically stems from the music of Webern. There are several derivatives. Serial music involves manipulation of an initial series of notes, whether all twelve tones or fewer, in which the series is subject to inversion, retrograde motion or retrograde inversion. The twelve-tone concepts of Schoenberg, which led to serial music, have been extended to include total organization of all elements—rhythm, dynamics, and about everything else.

Another concept involves free choice. Here the performer is given leeway by the composer to bend the materials to his own desires, within or even without certain limits. Still another involves a sort of neo-Dada, represented by John Cage and his followers. And, of course, there is the phenomenon of electronic music. This is coming up very fast, and may be—much more than serial composition—the real music of the future, both on its own and as an adjunct to more orthodox musical means of expression.

It is a revolution, all right. It even may already have been won. But if it has been won, the victors occupy only a tiny kingdom and have only a tiny group of subjects. By and large, the overwhelming majority of the public—yes and of professional musicians, too—could not care less. In the tiny kingdom of the musical avant-garde, the people live by taking in each other's washing, analyzing each other's compositions, and sneering at the various religions within the principality. (If you wish to gaze upon the art of sneering carried to its highest manifestation, observe the look on the face of a Babbitt-type composer talking about the music of a Cage-type composer.)

Part of the revolution concerns the type of ensemble preferred by the new school. By and large, the avant-garde does not write for the symphony orchestra.

For this there are many reasons—technical, sociological, economic. When the new music is occasionally presented by major symphonic organizations, as the New York Philharmonic did in Mr. Bernstein's "Music of the Avant-Garde" two seasons back, it generally ends in disaster, if for no other reason than the fact that the members of the orchestra actively resist the new ideas and are not equipped to handle them.

The avant-garde says: Wait! A new generation is coming up to whom this new music is meat and drink! And this is true in isolated instances. But it has been the experience of quite a few observers that the majority of youngsters coming out of the conservatories are as ill-equipped to deal with the new music as are their elders.

It all ends up with Mr. Bernstein's questions answering themselves. Is the symphony orchestra dead? Of course it is, if the new music really is going to be the music of the future. There is every indication though, that the new music is most definitely not going to be the music of the future, and this the liberal is afraid to say for fear of being labeled a conservative.

Right now the youngsters are experimenting like mad. Orthodox serialism is out. Style rather than content is the rage, the musical equivalents of op and pop. Tonality is not as dead as it seems; and, anyway, the composers who abjure tonality are but a tiny percentage of living composers.

There seems to be the beginning of synthesis in the avant-garde, with serial, electronic and aleatoric elements brought together in a wild mélange. Jazz also plays a strong part. All of this composition is generally quite far-out. Melody is generally of a disjunct, pointillistic nature; dissonance is total; and unorthodox combinations of instruments are brought into play. The avant-garde is hypnotized by new kinds of percussion, and the "official" instrument is the vibraphone. Most compositions in this style tend to be short, about 10 minutes in length (serial composition does not normally lend itself to extended developments). Very often a correlation with mathematics, or what the composer fondly imagines is mathematics, is served up, and names like Heisenberg, Einstein and Bohr are thrown around. And there also is in evidence, especially among the composers of the John Cage school, a strong correlation with avant-garde painting.

What most likely is going to happen is that elements of the avant-garde thinking are going to find their way into music of a more traditional nature. That has been the history of music up to now, and there seems to be no reason why any change should be anticipated. At the present moment the musical avant-garde is in a whirl, not knowing where it is headed, often frankly admitting its music is experimental, faced with the problem of establishing some sort of audience communication, faced even with the problem of finding musicians to play its music. The various sects are headed by theorists rather than strong creative minds, some of them actively engaged in diddling the public.

The new music awaits the arrival of its great leader, the kind of leader who took charge of previous avant-garde movements. Schumann, Berlioz, Wagner, Liszt, Stravinsky . . . I wish I could be as sure of the genius of Lukas Foss and Pierre Boulez as Mr. Bernstein seems to be. Boulez composes very little, and has in recent years dropped considerably even in the estimation of the avant-garde. He is beginning to be considered old hat, a renegade, an important theorist in his day who did not live up to his promise. As for Foss, he has always impressed me as a musical fashion-plate, dressing this way and that as current styles dictate: always impeccably turned out, but something more elegant than substantial.

And these are the only two names Mr. Bernstein chooses to cite! Does either of them weigh enough to imprint any footprints on the sands of time? And, apropos, what is it James Branch Cabell once wrote: "While it is well enough to leave footprints on the sands of time, it is even more important to make sure they point in a commendable direction."

AUG. 24, 1961

When Pierre Boulez came to New York it soon became apparent that he knew only one thing supremely well, and that was the new music. For that he was a fervent proselytizer, a believer, and he did his best to educate an audience that refused to be educated. Others had failed before him. Leonard Bernstein had tried an avant-garde series with the Philharmonic and it was a disaster, part of which was due to the resistance of the orchestra itself. (And Lenny, the orchestra said, did not like the stuff either.) Boulez could do no better; and, as suggested below, there was little he could do with the second-rate music he was trying to sell.

Boulez Trips Up Downtown

THE MARTINSON HALL in the New York Shakespeare Festival Public Theater is on the third floor of the old building on Lafayette Street. It is a rather small, close room, seating about three hundred, though about three hundred fifty tickets were sold for the first of the Prospective Encounters the other Friday. The overflow was accommodated on pillows strewn all over the floor.

There was Pierre Boulez, a lavaliere microphone around his neck, exhorting the troops. Never did a commander have a more faithful or worshiping army. The four-concert series was Boulez's idea. Disturbed by the lag between composer and audience, committed to the avant-garde, realizing that the New York Philharmonic is not the arena for experimentation, Boulez conceived the idea of four downtown concerts aimed at bridging the gap.

This was a long evening, seven to midnight. At least, the official starting time was listed as seven, but not until twenty minutes after that did Joseph Papp, the "owner" of the theater, get up to introduce Boulez. Papp made approving noises about the "decentralization" of the New York Philharmonic and of the arts in general. Then Boulez eagerly took over. He was wearing a gray striped suit, a blue turtleneck sweater and brown suede shoes (the jacket was shortly discarded; it was hot in Martinson Hall, and soon most of the men in the audience also doffed jackets and loosened neckties).

Boulez, speaking staccato English with a ripe French accent, was a happy man. This was close to his heart. He spoke for about a half hour on the purpose of the series. New York, he said, needed a new musical service in a different place in a different way. Contemporary music needed to be placed into proper perspective. He decided to forgo the use of the word "concert" in this series. There was too much "tradition" in concerts, and tradition was something that all of us had to fight. These "encounters" would institute a dialogue among composers, performers and the public. They were to be held in a free and informal manner. It is very important, insisted Boulez, that composers talk to the audience. Otherwise there could never be a direct relationship.

Why Martinson Hall? Because it was outside the normal limits of concert halls. Composers want to go beyond the feeling of pure music and establish a unity. More and more, composers hate precise borders. They want to dissolve the gap between pure music and theater. As for the actual music on these programs, Boulez said, he had selected pieces that were short. That way it would be easy to repeat any work that aroused attention, and such music also is easier to analyze. Any questions?

There were no questions. Boulez looked chagrined and disappointed. He looked this way and that, and there was an awkward
pause. Finally somebody took pity on him and asked a question.
The ice broken, questions then came one after the other. Boulez
fielded them deftly. He is a voluble speaker, and more: he is a
believer. There is a startling lack of pomposity in his approach.
He is not out to impress anybody, or to build himself up, or
satisfy his own ego. Rather, when he talks about modern music
(and modernism in general) he is something like Cicero address-
ing the Athenians: learned, reasoned, reasonable. And under-
neath is a burning fanaticism coupled to a powerful intellect.

Boulez completed the question period, even making a few
mild funnies as he went along. Then came the music. There
were two works, Mario Davidovsky's *Synchronisms* No. 6 for
piano and synthesized tape, and Charles Wuorinen's *The Politics of Harmony*, a theater piece for mime, actors, three singers
(within the orchestra) and small ensemble.

While Boulez was making out his case, one listened admiringly. It would be so nice to go along with everything he said.
There *is* a gap between composer and audience, a bigger gap than
there ever has been in history. This gap *should* be bridged, if the
state of music is to remain healthy. The repertory *has* to be
replenished. Symphony orchestras and opera houses *need* the
stimulus of new sounds, new forms, new philosophies. No argument anywhere. Boulez is right.

Then one listened to the music. The Davidovsky was an
academic-sounding collection of predictable synthesized effects
with a post-serial piano part. To anybody who has had any experience with tape music, this work was tired-sounding and
unoriginal. Paul Jacobs, who played it, told the audience what it
was all about (the composer, who was supposed to be present,
was in bed with a slipped disc). Jacobs's analysis was technical;
he said very little about the expressive qualities of the music
until somebody in the audience gave him the question direct,
whereupon he said that he liked it. There was a repeat of the
seven-minute work. It sounded no better the second time
around. Again Jacobs was asked about the emotional qualities of
the music. "I don't think of music in those terms," he said. "I

enjoy the piece. It has low levels of tension, uncomplex materials . . . it is not severe music."

There was a twenty-minute break, and then Wuorinen appeared. He had a few words to say about his score. It could, he said, be regarded as a purely musical experience. Or a theatrical experience. Or a combination of the two. Basically it was an attempt at cultural intercommunication—ancient Chinese in source, Western in treatment. The work was played; it ran some forty dismal minutes, with the singers maltreating the English language in extended twelve-tone syllabic extensions, with the usual academic kind of organization, with a 1960's kind of athematicism, with virtually no personality, with not a trace of charm.

Boulez analyzed it. He showed various relationships, various compositional techniques, and all one could think of was George Bernard Shaw's analysis of the Hamlet soliloquy: "Shakespear [Shaw's spelling], dispensing with the customary exordium, announces his subject at once in the infinitive, in which mood it is presently repeated after a short connecting passage in which, brief as it is, we recognize the alternative and negative forms on which so much of the significance of repetiton depends. Here we reach a colon . . ."

And that is Boulez's error, as it is the error of so many propagandists for the new music. The form of the work seems to be the end in itself, and not the quality of idea or expressive meaning. Wuorinen's score, whatever its compositional niceties, is a pompous bore, and most in the audience seemed to agree.

By the time it was over, many in the audience had drifted away, and there were about one hundred left to attend the final question and answer panel. With Boulez as master of ceremonies, there were Wuorinen, Richard Howard and James Seawright. There was much talk about the dead weight of "tradition." There was much bemoaning of the fifty-year cultural lag. It did not seem to occur to anybody that if a work of art has not established itself in fifty years, it conceivably, just conceivably, might be the fault of the work of art and not the public.

It was a very dull conversation. There was no basic disagreement among the panel members. All were on the side of Boulez's angels. In the meantime Boulez himself was employing his bright intellect to keep the subject moving along. But when it was all over he sounded like the barker at a carnival trying hard to entice an audience to enter. He would have had a more convincing case had he selected a better grade of merchandise. If these unattractive Columbia-Princeton hunks of academia are going to be characteristic of the Encounter evenings, it is hard to see many customers being enticed into the Boulez sideshow.

Oct. 17, 1971

PART V

Opera

If you want to know what an opera is, I tell you that it is a bizarre mixture of poetry and music where the writer and the composer, equally embarrassed by each other, go to a lot of trouble to create an execrable work.

—SAINT-EVREMOND

When I wrote this piece, the first of several on the subject, the Metropolitan Opera was gingerly approaching translated opera. Fortunately its approach has remained gingerly, whereas the New York City Opera is going more heavily every year into translated opera. To me, translated opera (except for operas in exotic languages where casts cannot be readily assembled) means provincial opera. In 1961, the big houses of France and Germany were using translations. Today that practice has virtually disappeared. I am not impressed by the argument that Verdi, among others, was insistent on his operas being sung in translation. Opera composers want performances, and if the Paris Opéra in Verdi's day always used French, then Verdi was going to be happy to have Don Carlo or whatever sung in French, with the best translation he could oversee.

The Metropolitan Opera now has admirable synopses in its program books, which it did not have in 1961, and those are enough to make the opera's action thoroughly understandable. One of the fallacies of translated opera, I have always felt, was the assumption that the words would be understood. But they almost never are. So why not remain with the originals, where at least the relation of words to music is what originally was in the composer's ear? In the early 1950's, Rudolf Bing tried a few operas in English translation. At a dress rehearsal of Gianni Schicchi one afternoon, Mr. Bing was unhappily slouched in a seat, listening unhappily as Salvatore Baccaloni and the others in the cast sang incomprehensible gibberish. Suddenly the curtain came down, then up, and the entire cast advanced to the footlights and sang "Happy Birthday to You." It was indeed Mr. Bing's birthday. He rose. "Thank you, ladies and gentlemen," *he said. "Those were the first words I understood all after-noon."*

The Easy Way Out: Translations

A WEEK ago last Thursday, Flotow's *Martha* was revived at the Metropolitan Opera, in English translation. To nobody's great surprise, not much of the translation came through. Most opera singers produce their pear-shaped tones with the proper orotundity, and they make agreeable noises indeed; but when it comes to singing English, the words come out as if their mouths were filled with oatmeal mush.

But even if every word were understood, the esthetics of opera in English—that is, opera written in another tongue and translated into English—are open to question. This subject of opera in English has been very much with us in the last decade. With the widespread development of the opera workshop, with an occasional opera on television and with the establishment of opera companies in several large American cities, there has come in many quarters the plea for a more "accessible" approach—that is, to give opera in English, "so that the public will understand what is going on."

Do not most foreign countries present opera in their own tongue? Would not the gain in understanding benefit the public as well as make the music itself more intelligible? So runs the argument. It has attracted many supporters (most of them, to be sure, with an axe to grind), and it has come to the point where it is next to un-American to question the desirability of opera in English.

But the question must be raised. The fact that the Paris Opéra does Verdi in French, or the Berlin Staatsoper does Puccini in German, does not necessarily mean the procedure is right. Have you ever heard *Otello* in French? Sounds just like Massenet. The music itself is different. Take *Die Meistersinger.* A phrase like

"So riff der Lenz in den Wald, dass laut es ihn durchhalt" may mean the same as "So cries the spring through the woods and makes them loudly ring," but the sound is quite different; and Wagner was as much concerned with the sound of his words as with the sound of his music. One determined the other, to a certain extent, and, no matter how skilled the translator, there will be a different set of sound values to fit into the musical line.

Some operas would defy translation completely. How could *Pelléas et Mélisande* be converted? The vowels and liquids of the French language—*"Viens ici: ne reste pas au bord du clair de lune. . . . Viens ici dans l'ombre du tilleul"*—have no equivalent melody in our tongue. Translate an opera into English and you have different music, together with the fact that (singers being what they are) the translation probably wouldn't be understood anyway. Which seems like deliberately going a good distance out of the way to arrive at undesirable results. As Rosalind tells Jaques, who brags that his travels have wrapped him in sadness: "And to travel for it too!"

If translation involves a loss in purely musical values—and it has to—then what the opera-in-English people want to do has its immoral aspects. Instead of wanting to bring people up to the level of music, they are demanding that music be brought down to the level of the people. Their idea is to get people into the opera houses by offering inducements and bribery. Anything goes. Too many people today are making a living by showing the public how to evade its mental responsibilities. Simplifications, popularizations, short cuts, condensations—anything but the real thing.

These things must be fought; and when they are under the sponsorship of so prestigious an institution as the Metropolitan Opera they must be fought all the more. Every lowering of standards means a point gained for the enemy; and then the time comes when low standards are expected as the norm. Even so dated an opera as *Martha* deserves as honest and faithful a performance as ingenuity and taste can devise.

The public should be made to realize that opera, just like any other form of art, demands a certain amount of intellectual preparation and participation. Opera is not a blown-up girlie show or

musical extravaganza. When an opera company presents a score
in English translation, with interpolated ballets and half-nude
boys and girls dancing out complicated sex orgies, all it is doing
is cheapening the opera and appealing to people's laziness. We
will do all the work for you, runs the appeal. Just come in and
relax. But is that the way to build an intelligent audience of
opera-goers? Behold the death-rattle of opera, murdered by its
friends.

Admittedly the public does not have the time or inclination
to put into music the mental effort it expends on bridge, or horse
racing. But the least—the very least—it can do before going to
the opera, though, is to buy a libretto and read it carefully. That
is an expenditure of about seventy cents in cash and less than
an hour of time. And that is enough to make the whole concept
of opera in English unnecessary. If people are not willing to
make that tiny investment for something they will have for the
rest of their lives, they have no business going to the opera in
the first place.

It is not hard to read an opera libretto. Very few of them
qualify as literature. Characters generally are one-dimensional,
and the dialogue is on the level of subtlety of the Sunday comic
strips. In opera, of course, we have to know what is going on,
and hence a knowledge of the libretto is mandatory; but the last
thing we ever go to the opera for is to see a play.

We go to hear music and singing. And, in the weaker operas of
the repertory, we go to hear singing, period. Those who consider
book and music of an equal nature in opera are making a great
mistake. Of course, one or two exceptions might be pointed out;
there always are exceptions to everything. But, by and large, it
is the music that counts. The composer might have spent
months or years fitting music to word. Once the opera is
mounted though, and after we have heard it five, ten, fifty times,
the opera lives or dies through its music, not its book. It is not
necessary to belabor the point. Never in history has a good libretto saved a bad opera; but many bad librettos live on because
of the music that accompanies them.

Even a fairly lengthy synopsis, such as is supplied in the New
York City Opera programs, can help. The Metropolitan Opera,

which says it is so interested in making friends, has no synopses at all in its program book. What it does have is an essay about the evening's opera and a lot of pictures of Metropolitan personalities. The Metropolitan has always had a tendency to glamorize personalities instead of music, a procedure analogous in the long run to a soup manufacturer's advertising the high quality of his container instead of the product that goes into it.

Fortunately the Metropolitan up to now has only gingerly approached opera in English. A survey recently showed that the majority of its subscribers did not want it. In that, the subscribers are showing better sense than the management. The best way for the Metropolitan to make friends is to present the world's best operas in the language in which they were written, with the best singers that can be obtained, as honestly as possible and with none of the fussiness and artificial staging that have marred so many of its recent productions. If the Metropolitan will not adhere to such a standard, who will?

FEB. 5, 1961

Rudolf Bing, in his twenty-two years (1950–72) as general manager of the Metropolitan Opera, did not like music critics, and he especially disliked the senior music critic of The New York Times. *During the 1960's there was much talk about the "feud" between Mr. Bing and Mr. Schonberg. But it wasn't that at all. A feud presupposes two people who know each other and dislike each other intensely. The fact is that I did not know Mr. Bing at all, except from hearsay. In the twenty-two years of his tenure, I interviewed him once for a* Times *magazine piece and had lunch with him twice. I did not dislike him: he was charming, formidably intelligent and very witty. He also had a thin skin and took everything very personally. Had positions been reversed, I might have acted the same way. Mr. Bing had as firm a belief in his flawless judgment as I had in mine.*

Of the operas I suggested below to flesh out Mr. Bing's limited repertory ideas, several were later staged during his regime and others after he retired. The million-dollar deficit in 1964 is currently (1979–1980) in the vicinity of seven million dollars.

Rudolf Bing: A Leader or a Follower?

LAST WEEK, looking at some of the problems of the Metropolitan Opera, we quoted Rudolf Bing on the repertory. Mr. Bing made the point that the Metropolitan had to have sellouts in order to exist; that the repertory was conservative because it had to be; that in any case it was no more the function of the Metropolitan Opera to do modern opera than it was the function of the Metropolitan Museum to show modern art.

Mr. Bing gave some statistics. "The difference between our average income and a 'poor' house may be $5000. If we have only two such works"—that is, operas with poor box-office pull—"each performed perhaps six times, that results in a box office loss of $60,000. Even so, we usually have at least two nonstandard works in every season. The critic has no responsibility whatever for the life or death of the house. I do; and if, by following the critics' advice, I should bring the Metropolitan to financial ruin, I doubt if even the press would thank me for it."

Several things. The analogy between the Metropolitan Opera and the Metropolitan Museum is far from exact. The museum presents art of the past in all of its periods: Egyptian and Greek through the renaissance up to the impressionists and even beyond. The Metropolitan Opera, on the other hand, has primarily been an Italian opera house ever since Mr. Bing took over. As such, it has concentrated only on one side of operatic history. Last season was typical—fifteen operas in Italian, three in German, four in English (all four translated), two in French, one half-English, half-German (that was *Ariadne auf Naxos*).

Next season will see much the same ratio—twelve operas in Italian, five in German, three in French, one in English and three in English translation. The three new productions will be *Lucia*, for Joan Sutherland, *Salome* for Birgit Nilsson and *Samson et Dalila* for Rita Gorr and Jess Thomas. The story behind *Lucia* is a commentary on opera in America—or, more precisely, opera at the Metropolitan. Mr. Bing has indicated that he would have preferred to set Miss Sutherland off in something more exhilarating than the tired Donizetti work. But this season, when she sang in the relatively unfamiliar *Sonnambula*, it was not to full houses. The Met became frightened. If even Sutherland could not draw in *Sonnambula*, whoa! Back to something that will please the dear somnolent ladies and gentlemen of the audience.

Thus, Mr. Bing does have a problem. His deficit runs well over one million dollars ($1,390,000 for the 1962–63 season), and he cannot ignore the imperative of the box office. And while he may have chosen an inexact analogy, there is truth in his statement that the Metropolitan Opera, like the Metropolitan Museum, is geared more for art works of the past rather than those of the present. The history and operation of the Met are against the avant-garde, and perhaps it has to be. With financial stability and a rethinking of philosophy (plus a reorientation of its clientele) it conceivably could be more of a spokesman for the twentieth century. Right now that is out of the question, and the Metropolitan Opera remains a coach-and-four in a jet age—but, at its best, a remarkably comfortable coach that in stately manner can go from here to there at a comfortably reliable trot.

With all that, the still, small voice whispers that Mr. Bing's attitude is equivalent to artistic abdication. For his repertory is such that the Met does not even go from here to there. It moves up and down without covering any ground.

His policy means that year in and year out we shall be having the same operas. It also means that the Metropolitan Opera is following public taste, not leading it. In which case, how can the Metropolitan Opera be taken seriously when it calls itself a cultural force? A cultural force presupposes a certain amount of initiative, daring, imagination. How much of that is there at the Met?

It seems to some of us that the externals are being put before the internals; that a new opera house is being built—for what? To commemorate a cultural archaism? And yet an enormous sum of money is being raised for that new opera house. Somehow the Metropolitan manages to get money for its new productions (and some of those productions are very expensive as well as exciting: *Meistersinger* a year ago; *Falstaff* this season). Somehow the Metropolitan manages to do the things it wants to do. There is a sneaking suspicion here that if the Metropolitan Opera wanted—really, desperately wanted—to give us a more interesting repertory, it would somehow find the means to do so.

And by interesting repertory is not necessarily meant twentieth-century or avant-garde operas that might alienate the very conservative public of the Metropolitan Opera. But the Metropolitan has to get out of its deadly rut. Surely it could consider operas like Boïto's *Mefistofele,* Charpentier's *Louise,* Chabrier's *Gwendoline* (Wagnerian in plot but not nearly as Wagnerian in music as some writers would have us believe), Poulenc's *Carmelites,* Tchaikovsky's *Pique Dame,* any one of several Janáşcek operas, any one of several Strauss operas, Mascagni's *L'Amico Fritz* (a little darling), Cornelius' *Barber of Bagdad,* one of the better comic operas by Rossini, Busoni's *Doktor Faust,* Mozart's *Abduction from the Seraglio,* Dukas's *Ariane et Barbe-Bleue,* Weber's *Freischütz,* Smetana's *Bartered Bride* and *The Kiss*— but why go on? With a little imagination the Metropolitan could flesh out its repertory without difficulty.

Instead, when anybody raises the repertory problem, the Metropolitan management feels abused, says that nobody understands its problems and waves the deficit flag.

Of course the Metropolitan has problems. Who hasn't? But until the Metropolitan thoroughly overhauls its musical staff and gets conductors who have the ability and temperament to put life into the performances (this season's roster was a disaster, and next season's does not look any more promising); and until the Metropolitan is ready to provide a more varied and interesting repertory, the old Metropolitan Opera House will have nobody but itself to blame if it loses the support of the critics and of the intellectual audience.

APRIL 19, 1964

I should have made it clear in this piece that my only experience with L'Amico Fritz *had been on records—the Tagliavini-Tassinari album released shortly after the war. Later the superb Pavarotti-Freni recording was to come, with the young Pavarotti in a spectacular outpouring of sweet, unforced lyricism. Whenever I was in Europe the opera was not on the boards at the time; and, of course, it was not in the American repertory at all. Several readers wrote in to tell me that the Schipa-Favero* Cherry Duet *was available in one of the Angel historical releases. When George Bernard Shaw reviewed* L'Amico Fritz, *he said that the* Cherry Duet *really should be hung in the Royal Academy.*

"L'Amico Fritz": A Sweet, Simple Thing

NEW YORKERS who like Mascagni's sweet little opera, *L'Amico Fritz*, will have a chance to hear it under reasonably professional auspices on Friday and Saturday. The Manhattan School of Music's John Brownlee Opera Theater is staging it at the Borden Auditorium. By coincidence, there was also a performance last April 25 by the Ruffino Opera Company at Town Hall. These performances seem to be the first by any opera company in New York since the Metropolitan Opera last staged the work, in 1924.

Mascagni turned to *L'Amico Fritz* directly after his international triumph with *Cavalleria Rusticana* at the age of twenty-seven. The brilliant one-acter had its première in Rome on May 17, 1890, and it made Mascagni a famous man. The following year, 1891, he came out with *L'Amico Fritz* (the première was also in Rome, on Oct. 31), an opera adapted from the Erckmann-Chatrian novel. Those who attended *L'Amico Fritz* expecting a continuation of the blood-and-thunder verismo of *Cavalleria Rusticana* were disappointed. The new opera was an idyll, and most people walked away shaking their heads. They still do. *L'Amico Fritz* has its admirers—I, for one, adore it—but although it turns up now and then on the international circuit, it never has been very popular.

So Mascagni remains a one-work man. It was not for lack of trying, but he was never able to duplicate his initial success. Later in life he was philosophical about it. "It was a pity I wrote *Cavalleria* first," he said. "I was crowned before I was king." Yet he had real talent, and it is a sad waste that it was never fully realized.

Mascagni was born in 1863 and became a musician over his father's objections. As with most composers, his talent asserted itself at a very early age, but his father wanted him to be a lawyer. Young Pietro secretly entered a music school, and was doing fine until his father discovered what he was up to. There was a fine Italian explosion, and only the intervention of an uncle kept Pietro in music. So rapid was his progress that an Italian nobleman sent him to the conservatory at Milan, where Mascagni worked for a while with Ponchielli, the famous composer of *La Gioconda*.

But Mascagni was not at the conservatory for long. He hated the study of counterpoint, and spent most of his time during 1883 waltzing around Milan with his roommate, a man named Giacomo Puccini. It was a *vie de bohème* for both of those young blades. They liked girls very much indeed, neither had much money, and they lived the kind of life later explicitly detailed in the Puccini opera about bohemians. When Mascagni's creditors appeared, he would hide in the wardrobe and Puccini would gravely explain that Mascagni was not in. Mascagni did the same for Puccini. They were not supposed to eat in their room and when one of the composers did some illegal cooking the other would go to the piano and play at a furious fortissimo to drown out the noises of the utensils. Mascagni and Puccini frequented the Osteria Aida, and the good-natured owner kept their credit alive for many years before finally being paid in full.

Puccini stayed at the conservatory, but Mascagni fled after a year. He became a conductor with various traveling opera companies, married (it is said that his wife caused a breach in his friendship with Puccini), lived from hand to mouth, and finally submitted an opera in a competition sponsored by the publisher Sonzogno. The opera was *Cavalleria Rusticana.* With it, the verismo school was launched.

But Mascagni did not pursue verismo opera. He went off in different directions, perhaps searching for a style, and composed a long series of failures or near-misses. There were such operas as *I Rantzau, Guglielmo Ratcliff, Silvano* and *Zanetto.* No matter. Mascagni remained the composer of *Cavalleria Rusticana,* and each new work of his was expectantly greeted. He was still so famous that in 1901 his new opera, *Le Maschere,* was given its première simultaneously in seven Italian cities. The opera failed. He doggedly kept on. *Amica, Isabeau, Lodoletta, Parisina, Il Piccolo Marat, Nerone*—all followed one another in dreary succession. The only opera that caused something of a stir was *Iris* in 1898. It was the first Italian opera on a Japanese subject, and contains many arias that singers of a previous generation admired. Puccini's Japanese opera six years later drove *Iris* from the boards. Mascagni lived until 1945, venerated but not performed very much.

He can be heard as a conductor in two complete recordings of his operas, *Cavalleria,* of course, and *L'Amico Fritz.* Libretto trouble is the major factor in keeping the latter out of the steady repertory. Nothing much happens in *L'Amico Fritz.* There is a quiet love affair, some interpolated music, and that is all. The interpolations occur when the almost nonexistent action comes to a halt, and the desperate librettist and composer had to fill in somehow. They added a number or two that has little to do with the action.

But there is something very sweet and genuine about the opera, and it has one section that impresses some listeners as the most lyrical moment in the entire body of Italian post-Romantic opera, Puccini included. That is the famous second-act *Cherry Duet*, in which Fritz and Suzel rapturously blend their voices. It is a sensuous piece of writing, delicately colored, harmonically ingenious. Mascagni had a feeling for the orchestra, and the wonderfully atmospheric evocation of growing love in the *Cherry Duet* is expressed against an exceedingly sensitive instrumental background. (Has the great recording of the duet by Mafalda Favero and Tito Schipa ever been transferred to LP?)

There are other lovely things in *L'Amico Fritz*. One has only to think of Suzel's *Son pochi fiori* and *Non mi resta*, or Fritz's *O, amore*, or the Intermezzo to the third act, which is a much more subtle piece of writing than the more famous *Cavalleria* intermezzo. There also is one unconsciously funny spot in *L'Amico Fritz*. It occurs where Rabbi David asks Suzel to narrate the story of Rebecca. She does, against a curtain of harmonies that could have come right out of the Vatican Choir. Rabbi David must have been a Reform Jew. Yet this musical naivete is terribly endearing, and actually helps make *L'Amico Fritz* the sweet, simple thing it is.

MAY 10, 1970

As early as 1961, on my first visit to Bayreuth, I was complaining about the Wolfgang and Wieland Wagner stagings, calling them alien to the spirit of the Ring *cycle. They may have been full of psychological significance and Jungian archetypes, but in the process whatever happened to Wagner's own wishes, so explicitly written down? The age of the Director-as-Hero was upon us. I set myself up as watchdog, barking myself hoarse and writing many columns about the decline of the West. It made no difference.*

When Jazzing Up Opera Becomes Vandalism

LAST MONTH, writing in the *Times Literary Supplement*, Erich Leinsdorf got some things off his mind about The New Staging, which is as much a part of the contemporary opera scene as The New Criticism used to be in literary circles some years back. Leinsdorf decried the directors and producers who make "a brilliant career on the back of defenseless Verdi or Mozart." If this goes on, he says, "Ultimately the public will be alienated, and the opera house will become an experimental laboratory for a small set of kooks."

It is a belief that has been echoed in this column time and again. There was a time when singers all but ran opera houses. Composers catered to their wishes; regisseurs designed productions around them. Then there was the period, starting roughly when Mahler took over the Vienna Opera in 1897, when the conductor was the axle around which the opera house revolved. Now the stage men are moving in, to redesign and reinterpret the operas for the unwashed.

Last month saw this writer on a tour of European opera houses, and that brings us to the Hamburg Opera's production of Massenet's *Don Quichotte* staged by Götz Friedrich. It is absolutely brilliant. Those who saw Sarah Caldwell's production of the Massenet opera in Boston—a production largely designed from Friedrich's original concept at the Komische Oper in East Berlin in 1971—will know what a striking impression it gives. Friedrich has taken the faded but pretty and sentimental *Don Quichotte* by the neck and twisted it out of all scenic and psychological recognition. There is a decadent, Fellini-like atmosphere; the sexual elements are transformed into kinky sex;

the Don is an innocent madman centuries removed from Cervantes; the locale has been shifted to Monte Carlo at the turn of this century.

All this is doubtless very stimulating, but it has very little to do with the actual opera. Friedrich, a protégé of Walter Felsenstein, in effect is showing contempt for the original. He will defend his approach by saying that the original is thin, which it is; that opera has to be brought into the twentieth century and interpreted by modern canons. But what he has done in *Don Quichotte* is similar to fitting a new Detroit chassis over a 1904 Olds. It is esthetic vandalism, really, and not all of Friedrich's brilliance can make up for it.

Then there was the *Nozze di Figaro* of Friedrich's mentor, Felsenstein, a few weeks ago at the Komische Oper. Felsenstein for years has been saying that nobody really understands the Mozart opera, and that itself was a funny statement. *Figaro,* which has been written about for almost two hundred years in contexts ranging from the radicalism of Beaumarchais to strict harmonic analysis! So Felsenstein gave us a social-conscious *Figaro.* All right; that's an interpretation that might be implicit in the score. Mozart as well as Beaumarchais was a revolutionary. But Felsenstein's heavy-handed, mackerel-in-the-face attempts to underline Marx-in-Mozart, his quaint notions of what constitutes modern scenery (a rag, a bone, a hank of hair), his arrogance in casting the opera with no-voice singers who at best had a primitive idea of Mozart style—this was an ego trip at Mozart's expense, and it was unpardonable.

This kind of staging is found all over Europe. In Vienna there were Herbert von Karajan's ideas about *Il Trovatore,* all in blackness and heavy symbolism. In London, at Covent Garden, there was the Vaclav Kaslik *Tannhäuser,* on a stage that had little more than two diagonal ramps and a back curtain of projections. Wagner, who was so explicit in his directions about the voluptuousness of the Venusberg scene, would have had a heart attack in seeing this kind of nonsense. In Munich there was an *Aïda* dominated throughout by long rectangular drops that pitifully tried to suggest Egyptian columns.

And in Berlin there was Ernst Schroeder's *Ballo in Maschera.*

This was unbelievable. We all know the history of the opera: how Verdi originally set it in Sweden; how the censors objected when faced with the assassination of a king; how Verdi transplanted it to Boston. Nearly everybody today puts the action back in Sweden. Not Schroeder. He took an unnamed city in the American South (New Orleans, judging from the architectural motif), established a dictator, had Ulrica singing voodoo out on the ol' plantation, and in general indulged himself at Verdi's expense.

But why? Why? In these cases are the directors so arrogant that they willfully ignore the specifications of the libretto? (Take the current *Walküre* at the Metropolitan, where instead of Siegmund's breaking his sword on Wotan's spear, as Wagner specifically directed, the deed is accomplished long distance against *Hunding's* spear, with Wotan far off on the side of the stage.) Or are they so doubtful about the intrinsic worth of the operas that they feel they have to jazz them up? Whatever the reason, the result is vandalism.

It is not that operas are untouchable. A skillful and imaginative director can of course reinterpret, provided that it is done in the spirit of the original. August Everding did that in the Metropolitan Opera's *Tristan und Isolde* some years back. Modern technology, after all, can provide legitimate effects that the composer would have welcomed: the use of film devices to bring up the Dutchman's ship in the Vienna production of Wagner's *Fliegende Holländer*, for example; or the all-film *Village Romeo and Juliet* at the New York City Opera; or the splendidly realized maze scene in the final act of Mozart's *Figaro* at the Staatsoper in Munich.

Not even old-fashioned operas have to be traditionally realistic. In Paris, the Capobianco production of *Il Trovatore* uses semi-stylized sets and props, all with enough relation to the real thing to augment the Verdian atmosphere. Capobianco works with taste and sympathy in this *Trovatore* and that makes all the difference. Similarly, in the Paris *Don Carlo*, with Margherita Wallmann's mise-en-scène, there is a stylized Baroque element intended to suggest the panoply and decadence of the Spanish court. It is not "realistic," but in so many respects it strikes deeper than mere realism. Here again there is a stage director with taste.

How different it was at Mauro Bolognini's production of *Norma* at La Scala, which was dominated by the ugly set of Mario Ceroli. Presumably the idea was to suggest Stonehenge. The set, which is revolved for the various scenes, is a massive series of symmetrically arranged rectangular blocks. The sacred tree, seen only in the first scene, branches off into a series of wide-open hands instead of leaves. There are no props, everything is bare. To compensate, there are some of the most ludicrous costumes ever seen since the great days of the M-G-M musical. In the dark, at least, the set achieved a certain looming dignity. In the light, and a good part of the opera was well lit, the set looked as though it was patched together with bandaids and flour paste.

There is a large esthetic point involved. An opera suggests a period by virtue of its music alone. Verdi and Wagner are as much nineteenth-century opera composers as Mozart is eighteenth and Berg is twentieth. When they composed their operas, they had in their minds the stage conventions of their own period. Music and convention are interlocked. By and large, no director today would dare touch the music of a great opera (there are, of course, exceptions even to that rule), but they very much alter the stage conventions that went along with it. The result often is an esthetic imbalance, an imbalance just as bad as Bach-Stokowski or a Mozart symphony played by the full complement of the modern orchestra.

The stage conventions of operas of the past have to be respected as much as the actual music is respected. Directors can have all the leeway they want working within those conventions. But those who break the conventions are also breaking the opera itself, adding meanings that are alien to the original, introducing the esthetic of a later period, and in general setting themselves up as scientists who practice genetic alteration rather than as artists who are responsive to style and period.

MARCH 23, 1975

While in Europe for the Bayreuth centennial, I went into train-ing for the Ring *cycle. About two weeks before the opening, I was in Munich, listening to the* Ring *as conducted by Wolfgang Sawallisch. Some of the Munich singers were to be at Bayreuth two weeks later, and that too was interesting. Would their con-ception and actual singing be different? The Munich* Ring *turned out not to be very exciting, but it was a model of probity compared to what Patrice Chéreau did to the* Ring *in Bayreuth. It could well be that the Bayreuth* Ring *was the most cynical production of any stage work I have ever experienced: an out-rageously calculated attempt to* épater les bourgeois. *Of course it had a "conception." The only trouble was that Chéreau's conception was not Wagner's.*

A Bayreuth "Ring" That Alarmed the Old Guard

FOR THE 100th anniversary of the Bayreuth Festival, coinciden-tal with the 100th anniversary of the first performance of the entire *Ring* cycle, something special had been expected. And something special the audience did get, though it may not have been exactly what many Bayreuth regulars had in mind. Wolf-gang Wagner, the composer's grandson, is the boss of Bayreuth, and for this very special *Ring* he went to two Frenchmen, nei-ther of whom had had any direct experience with the four operas of the Wagnerian tetralogy.

Patrice Chéreau, the thirty-year-old French director, had staged only two operas in his life. One was recent—the much talked about *Tales of Hoffmann* for the Paris Opéra. Rolf Lieber-mann, who is the head of the Paris Opéra, was delighted with this unconventional production, and he became one of Chér-eau's most enthusiastic supporters. It is being said in Bayreuth that Liebermann's endorsement had a good deal to do with Chér-eau's appointment for the *Ring*. The other Frenchman was Pierre Boulez, who had conducted *Parsifal* at Bayreuth with great success some years ago and *Tristan* with the Bayreuth company in Japan but who had never been involved with other Wagner operas.

Thus the two chief protagonists of the centennial *Ring* —director and conductor—were not bound by "tradition." They were going to look at the operas with fresh eyes. Chéreau certainly did. He broke away entirely from the symbolic presentations that have been *de rigueur* with the *Ring* cycle in international opera houses ever since the revolutionary ideas of the Wagner brothers—Wolfgang and Wieland—in the early 1950's.

One of the complaints of the Bayreuth old guard—and, of course, the old guard everywhere—is the lack of naturalism in the neo-Bayreuth stagings. Traditionalists grew up with the lush, literal settings in vogue from 1876 to World War II, and they want the full panoply of Wagnerian stage directions. Chéreau, unexpectedly, gave them naturalism with a vengeance. There was a rainbow to Valhalla. There were real horses in *Die Walküre*. In *Siegfried* there was not only a bear but also a dragon that moved its paws and wings. *Rheingold* had giants that were ten feet tall. The forest had real trees. You'd think that the old guard would have been delighted.

But along with that Chéreau decided to reinterpret the *Ring*. The results were pretty chaotic, but as much as one can figure out, Chéreau tried to put the *Ring* in a modern setting to show that the basic issues in the days of Nibelheim and Valhalla remain basic issues in our own day. Thus where some traditional trappings were retained—the Valkyries wore breastplates and carried spears—the gods and dwarfs wore Victorian or even modern dress.

Gunther in *Götterdämmerung* is clearly a rich landowner, and he looks over his estate while wearing a very up-to-date dinner jacket. Later Siegfried himself appears in a dinner jacket, and if you don't think *that* didn't upset the Bayreuth regulars you have another think coming. Another little piece of stage business that infuriated the regulars was the Forest Bird in *Siegfried*, which sings from a wooden cage. The performance nearly broke up when the bird cage was introduced. Hunding is the owner of a factory and is attended by a bunch of thugs. The opening scene of *Rheingold* is set at a hydroelectric dam, and the three Rhine-maidens are prostitutes. At the fatal hunting party in *Götter-dämmerung* many of Gunther's vassals are carrying modern rifles.

One can go on and on. Fafner the dragon lives in a handsome summer house set in a forest clearing. Wotan is treated as an insensitive bully and sadist who spears his son Siegmund in the back. Chéreau obviously has little regard for him. Nibelheim is the basement of a skyscraper. Valhalla has a New York skyline and is enthusiastically destroyed at the end. Hunding receives Siegmund in the courtyard of his factory and his retainers are constantly on the scene. Mime in *Siegfried* is a comic vaudeville figure. Siegfried makes his sword in an immense Industrial Revolution forge that does all his work for him.

There have in recent years been reinterpretations and modern adaptations of the *Ring* in various European opera houses; but in Bayreuth, the very heart of Wagnerland, where every note is supposed to be pure and sacred, where every one of Der Meister's stage indications is supposed to be taken literally, where the very streets of the city are named after Wagnerian operas and characters, nothing like this had ever been seen before.

There was an uproar. Every opera of the cycle received hearty booing and at the end there was a demonstration against the conception by a group of traditionalists.

There were also those who liked what Chéreau had done. Their position was that for everything that did not come off, there was somewhere else a shrewd thrust or an illuminating passage. Chéreau, they said, was an absolute man of the theater, full of ideas, with the ability to bend singers to his will and actually make actors of them. Was there ever, they rhetorically asked, a *Ring* cycle that was so well acted? The answer all agreed, even the opposition, was never.

The morning after the *Götterdämmerung* that ended the cycle, there was a press conference in which Boulez and Chéreau faced a large roomful of skeptical international music critics. Boulez had nothing to worry about, and as it turned out no questions came his way. Boulez, to the surprise of some, had turned out to be an exemplary *Ring* conductor. He had led the operas with a firm hand, using traditional tempos, adopting a refined approach, holding down the fortissimos to give the singers a chance to be heard. But this was not the kind of chamber-music Wagner that Karajan had brought to New York some years previously. Boulez had more strength than that, and his broad, unhurried pacings captured the flowing musical line. His was not a Romantic approach—Boulez is not built that way—but it was indubitably grand and moving.

Boulez's conducting was universally praised. At the press conference, one of the German critics, intending to praise Boulez, said something to the effect that he had never heard such precision from a Bayreuth conductor, and if here and there a tiny little thing had gone wrong, well, even Herbert von Karajan was not perfect. Boulez smiled a sour smile and said nothing.

It was Chéreau to whom all questions at the press conference were addressed. He was accused of playing fast and loose with Wagner, of ignoring stage directions, of misinterpretation. Much was made, for instance, of the non-raising of the dead Siegfried's hand. In the libretto, Hagen rushes to the body in the hall of the Gibichungs to seize the ring. The dead man raises his arm in a threatening gesture and Hagen retreats in confusion. Why, Chéreau was asked, had he dropped that traditional piece of stage business? (It might be mentioned that the Günther Rennert staging of the *Ring* in Munich also dispenses with the raising of the hand.)

Chéreau said that he had dropped it because "I don't think that Hagen would be afraid. He's too strong, too tough." But, a German critic insisted, that was beside the point. It was a miracle, and Wagner intended it as such.

"I don't believe in miracles," Chéreau curtly replied. And that was that.

Chéreau, young, very mod, handsome with black hair curling down to his shoulders, chain-smoking, speaking in German—gave some clues to his conception of the *Ring*.

He said that when the curtain goes up, nature already has been spoiled and corrupted. The much talked-about hydroelectric dam "represents industry and is also a mythical symbol." Chéreau said that nobody today could take all aspects of the *Ring* seriously. He himself purposely ignored most of the cosmic and mythical elements. "I am interested only in the human psyche and emotions. Those are much more important than myths." In short, Chéreau deliberately admitted to ignoring what was of overwhelming importance to Wagner—the mythic elements—and said as much. His remarks often were of rather breathtaking loftiness in respect to the *Ring* librettos. For instance, the figure of Hagen at the very end is treated by Chéreau with peculiar nonchalance. Hagen really does make a half-hearted attempt to get the ring from the funeral pyre, tangles briefly with the Rhinemaidens, and then walks off in complete defiance of Wagner's directions.

Why? Why? Chéreau was asked. His answer was indicative of the current usurpation of stage director over composer. Hagen, explained Chéreau, is not really interested in the ring. He already has had several chances to take it and didn't take advantage of any.

Which may be true. But that is Wagner's fault. As a stage work the *Ring* is full of holes and inconsistencies. But a sympathetic and understanding director can at least smooth those over. Chéreau is not interested in this. He wants to reinterpret according to his twentieth-century (and, one is afraid, adolescent) ideas about the operas.

Wagner himself had something to say about the subject, and his comments should be read to all of those directors—Wolfgang Wagner included—who constantly talk about adapting opera for modern audiences, about "bringing opera into the twentieth century."

In Wagner's own day Mozart's *Don Giovanni* and other great operas were constantly being "brought up to date," and being mangled in the process. Wagner, one of the greatest conductors of his day, objected strenuously. "Transported into today's conditions," he wrote, "that which is eternal in these works suffers a distortion. . . . Almost every director sets about producing *Don Giovanni* in the style of his own time; whereas any intelligent person knows that, if we are to be in tune with Mozart, it is not the work that should be adapted to our age but we who should adapt ourselves to the age of *Don Giovanni.*"

Aug. 8, 1976

Patrick Smith was good enough to send me an advance copy of his Opera News *article, and I gleefully fell upon it. If his list of "viable" operas of the 1950–60 period was so weak—and I don't think many will disagree with that estimate—it cemented the point I was making. There are hardly any operas after* Turandot *in 1925 that have had any kind of international appeal. Nor is it that composers are not writing operas. A glance at the compilations assembled by the Central Opera Service shows an incredible number of new works composed annually, generally for the smaller groups that have so proliferated in America during the last decade. From a sense of duty the New York City Opera and the Metropolitan Opera occasionally stage ambitious works by American composers. But those enjoy a season and disappear, never to return. Probably the only American operas of real worth are Virgil Thomson's* Four Saints in Three Acts *and* The Mother of Us All—*and those appeal only to specialized audiences. It is a sad state of affairs. Nor does anybody seem to be coming up, anywhere, who has the imagination and the vision to compose operas that seize the public.*

Opera Is in the Air—and It Has a Most Familiar Ring

WHAT WITH the memory of Bayreuth still resounding in the ear (and smarting in the eye), what with La Scala opening on Tuesday in Washington and the Paris Opéra opening in New York the very next day, what with the New York City Opera already under way, what with the Metropolitan Opera making noises prefatory to its Oct. 11 opening, one might safely say that opera is in the air.

It was only a few years ago that Pierre Boulez was issuing manifestos saying that opera was dead and that opera houses should be burned to the ground. And it is true that most opera houses of the world are as much museums, curators of tradition, as the Metropolitan Museum of Art or the Hermitage. Look at the Scala repertory: two Verdi operas—*Macbeth* and *Simon Boccanegra*—along with Puccini's *La Bohème* and Rossini's *La Cenerentola*. And what is Paris bringing? Verdi's *Otello*, Mozart's *Le Nozze di Figaro* and Gounod's *Faust*.

There was a certain amount of unrest in intellectual circles when the Paris repertory was announced. From La Scala one did expect traditional opera. It never has been an avant-garde house, though it does present a more adventurous repertory than many realize. But the Paris Opéra, reconstituted in 1973 under Rolf Liebermann, does stand for a degree of modernism. In Hamburg, Liebermann had created a house that was wildly avant-garde, as opera houses go. In Paris he had to start from scratch with repertory. But he did present Schoenberg's *Moses and Aaron*, conducted by his musical adviser, Georg Solti. He did bring in such relatively unfamiliar works as Massenet's *Don Quichotte* and Paul Dukas's *Ariane et Barbe-Bleue*.

Thus, had he come to New York with the Massenet and Dukas works (he probably would not have been allowed to take a chance on the Schoenberg), he would have (a) introduced audiences to an unusual and rewarding pair of unfamiliar operas, (b) showed a great deal of enterprise, (c) given his company a chance to excel in scores that few if any other opera houses can idiomatically handle (for only French singers can present French opera in a completely idiosyncratic manner) and (d) avoided invidious comparisons.

But there is something to be said for Liebermann's choice, and it is reflective of the worldwide malaise that afflicts opera. Liebermann did not have many options, and neither did La Scala.

Since there is no such thing as a successful modern opera, Liebermann and Paolo Grassi (the Scala manager) necessarily had to fall back on standard repertory.

It can be said, however, that the 1976–77 season at, of all places, the Metropolitan Opera will show a degree of adventure rare in this staid old house. One says of all places, because the Metropolitan's repertory consistently has avoided controversial opera. But here comes Berg's *Lulu,* left unfinished at the composer's death in 1935; and also Poulenc's *Dialogues des Carmélites* of 1957. The Berg, of course, is still modern by any standards. And two more of the six new productions are, if not examples of contemporary opera, at least unfamiliar enough to be well outside normal Metropolitan programming. Those are Massenet's *Esclarmonde* and Meyerbeer's *Le Prophète.* Otherwise the Metropolitan Opera season, which runs from Oct. 11 to April 16, will have the usual mixture of Verdi, Wagner, Puccini, Mozart and the other favorites. For once, the Metropolitan is outdoing the New York City Opera, which for its fall season is bringing in such "novelties" as Rossini's *Barbiere,* Wagner's *Fliegende Holländer,* Menotti's *The Saint of Bleecker Street* and Offenbach's *La Belle Hélène.*

The unhappy fact is that very little viable opera has been written since the great days of Richard Strauss and Giacomo Puccini. This is not exactly an original observation. Conservatives have been saying it for years. Proponents of "modern opera" counter by saying that contemporary music never has had a fair chance; that audiences have to learn how to listen to it; that it takes time for a new and difficult tonal language to insinuate itself into the heart of a lay audience.

There is always a cultural lag. Nobody is going to argue against that. But does that argument about contemporary music really hold true today? When audiences have been exposed to it for over fifty years and still stubbornly refuse to accept it? When recordings of the most difficult music proliferate? When anybody with the least inclination can immerse himself in the medium?

There is a basic fallacy in the argument. The proponents of contemporary opera (and contemporary music in general) seem to argue that it is the *duty* of the listener to sit stoically through new music, no matter how painful or unmusical it may be. The argument also presupposes that modern music must be listened to merely because it is new, not because it is good.

But experienced composers—Verdi was a good example—know differently. Verdi said time and again that only the public was the final judge; that a good work would make its way and a bad work would fail. History bears him out. Opera came into being almost four hundred years ago. Since that time, thousands upon thousands of operas have been composed. Of that stupendous number, how many have become repertory pieces? A hundred (to stretch the point)? The fact is that the dearth of viable opera is not a new phenomenon. Take Italy in the period between the death of Donizetti and the emergence of Ponchielli and the verismo composers who followed him. There was Verdi, of course. There was Boito with *Mefistofele.* And then there was —who? Can you name a single one? But in 1869, to pick one year, Italy saw new operas by Sampieri, Mancini, Ricci, Monti, Petrella, Morales, Vera, Montuoro, Marchetti, Perelli, Vezzossi, Battista, Germano, Alberti, Zecchini, Tancioni, Libani and Grondona. Not one of those rates even a footnote in any history of music.

Take our own day. Patrick Smith, a knowledgeable critic and scholar, has written an article for *Opera News* (as yet unpublished) that looks at the decade between 1950 and 1960 with a view to picking viable operas. Here is what he has come up with: Menotti's *The Consul,* Poulenc's *Carmélites* and *La Voix Humaine,* Britten's *Turn of the Screw,* Tippett's *Midsummer Marriage,* Dallapiccola's *Il Prigioniero,* Blomdahl's *Aniara,* Moore's *Ballad of Baby Doe,* Weisgall's *Six Characters in Search of an Author* and Stravinsky's *The Rake's Progress.*

It is not a very impressive list. Some of these operas are forgotten already—the Blomdahl, Weisgall and Dallapiccola. The Menotti and Moore are lightweight by any standards. Stravinsky's *Rake* never really took hold with any company, and only the overpowering name of its composer has kept it in the periphery of the repertory. Only Poulenc's *Carmélites* seems to have a chance to survive.

The point is not that these operas were produced here and abroad. They had to be; the public had to be exposed to them. No argument there. But if they are tried and found wanting, there seems to be no reason why they should be forced down the public's throat because they happen to be "modern." (Not that Britten or Menotti are "modern" composers; the term is used here in a highly general sense.)

But times are changing. Fifteen years ago anybody who argued against international postserialism and its chokingly dull abstractions was hooted down and called a reactionary. Today it is taken pretty much for granted that serialism is dead; that the entire serial movement produced nothing of lasting value. Not only are people speaking up against it; composers themselves are abandoning serialism and introducing Neoromantic elements into their music.

Serialism, with its strange use of the human voice and its reductio ad absurdum of expressionism, had a good deal to do with the age's dearth of opera. The energies of all advanced composers seemed placed at the service of a terribly mathematical kind of music that was anti-opera all the way through. The composers ended up writing for each other.

It was a bad period. Even the conservative composers, like Benjamin Britten, started experimenting with a type of melodic line that sounded contrived and constipated.

But opera is singing, and don't let anybody tell you otherwise. Yes, we all want good, intelligent librettos with strong plot lines and believable characters. Yes, we all want imaginative productions. Opera is drama—to a point. But opera transcends drama. The music is the important thing. It is the music that underlines character and sets the mood. It is the music that one remembers, not the words of the libretto. Great music can triumph over the weakest libretto (vide La Forza del Destino or Aïda). But if the music is uninteresting, no libretto, however strong, can save the opera.

Another thing: opera is probably the most visceral form of music, and that goes for such "intellectual" composers as Wagner and even for such pure composers as Mozart. But the anti-Romantic movement that came into being after World War I despised Romanticism and its gestures. The culmination came with the serialism, electronic music and total dissonance of music after 1950. Opera simply could not be composed under those circumstances—or, at least, opera that the public would listen to.

Today there is a different attitude, and one that bodes well for the re-establishment of opera. If nothing else, a visceral element is beginning to creep back into music. Composers are trying to recapture an alienated audience, and they are no longer afraid to use broad melodic gestures.

That does not mean they are writing in nineteenth-century style. They aren't. Rather they are evolving a medium that is a new kind of *Gesamtkunstwerk*. It is an eclectic medium that calls upon the entire history of music, from the Renaissance and classical raga through Broadway and serialism. Electronic music may be unselfconsciously introduced, as another instrument in the orchestra. Certainly the direction taken by such composers as Peter Maxwell Davies in England and Stanley Silverman in New York hint at a future kind of lyric drama in which intellectuality and visceral impact come together in an exciting mixture.

But nobody as yet has come along to fuse the new materials into a kind of opera that means to this age what Wagner meant to his. In opera there currently are no big men around. So Milan and Paris come to New York with Verdi, Mozart, Puccini and Co. That is the fault of composers the last fifty years or so.

SEPT. 5, 1976

While writing this piece about Meyerbeer's Le Prophète, *I did not want to prejudge the performance, though I had a very good idea of what I would think of the music. As it turned out, the John Dexter production was all but universally condemned, and it was in all truth pretty bad. Nor did I find much of inter-est in the music. Meyerbeer did not have a very original mind; he was much more a technician and entertainer rather than a powerful creative figure.* Les Huguenots, *which I heard on a pirated tape, impressed me as equally bad. But Meyerbeer was an interesting and important phenomenon who did put his mark on the history of opera, and I am perfectly willing to concede that there may be much more in his music than is apparent to me.*

Meyerbeer, Once the Most Idolized Opera Composer

WHEN THE Metropolitan Opera stages its new production of Meyerbeer's *Le Prophète* on Tuesday, it will be reviving an opera that has been out of its repertory for about fifty years. It also will be focusing attention on a composer who was by far the most popular, most imitated, idolized concocter of operas through most of the century after 1831, when he sprang *Robert le Diable* on the world. There had been nothing like the Meyer-beer craze, not even the Rossini craze in *his* day, and Heinrich Heine observed that Meyerbeer's mother was the second woman in history to see her son accepted as divine.

He was admired, and also hated. Wagner all but frothed at the mouth when discussing the Meyerbeer operas. He compared Meyerbeer to "a starling who follows the plowshare down the field and merrily picks up the earthworm just uncovered in the furrow." He poked fun at the operas, which he described as "monstrous, piebald, historico-romantic, diabolico-religious, fanatico-libidinous, sacro-frivolous, mysterio-criminal, autol-yco-sentimental. . . ." The fact that Meyerbeer was a Jew—and, worse yet, a rich, successful Jew—did not sit well with the great-est anti-Semite of the century.

But Wagner was not alone. The serious musicians of the time could find little to admire in the Meyerbeer operas. "Something for everybody, but there's no heart in it," said Mendelssohn, putting his finger exactly on the Meyerbeer problem. Schumann was furious when he heard *Les Huguenots:* ". . . commonness, distortion, unnaturalness, immorality and unmusicality." Berlioz, not as hostile, admitted Meyerbeer's "genuine eclectic talent," but also had fun describing the operas as consisting of "high C's from every type of chest, bass drums, snare drums, organs, military bands, antique trumpets, tubas as big as locomotive smokestacks, bells, cannon, horses, cardinals under a canopy, emperors, queens in tiaras, funerals, fêtes, weddings, jugglers, skaters, choirboys, censers, monstrances, crosses, taverns, processions, orgies of priests and naked women . . . the five hundred fiends of hell and what have you . . ."

Meyerbeer started composing his operas in Paris at just the right time. Rossini had just retired, the Opéra had a new and innovative manager, and the public was ripe for the new Romanticism that was sweeping Europe. Meyerbeer, Berlin-born, a piano prodigy, a composer who had studied with the right people and who had achieved some success with his operas in Italy, gave the Parisian public exactly what it wanted. What it wanted was spectacle, operas on historical subjects, ballet, the grand panoply, lusty singing. Meyerbeer supplied all that— in spades.

Robert le Diable of 1831 was followed by *Les Huguenots* in 1836, *Le Prophète* in 1849, *L'Etoile du Nord* in 1854, *Dinorah* in 1859 and the posthumous *L'Africaine* in 1865 (Meyerbeer died in 1864). Most of these had librettos by Eugène Scribe. They enjoyed phenomenal successes. Indeed, they were inescapable. Military bands blared out themes from the Meyerbeer operas. Restaurant orchestras played them. One of Europe's important minor industries was the creation of potpourris on Meyerbeer themes. Pianists also composed transcriptions of Meyerbeer themes—among the pianists being Franz Liszt, who wrote a blazing virtuoso organ piece on the *Ad nos, ad salutarem undam* from *Prophète.*

Every opera house had several Meyerbeer operas simultaneously in the repertory. Naturally he was much heard at the Metropolitan after it opened in 1883; and in those days the Metropolitan could stage the operas with such singers as Lilli Lehmann, the de Reszke brothers and Pol Plançon; or, later, with a *Prophète* cast containing Muzio, Matzenauer, Caruso, Didur and Mardones.

But after World War I, with Romanticism in retreat, the Meyerbeer operas fell upon hard times. Seldom has so overwhelming a reputation been so reduced to shreds. Meyerbeer soon became synonymous with vulgarity, cheapness, effect over substance. Virtually everybody condemned him, and by the 1940's Meyerbeer virtually disappeared from the repertory. Only in recent years has there been the beginning of a Meyerbeer revival, and that has not taken hold the way the bel canto revival of the 1950's had done. But Romanticism has been in the air the last five years or so, forgotten 19th-century works are being re-examined, and it may be that Meyerbeer once again will have something to say to international opera lovers.

The Metropolitan Opera is giving Meyerbeer a chance with its new production of *Le Prophète*. Like many Scribe librettos, this one has some basis in history, and it is based on the Anabaptist movement of the early 1500's. Anabaptist is the name given to certain sects in Martin Luther's day that denied the validity of baptism. It was an anti-ecclesiastical movement, and it held that divine revelation came not from the church or from preachers but from the very spirit of God. Anabaptists practiced primitive Christianity. In many ways it was a communistic movement. Naturally the Anabaptists were persecuted. But from them developed the modern Baptist movement.

In 1521 three "prophets" appeared in Wittenberg. These three Anabaptists preached that feudalism should be abolished. Luther condemned them, and they took to preaching in the countryside. The Peasants' War of 1525 was one result. The best-known of the Anabaptist leaders—and one entirely untypical of the movement—was a man from Leyden named Johann Bockholdt or Bockelson (authorities disagree). He claimed to be the successor of David and demanded absolute power in the new Zion. Among other things, he legalized polygamy and took unto himself four wives. In 1536, in Westphalia, he was captured, tortured and executed.

It is this John of Leyden who is the central male character of the Meyerbeer opera, which also contains the three Anabaptist prophets (an evil force in *Le Prophète*). Scribe invented everything else, making John an innkeeper, introducing a love interest and a mother who is continually seeking her son, and a villainous lord. The opera is *echt*-Meyerbeer. It has big choruses, ballet music, battle music, a bouffe trio, demanding vocal parts, a final scene in which a castle is burned and destroyed.

Some of the music may be familiar. The fifth-act contralto solo, *O prêtres de Baal*, can be heard on any number of discs by virtuoso singers. The third-act ballet of skaters will be familiar through Ashton's popular ballet, *Les Patineurs*. (The roller skate had just been invented in 1849, and the choreographer for *Le Prophète* trained his dancers to use that new invention, simulating ice-skating on the frozen river.) Piano and organ fanciers, too, will recognize the *Ad nos, ad salutarem undam* theme through the Liszt transcription. Then there is the once-famous *Coronation March*.

Whatever one thinks of the musical substance of the opera, there can be no denying the skill with which it is put together. There even is a use of something resembling leitmotifs. Thus in Act II, just before Jean's big monologue, there is an allusion to the *Coronation* theme that later plays such a big part in Act IV. The sinister Anabaptist theme weaves through the entire opera: another thematic linkage that creates a unifying force. The orchestration is full of deft touches; and when orchestra, chorus and soloists are going all out in one of the big Meyerbeer climaxes, there is a visceral response that cannot easily be shrugged off. It is only later that one asks oneself what all the excitement was about.

A recording of *Le Prophète*, with much of the Metropolitan Opera cast, will shortly be released by Columbia. Thus a wider audience than that at the Metropolitan alone will be in a position to immerse itself in the music and draw its own conclusions. It will be interesting to see how *Le Prophète* makes out on records. For it could well be that this is an opera in which the visual aspects are just as important as the musical ones; and if that is true, *Le Prophète* will make nowhere near the impact that it does in the opera house.

Nor is *Le Prophète* for every opera house. It demands literalism and lavishness; that was what French opera in the 1830's through the 1860's was all about. Read this description of a representative production in 1835. The opera was *La Juive*, but it could just as well have been a Meyerbeer one: "The costumes of the warriors, civilians and ecclesiastics are not imitated but reproduced in their smallest details. The armor is no longer pasteboard; it is made of real metal. One sees men of iron, men of silver, men of gold! The Emperor Sigismond, for instance, is a glittering ingot from head to foot. The horses, not less historically outfitted than their riders, turn and prance." The Metropolitan Opera, in producing *Le Prophète*, has a real job on its hands.

JAN. 16, 1977

I am very fond of four Puccini operas. La Bohème, I think, is one of the few perfect operas ever written: short, one fine musical idea following another, sensitively orchestrated, no long and sentimental reprises in the last act, and with a libretto that remains eternally youthful and appealing. Gianni Schicchi is a gem throughout, Puccini's answer to Verdi's Falstaff. The massive Turandot is rich-sounding and exciting, given a heroic pair of singers who can handle the terrible demands. And then there is the often-derided Fanciulla del West, which I find the most unusual of all. To me there is something dreamlike about it: those curiously vague, pastel harmonies; those Never-Neverland characters; the unconsciously funny things in it; its prevailing sweetness. There also is that crazy poker game which, as a veteran of a stern monthly, table-stakes game, I felt qualified to write about.

Don't Sneer at Puccini's Horse Opera

WHEN THE Metropolitan Opera brought back Puccini's *La Fanciulla del West—The Girl of the Golden West*—to open its 1961–62 season, this column wondered if the time was ripe for the opera to capture the public's imagination. It may have been a tearjerker, full of impossible melodrama, but perhaps it would be possible to accept it as a period piece. And there was some wonderful music in it.

Well, *Fanciulla del West* came, but it did not exactly conquer, though it was in and out of the Metropolitan Opera repertory for some years. Now it is out. But tonight the New York City Opera is taking a look at the work. Never before staged by the company, the opera will have Maralin Niska in the title role of Minnie, the innocent California girl who defends her honor with a revolver, teaches Bible classes to the tough gold miners, plays poker with the sheriff for her lover's life (she wins by cheating) and comes galloping—literally: on a horse—to his rescue when he is about to be lynched.

A generation ago *La Fanciulla* was not discussed in intellectual musical circles. The libretto was considered too embarrassing, and that was enough to kill it. Critics who loudly condemned it probably had never heard the score; it had disappeared from the American repertory around 1932, and seldom turned up overseas. Nor was there a recording in pre-LP days (not that there are many of *La Fanciulla* today). Some Italian opera enthusiasts wrote glowingly of the music. They pointed out that *La Fanciulla* had a new depth for Puccini, much more ambitious orchestration, some modern devices stemming from Debussy and even Schoenberg. Nobody listened to them.

Puccini had been in New York early in 1907. The Metropolitan Opera was in effect giving a Puccini festival, culminating in a new production of *Manon Lescaut,* never before staged by the company. Puccini was invited over, for a fee of $8,000—a considerable sum then. During his five-week stay he attended a performance of David Belasco's play, *The Girl of the Golden West*. Belasco went all-out: he used projections, a moving panorama, "authentic" California minstrels (singer, concertina, banjo, xylophone for the "bones"), and had thirty-two men backstage operating the wind and snow machines. No wonder Broadway went wild.

Although he was interested, Puccini blew hot and cold. "Never a clear line of development," he wrote. "It's all a hodgepodge and sometimes in very bad taste and *vieux jeu*." But he had wanted to write an opera on the exotic Wild West, and on his return to Europe he got in touch with Belasco, indicating that with some modifications a libretto could be derived from the play. By July, 1908, Puccini decided to go ahead. As was his custom, he immersed himself in what he thought was authentic American material, studying popular songs, Indian melodies, American rhythms. Some of these play a prominent part in the opera, especially the tune known as "Old Dog Tray."

Composition went slowly, but *Fanciulla* was finished in 1910 and the Metropolitan gave the world première on Dec. 10 of that year. What a cast! The three principals were Emmy Destinn, Enrico Caruso and Pasquale Amato, with such stalwarts as Andrés de Segurola and Adamo Didur also on prominent display. Toscanini conducted. Belasco himself worked on the production, determined "to make the artists act as well as sing." It was the most publicized première in the history of the Metropolitan Opera. Tickets were impossible to get; the scalpers had a field day. Day after day, before and after the première, the New York newspapers ran story after story about Puccini and his opera.

The composer felt that he would have a hit on his hands. A few days before the première he wrote to his wife: "The rehearsals are going very well. I believe it will be a success and let's hope it will be a big one. Tomorrow is the dress rehearsal. After the performance there will be a supper and reception at the Vanderbilts' and perhaps others to follow—what a pleasure! . . . The opera emerges splendidly, the first act a little long but the second act magnificent and the third act grandiose. . . . Caruso is magnificent in his part, Destinn not bad but she needs more energy. Toscanini the *zenith!*—kind, good, adorable—in short I am content with my work and I hope for the best. But how tremendously difficult it is, this music and the staging!"

Indeed, *Fanciulla* does pose more problems than any Puccini opera to that point. He asked a great deal from the producers (and was happy to see that they gave him eight horses on stage for the third act), and the music itself marked something of a departure. In *Fanciulla* there are relatively few of the knock-'em-dead arias that there are in the previous operas. The chorus is much more prominent; the orchestral texture is far richer: there is a striving for the kind of intensity and local color that was to come to fruition many years later in *Turandot*.

There are many anticipations of *Turandot* in *La Fanciulla del West*. The first-act chorus, starting with the miners singing *Quanto piangera*, is strongly reminiscent of the Moon Chorus in the later opera. The slithery harmonies of Rance's *Minnie, dalla mia casa*—a gorgeous piece of music—are new to Puccini and those, too, were to find their echo in *Turandot*. There are some breathtakingly beautiful things in *Fanciulla*, and it deserves to be a repertory piece. As for its libretto—well, what American, weaned on horse operas, sympathetic to that curious art form named the cowboy movie (*Fanciulla* is about gold miners, but it still remains basically an oater), can sneer at it? We have had much worse than this libretto on film and television, and will continue to have worse. In its way, the libretto of *La Fanciulla del West* is a wonderful period piece. Just sit back and enjoy it.

Then there is that famous poker game between Minnie and Jack Rance. No musicologist has taken a close look at it; musicologists do not apparently have much expertise in that noble game. It demonstrates, if nothing else, that Minnie was an awful poker player. No wonder she felt she had to cheat.

Here's the situation. Rance has cornered the wounded Dick Johnson in Minnie's cabin. Rance is madly in love with her. She of course loves Johnson. Minnie appeals to Rance's gambling instincts. Let's settle this between ourselves, she says. We'll play poker, best two games out of three. If you win you'll get Johnson and me also. If I win, you go away and keep your mouth shut.

Rance agrees. Minnie goes to one side, to get a new pack of cards. We see her lift her skirt and put five cards into her stocking. Then she returns to the table. Minnie and Rance are playing draw poker. One would think they would play three showdown hands, in which five cards are opened up, one by one. But no; they draw.

Game No. 1: Minnie draws two cards and wins the hand with king high. Rance also has king high, but Minnie's queen tops Rance's jack. The question is: Why did Minnie draw two cards? She did not have a pair. Was she trying to draw two to a straight or flush? Terrible poker.

Game No. 2: Rance draws one. Minnie again draws two. Rance announces aces up: *"Due assi e un paio."* Two aces and a pair. He wins. Again one can well ask: Why did Minnie draw only two cards?

Game No. 3: Rance shuffles and offers the pack to Minnie. "Cut!" He deals and they pick up their hands. "Discard," says Rance. Minnie discards—what? Two cards again, the silly girl. Jack discards three. He gleefully announces three kings. "I have won!" Minnie creates a diversion, switches her hand and announces a full house—three aces and a pair. Rance honors his debt and slinks off.

What would have happened had Rance held a pair of aces in that third game?

The poker game was even funnier when Dorothy Kirsten was singing Minnie at the Metropolitan. Kirsten dealt all the hands and never bothered to put the discards back into the deck, pushing completed hands to one side and dealing what was left of the pack. In Game No. 2 Rance had two aces. In Game No. 3, Minnie has three. The besotted Rance did not notice there were five aces in that particular pack of cards. But there were some in the audience who did, and they were amused no end. Doesn't anybody at the Met, they were asking, play poker?

OCT. 16, 1977

The première of the complete, three-act Lulu *at the Paris Opéra on Feb. 24, 1979 was probably the most glamorous operatic event since World War II. Everybody was there. Those who had been worried about the staging had their fears fully borne out. The same Patrice Chéreau, who had mangled the* Ring *cycle at the Bayreuth Centennial in 1976, did an equivalent job on* Lulu. *He contemptuously disregarded Berg's own stage directions and even—for the sake of a cheap stage effect—actually distorted a key element in the final scene. Berg specialists were furious. There was nothing but praise, however, for the conducting of Pierre Boulez and the Cerha reconstruction of the last act. I thought Cerha's work was brilliant, and said so in my review, but I was willing to defer ultimate judgment until a superspecialist like George Perle heard it. In Paris I managed to get a pirated cassette of the last act. That was on the day I was leaving for home. At the airport in Paris I called Mr. Perle. Would he like to hear the cassette that evening? Would he! I arrived home around 6 P.M., phoned Mr. Perle, and he came right over. We pulled out the piano score, started the cassette and followed the opera. When it was over, Mr. Perle looked at me. "It's very, very good," he simply said.*

Awaiting the Complete "Lulu"

THE STRIKE in the opera houses of Paris is over, and on Saturday the Opéra will go on with Alban Berg's *Lulu* as scheduled. But this is not an ordinary *Lulu*. It will be the first staging ever of the complete work, with its third act reconstructed by an Austrian composer-conductor named Friedrich Cerha. (Up to now, *Lulu* has been staged as a two-act opera, though in recent years parts of the third act have been used. Those sections are taken from the published *Lulu* Suite, which contains materials from the last act.) Pierre Boulez will conduct the première, the title role will be sung by Teresa Stratas, and from all over the world people are rushing to Paris for this unusual and prestigious event. Rolf Liebermann, the director of the Paris Opéra, must be going out of his mind trying to fill ticket requests for the first night.

It is by no means the first time in musical history that an unfinished work by a major composer has been brought to completion. Bach, for instance, never finished his *Kunst der Fuge,* and experts have been playing around with it ever since. Mozart's pupil Süssmayr finished the Requiem. Puccini left *Turandot* in an incomplete state, and Franco Alfano completed it. It was Philip Jarnach who brought Busoni's opera *Doktor Faust* to its conclusion. Russian musicologists have given us Tchaikovsky's Seventh Symphony, to their own satisfaction if nobody else's. And so on.

But a complete third act of an opera? Can this be the real thing, or is it a mere approximation of what Berg had in mind?

The answer can be pieced together, mostly through the work of the American composer and Berg specialist, George Perle. Mr. Perle has spent decades working on the problem of *Lulu,* and has written a great deal about it. The current issue of the *Musical Times* in London has a piece by him that is a summation of the events leading up to the forthcoming *Lulu.* Conversations with former and current editors of Universal Edition, Berg's publisher, have helped fill out the picture. It turns out that there is no great secret about the unfinished third act of *Lulu.* The only secret seems to be why the publisher has never brought out any of the voluminous materials relating to the opera—and that, too, is being explained by the attitude of Berg's widow, Helene.

The chronological survey would start with the last years of Berg's life. He was working on *Lulu.* In 1934 he wrote a letter to Anton Webern saying that he had finished the work and was going to retouch it. Berg died on Dec. 24, 1935. He never did fully orchestrate Act III. But he left a "Particell"—a short score, with some indications of orchestration. Every note of the third act except for a few measures of a vocal quartet is contained in the Particell. Berg also left sketches and other materials, including the typescript of the Act III libretto.

Erwin Stein, who had made the piano score of the first two

acts (which were published) also prepared Act III in its entirety. (A vocal score has all of the vocal lines, with the orchestration condensed into a realization for solo piano.) Universal started to engrave Stein's vocal score. Then came the Anschluss, and Hitler took over. Berg was one of the composers on the hate list of National Socialism. All work on *Lulu* was instantly dropped. *Lulu* had had its world première in Zurich in 1937. There were to be no further productions until after the war.

Then why did not Universal hasten to publish Stein's definitive Act III after 1945? The answer has to do with Mrs. Berg. She appears to have been mildly dotty. She claimed to be in communication with her late husband. They spoke to each other every day. He kept telling her that *Lulu* was not to be completed. Not only that. Arnold Schoenberg, Anton Webern and Alexander Zemlinsky, Berg's closest friends and associates (Schoenberg had been Berg's teacher) had told her that *Lulu* would be impossible to complete. So said Mrs. Berg.

Stein died in 1958. Universal, honoring Mrs. Berg's wishes (she also was the executrix of the estate), firmly sat on all *Lulu* materials. Nobody was allowed to see anything. Mr. Perle tried desperately to view the *Lulu* relicts. He was turned down. He was also told by Universal that there were no plans to publish Stein's vocal score of Act III.

So matters remained until 1963. In that year Mr. Perle was given permission to go to the Universal headquarters in Vienna and examine the *Lulu* material. The Particell and the libretto were placed before him. Mr. Perle was electrified. *Lulu,* from what he could see, was eminently capable of being completed. Indeed, it would not be that difficult a task. He set forth his findings in a long letter to Dr. Alfred A. Kalmus of Universal. The letter was published in the spring-summer 1964 issue of *Perspectives of New Music.*

"With the exception of not more than 20 bars in Act III, Scene 2," Mr. Perle wrote, "which are almost but not entirely completed, the third act of *Lulu* is complete, both musically and dramatically, including the full orchestration of three-fifths of Scene 2 and almost the same proportion of Scene 1." Mr. Perle, who is a specialist in twelve-tone music, took a close look at the few incomplete bars, and found many indications by Berg that suggested those bars were not, after all, "incomplete." No problems were posed, said Mr. Perle. "With the assistance of the suggestions provided by Berg himself, I cannot see why a satisfactory solution should require more than a few hours of work."

Mr. Perle pointed out that the Particell of *Lulu* was not in any sense a sketch. "It is, on the contrary, a final statement of the music and text, indicating (with the negligible exceptions referred to above) every note of music, every metronome mark, every word of text, and every stage direction, preparatory to the final realization of the work in full score." A study of the Particell "reveals Berg's explicit intentions regarding the exact orchestration . . . beyond any reasonable doubt. In fact, Berg omits instrumental indications because the exact scoring of these passages has already been determined and can be reconstructed easily without the aid of such indications."

Other interesting points are discussed by Mr. Perle. He mentions a letter from Berg to Schoenberg in which Berg discusses certain ideas in the last act, among which is the plan of having Lulu's clients (in Act III she is a prostitute in London) played by the same characters who had been Lulu's victims in the first two acts. Thus a parallel would be drawn. The Doctor returns as the Professor; the Painter as the Negro; Dr. Schön as Jack the Ripper. Mr. Perle and other Berg specialists are grimly waiting to see if the Paris production, staged by Patrice Chéreau, follows this plan. For some reason they seem to have no great confidence in Mr. Chéreau. They have seen, or read about, what Mr. Chéreau did to Wagner's *Ring* at the 1976 Bayreuth Festival.

One point made by Mr. Perle about this plan in Act III is that the music of the new characters, who are alter egos of the old characters, duplicates the music of the previous two acts. Since the earlier music had been fully scored by Berg, the same or a similar orchestration could apply to the equivalent episodes in Act III, making the task of reconstruction that much easier.

Therefore, concludes Mr. Perle, "I would go so far as to say that it is an error to speak of another person 'completing' *Lulu* for in every essential respect this has already been done by Alban Berg."

Mr. Perle, who knows more about *Lulu* than, possibly, the composer himself, would have been happy to have scored Act III. But Universal preferred somebody closer to home, and Mr. Cerha was chosen. Friedrich Cerha, born in Vienna in 1926, is a specialist in avant-garde music. He conducts, composes and teaches. Apparently his name was being discussed about a decade ago in relation to a completion of *Lulu*. Gossip has it that Mr. Boulez was approached, but he said that he was too busy. Gossip also has it that Universal selected Mr. Cerha on Mr. Boulez's recommendation.

The tightly inbred world of modern music being what it is, there is by no means unanimous happiness about the choice of Mr. Boulez as the *Lulu* conductor and, presumably, the overseer of the Cerha orchestration. There are those who have little respect for Mr. Boulez, calling him "an opportunist" and a person who takes the easy way out. Many specialists who have devoted years to the Schoenberg-Berg-Webern school consider the Boulez recording of *Wozzeck* to be an absolute disgrace. Those critics are going to be awaiting the Paris première with sharpened knives. It's going to be a hot time in the old town come the evening of February 24.

FEB. 18, 1979

Perhaps there is no clear line between musical comedy and opera, but Marcel Prawy raised the question and an answer had to be attempted. Some six months later I interviewed Franz Allers. He has a foot in both camps, and I posed the question to him. A musical comedy is not opera and never can be, he said. "Opera demands so much more in the way of singing. Its architecture is so much more complex. . . . And in opera the words carry the music. In musicals, the music carries the words." Opera, he concluded, was much more complicated than even the most ambitious musical.

Why Isn't a Musical Comedy
an Opera?

MARCEL PRAWY asked a hard question the other week in Washington, during the visit of the Vienna State Opera. The occasion was a panel on opera set up by the Music Critics Association. Mr. Prawy, an urbane, trilingual, knowledgeable man, is an official of the Vienna State Opera. He also is an admirer of Leonard Bernstein, and he simply cannot understand why certain American critics refuse to recognize the clearly obvious fact that Mr. Bernstein is the greatest thing that has happened to music in America since Thomas Jefferson played the fiddle.

Anyway, the subject of repertory was being discussed. Mr. Prawy said that the repertory in many European opera houses, including the Vienna State Opera, is much more flexible than it is in American houses. In Vienna, he said, you might have Wagner one night and Johann Strauss the next. Puccini may jostle *My Fair Lady*.

"Tell me," said Mr. Prawy, "why is not *West Side Story* as much an opera as *Le Nozze di Figaro?* I ask this question in all sincerity and humility. Will somebody tell me why *West Side Story* is not an opera?"

But answers there were none. There was a somewhat embarrassed sputter as the panel and the critics in the audience tentatively groped with the problem. Everybody except Mr. Prawy seemed to think that *West Side Story* was not an opera, but nobody could say exactly why. Mr. Prawy, a gentleman of impeccable manners, did not exactly gloat, but he did look a bit smug.

The question is an irritating one, easier asked than answered. Years back this column suggested that Mozart's *Magic Flute* was, in its way, a musical comedy: it had spoken dialogue, it had strong elements of humor, it was topical (the characters, it is generally conceded, represented such figures of the day as

Empress Maria Theresa), it moved fast. The same, of course, can be said of *West Side Story.* So is the Bernstein musical comedy also an opera?

Or what about the *Mahagonny* of Kurt Weill and Bertolt Brecht, which the Metropolitan Opera staged on Nov. 16? Many look down on it because of its jazz, its cabaret elements and its basic simplicity. But Weill insisted that it was an opera. Which does not necessarily make it so. Or what about the Stephen Sondheim *Sweeney Todd,* which Beverly Sills is thinking about producing at the New York City Opera? This ambitious work is almost through-composed, and a good case can be made for it as opera, even with its lengthy dialogue. *Candide, Porgy and Bess* —there are many works from the Broadway stage that have operatic pretensions. But are they operas?

The standard definition of opera calls the form a drama, either tragic or comic, usually sung throughout (though, as in *The Magic Flute,* it also may have spoken dialogue), with orchestral accompaniment and scenic investiture. The conventions of opera—recitative, singing emotions instead of speaking them, the constant repetition of words within an aria or ensemble, and so on—have excited ridicule from the days of Addison and Steele. Opera has been described as a mélange of the arts that spoils all of them. Saint-Evremonde described opera as "A bizarre affair of poetry and music in which the poet and the musician, each equally obstructed by the other, give themselves no end of trouble to produce a wretched result."

But most people happily accept the conventions, and opera remains a thriving art form. What about comic opera as opposed to opera? Has it any special characteristics? The Harvard Dictionary of Music defines operetta as the "general name for an opera or other dramatic work with a large admixture of music, on a light or sentimental subject, with a happy ending, and in which the comic element plays a certain part. The term thus comprises a number of types, such as the operetta, opéra-bouffe, musical comedy, etc., the distinctions between which are not clearly marked."

That's the trouble. The distinctions are not clearly marked. But it seems to this writer that the *aim* of the work has to enter into the definition. Is the work intended as pure entertainment or does it aim at something higher? Is its message universal or ephemeral?

We all know that no opera composer ever despised money or artistic success. But we also like to think that Mozart composed *Die Zauberflöte* or that Verdi composed *La Traviata* out of passionate conviction, backed by genius, and there is every indication that those two composers wrote without ever lowering their Olympian standards. They might have changed an aria, or recast an opera that needed revision, but they did so according to their own dictates and not the dictates of immediate audience success.

That is not true of the Broadway musical. The musical is *entirely* governed by what the composer, director, producer and backers think will "go." It is a commercial venture. As such it has to appeal to a mass common denominator.

That is not to say that a skilled composer—a Kurt Weill in *Lady in the Dark* or a Bernstein in *On the Town*—cannot get a good deal of sophistication into his writing. But it is a writing that necessarily must avoid pronounced subtlety, and almost always it reflects the popular music of the period. At the turn of the century it was ragtime, or ballads. In the 1920's it was jazz. In recent years it has been rock in one or another of its manifestations. The Broadway musical is a carefully assembled package, reflecting whatever is in fashion at the moment. There is no art for art's sake nonsense here. Before it comes to Broadway, a musical is carefully tested for audience reaction on the road. Songs or ensembles, no matter how brilliantly composed, are ruthlessly discarded if they do not work—that is, if audiences do not immediately respond.

Nor does the composer of a Broadway musical, even so highly regarded a composer as Bernstein, score his own show. Experts are called in. For decades it was Robert Russell Bennett. More recently such specialists as Hershy Kay have been taking over that specialized job. Presumably the feeling is that the composer of a Broadway musical does not have his finger on the public pulse. We can't risk a million-dollar investment with an orchestration that is different from all other tried and true orchestrations, can we? The public is used to a certain kind of sound, and that sound it gets.

Also, as Cecil Smith pointed out in his valuable little book, *Musical Comedy in America,* there is an additional element that is a unique feature of musical comedy. "Musical comedy," Smith wrote, "may be distinguished from such other forms of entertainment as comic opera and burlesque by its direct and essentially unstylized appropriation of vernacular types of song, dance and subject matter; and it may be distinguished from its chief source of inspiration, the variety show, by its employment of a plot and, at least in some slight degree, of consistent characterization."

So the Broadway musical, as opposed to opera or comic opera, does have certain identifying characteristics. It is much more a collaborative effort (in which an orchestrator is called in to help the composer), it is governed exclusively by commercial considerations, it is always in the vernacular, it almost always reflects the most popular musical trends of the period, and it is much simpler and less sophisticated or musically inventive than opera or comic opera. Which, alas, still does not clearly answer the question about *Sweeney Todd, Mahagonny, Candide* and the other lyric stage works that have a foot in both camps. Most likely a classification is impossible, and one can put up as good an argument for them being "musicals" as for being "operas."

All of the above is in the nature of trying to pin things down, and is not meant to be pejorative. One would have to be deaf and completely unaware of what history means not to realize that the American musical stage has given the world a body of songs with incomparably more life and staying power than anything our "serious" composers have ever been able to create. Name one tune from an American opera. You won't get very far. But dozens of wonderful tunes from American musicals can instantly be cited. They have remained popular through the years, as much loved in Europe as they are in America. The best American tunesmiths always knew how to work within the formulas, just as the same can be said of a British dramatist named William Shakespeare. If they did not have the genius and scope of the great composers, the best composers of musical comedy at least have had the ability to write songs that have managed to evoke a universal response. This is art, and it cannot be dismissed or placed in a lower category than "art music" or "serious music." If longevity means anything, it has to be placed in a *higher* category. For very little music composed by serious American composers this century has lived, but an amazing number of songs from musical comedy have remained as fixtures in the American consciousness, and subconscious too, for 50 years and more.

Nov. 21, 1979

PART VI

Singers and Singing

That his [Nicola Porpora's] pupils were extraordinary singers is not a figment of the novelist's imagination. Specimens of the outrageous vocal feats which they habitually executed, and which they compelled composers to devise for them, may be seen in the works of Hasse, Porpora himself, Handel and Mozart. The only artists we have who can compare with these singers are our circus acrobats, who make their living by performing athletic impossibilities with grace, ease and perfect tranquility.

—GEORGE BERNARD SHAW

In 1956 I started writing articles for the Sunday magazine section of the Times, *and in 1957 I was sent to Chicago for the following Tebaldi interview. Conductors and press people at the Metropolitan Opera warned me that she would be a hard lady to confront. She did not talk much, she would rather play with her dolls, and Mama would be around to interfere. The implication was that Tebaldi was not a very intelligent woman. Before I visited her I sent a few dozen roses to her hotel room. That seemed to please her. I found her voluble, cheerful, delightful and utterly unpretentious. The* Times *refused to honor the price of the roses on my expense account. That still rankles.*

The figures on her earnings that I cited may sound like small beer today. In 1957 they were enormous.

Renata Tebaldi:
A Prima Donna Who
Doesn't Act Like One

ON HER American tour three years ago, Renata Tebaldi was accompanied by her mother, a secretary and some thirty pieces of luggage. Two years ago she came with mother, secretary and some forty pieces of luggage. This year she traveled with her mother, a secretary, a maid, a gray miniature French poodle named New (because it came from New Jersey), and some fifty pieces of luggage. This contents her admirers, who take the ever-increasing appurtenances as a symbol of her progress as a prima donna.

But few singers act less the prima donna. Miss Tebaldi seldom leaves her apartment, indulges in no great bursts of temperament, is shy, polite, quiet and dignified. She is the subject of absolutely no derogatory backstage gossip. Some years ago it was rumored that she was having a romance with a singer. That singer has since married and the rumors have long died down. There is no man in Miss Tebaldi's life. She is never in the newspapers, except for reviews of her work as a soprano who owns what many consider the finest Italian female voice before the public today.

It is a voice that has made her the toast of Italy, the joy of American opera houses, the comfort of managers and impresarios, the idol of about a hundred Renata Tebaldi Music Clubs throughout Europe and America, and which has given her an income that runs well into six figures annually. Her American royalties on records alone come to about $30,000 a year. As of last August, 629,993 of her discs had been sold here.

Miss Tebaldi is said to command the highest figure per performance of any singer before the public today. She is notably close-mouthed about her business affairs, but she is reputed to drive a hard bargain. "She may be naïve to a lot of people, but she's not naïve about money," one of her associates has said. A concert manager in New York says that she is charging the highest prices since Caruso—and getting them. For a recital engagement her fee is $5,000. So many cities have thrust forward $5,000 checks—with an extra thousand or so as an added inducement, in some cases—that Miss Tebaldi cannot begin to fill all the recital dates offered her. At the Chicago Opera her fee is probably close to $3,000 every time she sets foot on stage. At the Metropolitan Opera the maximum fee for any singer is supposed to be $1,500, but people in the business suggest that perhaps in Miss Tebaldi's case an upward revision or understanding of some sort may quietly have been made. This, of course, is indignantly cited by the Metropolitan as an instance of the depths to which base gossip can descend.

Impresarios find Miss Tebaldi well worth her fees. She opens her season at the Metropolitan on Thursday, as Tosca, and the house has long been sold out. It probably will be sold out for the ten other performances she will sing this season. She was, as always, the biggest attraction of the current Chicago Opera season. Ever since her first season in America, seven years ago, she has never sung to a house that was not entirely sold out.

She is admired and often adored by her colleagues. Even conductors like her, though not invariably. While cooperative and considerate, she has certain firm ideas about staging and tempo, and she generally has her way. She will never argue. She will cross her arms, cloak her regal body with dignity a yard thick, and slowly tap her foot on the stage. Minerva could do little more. Abashed conductors have been known to break into a sweat, gulp and apologize.

Because she is not, in the inelegant words of some opera singers, a curtain hog, and because she meets her colleagues more than halfway, astonished tenors find themselves doing things for her that they had not done since the age of seven in Sunday school. Not too long ago, in Puccini's *Manon Lescaut,* she refused to take a solo curtain after the third act because, as she said, "It is the tenor's act." The tenor in question nearly fainted; this had never happened to him before, in twenty-plus years of singing in opera houses throughout the world. It so happened that during the last-act duet, Miss Tebaldi made a bad attack on a note—something that seldom happens to her—and the tenor obligingly cut his own note short. After the performance he was told that he had done a rare and noble thing; and, in all truth, he probably was the first singer since Chauntecleer sang to Pertelote to let go of a good high note. He shrugged. "Oh, well," he said. "Glad to do it for her." He thought a moment and added, "After all, it wasn't ———," mentioning the name of a tempestuous and temperamental soprano.

In the Italian repertory, only one soprano offers Miss Tebaldi any real competition today. That is Maria Meneghini Callas. (Zinka Milanov, the great Yugoslav who specializes in the Italian repertory, belongs to another category, the dramatic soprano.) Miss Tebaldi's relations with Miss Callas are rather curious. "We are not rivals," Miss Tebaldi insists. "Our voices are too different. I have not run across her since Rio de Janeiro in 1951. All the stories that we are enemies are just publicity."

But then she contradicts herself and admits that perhaps there might be just a wee bit of rivalry between them. Miss Tebaldi was a star at La Scala when, in the early nineteen fifties, The Other One began to attract attention. (Friends of Miss Tebaldi never refer to Miss Callas by name; it is always The Other One.) At La Scala the Tebaldi and Callas factions created a great uproar. There were internal politics, about which Miss Tebaldi does not care to talk, and she left the house in 1954. She has not sung there since.

Ordinarily there are nothing but polite purrings when the two divas discuss each other, but last year Miss Callas went on record as accusing Miss Tebaldi of lacking spirit. For the first and only time, Miss Tebaldi struck back and, in a letter to a national magazine, she wrote, "Signora Callas admits to being a woman of character and says I have no backbone. I reply I have one great thing that she has not—a heart. . . . It was not Signora Callas who caused me to stay away from La Scala. I sang there before she did and I consider myself a *creatura de La Scala.* I stayed away of my own free will because an atmosphere not at all pleasant had been created there."

It is safe to say that there is no love lost between the two prima donnas. Yet when The Other One made her debut at the Metropolitan, Miss Tebaldi deplored the "bad taste" of another soprano who flounced down the aisle on opening night. "It was Callas' night," Miss Tebaldi said. "It should have been left to her."

Miss Tebaldi's voice is described by the Italians as a *lirico spinto.* This is a vocal category between a lyric and a dramatic soprano. Butterfly for example, is a lyric role. Aïda is a dramatic one. Tosca is a characteristic *spinto* role. A good *spinto* can manage lyric and dramatic roles as well. Miss Tebaldi's Aïda and Tosca are well known to American operagoers and, after her Metropolitan appearances, she will sing her first Butterfly anywhere at the opera house in Barcelona.

She claims a three-octave compass for her voice—high C to the first C in the bass clef. This is a fairly unusual range, and that low C is something even few contraltos would dare attempt. But it is not her range that makes Miss Tebaldi's voice so individual. Vocal characteristics are difficult to describe and many of her admirers have talked themselves hoarse in a vain effort to pin down the elusive characteristics of her style.

Their conclusions can be summarized somewhat as follows: she has the most even range, they say, of any soprano now active, and there is no shifting of gears when she comes to a different register; her pitch is near-perfect, and almost never does she depart from the dead center of a note; the timbre of the voice is velvety, sweet and intensely feminine; she produces her tones with clarity and purity, without the tremolo, or wobble, that afflicts some otherwise great singers. "She's all woman, that's the way I look at it," says one of her admirers.

Miss Tebaldi has about thirty-six roles at her call (not one of which requires anything so out-of-the-way as a low C), among them the leading soprano parts in such curiosities as Spontini's *Fernando Cortez* and *Olympie,* Rossini's *Siege of Corinth* and *L'Assedio di Cortino,* Handel's *Julius Caesar* and Verdi's *Joan of Arc.* Two roles she would love to sing at the Metropolitan are Fedora and Adriana Lecouvreur in the Giordano and Cilea operas of the same names.

She started almost at the top and she reached it without any great effort. Born in Pesaro (the birthplace of Rossini) on Feb. 1, 1922, she was an earnest piano student when she discovered certain vocal possibilities. Several years at the Conservatory of Parma followed—her father, now retired, played the cello in an orchestra there—and were topped off by study with Carmen Melis at the Pesaro Conservatory. Melis, who sang with the Hammerstein Opera in New York and later appeared in Chicago, was one of the great Toscas of all time.

Miss Tebaldi made her debut in Rovigo as Elena in Boito's *Mefistofele.* It was on May 23 or 24, 1944; she forgets the exact date. She then stopped her operatic career until the war was over. Her first big success came with her Desdemona in *Otello* at La Scala in 1947, though the previous year she had been chosen by Toscanini for Verdi's *Te Deum* at the Scala inaugural concert after the hostilities. She was scared, "but Maestro was very kind to me." (Once again she was to sing with Toscanini. That was also at the Scala, in Verdi's Requiem in 1951, and Toscanini told friends that she sang like an angel. The Metropolitan Opera press department once asked her what she considered her outstanding achievement. "Satisfying Maestro Toscanini," she answered.)

After her Italian success, Miss Tebaldi began the international operatic trek. Lisbon in 1947. San Francisco in 1950. South America in 1951. France the same year. New York in 1955. Stuttgart in 1956. She has not yet sung at the Vienna Staatsoper, but that deficiency will be remedied next season. The Viennese will hear her Tosca and Desdemona.

She sings only in Italian and that includes three Wagnerian roles as well as Marguerite in *Faust*. It is her theory that it is necessary to change the position of the voice when singing in other languages. French, she says, is too nasal for her; German, too guttural. Anyway, she has not been brought up in those languages and shudders at the idea of singing French and German with an Italian accent. She realizes, though, that sooner or later she will have to make the attempt to learn roles outside the Italian repertory.

Often queried about her favorite roles, Miss Tebaldi has a standard answer: "Everything." But it is no secret that she has a special fondness for Desdemona, Tosca and Adriana Lecouvreur.

She is a commanding figure on stage, though nobody has ever put in a claim that she is a great actress. Many think that she is about eight feet tall. She may give that impression, especially on stage, but on her vital statistics sheet at the Metropolitan Opera she is listed as five feet, eight inches. High heels may add another two inches. At that, she generally towers over most of the tenors who partner her. By some inexplicable rule of nature, tenors run short; and often, the louder the voice, the shorter the body.

She has blue eyes, dark brown hair, a nose with a slight upward tilt, a perfect complexion—a very handsome woman. In repose, her face has a madonna-like serenity. Audiences at the Metropolitan this week are going to see a Tebaldi sixteen pounds lighter than last year's model. People, she says, want to see a slim prima donna. Some singers feel that dieting is ruinous to the voice, but Miss Tebaldi does not seem to worry.

At home she does no vocalizing at all. Nor will she sing full voice at any rehearsal but the final one. On the evenings of her performances, she gets to the opera house early. She brings the vocal score with her, and also a bag of little dolls dressed in operatic costumes. (Miss Tebaldi likes to play with dolls; in Toronto one year, on tour with the Metropolitan, she and a teddy bear had a great affair, and she added it to a huge collection she keeps in her home in Italy.)

When she enters her dressing room, she prays; she is very religious. Then she goes to a rehearsal room and plays through the opera on the piano, humming her role. Next, she gets into costume. Her mother always helps her and also does her hair. Miss Tebaldi and her mother are inseparable; seldom has anybody seen them apart. Finally she crosses herself, kisses Mama and steps on stage.

She says that she is nervous during the five minutes preceding her entry. As soon as she hears her cue, she forgets everything but the task at hand. On stage, she is described as strictly business, with no departures from an expected pattern. It would never occur to her to unbend as some sopranos do. Once, during *Aïda*, just after George London finished a solo, Zinka Milanov turned her back to the audience and whispered: "George, how is the baby? I understand she's a darling." If Tebaldi ever did that, her colleagues would stop singing from shock. On the other hand, she has helped many a nervous debutante, and once she ushered a singer in a minor role up front so that he could see the conductor's cues.

Once the performance is out of the way, she forgets about it. She does not brood about a mistake, unlike one of her colleagues who, if he fluffs a note, goes to his dressing room, literally bangs his head against the wall, smashes the piano and screams that his career is finished. Miss Tebaldi takes things in stride. In any case, she seldom makes a musical mistake. Conductors say that she is a perfectionist, almost never misses an entry, has good rhythm, is a good ensemble partner and is always considerate on stage.

But she does not have a driving temperament. Several of her friends feel that things have come too easily for her. They would like her to assert herself to a greater degree, to break the placidity in which she has enveloped herself. "She's never irritated," says one friend, with real irritation. "She hasn't even got any enemies to get irritated at."

Her friends have all kinds of theories to account for her quiet, secluded life. One says that she has an inferiority complex. Another says that it is really a child, a sweet and simple child, who sits at home with Mama wrapped uncomfortably in the apparel of the great diva. They would like her to have the burning ambition and temperament of The Other One. Then, they say, she would be the greatest singer who ever lived.

But none of this bothers her public, many of whom do regard her as the greatest singer who ever lived. Least of all does it bother the members of the New York chapter of the Renata Tebaldi Music Club. Recently, one of the members, attempting to describe her, started out by saying, "She looks like a vision and sings like a goddess," and went on in ascending terms from there. This fan, a dedicated gentleman with a successful business and a Tebaldi complex that boils like the interior of the sun, once saw her off on a trip. "I offered her a pack of chewing gum," he said, "and do you know? She . . . she . . ."—and his voice broke—"she *took* it!"

Nov. 15, 1957

Less than six months after this magazine profile appeared, Leonard Warren was dead. On March 4, 1960, he was singing in Verdi's La Forza del Destino *and, toward the end of the third act, pitched forward and died. Howard Taubman was reviewing the performance. Because of the deadline pressures those days, he had left after the* Solenne in quest'ora *duet and was not in the audience when the tragedy occurred. His wife phoned him, and she and the Metropolitan kept feeding him information while he wrote the news story. I wandered into the office after my concert, and Mr. Taubman told me to drop everything and write the obituary notice. As I had written the magazine story only such a short time before, I had the material at my fingertips. A unique voice had gone.*

The Big Voice and Big Temperament of Leonard Warren

LEONARD WARREN, who will sing the leading baritone role in *Il Trovatore* when the Metropolitan Opera opens its seventy-fifth season tomorrow night, is a human bellows mounted on matchsticks who, many believe, is the greatest baritone in the Italian repertory today. This will not be his first opening night; he has participated in four previous ones since his debut at the Met in 1938. American-born, American-trained, he is very much a prophet with honor in his own land. With his fifty-one-inch chest (unexpanded), size 17½ collar, massive head, almost six feet of height, generous abdominal proportions and well over 200 pounds of weight—all supported on a pair of thin-looking legs—he has a habit of dominating any stage on which he appears.

He did not burst upon the scene, and for his first few years at the Met he sang only minor roles, although even at the beginning critics expressed amazement at the size and quality of his voice. When he moved to leading roles he was more or less taken for granted, and it has been only within the past decade that he has enjoyed the exalted place he now holds.

One reason is that Warren is a musician who constantly tries to improve himself, and his art is in a process of constant development. He has progressed from singer to artist. Every year sees a new, and usually effective, bit of stage business added to this or that role, and in certain parts—Rigoletto, say, or Iago—his pre-eminence is unquestioned. He has learned, among other things, how to act with his voice as well as with his body. His stage gestures are inclined to be broad, and when he registers scorn, hate or love nobody could possibly mistake his meaning, not even the soprano opposite him. But while he can be called a serviceable actor, there are subtleties in his voice that his acting has never attained, and when he sings *Era la notte,* from *Otello,* all in an insinuating, oily pianissimo, it is a triumph of the vocal art.

Warren is rather proud of his acting ability, though some of the public are amused instead of awed by his gifts in that direction. When it comes to the purely vocal aspects of his art, however, he has conquered all criticism, and offhand one cannot think of a Warren review that expresses anything but admiration for his noble, full-throated and flexible voice.

Through the years he has sung a total of 636 performances of twenty-two roles at the Met (over a fifth of them as Rigoletto) and until last season, when the Asian flu hit him, he almost never canceled. His voice starts at a low G and runs without a perceptible break to a high B flat. When he feels exceptionally good he can take a high C, and at parties he may amuse the guests by singing tenor arias in the original key, shaking the walls with a thunderous high C in *Di quella pira.*

He is proud of that high range. Very few baritones have ever had it. Last summer he was making records in Rome. He and his wife, accompanied by the tenor Richard Tucker and his wife and a few other Met singers and officials, got together one night and went to a restaurant for a good meal. By the time they were finished it was rather late, the place was clearing out, and a tired guitar player was plucking away at Italian songs.

Suddenly Warren threw his head back and let loose. Tucker got into the spirit of the occasion and also started singing. The others joined in. All the diners rushed back to hear the impromptu concert, and all the singers at Warren's table tried to outdo one another.

Matters followed a natural course and Warren tried his high

C. He broke on the note, looked fearfully ashamed and ran his finger around his collar. Everybody tried to comfort him: a busy day, tired, a full meal . . . Warren glowered. He stood up. "Again!" he told the guitarist. This time he landed square on the note. The sound brought the kitchen help into the act; they rushed out to observe the maker of miracles. Then they, too, joined in the singing. "It was quite an evening," says one of the participants, in a gorgeous understatement.

Like most front-line singers, Warren is temperamental. Not much has been made public about his backstage flurries, but at the Met he is regarded in certain quarters with mixed emotions. He tells other singers how to sing, conductors how to conduct, directors how to direct, photographers how to photograph, recording engineers how to engineer and costumers how to costume; and, they say, if Verdi were around he would tell him how to compose. One backstage worker describes him as "a pain in the neck with a great voice," and that feeling is rather prevalent throughout the house.

In the hierarchy of operatic temperaments he ranks high, but leading singers are expected to be temperamental, and managers have learned to put up with them. Gatti-Casazza once said to a person who complained of the flamboyant goings-on of one of the leading singers, "Madame, it is the custom of the opera." A great voice can make amends for any amount of personal idiosyncrasies, and Warren has a great voice. Therefore the Met, or any other opera house, will gladly accept his whimsies.

He is determined to have his way, not so much because he is stubborn as because he *knows* he is right, an opinion not always shared by his colleagues. Once, a few seasons back, he went up to his conductor, between the third and fourth acts of the evening's opera, and grabbed him by the throat. "What are you trying to do?" he snarled. "Kill us? We only have one pair of lungs. If you don't stick to the proper tempo, so help me I'll walk off the stage." Several conductors have threatened to quit because of him.

On curtain calls his attitude is an unyielding 200-plus pounds of stern, unmoving principle. He demands his rights. In *Macbeth* he would not let Leonie Rysanek take the final curtain; the opera was named *Macbeth*, and he was Macbeth, and it was *his* opera. She was a bit put out, but later said that she understood his point of view. Had it been *Aïda*, which would have made it *her* opera, he gladly would have let her take the curtain.

Some singers are not as understanding as Rysanek, and when Warren is in an opera with some other blue-blooded temperaments, mainly that of a certain volatile tenor, there can be backstage scenes and tantrums. If somebody tries to upstage Warren during the course of a performance, blood may be shed, and it will not be his. Not that he is a bad scene-stealer himself. "If you are in this crazy business," he says, "you'd better know all the tricks of the trade."

At rehearsals, too, he can be something of a trial. Last season, during one of the *Macbeth* run-throughs, he drove Carl Ebert wild with his suggestions. Finally the German director could take it no longer. "Will you please stop directing and just sing, Mr. Warren?" Ebert snapped.

Warren was not in the least abashed. He did sing. At one of those rehearsals, during an aria in which the baritone has a high A, conductor Erich Leinsdorf asked him whether he wanted to take a pianissimo on the note. Warren grinned, started pianissimo, swelled it to a fortissimo and made a decrescendo back to a pianissimo—an amazing bravura feat known as the *messa di voce*. (At the actual performance, though, he started fortissimo and stayed there; that, he knows, is what his public wants.) It is little feats like this that make him the most highly paid baritone in America, with an income of well above $100,000 a year.

One reason Warren did not immediately assume the place his voice ordinarily would have guaranteed him was the fact that when he came upon the scene he had virtually no experience or repertory. At the time he was engaged by the Metropolitan he had seen only one opera in his life. That was *La Traviata*, when he was 22 years old. He says he cried like a baby.

Not only had he never seen an opera before then but the only time he had ever been near a stage was in high school, where he played an Indian in a drama about Daniel Boone. His voice had changed when he was between 16 and 17, and he had spent his time at neighborhood music schools in New York (he went to public school and graduated from Evander Childs High) instead of playing ball with the kids. "I was very much to myself, the dreamer type," he says with a nervous giggle.

He had no definite idea of making a career in music. He never was inspired by a particular singer for the simple reason that he had never heard a great singer except Caruso—on phonograph records—and Caruso was a tenor. He worked in his father's fur business before landing in music.

As he tells the story, "One day I went to Radio City Music Hall and saw a bass on stage. 'Well,' I said to myself, 'if he can get the job, I certainly can.' So I went backstage and asked for an audition. I got it, and the job." That was in 1935, and Warren stayed at Radio City for three years, spending all of that time in the chorus. He never was given the chance to make a solo turn.

His first important teacher was Sidney Dietch. Warren was still in the chorus at that time, Dietch remembers. "When I first heard the voice," he says, "it was of very fine basic material but the quality was not so good. A little rough. I would never have expected him to make the career he has made. But all of a sudden, after two years or so, the voice grew in size, got its characteristic color, and I realized it was a great organ."

Warren came to the Met via the "Auditions of the Air" in 1938. He was dared into entering by fellow chorus members. When he sang for Wilfrid Pelletier, the conductor thought a ringer had been brought in. Warren then went to Italy to prepare some repertoire. He did not have a single operatic role at that time. Working under Giuseppe Pais and Ricardo Piccozi, in Rome and Milan, he managed to learn seven roles in seven months. (He is not considered a fast study, but once he has learned a role he has it for good.) It was in Italy that he met Agatha Leifflen, a voice student from the Juilliard School. They were married in 1941.

On Nov. 27, 1938, he made his official Met debut at one of the Sunday evening concerts. Not long after, he appeared as one of the subsidiary singers in Verdi's *Simon Boccanegra,* the opera in which he will sing the title role when it is revived this February. The Met brought Warren along slowly, and for that he is grateful; he has seen too many singers ruin their careers by taking on roles for which they were not ready.

Year by year the Met gave him more responsibility. Now he is the bellwether of the Italian repertory and has sung the leading baritone roles in all the Verdi operas the Met has produced. He also has sung in La Scala, the Colón in Buenos Aires, the Bolshoi and other houses. These days, however, he restricts his activities pretty much to the Met. He will sing forty-five performances there this season, at $1,500 a performance, and will also sing two dozen or so concert dates at about $2,500 a concert.

When he studies a role he engages in an awesome amount of research that never stops. "They can say he lives in a fog, but when it comes to his roles he thinks like a fiend," one of his colleagues admiringly reports.

For *Rigoletto,* he read all he could lay his hands on about Italian history. He made a study of Italian life in the sixteenth century, with special reference to Mantua. He looked at Renaissance paintings and closely examined the costumes of the day. The design for his most recent Rigoletto costume was adapted from an old print he happened to find.

For his *Macbeth* role he became a Shakespearean scholar. He read Bradley, Chambers, Dover Wilson, and went to Columbia University for consultations with an authority on Shakespeare. One of his prized possessions is a Furness variorum edition of the play given him by Francis Robinson, assistant manager of the Metropolitan. For Scarpia in *Tosca* he went to a man in Rome to view a pair of eyeglasses of the period.

Warren knows all about Scarpia. "He was a Sicilian, a social climber," he says. "He was a very powerful man in his day. Did you know that he got a decoration from the Vatican? I managed to get a copy of it made for my costume. I was trying to figure out the one thing that signifies the man himself. I came to the conclusion that it was his dress. Sicilians like to dress up, the fancier the better. So I ordered long black stockings with a red clock. Those are the kind of stockings that a man of that type would wear. He is so vain, so powerful, that he has to have a touch of color, even though he dresses entirely in black. The red clock, I think, allies Scarpia to the Sicilians."

The fact that nobody in the audience beyond the first few rows sees that red clock is of no special concern to Warren. He is content, for he feels that he is being historically exact.

Scarpia, however, is not one of his favorite roles. "They kill me off after the second act," he explains, with real indignation. Anyway, he is fonder of Verdi than of Puccini. His favorite roles are Rigoletto, Falstaff, Macbeth, Simon Boccanegra—the name roles in as many Verdi operas, in short.

He no longer pampers his throat. There was a time when he was a hypochondriac about it. This he got from Ezio Pinza, who was always worried about coming down with a cold. For a long time Warren's major recreation was playing with model railroads in a hermetically sealed room, but now the trains have been dismantled and Warren leads more of an outdoor life.

During the summer, at his country home near Greenwich, Conn., he goes boating and fishing. He has a well-outfitted cruiser and is very proud of it. A press agent once spent an afternoon with him, desperately trying to work up some angle that would interest a national publication. Warren was, for once, completely uncooperative; his mind appeared to be on other things. Then it finally came out: what he wanted, more than anything, was an interview in *Yachting*.

If there is one thing above all others about which Warren is proud it is The Episode of the Cracked Mirror. For years Warren had been reading about Caruso's trick of cracking a glass or a mirror while singing a powerful sustained note—a completely unauthenticated and most dubious story, by the way. One day he was at a recording session at the Manhattan Center and, while he was singing, a mirror began to shatter all over the floor. Warren was ecstatic. He felt this really was *it*. He had now arrived among the truly great. Gleefully he told one and all about it.

"Warren firmly believes he cracked the mirror," a Victor official says. "Maybe he did. Of course, it was an old mirror. It was one of those big, old-fashioned jobs made up of little squares. It was also falling to pieces, and those squares were all over the floor when we started the session. A section happened to fall down while he was singing. As I say, maybe he did crack it. Don't ask *me*."

Oct. 25, 1959

The young Birgit Nilsson was a phenomenon, and in this magazine piece I guessed correctly that she would be around for a long time. I had first heard her in 1956, at the Maggio Musicale in Florence, and knew in advance what to expect from her New York debut. In this piece I also was worried about the Heldentenor situation, and unfortunately was correct there too. When Lauritz Melchior stopped singing, there was nobody to replace him. The only one in our time who has come near that greatest of all Wagnerian tenors has been Jon Vickers.

In the years she was active, Nilsson became a legend in more ways than one, and splendid stories about her entered the public domain: how, in filling out her tax form, she entered Rudolf Bing as a dependent; her advice to a young soprano on how to sing Isolde ("Get a comfortable pair of shoes"); how, at a Karajan Ring *rehearsal, with its prevailing darkness, she put on a miner's hat with a lamp on it. Singers and opera buffs spend hours swapping Nilsson stories, of which there are even more than Zinka Milanov stories.*

Of Wagnerian Sopranos

Iᴛ ɪs a truism of the opera house that a big voice is found in a big body, and the bigger the voice the bigger the body. The Wagnerian operas require the biggest voices of all, and the breed of Wagnerian sopranos runs largest of all. It was not long after Darwin that the vocal art was described as the survival of the fattest, and while this may not be so true today it still applies to those sopranos who aspire to the big roles in Wagner.

Historically, a Wagnerian soprano is a body filled with a vast amount of empty space—the cubature, say, of a barrage balloon—and that space can be filled with air which can then be sent forth to create an unprecedented quantity of sound. Even at the turn of the century, when singers from coloratura sopranos down (or up, depending on how you look at it) were ample of hip and bosom, and proud of it, the Wagnerian soprano stood out like a St. Bernard in a pack of cocker spaniels—majestic, serious of mien, commanding of stance and physique.

The Wagnerian soprano needs heft. "It takes stuffing to sing Isolde," Helen Traubel once said. Wagner thinks nothing of letting a soprano run on, at full voice, for twenty minutes or so. To carry it off, to ride the great volume of orchestral sound without faltering, to achieve the full-throated climax of the *Liebestod* or *Todesverkündigung*, a soprano requires big lungs, stamina, and a special kind of physique. Such a phenomenon is rare in any age and actually unique in the present one. Hence the page one excitement recently after Birgit Nilsson made her Metropolitan Opera debut as Isolde.

For the Wagnerian breed seems to be vanishing, and that goes not only for sopranos. The world has not seen a true Heldentenor since Melchior was in his prime, and there are no signs of anyone coming along to replace him. The last of the heroic sopranos, up to the time of Nilsson, were Traubel and Flagstad. (Eileen Farrell, who seems to have the voice, has done very little opera and no Wagner at all in New York.)

During the early years of this century, though, and into the nineteen-forties, the Wagnerian soprano throve. When the great Lilli Lehmann reached the end of her career, Lillian Nordica was around to carry on, and from her the line passed to Olive Fremstad, Johanna Gadski and Frida Leider, to mention but three great sopranos. There were many more.

They were a marvelous group of vocal battleships. All were big, lusty, domineering women. Nordica, the idol of the opera-going public around 1900, was described by her great admirer, Henry T. Finck, as a "living Titian." She made an enormous impression on Finck by dining with him and ending the meal with six kinds of pie. Other commentators agreed that she had Titianesque qualities, but added that she was so big that she tended to be ridiculous on stage.

Nordica, an American girl (Lilly Norton was her real name), was married three times, once to a balloonist who attempted a Channel crossing. He got off the ground all right, but was never heard of again. The name of Nordica still brings horrified shudders in the older sections of Boston; she once told the Boston Symphony that it played like a band from Kalamazoo.

Judging from her pictures, the great Lilli Lehmann was built, to put it mildly, on matronly lines. In her day she was described as a "handsome, fine-figured woman." Translated from the Victorian, this meant that she was tall and stout. She sang in the first Bayreuth *Rheingold,* and in her autobiography she describes the trouble the stagehands had when they tried to strap her in the harness that would "swim" her through the Rhine. She was so terrified that stress-and-strain specialists were called in; the very pages of her book tremble with the experience.

Lehmann could be tart, and it may be that, being the greatest soprano of her day, she resented the appearance of a challenger. In 1894, when Nordica scored a triumph at Bayreuth, she (Nordica) approached Lehmann humbly for an appointment to pay her respects. Lehmann, making sure that her voice carried over the lobby, said "No, my dear. I'm not taking any pupils this season."

Fremstad—she of the gigantic voice—was of average height but had a remarkable thickness of diaphragm. She was a little self-conscious about it, thinking people might get the wrong idea. "That is my bellows, not my belly," she would explain. At her couturier's she would proudly hold herself erect during fittings. "I am not one of your dumpy South American clients," she would complain. "Give me more material, I tell you!"

Like all her colleagues, Fremstad was a woman of great temperament. She was also a woman who knew what was due her and who insisted on her rights. Even so temperamental a star as Maria Callas would be put to it keeping up with that kind of company. Fremstad, for example, would not step foot on the Metropolitan stage unless she had her check for the performance. But the Met refused to give her the check until she was in costume and ready to go on. Thus the timing was a delicate matter. She would wait in the wings until her secretary, clutching the check, gave the signal. If the signal was late, so was the curtain. Since there was no doubt in anybody's mind that there would be no Fremstad on stage if the check wasn't ready, a check was always prepared.

Fremstad and Gadski had little use for each other. At one *Walküre* performance around 1910, in which Fremstad was singing Sieglinde and Gadski Brünnhilde, Fremstad came off stage with blood all over her arm. She was furious, insisting that Gadski had pulled her arm across the metal breastplate that is the chief adornment of all Brünnhildes, past or present. "She wants to keep me from coming out for applause! Ha, but she will be sorry!" Fremstad screamed.

She refused to have the wound dressed, and took her curtain calls clutching Gadski's hand. Apparently nobody in the audience noticed the blood. "My, how those two great singers love each other!" was the general reaction.

Yes, they grew 'em big every way in those days, and until a few weeks ago, most people thought that the breed was extinct. If not for Nilsson, it would be. What has happened?

The late Noel Straus, a critic on the *Times* for many years and a lover of good singing, blamed it all on the craze for dieting. Straus maintained, with considerable fervor, that a slim singer could not sing Wagner, or any dramatic role, for that matter. "As well expect a nightingale to roar!" he would snort. He cited with approval Traubel's statement about stuffing and Wagner, and he maintained that the universal urge of contemporary women to slim down was the death-knell of singing. "Who cares what they look like?" he would cry. "We go to hear 'em, not to see 'em."

Straus was a wag, but he had a point. The sheer physical effort involved in singing a major Wagnerian role demands a powerful body. Ask any singer what the basic requirement is, and the one word that comes to everybody's lips is "stamina."

It is expected that a singer's voice be perfectly placed and produced, but that is only the start of the Wagnerian singer's problems. Grete Stückgold, who had her share of experiences as a member of the German wing of the Metropolitan Opera, likens Wagnerian singing to intense muscular work. "It's absolutely like prizefighting," she says. "For Wagner you have to be a heavyweight."

In Italian opera the voice—pure voice—is the thing, and composers calculated their vocal writing so that the voice is the primary instrument. Not until Verdi's later work, the prime example being his last opera, *Falstaff,* did the orchestra take on a function equal to that of the singers. But almost from the beginning Wagner had a different idea. He was going to synthesize drama and music. His orchestra was not going to go tum-ti-tum in *La donna è mobile* fashion; his orchestra was going to comment on the action, develop the drama, underline mood, personality and emotion.

Which it did. But in the process it threw up a richness of sound that demanded singers with enormous voices to sing over it. It is not that the vocal parts are of extraordinary technical difficulty. In the average Italian opera, for example, there are more high C's than in any Wagnerian opera, and there is much more vocal display. Lilli Lehmann once said that she would rather sing three Brünnhildes than one Norma.

But whereas Norma requires more vocal agility than Brünn-hilde, the latter requires infinitely more strength and—there's that word again—stamina. And experience, too. Seldom does a young singer take on a major Wagnerian role.

Lauritz Melchior holds that the Wagnerian singer does not have a born voice; it is a made voice, he says. It takes time for any voice to settle and to develop in size. And once it has developed it must be carefully built. While a singer who specializes only in Italian opera can make a career on four or five high notes, a Wagnerian singer needs a well-developed range. The role of Isolde, for example, encompasses a low A and a high C.

Many promising singers have ruined themselves by undertaking Wagnerian roles before they were ready for them. Melchior, like many other musicians, believes one reason for the dearth of Wagnerian sopranos and tenors today is that young singers will not take the necessary time to develop. Either that, or they jump into Wagner before their voices have set.

In either case the result is ruination for singer and composer. It is interesting to note that Melchior, who, like his great predecessor Jean de Reszke, started as a high baritone, sang for eight years before taking on a Wagnerian role: his first was the relatively light tenor lead in *Tannhäuser*.

Nilsson, too, has taken her time. She made her official debut in Stockholm in 1947 as Lady Macbeth in the Verdi opera (she previously had been a last minute replacement for an indisposed soprano in *Der Freischütz*, but that was a traumatic experience she prefers to forget). Three years later she started to wade into the Wagnerian ocean.

She sang lyric roles like Senta in *The Flying Dutchman* at first. After she sang her first Brünnhilde—"and I was forced to do it"—she didn't touch it for the rest of the year. It was not until 1955 that she felt enough vocal security to attempt the last three operas of the *Ring* cycle. "And at that time my voice was not as strong in its middle register as it now is," she says.

Physically, Nilsson is built on the classic lines of a Wagnerian soprano, although she is not as monumental in configuration as a Traubel or a Flagstad. She weighs about 150 pounds and is 5 feet, 8 inches tall. Solid but not stout, she gives the impression that she could carry an operatic Siegfried over each shoulder without staggering. Her chest cavity is extraordinarily large and her neck unusually thick. It is the neck of a female Caruso. Yet Nilsson, with her perfect complexion, gay smile and well-turned legs, never gives the impression of masculinity.

What the first-nighters at Nilsson's debut in *Tristan* heard was a perfectly produced voice. It was exactly in focus, and enormous in size without ever becoming edgy. With no apparent effort it rose over the orchestra and into the ears of every listener in the house. Those big lungs and that thick throat combined to sustain without waver a massive column of tone that, according to the dictates of human logic, could not come from one body. All great Wagnerian singers have this awesome ability to defy physiology.

Nilsson's is not the most colorful voice extant. It is even a bit "white," produced virtually without a vibrato to soften it. Thus it is a rather cool voice, despite its size; but it probably will darken in a few years. Nilsson is quite young (she declines to tell her age), and as she continues to sing, her voice will achieve more resonance and even more solidity in its lower compass.

Wagnerian sopranos grow deeper in vocal range as they grow older. Toward the end of her career, Traubel had completely lost her top notes, but had added what appeared to be the bass notes of an organ to the lower register; she would have made the most spectacular contralto since Clara Butt. Flagstad, too, started to have trouble with her top notes in the last years of her Metropolitan career. In her last recording she was heard in the mezzo role of Fricka in Wagner's *Rheingold*.

None of the great Wagnerian sopranos of history was considered a great actress, and in this, too, Nilsson is following tradition. Flagstad, the greatest Wagnerian soprano of our times, was largely content to stand motionless and let her voice do the work. The heroic Traubel was not exactly a broken-field runner either. By far the best-acted Brünnhilde of the generation came from Martha Moedl three years ago at the Met. She had musicianship and intensity, and was the trimmest Brünnhilde within the memory of man. But her singing simply did not have the splendor for the role. While Nilsson's gestures are conventional, she does have the vocal splendor.

Nilsson does not intend to type herself as a Wagnerian singer. In any case, few Wagnerian singers concentrate only on Wagner. Flagstad was an exception. An all-purpose soprano like Lilli Lehmann would be singing Brünnhilde one week and the coloratura Philine in *Mignon* the following week. *That* kind of versatility has disappeared from the world, and not even Callas would attempt to duplicate such a tour de force.

But, if we no longer have the likes of a Lilli Lehmann, there is no reason why a good Brünnhilde cannot make a good Aïda, and that is the rule these days. Indeed, Nilsson thinks it mandatory for a Wagnerian soprano to alternate with Italian roles.

"Otherwise," she says, "the voice may get *too* big." She speaks clear and rapid English. "It is important for a singer to vary her way of singing. In Verdi a singer has to cut down, to frame the voice a little differently. Verdi singing, technically, is completely unlike Wagner singing. It demands different adjustments."

As part of her regimen of change, Nilsson will be singing Leonora in Beethoven's *Fidelio* later this year at the Metropolitan Opera, and next year she will be heard in something eagerly anticipated by opera lovers—the Princess in Puccini's *Turandot*. This is one of the most fiendish parts ever conceived, lying high in the voice and demanding fortissimo piled on fortissimo. And America has not heard a great Turandot since the days of Jeritza and Raisa some thirty years ago.

Nilsson apparently has always had a big voice, something that a singer is born with; and she has survived inferior teaching, something that very few singers can survive. She says that she had to teach herself almost everything. "In Stockholm I had two teachers. One made me sing edgy, like a knife. The other made me grunt like a bull. How my voice was not ruined, I do not know."

The trouble with a big voice like hers is that today there is not a man who can match it in the Wagner repertory. When she appears on stage with a shrinking flower of a Heldentenor, it is like a glorious girl being escorted by a midget. Nilsson will be around for a great many years. She has youth and a brilliant voice, and with her relaxed style of singing she will not easily wear out her vocal cords. But, despite her appearance on the scene, there still may not be a Wagner renaissance, as there was when Flagstad electrified the operatic world a generation ago. Flagstad had her Melchior. For Nilsson's Isolde there is no Tristan; for her Brünnhilde no Siegfried. In Wagner she is the poor little rich girl who has no playmate.

JAN. 10, 1960

The 1950's were a bad period for singing. Perhaps the war was to blame. How many promising talents died on the battlefield or in concentration camps? In the 1950's it was hard to think of more than half a dozen artists anywhere in the world who would have been allowed to sing leading roles at the Metropolitan Opera fifty years previously. There was a strong improvement in the 1960's. Today (1980) the curve has again dropped. Managers and conductors all over are desperate for dramatic or Wagnerian voices. The Metropolitan's music director, James Levine, has said that it is next to impossible to cast an Aïda. The Bayreuth Festival gives its Wagner with pipsqueak tenors and is desperate for a great Wotan or Sachs. And with Birgit Nilsson nearing the end of her career, what are we going to do for Wagnerian sopranos?

A Decline in Performance

Every age has a tendency to think that it is going to Hades in a handbarrow, and it is always the previous age that is upheld as the exemplar. In the art of singing such thinking is standard procedure. Rossini bewailed the fact that the days of the castrati were over. His own days were merely the days of Lablache and Malibran. In the eighteen nineties George Bernard Shaw complained that the singers of his day could not hold a candle to the aforesaid Lablache and Malibran. In the great days of opera at the Metropolitan and Hammerstein houses the singers the old-timers were talking about were not Caruso, Melba and Gerville-Réache; they were upholding singers like Lilli Lehmann and Jean de Reszke. Today we are reminiscent about Flagstad, Rethberg, Gigli and Melchior.

But perhaps the irony is that the old-timers knew what they were talking about. Perhaps vocal art really has been on the decline since Handel's day. Certainly one fact is indisputable. Fifty years ago there seems to have been enough great singers to form a division. Today we are lucky if we can get a platoon. As an indication, there does not seem to be a true heldentenor anywhere in the world. As for coloratura sopranos in the Hempel or Galli-Curci tradition, well . . .

In one respect we have improved and that is in the status of musicianship among today's singers. Very few of them will pull the tricks that some of the respected names of previous generations did. Singers today have a more cultivated style, securer rhythm and greater respect for the composer.

But very, very few have the vocal techniques of their predecessors. When it comes to the really difficult things in the repertory the results can be painful, even among the great voices of today. Yet such has been the lowering of vocal standards that we are not only likely to take sloppy singing for granted; we also are happy to applaud it.

The Metropolitan Opera is one of the great houses, and its

vocal standards are representative of the best that obtain anywhere in the world. When it revived Donizetti's *L'Elisir
d'Amore* last month it presumably assembled the finest cast
within its power. The Metropolitan did put on a nice show,
what with the tuneful music, elaborate sets and a cast that cn-
tered fully into the spirit of the proceedings. When it came to
the vocal letter of the score, though, the results were anything
but what the composer would have wanted.

Is it demanding too much for singers to handle coloratura
passages with neatness, to sing on pitch, and not to run out of
breath before a phrase is ended? And, as a concomitant, would it
perhaps be wiser for the Metropolitan, or any other house, to
avoid operas that demand a vocal technique apparently alien to
singers of today?

While we have many singers who can handle lyric or dramatic
roles, we have few who can sing coloratura with any flair. It is
not that today's voices are any less beautiful, as voices, than in
preceding generations. Lungs and vocal cords are still manufac-
tured much the same old way. The trouble seems to be that
hardly anybody around can take a young singer and instill a
technique capable of handling a role like Donna Anna in *Don
Giovanni* or Adina in *L'Elisir*.

Thus in *L'Elisir* we had a baritone who often did not even
attempt to handle the vocal flourishes with any clarity. We had
a soprano with a basically beautiful voice, one to which a high
C holds no terrors. In a straight lyric line her singing was enchanting. As soon as a few cadenzas came around, as soon as the
line became florid, her voice became spread and edgy. She managed to get up and down the scale, but the results were not very
pleasant.

And yet it is not so long ago that any number of sopranos
could have swarmed all over a role like Adina. Many names
come immediately to mind: Ivogün, Kurz, Hempel, Galli-Curci,
Bori, Tetrazzini. We have not only the testament of memory.
We also have phonograph recordings, made in the days when
there was no fakery to records. These singers sang coloratura
roles as naturally as they breathed, effortlessly and brilliantly,
right on pitch, with the voice never losing quality above the

staff. Arpeggios, leaps, trills, staccato scales, a flowing line—all were in their armory. They did not pinch at about a B flat; they ascended surely to E in alt and above.

That school of singing has all but vanished from the scene. Which is why, when a Joan Sutherland comes along, there is such excitement. For she is a throwback—a singer who can handle both Donna Anna and Adina; a singer with a good-sized voice that also has enough flexibility to do coloratura work. This may not have been so uncommon fifty years ago. Today it puts Miss Sutherland in a class with the coelacanth. Not a very gallant metaphor, perhaps; but the analogy is strongly there.

What has happened? And why is it that vocal technique is at such a low ebb? Part of the answer is, of course, in the teaching.

It is no great secret that in our decades vocal teachers have ruined many promising voices. You, I, anybody can hang out a shingle and teach voice, loudly announcing ourselves as the only true exponent of the coup de glotte as taught by de Reszke and handed to us personally by his ghost. Or we can invent the laryngo-thyro-crico-aryteno system of muscular untension, every applicant guaranteed to have the sinuses expanded, the diaphragm unfastened, and two octaves added to the upper and lower registers. All, of course, provided that The System is followed. At $50 the weekly lesson.

Teaching aside, many singers have no one but themselves to blame for not living up to their potential. How many around today have the restraint of Kirsten Flagstad, who was content to sing light and even subsidiary roles for many years? Not until she knew she was ready did she turn to Wagner. Singers like her, like Giuseppe de Luca and Léon Rothier, could go on singing apparently forever because they had never forced their voices as young artists. A young singer can do things by sheer lung power and get away with it for a while; but that singer is ruining a voice. When one thinks of all the brilliant talents of the last twenty years who rushed into roles beyond them and ended up with a ten-year instead of a thirty-year career, one could weep.

Management is at fault, too. Management only too often seizes a promising singer and, literally, works the young artist to vocal death. Opera and concert tours; recording sessions; in

San Francisco one day and London the next; rush, rush, rush. How can an artist be expected to mature, artistically and vocally, under these circumstances? Today an opera singer seems to be proud if she has learned twenty or twenty-five roles. Lilli Lehmann is said to have had around two hundred fifty. And those were roles that ranged from Philine in *Mignon* and Constanza in *Die Entführung aus dem Serail* to Brünnhilde in *Götterdämmerung.* Of her it could not be said, as it can with so many singers these days, "O good my lord, tax not so bad a voice to slander music any more than once."

DEC. 4, 1960

Naturally the Times *girded itself for the demise of the old Metropolitan Opera and its reincarnation in Lincoln Center. As early as the beginning of the 1965–66 season—the Metropolitan's last at Thirty-ninth Street—I was asked by the Sunday magazine to write an article on the old house and what it represented. I had been going there steadily since 1927—my first opera was* Die Meistersinger, *with Laubenthal, Stückgold and Whitehill—and the article was a labor of love.*

A Farewell to the Old Metropolitan Opera House

ON OCTOBER 22, 1883, the Vanderbilts, Whitneys, Roosevelts, Goelets, Goulds, Drexels, Morgans and certain other denizens of Fifth Avenue, Newport, Wall Street and Delmonico's, having most democratically drawn lots to see which box would belong to whom, settled down in the new Metropolitan Opera House to enjoy what their $1,732,478.71 had created and, concurrently, a performance of *Faust* in which Christine Nilsson, Giuseppe Campanari and Franco Novara took the leads. On September 27, 1965, *Faust* opened another new season at the Met—and its final season at the old homestead. On a day sometime in May (unless the Landmarks Commission steps in or an equivalent miracle takes place), a crew of wreckers will move into the building. The house is tired, the Old Lady of Thirty-ninth Street has seen her day, and the wreckers will apply the *coup de grâce.*

With ax and crowbar they will toll a melancholy requiem to the house of Grau, Conried, Gatti-Casazza and Bing. Their sledges will ring as loudly as ever Siegfried's did, tearing into the stage over which trod Caruso, Melba, Jean de Reszke, Flagstad and Melchior. The steel ball will smash the dressing rooms over which great prima donnas fought and wept. Overalled and uncaring figures, chewing cigars and wearing steel hats, will pick at the great proscenium and send it tumbling down, down, down, along with those noble names on top—Mozart, Verdi, Wagner and the others. Not by clean fire will come this Götterdämmerung, but in a mean cloud of dirt, dust and rubble. Then everything will be gone but the memories. Those are eternal.

For the old Met has become part of the legend of music, and the figures who appeared there have become even more legendary. It was thus from the beginning, though hardly anybody is around who can remember the first decade of the Met, when all of the Wagner operas after *Lohengrin* were introduced to America. And there cannot be many who were there at the first—and, for many years, the only—production of Strauss's *Salome.* That was in 1907, and at that performance too many people discovered the meaning of musical sin. But the two great Puccini world premières—*La Fanciulla del West* in 1910 and *Il Trittico* in 1918, both with the composer present—are well remembered by the old-timers.

The Metropolitan Opera, however, is not notable for world premières. It never has been that kind of house. For the overwhelming part, those world premières it *has* had have promptly been forgotten. Who today remembers Humperdinck's *Königskinder,* Parker's *Mona,* Damrosch's *Cyrano de Bergerac,* Gior-

dano's *Madame Sans-Gêne*, Wolff's *Oiseau Bleu*, Hanson's *Merry Mount*, Taylor's *Peter Ibbetson* and the many others that died aborning? The more important operas of the century have been ignored by the Met, traditionally a conservative house, a museum-like repository of great works of the past. From the beginning—at least after the eighteen-nineties—it has been well content to concentrate on great singing and sumptuous productions rather than on controversial music that would disturb the patrons and customers. Its percentage of new music is probably the lowest of any major opera house in the world.

Singing—that is where the Met shines, even today when great singing is in short supply. Impresarios during the last two decades or so have talked about the virtues of ensemble opera and the perils of the star system. But the talk is loudest from those impresarios who have no access to great singers. Opera may be many things, but it is first and foremost singing. That is one law that is never going to be repealed. Well known is part of the story about Geraldine Farrar and Arturo Toscanini. She stopped him during a rehearsal and said, "Maestro, I have to remind you that I am the star here." Toscanini answered succinctly: "Madame, there are stars only in heaven." Not too well known is Farrar's riposte: "But the public pays to see my face and not your back." Farrar had her way, as she knew she would.

It must be remembered that stars are stars because they do certain things better than anybody else. From the day it opened, the Metropolitan Opera has had more than its share of them. It may never have been a haven for new music, nor has it traditionally been a house for great conducting (though the 1908–09 season brought together Alfred Hertz, Gustav Mahler and Arturo Toscanini; and shortly after the start of World War II it extended its arms to Beecham, Busch, Reiner, Walter and Szell). But as a repository of sheer voice it has ranked with any house anywhere.

How can one make a list of the outstanding singers who have appeared there? Impossible. There are too many. Mention Flagstad, and you have to mention the other great Wagnerian sopranos—Leider, Matzenauer, Larsen-Todsen, Nordica, Fremstad, Gadski and so back to Materna and Lilli Lehmann. If you mention Sembrich, Melba, Bori, Galli-Curci, Barrientos and

Tetrazzini in an all-time list of great Met singers of the past (names of singers currently in action are studiously avoided here), it would be sheer insult not to mention also Eames, Rethberg, Muzio, Ternina, Calvé, Jeritza, Destinn, Ponselle, Hempel, Lotte Lehmann. The royal line of tenors from Tamagno, van Dyck, Jean de Reszke and Caruso must be extended to cover Pertile, Slezak, Gigli, Schipa, Martinelli, Melchior, Bjoerling.

Nor does an opera house exist on high voices alone, even if many of the claque obviously wish it did. Chaliapin, Onegin, Schumann-Heink, Homer, Branzell, Journet, Scotti, Edouard de Reszke, Plançon, Pinza, Amato, de Luca, Rothier, Ruffo, Mardones, Schorr, Bohnen, Baccaloni—those names ring out like the overtones from a great bell. And the line of American singers —Easton, Farrar, Ponselle, Whitehill, Moore, Jagel, Swarthout, Traubel, Tibbett, Warren, Bampton, Bonelli, Crooks, Thomas, Thebom, Stevens. A few dozen other names could easily be added to an all-star list. It would include Albert Niemann, the great Bayreuth tenor; and Max Alvary, the first to sing Siegfried in America; and Lina Cavalieri, if only for her ravishing good looks; and Lucienne Bréval, the big-voiced queen of the Paris Opera; and the fabled Sofia Scalchi, who sang in the first Met season; and Charles Hackett of the smooth voice and the lyric line; and—but a stop has to be made somewhere!

They are magic names, all of them; the public's love, often the manager's despair. Temperamental, childlike, rotten, spoiled, sometimes sheerly unmusical, naive, superstitious, frequently oversexed ("Look at all those expectant mothers," Edward Johnson once said of a litter of bobbysoxers outside the stage door on West Fortieth Street, waiting for their favorite tenor to emerge), generally mountainous in size, they all had one thing in common—the ability to sing out and reduce listeners to an emotional blob. As such they always have been a race apart, even enjoying front-page play in the newspapers, as Birgit Nilsson witnessed when she made her unforgettable debut, or as Farrar witnessed when she retired in 1922. The gerryflappers all but tore down the Met, waving flags, unfurling banners, crying, cheering, carrying on.

How can one mention individual high spots when there have

been so many of them? One can go back to the 1900–01 season, when Jean de Reszke sang ten different roles, in three languages, over a three-week period. It was his last season, he was the greatest tenor of his day, and he wanted to go out like a hero. Or one can look back to 1925 when Lawrence Tibbett, all but unknown, sang the role of Ford in Verdi's *Falstaff* and reduced the audience to savage, shrieking beasts. Antonio Scotti was singing the title role, and was convinced that the applause was all for him. He came forward beaming, taking bow after bow, not realizing that the audience wanted him off the stage. Not until ten minutes later did Tibbett take a solo curtain, after which the performance could proceed.

Closer to our day was the 1935 matinee of *Die Walküre*, in which an unknown named Kirsten Flagstad made her debut. Farrar was the intermission commentator, and she threw away her script. "Ladies and gentlemen," she told the radio audience, "you have just been in on the most exciting thing that can happen in the theater—the birth of a new star." Such a star did Flagstad turn out to be that she became one of the only two singers in Metropolitan Opera history to have her own dressing room—No. 15, not very big, not very comfortable, but her very own, with her very own key. The other singer was Farrar, who also had No. 15.

In recent years, the debut and the first night that caused the most excitement was the evening of February 4, 1949, when *Salome* was revived, with Fritz Reiner in the pit and a new soprano named Ljuba Welitsch. To this day those at the Met refer to it simply as "that night," and everybody nods understandingly. Welitsch came out, big, commanding, in a red wig, moving like a tigress, and people got hysterical. "They were leaning forward, and more forward, and I thought they'd fall out of the balcony into the orchestra," recalls a Met official. "I have never seen anything like it. It was hypnotism at work. I can't find any other way to describe it. People held their breath, and at the end you never heard such a yell. The Tebaldi and Callas premières were exciting, and so was Sutherland's, but there has been nothing like that since. People are still talking about it."

Poor Welitsch lost her voice about a season later. But not her temperament. One of her last appearances was as Musetta in *La Bohème*, early in 1952. She thought the baritone, Paolo Silveri, was trying to upstage her, and in the second-act "Waltz" she elbowed him out of the way and climbed on a chair, singing lustily away. She was right. Silveri was most definitely trying to upstage her. He glared defiance, pushed everybody out of the way, and climbed up beside her. They sang, if that is the word, together, trying to knock each other down, bellowing as loud as they could. Alberto Erede was the conductor, and he might as well have been in Siberia. When the curtain came down he fled backstage, mopping his brow, yelling unprintable comments about "that woman." His yells were louder than those of both singers together, and they had very big voices in very big bodies.

Yes, the history of the Met is in its singers—in their great voices, their great temperaments, their feuds, loves, public and private lives. How else would the name of Mrs. Hannah Stanhope have a footnote in musical history? It was she whom Enrico Caruso pinched in a place where ardent young Italians generally pinch attractive young women. The date was November 16, 1906, and the scene of the dastardly crime was, of all places, the monkey house in the Central Park Zoo. Caruso was pretty new to New York at the time. He had made his debut in 1903, and the notices were respectful but scarcely spectacular. Of course he did get better year after year; his records bear this out.

Enrico Caruso! He of the clarion voice, the perfect vocal technique, the eternal boyishness, the incredible stamina (in 1907–08 he sang fifty-one times, or a third of all the season's performances; he was the big counterattraction to Hammerstein's Manhattan Opera House). The greatest single star in Metropolitan Opera history, he appeared in every opening night from 1904–05 to his last season, 1920–21, with but one exception. In all he sang 607 performances of thirty-six roles, most of them at $2,500 a performance. He could have received more money had he wished; it is said that the management once sent him a blank contract for him to fill in as he desired.

The great tenor probably had the maturity of a boy of thirteen.

Money meant nothing to him, and he would pass around fifty-dollar tips as though he were Diamond Jim Brady. His idea of a joke was to fill a colleague's hat with water or flour, and watch what happened when he put it on. At one performance he sewed up the sleeve of Vittorio Arimondi's coat and waited eagerly for the end of the *Vecchia zimarra* aria in *La Bohème*. When Arimondi tried to put the coat on, Caruso nearly collapsed from joy. Criticism bothered him. Once, after a performance that received unanimously bad reviews, he sent in his resignation. Gatti-Casazza almost died. Along with the opera patron Otto Kahn, he rushed to Caruso's apartment. Gatti wept, and Kahn got on his knees until Caruso, who was enjoying every bit of it, relented.

Withal, he was a sweet man, a gallant one, and a trouper. None but an authentic hero would have tried to carry on at the Brooklyn Academy on December 11, 1920. It was a performance of *L'Elisir d'Amore,* and Caruso had a throat hemorrhage as soon as he started singing. He filled handkerchief after handkerchief with blood, and still insisted on trying to continue after the first act. The audience was told of the situation. "No! No! Stop the performance!" was the cry. The curtain never rose on the second act. Almost two weeks later, on December 24, the ailing Caruso sang his last performance at the Met. He died the following year, on August 2, 1921.

Caruso was the best of the Italian tenors, but there were other fine ones, and one of them contributed a dramatic moment to Met history. Giovanni Martinelli went along for thirty years after his debut in 1913, apparently indestructible except for his famous bellyache on February 26, 1938. He had eaten crabmeat the night before that particular *Aïda,* came down with ptomaine poisoning, but insisted on singing anyway. His contribution to the performance ended about ten minutes after the curtain went up. He collapsed during *Celeste Aïda,* and backstage they thought he was literally dying.

Thus the curtain came down for the first time in Met history during the course of an opera. (The only other time was when Leonard Warren died on stage during a performance of *La Forza del Destino* in 1960, the most horrible moment in Met history, although back in 1897 Armand Castelmary died in the arms of Jean de Reszke during a performance of *Martha*.)

To this day nobody can mention shellfish to Martinelli. There were some byproducts to the incident. Milton Cross, in an intermission broadcast, told about the awesome results of Martinelli's crabmeat binge. Whereupon there was a roar from the crabmeat lobby. Cross had to apologize the next week. "I *like* crabmeat," he plaintively said.

Martinelli got along very well with his colleagues, which is more than can be said of most singers. Opera houses are notoriously torn by feuds, and the Met is no exception. Emma Eames was hard to get along with, and she and Calvé could never be in the house at the same time. For a singer supposed to be cold, Eames had a violent temper, and during the 1904–05 season she once hauled off and slapped the face of contralto Katherine Senger-Bettaque during a performance of *Lohengrin*. Reporters descended upon the contralto and asked her how she felt about it. "I did not resent it," Senger-Bettaque said. "I was really surprised and delighted to see *any* evidence of emotion in Madame Eames."

A decade later, Fremstad and Gadski, both mighty women, and both sublime Wagnerians, were constantly having at each other. A performance of *Die Walküre* saw Gadski grab Fremstad's arm and roughly draw it across her breastplate, drawing blood. Fremstad let the blood flow all over Gadski's costume, refused to stanch it, and at the curtain held her so that the audience could see the carnage.

Farrar and the normally good-natured Caruso occasionally were at odds, and during a *Carmen* in 1916 she threw herself into the action wholeheartedly, slapping him until his teeth rattled. The sequence is a little confused, but it appears that Caruso lost his temper, grabbed her wrist and bit it. So she hit him back. Before they started eating each other, he threw her to the floor. At the curtain calls there was much sweetness, smiling and gallantry between them; backstage there was hell to pay —great crying, hysterics and rounded Neapolitan oaths.

At least those two kept it to themselves. Jeritza once called a press conference and said that Gigli was a murderer; another time she stepped before the curtain, sobbing, and told the audience that Gigli was not nice to her. In the nineteen-thirties there was no great love between Grace Moore and Jan Kiepura. Among other things, he was constantly moving a chair in *La Bohème*, and it would drive her crazy. He would move it, and she would move it back, and he would move it again. "I'll fix him!" She ordered the stagehands before one performance to nail the damn thing to the floor. They say that when Kiepura tried to move it, his face was something to see.

The conductors have had their share of temperament. Roughest of all, it will come as no surprise, was Toscanini, who arrived at the Met with Gatti-Casazza in 1908. He left in a rage in 1915, under circumstances that are still unexplained. The best guess is that he had demanded, and was promised, more control over artistic policy, a promise that was not fulfilled. Later the Met offered him every inducement to return, on his own terms. Once Toscanini had made up his mind, though, he was immovable. The man never forgave. "I will conduct over the ashes of the Metropolitan!" he growled. But that never kept him from listening to the broadcasts, making powerful comments about them and spitting at the radio when the performances irritated him beyond human endurance.

In recent years the tolerance of opera lovers has often been pushed to that point. Singing today is not what it was in the past. How many leading artists at the Met today could have sung leading roles there at the turn of the century? Four? Five? Everybody is concerned about the problem, but not much can be done about it.

Various reasons have been given for the decline in singing, some unconvincing, some making sense. Probably the answer is in the pace of modern life. It is not so much that singers are being rushed in their careers too fast. Great singers nearly always start early. But today they are in constant demand, and they do not rest. They do not even study very much. Lilli Lehmann is reputed to have had some two hundred fifty roles. Today's singers can make a reputation on twenty or fewer. They split their winter seasons at various opera houses, give concerts, make records, and in the summer months sing in festivals all over the world. They cash in, but their careers are considerably shortened. Vocal cords can take just so much wear and tear.

Whatever the reasons for the decline, it is clear that the Golden Age—1890 through 1908 is the commonly accepted span at the Met, though some would extend it to 1920—brought together more and greater vocalists than at any other time in modern history. And in Chicago and Europe were groups just as luminous who, for one reason or another, did not sing at the Met. The old recordings are ample testimony. Every important singer from 1900 on made records, and there is no mistaking the brilliance, fluency and vocal splendor that coruscate through the old shellac. There also is the remarkable testimony of the Mapleson cylinders.

Lionel Mapleson, the librarian of the Met, was given a cylinder machine by Edison in 1900. From 1901 to 1903 he set it up in the wings of the house, or on the catwalk, and recorded hundreds of fragments of actual performances. (A pair of LP repressings was issued some ten years ago by the International Record Collectors Club, 318 Reservoir Avenue, Bridgeport, Conn.) Listening to them is an eerie, spine-tingling, even awesome experience. Constant exposure and study is needed, though. The surface noise is appallingly high, and through the overwhelming roar one hears in the far background only the silvery, ghostlike threads of voices.

More than enough comes through, however, to suggest that there were indeed giants in those days. One can hear the thrilling high C that Nordica takes at the end of *Siegfried;* or the warmer sound of Gadski as Brünnhilde in *Die Walküre.* There are tantalizing snatches of Jean de Reszke's voice, and a fantastic, even overwhelming series of snippets from *Tosca* sung by Emma Eames. Melba in the *Jewel Song* produces a matched string of evenly graded notes. Calvé's *Jewel Song* is no less impressive, and the audience goes wild. (Hearing the applause come through is a spooky experience. It puts today's listener back in time and space: he is sharing the same experience that long-dead people were frantically acclaiming. Ghosts become alive.)

What all the great figures of the Met's past had was voice:

voices of heroic size, of a technical ease that only a tiny handful today can approximate; voices versatile enough to encompass all styles, from dramatic to lyric. And, above all, voices that give the impression of having untold power in reserve. There is no feeling of strain, of vocal cords being pushed, of purple faces and bulging veins. Those people were born to sing.

Could their heroic size have had a correlation with their heroic voices? Nobody in those days thought of dieting. They knew that the biggest voices come from the biggest bodies. How those old-timers loved to eat! They tell the story of Caruso walking into a restaurant and seeing Ernestine Schumann-Heink attacking a steak as big as a manhole cover. "Are you having that steak alone, Tina?" he asked, preparing to join her. "Ach, no," she said. "Mit soup, und spaghetti, und potatoes, und wegetables . . ."

All those memories, all those figures, all that tradition, all those stories, all that music—that is what makes the Met. At the old building on Thirty-ninth Street we have enjoyed a form of spiritual identity with our ancestors, and any heart beats a little faster entering the premises. The new Metropolitan Opera House in Lincoln Center will probably be handsome, it may even work acoustically, and it will certainly be a more efficient plant. But it will also be antiseptic, a new-born babe without any characteristics of its own, a *tabula rasa* needing the weight of years and experience before it achieves its own profile, its own mythology. This will come. It has to come. But, singing and personalities today being what they are, the new Met never can conceivably be much more than an abstract, a non-objective, compared to the grimy but romantic palace of music in the garment district.

OCT. 24, 1965

When a famous musician dies, it is part of the critic's job to supply an appreciation; and when the person is of great renown, as in the case of Mary Garden, a Sunday piece almost invariably results.

The Death of Mary Garden

MARY GARDEN! I never heard her sing, except on records, and I never met her, but I knew her very well. What opera buff didn't? Indeed, who of a certain age didn't? Anybody as much in the papers as Mary Garden was is not going to be easily forgotten. She was Sir Thomas Beecham, Maria Callas and Geraldine Farrar rolled into one: lively, indomitable, glamorous, witty, imperious, publicity-minded, capricious and a great artist on top of all that. She died two weeks ago at the age of ninety-two. Only Farrar is left.

Debussy's Mary Garden, Charpentier's Mary Garden, Massenet's Mary Garden, the Turkish Pascha's Mary Garden. The Pascha needs some explaining. Mary (let's call her that; she was informal) arrived in Chicago in 1910 to help launch the first season of the Grand Opera Company. She arrived with a foreign accent (this Scots girl who had spent her formative years in America), a valet, a French maid, a few billion dollars worth of jewels, a monocle and an engagement ring. The ring, she gravely said, came from a Turkish Pascha to whom she was engaged.

A Pascha! The news went around Chicago, and thence America, with the speed of a flood when the dam is broken. Mary Garden is going to marry a Turkish Pascha, with a harem! Newspaper editors and reporters were enchanted. They descended upon Mary, whose press conferences were as celebrated as her portrayals of Mélisande and Louise. Mary always had a breezy way with newspaper people. She would quip, banter, exchange jokes. When the air got too heavy with cigarette smoke, which she detested, she would invite them into her bedroom and perhaps model her new costumes for them. ("I don't wear corsets, you know.")

Anyway, they asked her about the Pascha. Oh, yes, Mary said, flashing the ring. With a straight face, she provided corroborative detail. They rushed back to the office. Things pursued a normal course, as Mary knew they would. The papers were full of the Pascha and his seventy-eight wives, all of said females on the way to Chicago to plead with Mary not to marry him.

The *Chicago Tribune* gladly went along with the act. "Get the picture?" one news story ran. "Seventy-eight Turkish ladies in bifurcated hobble skirts parading down Michigan Avenue behind a brass band, with big banners reading: 'Mary, do not marry.'" (I am indebted for this delicious excerpt to Ronald Davis's chatty *Opera in Chicago*, published last year. Davis adds: "Needless to say, the wives never showed up. The Pascha himself was never heard of again after this season. And, of course, Mary never married anyone.")

Yes, Mary knew the value of publicity. There were those who sourly said that without the publicity, no opera house would have her, so bad was her voice. Fie on them! There was nothing wrong with Mary's voice, even if it did not have the poised perfection of an Eames, the flexibility of a Tetrazzini, the silvery quality of a Melba. Mary, who started singing professionally in 1900, was in competition with some of the greatest vocalists in history.

But that does not mean that, in her kind of repertory, she was not supreme. She knew that in direct competition with such as Eames and Melba she could not hold her own (though nobody alive could; it was no disgrace). And so she concentrated on a kind of repertory that few other singers touched. She did, of course, sing some standard roles—Tosca, Carmen, Violetta and so forth. But she was famous for other things: as Mélisande and Louise, as the Juggler of Notre Dame, as Thaïs, as Salome. She sang in such operas as Alfano's *Resurrection*, Honegger's *Judith*, Hamilton Forrest's *Camille*, Erlanger's *Aphrodite*, Février's *Monna Vanna*, Montemezzi's *L'Amore dei Tre Re*. There she had no competition, and there she could put to work her unique quality of voice and her equally unique acting ability.

The nonsense about Mary being an inferior vocalist should be laid to rest once and for all. She did not make many records, but she made enough to demonstrate that hers was a voice with character, beauty and size. As early as 1904 she was in the studios, with none less than Claude Debussy at the piano, singing three of his *Ariettes oubliées* and the Tower Scene (part of it, anyway) from *Pelléas et Mélisande.* Those records are fascinating. They show a soprano with an exceptionally even scale, with the booming chest notes favored by singers of the day, and with lovely, floating high notes. More than that: the singing is that of a supreme artist, one with wonderfully subtle rhythm, imaginative phrasing and musical authority.

She recorded *Depuis le jour* from Charpentier's *Louise*—her most famous role—more than once. Her most famous recording of the aria was made in 1926, toward the end of her career. She had the aria transposed down from G to F, and thus the climax is a high A instead of B. But how easily and beautifully she takes that note, and how elegant is the musical conception, and how purely the voice is projected! The performance is the most haunting I know. (Incidentally, the singer who impresses me as coming closest to Mary Garden in style and actual vocal timbre is the Maggie Teyte of the 1920's and 1930's.) One feels that, in this recording of *Depuis le jour,* Mary could have sung in the original key without any trouble—as effortlessly as she took the high C in her World War I recording of *Sempre libera.*

No; there was nothing wrong with Mary's voice. And as an actress she was in a class by herself. She was smaller and lighter than most of her operatic colleagues. She was 5 feet 4 inches in height, and her best fighting weight was 112 pounds. A great singer like Eames suggested extreme passion by slightly lifting one eyebrow. That was the norm of operatic activity those days. But Mary was the Duse, the Bernhardt, of the operatic stage. She had that quality—Callas has it today—of merely walking on stage and projecting her personality over the footlights with the force of heavy artillery. People reeled under the impact. Mary took her acting very seriously, much more seriously than her singing, which could be sloppy. She knew more about makeup and costumes than any operatic star of the day, she moved with grace, and she so could get into a role that often members of the audience would leave the theater weeping.

She was quick of mind and of tongue. One example of her verbal swordplay has become public domain. Everybody knows the story, but I am going to repeat it anyway. She was at a dinner party, seated next to Chauncey Depew, and she was her flashing best, bejeweled, tiaraed, and with a breathtaking strapless gown. Depew could not keep his eyes off the dress. He pondered. Finally he asked the question direct: "What keeps your gown up?" Mary's answer is deservedly famous. "Two things, Mr. Depew. Your age and my discretion."

JAN. 11, 1967

In my obituary piece on Mary Garden I mentioned that only Geraldine Farrar was left. About two months later Farrar died, and of course a Sunday piece was mandatory. My father, who had heard her and Caruso together for many years, once tried to tell me what she represented. "It was life *when she was on stage," he ended.*

The Goddess That Was Geraldine Farrar

NOW GERALDINE FARRAR is dead, only a short time after Mary Garden, and the Golden Age really has gone. She was the last of the great singers who came in at the turn of the century, and she was one of the greatest. Farrar was the *prima donna assoluta*, and she did not have to act the part. Not Farrar, with her talent, her glamour, her presence and her beautiful voice. She did not even have to put on Olympian airs. Everybody, except perhaps a few competing prima donnas, liked her. She was a regular girl.

Mary Watkins Cushing, who was the great Olive Fremstad's secretary, has written of the impact the Farrar presence could make. Cushing would be in the corridors of the old Met, and Farrar would sweep by. "Even I, dedicated heart and soul to another singer, felt my pulses quicken and the fatuous smile of the 'Gerry-flapper' spread across my face when, in a drift of delicious perfume, trailing furs, plumage and the sparkle of jewels, she brightened my exile in the drab gray hall."

Farrar was the Queen Bee of the Metropolitan all through her years there, from 1906 to April 22, 1922, when she made her farewell appearance as Zaza in the Leoncavallo opera of that name. Caruso was the King Bee, if there is any such thing. He and Farrar made the most popular singing team the Metropolitan Opera ever had. Farrar's years at the house saw her in competition with a number of immortals—sopranos like Fremstad, Gadski, Destinn, Boninsegna, Ponselle, Muzio. None of them was exactly a pushover. Yet Farrar rode over them all, even to the extent of having her private dressing room. This may not sound like much, but sopranos have been known to fight to the death for a favored dressing room, and it was a tribute to Farrar's supremacy that no soprano questioned her right to be thus singled out. She was the only one in Metropolitan Opera history until Flagstad to be so honored.

She was idolized in a manner hard to understand today. Part of this was because of her looks. Opera singers until recently did not worry about diet. The biggest voices came from the biggest bodies; and the great sopranos of the past, taken as a tribe, would not have been candidates for *Playboy* covers or inserts. Farrar was one of the exceptions. She was one of the relatively slender singers of the age (Garden was another) and had extraordinary beauty and femininity. And (again like Garden) she could act. She went far beyond the Emma Eames idea of expressing passion, and she threw herself into every role.

Sometimes she did this with a kind of realism that disconcerted the other singers. At one famous performance of *Carmen* in 1916, she slapped Caruso in the face, shoved a chorus girl around and, at the end, engaged in hand-to-hand combat with the tenor. The chorus girl didn't like it. Neither did Caruso.

Word got to Farrar. Very well, she said. If Caruso was unhappy, if he didn't like realistic acting, let the Metropolitan Opera look for another Carmen. Caruso was not to be outdone. No, no, he said. Let the Metropolitan Opera find another Don José. At the next *Carmen*, the New York press was present en masse. Would blood flow? Not a bit of it. Never was a *Carmen* more politely acted.

It was the eminent W. J. Henderson of the *New York Sun* who coined the word "gerryflapper." Henderson mused on the hysteria created by Farrar, especially among the young generation. "What is a gerryflapper? Simply a girl about the flapper age who has created in her own half baked mind a goddess which she names Geraldine Farrar." The gerryflapper contingent nearly tore the Met down at Farrar's farewell. Banners were hanging from the boxes. Balloons were released inside the house. Confetti flew. After Act II of *Zaza* she was presented with a crown and a scepter. At the end, Farrar made a speech, making it clear that "I am leaving this institution because I want to go." She said this because there was gossip that Farrar was leaving on account of the arrival of Maria Jeritza, the new star from Vienna.

But Farrar was telling the truth. She long previously had made up her mind to stop singing at the age of forty. She did not have to stop. Judging from her last series of records, her voice was as strong and vibrant as ever, though she avoided a high C when she could. How to describe her voice? It was a very strong lyric soprano—a spinto, as the Italians say—that could take in roles from Juliet and Violetta to Tosca and Elisabeth in *Tannhäuser*. In its early days it was a voice with considerable flexibility, enough to take care of any coloratura, as her 1905–06 records from Berlin illustrate. (One of them is the *Sempre libera*, with a gorgeous trill on the high A flat and an easy, even lazy, high C.) At the beginning she had a fairly large repertory, but for the most part was content to sing only a few roles after she established herself at the Metropolitan. Tosca, Butterfly, Manon, Mimi, Marguerite, Carmen, Zaza, the Goose Girl in *Königskinder* were among her specialties.

These she sang with a blazing personality that comes right through the old records. One interesting aspect of her singing is that it is very modern. She was almost always dead on pitch, she did not slide into notes, her rhythm was secure, her tempos a shade fast (nobody alive today can articulate the *Jewel Song* as Farrar did) and her singing was marked by unusual security. With Farrar there always was a feeling of something in reserve, and she made singing sound easy, almost an extension of speech.

She did not have the awesome vocal equipment of an Eames, though—like Eames—she used her voice in almost an instrumental manner. But her singing is much more expressive than that of almost anybody of her day. It was—what word can one use?—a *confident* voice: clear, unforced, vibrant, intense, colorful, used with utmost finesse and an unparalleled personality. It was a voice with not a single audible break from chest to head. Farrar cultivated her own style of singing. She well knew her limitations, even when studying with Lilli Lehmann, and she would not be pushed into roles unsuited for her.

A Farrar postscript should be added. It concerns her famous recording with Caruso of the duet from Act I of *Madama Butterfly*. The story goes that Caruso arrived at the studio by way of a restaurant and a bottle or so of wine, plus other alcoholic refreshment. Farrar said nothing, but while singing the duet, at the words *Si, per la vita,* she instead sang "He had a highball." On the relatively primitive recording equipment of the day, her interpolation passed unnoticed. At best the words are not easy to hear, and many believe the story is apocryphal. Deems Taylor, in his notes for the Victor LP reissue around 1950, has a footnote to the effect that the story is a pipe dream.

But it isn't. The other day I pulled out the record and played it. Sure enough, "He had a highball." Then, to make sure, I reduced the speed by a third (D flat to B flat) and this time, clear as a bell, no possible doubt at all, "He had a highball." Caruso, according to legend, is supposed to have sung, immediately after, "I had two." He didn't. But Geraldine now stands vindicated. Only Farrar could have thought of a thing like that. Only Farrar could have carried it off so irrepressibly on the spur of the moment. Naturally. She was Farrar.

MARCH 19, 1967

Years ago I had owned the Moreschi recordings, before losing them to a moving company, and found them spooky. The voice was neither male nor female, it had a curious kind of bleat and a peculiar singing method. Without knowing anything about the man, I found something inexpressibly sad in his singing. He was the last of his line, and probably not very good to begin with. The Handel Society performances started me thinking about castrato singers, and when I began to read up on the subject I was surprised at how little had been written about it in English. Some countertenors were active in the postwar period, and I imagine that their vocal quality was not unlike that of the castrati—but without the lung power, training and extraordinary vocal ranges of the evirati.

Alas, No More Castratos

THE CURRENT series of Handel Society opera performances— *Ariodante* will be given tomorrow in Carnegie Hall—and such presentations as the Clarion Concerts *Olimpiade* by Hasse the other week once again bring attention to a problem involving Baroque opera. There is at least one reason (among many others) why it is impossible to duplicate this kind of opera as it was done in the 18th century, and that is the disappearance of the singing machine for which many roles were created. I refer, of course, to the castratos. These *evirati* were, technically, the greatest singers who ever lived, these unfortunates with the lungs of a man and the voice of a woman.

We can only guess how they sounded. The recordings made in the first decade of this century by the only castrato who ever made discs, Alessandro Moreschi, give only a faint idea of what the castrato style represented. Moreschi, who sang with the Vatican chorus, was elderly when he recorded, and at his best was not a very commanding singer, certainly not one who could come anywhere near the great ones.

This is not guesswork or hearsay. There are too many descriptions by competent authorities—musicians of the caliber of Johann Quantz—that tell us exactly what those marvels could do. When Quantz writes that he timed Farinelli holding and deco- rating a note for about sixty seconds, which is about six times longer than the breath duration of any singer you or I have ever heard, there is no reason for disbelieving him, all the more in that other musicians with perfect ears back Quantz up. Castra- tos were trained to hold notes seemingly forever, and they had techniques unequaled by any singers before or since.

Henry Pleasants, in *The Great Singers*, and Ida Franca, in her *Manual of Bel Canto*, have a good deal to say about the castra- tos, and the interested reader can look them up (Simon and Schuster and Coward-McCann, respectively). Franca traces the castration of young boys (of pre-puberty age) for singing purposes back to the ancient Greeks. The medieval church found use for the *evirati*. For had not Saint Paul written: "Let your women keep silence in the churches"? and to Saint Timothy: "But I suffer not a woman to teach, nor to usurp authority over men, but to be in silence." Women were forbidden to speak, much less sing, in church. For a time, men who sang falsetto were used in the services. But the castratos had much more beautiful voices, and they were officially admitted to the Sistine Chapel in 1599 (though many had sung there previously).

In the eighteenth century they reached their height, leaving the church to sing in opera and give recitals. They were the first of the musical matinee idols, and the great ones died rich and respected. They had come up the hard way. Many greedy par- ents, nearly all of them in Italy, subjected their boys to the cruel operation, hoping they would be as rich and famous as Farinelli or Caffarelli. The operation was illegal. Parents would gravely explain that their boy had been involved in an accident—such as being butted in the testes by a goat—that necessitated the operation. Anyway the castratos were sent to singing school, and there they really worked.

Perhaps the most famous voice teacher was Nicola Porpora. In the morning he would have his pupils sing an hour of difficult passages, work on diction and enunciation for an hour, sing be- fore a mirror for an hour. In the afternoon there was a half hour of theory, a half hour of improvisation, an hour of counterpoint, another hour of diction and enunciation. The pupil also was expected to play the harpsichord and compose.

Improvisation and composition were very important. In those days it was expected, by the public and even by the more or less reluctant composer, that the leading singers would insert their own embellishments, cadenzas and even modifications of the vocal line. The better singers did this tastefully; the more exhibitionistic ones actually changed the music and overloaded it with monstrous excrescences. That was one reason for Gluck's famous operatic reforms; he wanted a return to simplicity and demanded that his singers sing exactly what was written in the score (though even he permitted a certain amount of tasteful embellishment).

When the castratos were ready for public performance, they were complete singers. Many had voices of three octaves in range, and a few came very close to four. Some voices were contralto-like, some were high sopranos. The sopranos could go far above the staff. Quantz reports that Farinelli had an F above high C in full voice (not falsetto). Their specialty was breath control; within one breath they could announce a melody, embellish it and add an impromptu cadenza. Giovanni Bontempi, himself a singer, has described the great Baldassare Ferri's voice as follows:

"What this noble singer expressed with his voice is beyond description. There was, to begin with, the purity of his voice and his success with every kind of passage, the impact of the trills, and the ease and grace with which he achieved every note. But beyond all that, after a very long and sustained passage beyond the lung capacity of any other singer, he would, without taking a breath, go into a very long and lovely trill and then into still another passage, more brilliant and beautiful than the first, and all this while remaining as still as a statue, and without any movement of the brow, the mouth or the body.

"To sing a descending chromatic scale, trilling on each note, from the high G and A to the same note in the lower octave, a feat if not impossible certainly very difficult for any other singer, was child's play for Ferri; for again, without taking a breath, he would continue on to other trills, passages and artistic wonders.

He often added a soft crescendo to these chromatic scales, building out the trills at the same time, a feat never previously accomplished or heard of."

Carlo Broschi (1705–82), who sang under the name of Farinelli, was considered the greatest of all castrato singers. Hence he was probably the greatest singer who ever lived. Quantz describes his voice as "a penetrating, well-rounded, luscious, clear and even soprano whose range at that time"—1726—"was from the low A to the D above high C. In later years it was extended several tones below without the loss of the high notes." Elsewhere Quantz refers to Farinelli's high F. "The result was that in many operas there would be an adagio for him in the contralto range, and another in the soprano. His intonation was pure, his trill beautiful, his lung capacity extraordinary and his throat very flexible, so that he could sing the most distant intervals in fast tempi and with the greatest ease and accuracy. In arbitrary embellishment of an adagio he was very inventive." Farinelli for years was the court singer and favorite of Philip V of Spain. Incorruptible, intelligent, a good administrator, he helped Philip in affairs of state, and in many respects he actually ran the country. There should be a fascinating biography in this remarkable man.

The vocal genius of the castratos did not extend to acting. It is hard to act when you are grotesque. Because of the operation, many castratos developed secondary sexual characteristics. They became stout, had huge torsos, spindly legs, the breasts of a woman. But it seems that their sexual life was untouched. Some were homosexuals. Others had affairs and a few even married. Women pursued these glamorous, wealthy, ungainly figures, especially decadent or bored women, out for a new kind of thrill. There were many such in the aristocracy of the eighteenth century. They also knew that, come what may, there would be no children. No wonder the castratos were spoiled.

But there never were singers like them, and one can only thrill in imagination to such a one as Farinelli—Farinelli with his powerful and sonorous voice, his unparalleled breath control, his perfectly equalized scales, his "creative genius that inspired him with embellishments so new and so astonishing that nobody was able to imitate them," his ability to take a breath "so softly and evenly that nobody could perceive where it began and died within him," his "union of the registers," his agility, "and a trill as admirable as it was rare." Time and time again admirers would refer to Farinelli's "divine trill." Ah Edison, Edison. Thou should'st been living at that hour.

MARCH 28, 1971

In over fifty years of exposure to great singing I never heard a female voice that equaled Rosa Ponselle's. This statement need not be taken on faith. She made many records, and from them one who never heard the great lady can thrill to the purity and intensity of the singing. She also—and this has never been stressed enough—was a superb musician, one who sang with taste and feeling as well as with prodigality. The very fact that she learned the principal roles in so many oddball operas indicates that she was much more than a dilettante blessed with a unique voice. I was all set to attend the gala honoring her seventy-fifth birthday. The Baltimore Symphony strike scuttled that, so I phoned Madame Ponselle and got something better —an exclusive interview.

There Was Nothing Like the Ponselle Sound, Ever

THE VOICE on the telephone sent shivers down the back. It was low, throaty, sexy, vibrant, expressive. "How nice that you would like to see me," said the voice. "Do come down tomorrow. Only a few hours? I do wish it could be longer. *Arrivederci!*"

It was the voice of Rosa Ponselle, and the dazed caller hung up and leaned back, transported in time some forty years back. Black Depression days, those; but somehow one could always manage to find seventy-five cents for standing room in the Family Circle of the Metropolitan Opera. When Rosa Ponselle was singing, the vast distance between stage and upstairs standing room seemed diminished. That big, pure, colorful golden voice would rise effortlessly, hitting the stunned listener in the face, rolling over the body, sliding down the shoulderblades, making one wiggle with sheer physical pleasure.

There are voices and voices, and the Metropolitan Opera in the 1930's had many great ones. But there was nothing like the Ponselle sound, ever. To many of us it was the greatest single voice in any category. Rethberg may have had the silvery purity. Melchior was a trumpet. Flagstad was monumental—and monumentally sexless. Bori had that sweet, ultrafeminine, cuddly sound. Gigli had the unparalleled sweetness. But Ponselle seemed to have everything. She could sing Violetta, and she also could sing Norma, and Rezia in *Oberon.* She had the low notes of a contralto, and a knockout high C; and there were no artificial registers to the voice—it went from bottom to top in the smoothest, most seamless of scales, with no shifting from chest to head. And that trill: that articulated br-r-r which no singer today is able to come near matching! And the emotionalism of her singing, withal combined with good taste! And the power when she let loose! And the delicacy of her pianissimos! And the flexibility in coloratura work! And that effortless production! And the accuracy of intonation! And the handsome figure on stage! The good fairy was very kind to Rosa Ponselle.

She made her debut on November 15, 1918 and, at the height of her career, in the full glory of her voice, abruptly called it quits after the 1936–37 season. She retired to her Villa Pace in Baltimore (*Pace, pace, mio Dio;* it was in *La Forza del Destino* that she had made her debut), was divorced from her husband about twenty years ago, and continues to live in her villa, acting as artistic director of the Baltimore Opera, interesting herself in young singers, giving her advice to many international headliners who come to her door.

And to humble admirers who come to her door. Last week she made a grand entrance into the living room, every bit the diva, accompanied by a half-dozen or so yipping toy poodles. It was a few days before her seventy-fifth birthday, which took place yesterday, and there was supposed to be a gala concert in her honor today. That was canceled because of the strike of the Baltimore Symphony players. "How sad!" she said. "I was so looking forward to it." Would she perhaps have sung at the gala? Madame Ponselle laughed. "If I were warmed up I could do it," she said. "Still."

She would have been nervous. She always was nervous. Her nervousness was a legend. In the old days she would arrive early on evenings she was singing, and walk around the old Met a half-dozen times before she got up enough nerve to go in. That was especially true if the opera was *Aïda*.

"I had a complex about the high C in *O patria mia*," she said. "In the early days high notes never bothered me. I could sing the C standing on my head. But one performance I got out of sick bed to sing *Aïda*, and when I got to the C, I couldn't hold it as long as I would have liked. That was at the Brooklyn Academy, I remember. It gave me such a complex! After *O patria mia* I was comfortable, and the rest of the Nile Scene did not bother me. But that first C! I went along like this for a long time, in terror, and then Serafin said: 'Why worry? We can transpose the ending of *O patria mia* a half-tone down. Everybody does it. Caruso used to transpose his C's down.' "

This had never occurred to Ponselle. It was a revelation. "*Now* you tell me," she said. So she sang a B in *O patria mia*, but only in that aria. All other high C's were easy for her. "I felt pounds lighter."

Madame Ponselle is seventy-five but she is full of joie de vivre, likes to rattle on in nonstop manner, likes to listen to her recordings, likes to talk about the old days. How she got into opera, for instance. She had never thought about it in 1918. Indeed, she had never learned an operatic role, and had attended only two operas in her life. In those days the attractive young lady from Meriden, Conn., the daughter of an Italian immigrant named Ponzillo, was singing in a sister act at the Palace vaudeville house with her elder sister Carmela. "Sister acts were a big thing in 1918."

Word got around about those two phenomenal voices ("Carmela and I ended our act with the *Faust* Trio!") and a voice teacher named William Thorner got interested in the two girls. Until then, Rosa never had had a lesson. Thorner did not teach her very much about singing. "I wouldn't let him *touch* my voice!" He did, however, coach her in some arias, and he had contacts at the Metropolitan.

What Ponselle did not know was that the Metropolitan Opera was looking for a dramatic soprano. Caruso wanted to revive *La Forza del Destino*, and there was nobody around who could sing Leonora. Some seasons previously, the great soprano Celestina Boninsegna was singing opposite Caruso, but he did not like her very much and, in addition, she was a short, dumpy woman. She did not last long at the Metropolitan.

So Caruso, tipped off by Thorner, walked into the studio with a few friends and listened to the young American. He heard enough in a few minutes to make up his mind.

"You will sing with me," he said. Ponselle remembers being paralyzed. But sing with him she did, about six months later. "Caruso," she says. "The sublime voice. You can't describe it. You die at the first note."

That was on November 15th. Only a little over two months later, Ponselle sang the role of Rezia in *Oberon*, and to the professional that is indeed significant. Here was a girl who was completely untrained in opera. She learns two major roles in short order, one of them (Rezia) little known and of extreme difficulty. Obviously she must have had brains and aptitude in addition to the once-in-a-century voice. The music critics of the day, Huneker and Henderson among them, refused to believe that Ponselle had come to the house without training.

During the following twenty years, Ponselle sang twenty-two roles, some of them very curious. She did appear in *Don Carlos*, *Ernani*, *La Gioconda*, *Andrea Chenier*, *Norma*, *Don Giovanni*, *Cavalleria Rusticana*, *La Traviata* and *Carmen*. But she also sang the leading soprano roles in such forgotten operas as Breil's *The Legend*, Rossini's *William Tell*, Meyerbeer's *L'Africaine*,

Spontini's *La Vestale,* Montemezzi's *L'Amore dei Tre Re* and *La Notte di Zoraima,* and Romani's *Fedra.* Gatti-Casazza, the general manager of the Metropolitan Opera, pressed those roles upon her, and like a good girl she said yes every time. Imagine the reaction if today's general manager asked one of his stars— *the* star, indeed—to sing in an opera by Montemezzi or Romani! Ponselle's repertory was indeed curious. She never sang Puccini, for instance, nor did she have any Wagner roles. A voice of that size and color could have made a sensation in the early Wagner operas.

"I would have loved to have done Elsa and Elisabeth," she says. "Not Brünnhilde, which Gatti asked me to do. I had more brains than that. I would have loved to sing Tosca. Desdemona. But I never had the time. I was always learning new roles in strange operas."

Finally, after twenty years, Ponselle asked the Met management for a role she dearly wanted to do—Adriana Lecouvreur, in the Cilèa opera of that name. Edward Johnson turned her down. Ponselle turned the Metropolitan down. Her contract was not renewed, and she had a nervous breakdown. Since 1936 she has not put foot into the Metropolitan Opera.

"I was demoralized," she says. "I always was sensitive, and people have to treat me like *this*"—stroking her forearm gently.

In 1953, at the age of fifty-six, she made a record at her home. It was a private recording, in which she and Carmela (who now lives in New York) and "some of my kids" (the Baltimore Opera youngsters) sang odds and ends to an electric organ background. It was all impromptu. But there are unforgettable sequences of sound when Ponselle opens her mouth. Now the voice is deep ruby-red instead of gold, but the tactile richness, the awesome authority, the smooth passage from register to register—all this is prime Ponselle.

Nobody around has this kind of sound. Why, one wondered. "Everything is too *fast* today," Ponselle said. "It's the greed for money in this jet age. Singers run everywhere, unprepared, and performances are sloppy and unintegrated. There is no real involvement, no *pride.*" She relaxed and listened to her record, her eyes shining. "Listen!" she said. *"Listen!"* when something especially good was to come up. She absentmindedly beat time, her mind probably back on the stage of the Met.

"I can't explain how I did it," she said. "Geraldine Farrar once said that voices like Caruso's and mine came from God."

JAN. 23, 1972

Just as Rosa Ponselle was the greatest dramatic soprano of my time, so Lauritz Melchior was the greatest tenor. His problem was that he had no competition in his chosen repertory. A singer—any artist—needs to be pushed, needs to measure up to something, needs challenge. Melchior was, simply, unique, and there was nobody remotely near him. Thus he became a law unto himself. It was not that he failed to discharge his artistic responsibilities (though sometimes his behavior on stage could *be perfunctory). Rather it was that he could have done so much more.*

The Heldentenor Species Died with Melchior

LAURITZ MELCHIOR lived a long and a full life, and he died full of honors, and he left his mark on singing in the twentieth century. Yet it was with a pang that one music lover heard about his death last Monday. In a way, Melchior was an integral part of the life of anybody who went to the Metropolitan Opera from 1926 to his retirement in 1950. He was there every season, singing the heroic Wagnerian roles—big, tireless, with *the* unique male voice after Caruso. When he retired, many of us had the feeling that an age was over, and we were right.

For, in a way, the Heldentenor species died with him. Certainly nobody since Melchior's retirement has begun to approximate the glory of that voice. The man may not have been the best actor, and he was constructed along the lines of a bull walrus, which meant that he was not the most credible figure as the young Siegfried or the warrior Tristan. (Although, come to think of it, Ludwig Schnorr, Wagner's first Tristan, was constructed along the lines of a watermelon.) But he had the most heroic voice of any singer of his day and, it could well be, any singer of history.

He made all other singers sound pale. In the 1930's there were such fine Wagnerian tenors as Max Lorenz and Franz Völker; and before them there was Leo Slezak; and before *them* the near-mythical Jean de Reszke. One can listen to their records with respect (there are some cylinder fragments of de Reszke's voice which, when studied carefully, give an index of his singing). None of them had the clarion sound of Melchior.

When Melchior sang, he not only could generate an awesome body of sound, he could also give the feeling that this was nothing, that he had an untold reserve to draw upon if he so wished. Most of today's Heldentenors have to sing all out, eyes popping, veins near bursting. They have to pace themselves carefully. Not Melchior, who gave carelessly and prodigally.

And he did this year after year, giving the lie to those who thought Wagner was death on the human voice. There was surprisingly little deterioration in Melchior's singing even toward the end of his career. The story is told around the Met that after one of his arguments with Rudolf Bing—the general manager had let it be known that Melchior's voice was gone, that he could not sustain a note any longer—Melchior and the conductor cooked up a deal for the tenor's next performance in *Walküre*. The conductor agreed to hold the orchestra on the *Wälse, Wälse* outburst as long as Melchior could hold the note. The performance came, and Melchior did just that, holding the two climaxes for an incredible length. "Like a signal generator," somebody said. "Steady, pure and loud." It may not have been good Wagner, but Melchior proved his point. He showed Mr. Bing.

There was talk in musical circles that Melchior was lazy. He probably was. His repertory was small, perhaps the smallest of any of the great singers of his day. At the Metropolitan, he confined himself exclusively to the Wagner roles, avoiding only the role of Walther in *Die Meistersinger.* There were so many things he could have sung: Otello, Florestan, Radames, Vasco da Gama. But no. Occasionally he recorded pieces out of his repertory, showing everybody what he could have done had he bestirred himself.

What Melchior did not realize was that he was stifling himself and his art. A singer needs challenge. Melchior, avoiding challenge, got to the point where he was doing things by rote. Nothing ever happened to his glorious voice. There was no diminution there. But year by year his acting got more and more perfunctory, and he must have driven stage directors out of their minds. His antics in *Parsifal* were a case in point, and Bing was perfectly correct in objecting. The tenor, during the Act I Grail scene in *Parsifal,* is supposed to stand motionless for about half an hour, listening to the service as one bemused. Melchior simply refused to do it. Perhaps his big body—he was a heavy man —objected to the strain. Perhaps he kept thinking of his card game with the stagehands. Whatever the reason, he would imperceptibly begin to sidle to the exit: an inch here, a step there. Suddenly he was gone and the scene would go on without him.

In his day he had some great sopranos to work with. Maria Mueller, Frida Leider, Grete Stückgold and Kirsten Flagstad were at the house with him in the 1930's, and in the 1940's came Helen Traubel. He worked best, of course, with Flagstad; they stimulated each other, and there never was a team like that. Both had godlike voices of comparable quality: huge, clear, accurate, instrumental-like, vibrato-free. Some critics were bothered with what they called Melchior's lack of musicianship and rhythmic freedom. But when he and Flagstad blended voices in the second act of *Tristan und Isolde,* or when they rose to the heavens in the final act of *Siegfried,* there simply could be no criticism. Never in the history of opera had two such extraordinarily endowed singers come together. Never in the history of opera had there been such a sheerly thrilling sound.

Melchior always maintained that all Heldentenors should follow his recipe: start as a baritone, and take plenty of time before singing the big Wagner roles. (Jean de Reszke, before the turn of the century, had also started as a baritone and sang the Heldentenor roles only toward the end of his career.) Wagner was, unlike Verdi, not a high-note composer. George Bernard Shaw was constantly pointing out that Verdi concentrated on the upper fifth of the register, whereas Wagner spread the singing throughout all the registers, using high notes relatively seldom. Hence the necessity for a baritonal underpinning in the Wagner tenor roles. It also was Shaw's thesis that—general belief to the contrary notwithstanding—Verdi was more ruinous to the singing voice than Wagner with all of the German composer's heavy orchestration and long-distance efforts.

And it is a fact that many Wagnerians have had long careers. Melchior had almost four decades before the public (he made his debut in 1913 and came to the Met in 1926), and his career was by no means unusual in that respect. Just think of such singers as Lilli Lehmann, who kept going nearly forever. The only difference was that the Lehmann type of artist sang everything, whereas Melchior was content to reign within only a small segment of the repertory. But within his limitations he was the absolute monarch of all time. And his tragedy—if indeed it is a tragedy, considering his accomplishment—is that he could have been the absolute monarch of all singing had he possessed the drive to do so.

March 25, 1973

PART VII
Piano

One does not sit down to play the piano in order to demonstrate a mathematical truth.

—FRIEDRICH HEBBEL

I used Sviatoslav Richter's New York debut as a springboard for a topic that greatly interested me. Emil Gilels in 1955 and David Oistrakh the following year were the first to come over from the Soviet Union, and they were followed by a small group of which Richter was the culmination. But even in Richter's playing—and he was the most serious and intellectual of them all—I was disturbed by certain gaucheries which, in a player of his strength, could only be attributed to provincialism. Hence the discussion of Soviet training and the need for Soviet musicians to enter the intellectual life of the West. Some did, with a vengeance, defecting. Today, after some twenty-five years of cultural interchange, Soviet musicians tend to sound like musicians everywhere else—except for high-voiced singers. For some reason, Russian sopranos and tenors sound shrill and edgy, squeezing from the throat—but I won't go into that here. To get back to Richter: he has not played much in the United States, and it is said that he does not like it here.

An Evaluation of
Sviatoslav Richter

WITH SVIATOSLAV RICHTER, recently departed shores, it was a clear case of venividivici. (Why word of it?) Certainly it was the most unparallele this writer has ever observed. Part of it was, of c But a very large part was sheer personality. T

who have better technical equipment—Cherkassky, say. There are pianists who are better rounded, such as Rubinstein. There are pianists who are superior colorists, such as Novaes, and pianists with more strength, such as Serkin. And there are many pianists with more scholarship.

But Richter had only to walk on the stage to make his audience swoon. There is something about his appearance that instantly overpowers the listener. Critical judgment seems to go by the wayside and mass hypnosis sets in. Richter at his best is a wonderful pianist, one of the elect, but he is not *that* good. Nobody ever was or will be.

The Russian pianist is obviously a dedicated artist and a sincere musician. In many respects he is a born pianist. His technique—and we can forget the many wrong notes that spattered through his recitals—is natural, flexible and all-encompassing. Most of all, his tone is nearly unparalleled today. He really makes the piano sing, and that is an art almost forgotten.

But he is an erratic pianist, and his recordings should have prepared American listeners for that. Often his ideas are unorthodox. Now, unorthodoxy in itself is nothing to condemn. Many great creators are unorthodox. But unorthodoxy that seems to have no basis in experience—using the word "experience" in its Platonic sense—means little except to the person himself. And some of Richter's ideas, as in the Tchaikovsky B flat minor Concerto, were hard to explain on any rationale, just as it was hard to explain how so experienced a musician could go so haywire in the coda of Beethoven's *Appassionata* Sonata.

Thus he has his limitations. Fortunately for us, his playing also has its moments of sheer glory. The man has imagination, and when everything fuses, the result is incandescent. And one other thing: his playing is always interesting, if for no other reason than one is always conscious of an unusual mind behind the music. Win, lose or draw, a Richter recital remains an event even when he is at his most inexplicable.

Perhaps the main trouble with Richter is that his has been a one-sided development. Up to last year he had never played in a non-Communist country. The inevitable result is that in some

respects his playing tends to be provincial. One has noticed this again and again with Russian artists coming to the West for the first time.

It is provincial in that it reflects only a specific school—the Russian. Admittedly there are various schools of pianism—the Slavic, the French, the American (recently), the English and the German. But all Western artists, whatever their origin or training, reflect a cosmopolitan point of view. As they travel around the world they cannot help but take in the best that colleagues everywhere have to offer.

Until recently, however, the Russians were isolated. They learned to make music a certain way; and that way had many elements that had been discarded by the West for many years. The Russian style is not normally noted for its subtlety. Russian musicians, ballet companies and even orchestras, when they first emerge from their homeland, make music (or dance) with the big gesture. Before the second subject of a sonata, for example, there invariably is a long ritard preparing the listener for the change in mood; and when the second subject does arrive, likely as not it will be in a slower tempo. They really let you know in advance what is going to happen.

But, one notices, by the time the Russian musician has made his third or fourth visit, there no longer is this type of provincialism. What has happened is that he has been talking with his colleagues in Germany, in England and America. He has been matching ideas (and not only musical ones, either), discarding some of his old notions, accepting some new ones. The intellectual climate of the non-Russian world has been revealed to him, and if he is anything but a pig-headed doctrinaire he takes advantage of them. (It works the other way around, too. No Westerner can fail to profit from studying the work of the Soviet musicians, for, goodness knows, they have plenty to offer.)

The career of Emil Gilels is a case in point. When he first came here there was no doubt that he could play the piano. But some interpretive crudities did raise doubt about the finish of his musicianship. Now that he has been playing in the West for a good part of the decade, he is a different musician entirely— one much more suave, assured and interesting. He has retained the best elements of the Russian style and added to them a patina that he could not possibly have achieved in his own country. I submit that this is not merely the case of an artist maturing as he grows older and more experienced. It is the case of an artist being exposed to a new and stimulating intellectual climate, without which he could not possibly have developed as he did, if at all.

Even the great David Oistrakh revealed amazing (to Western minds) deficiencies on his first visit here. His Mozart was unstylistic, played with the same throbbing vibrato that he applied to Bruch and Tchaikovsky. This was the way he had learned to play Mozart in Russia. Indeed, he played everything much the same way—with incredible polish and fluency, to be sure, but without the backbone one looked for. The playing by itself was sheer sensuous delight; the music-making tended to be limp. Later a sharper, more incisive approach was noted in his playing. Oistrakh will always remain the Romantic fiddler par excellence, but at least his vision has broadened a little—not as much as that of the younger Gilels, but enough to make an appreciable difference.

Thus it may be impertinent to say of an artist of Richter's stature that he has much to learn, but that happens very truly to be the case. He already has learned everything that his own country could offer him. Now he must adapt his thinking to new influences. He must browse in the cosmopolitan markets, sniffing this, tasting that, restocking his larder and consigning to the garbage heap some stale material.

As it is, he is one of the world's great pianists. If the Russians let him out of the country with regular frequency, his playing in the next ten years should develop into something extraordinary. (He is only forty-five years old.) He has everything in his favor, for he is singularly gifted—a pianist with unusual technical facility, a musician of integrity, and an altogether fascinating mind. All that is lacking is a real knowledge of the many directions that musical thought has taken outside of Russia in the last generation.

JAN. 8, 1961

*Artur (who now spells his first name Arthur) Rubinstein contin-
ued to play until the age of ninety, fifteen years after this Sunday piece was written. He also completed the two volumes of
his autobiography, took up with a young lady and finally—
when his eyesight began to fail (today he is almost blind)—left
the piano for good. There is a minor error in this article. Rubinstein was recording long before 1932. Some of his 1927 HMV
records even more strongly belie his oft-quoted statement that
he was a sloppy pianist. He plays such difficult things as the
Liszt Tenth Rhapsody and the Albeniz Navarra with irresistible
elan and flawless finger work. I would also like to tone down
my remarks about the older generation of pianists. Not all of
them took the liberties I describe, and many of the great ones
were, if anything, classic. Rubinstein, by the way, never did get
around to recording the Rimsky-Korsakov or Rubinstein D
minor concertos. But he did finish his two-volume autobiography.*

The Rubinstein Touch

SEVERAL YEARS ago Artur Rubinstein was discussing young
American pianists. "You know," he said, "they are fabulous.
They play better than I do. No, I am not joking. I mean it. Such
technique! Such musicianship! They do things I wouldn't begin
to attempt."

Rubinstein paused to let the point sink in.

"But when they come on stage," he said, "they might as well
be soda jerks."

Nobody has ever accused Rubinstein of coming on stage like
a soda jerk. When he strides out, walking briskly and as often as
not dodging the people who were lucky enough to get seats on
the stage at the last minute, it is one of the few regal entrances
music has left to offer. Not a tall man (he is a little under 5 feet
8 inches), he nevertheless looks like Gog rolled into Magog as
he confidently approaches the piano.

Without trying, he lets the audience immediately feel that it is facing a Presence. Look, my lord, it comes. Polite, agreeable, not gushing, he accepts the homage due him. He seats himself, and his nose points toward the stratosphere like the prow of a jet going upstairs. The audience waits, breathless. Rubinstein is in no hurry. He must compose himself; he must think of the opening piece; he must wait for the last cough to dissipate before he puts his hands on the keyboard. Suddenly the auditorium is filled with golden piano sound. A typical Rubinstein concert is under way.

Rubinstein will be seventy-five years old on Tuesday, and he has been playing the piano for about seventy-one of those years. At the age of four he already was a famous citizen of Lodz, and was passing out engraved cards on which was written "Artur the Great Piano Virtuoso." Seventy-one years later he is going strong. His colleagues consider him a miracle, geriatrics experts mumble when they talk about him, and nobody will put up much of an argument when he is called the greatest living pianist. Vladimir Horowitz may have a more glittering technique, Rudolf Serkin may have a better way with German music, Rosalyn Tureck more of an affinity for Bach, Sviatoslav Richter for Prokofiev and Scriabin, and Claudio Arrau may have a bigger repertory. But no pianist has put everything together the way Rubinstein has. Others may be superior in specific things, but Rubinstein is the complete pianist.

At seventy-five, an age when the coordination of most instrumentalists is gone, Rubinstein seems to play with ever-increasing steadiness. About ten years ago he recorded the Schumann *Carnaval*. Last year he re-recorded the work, and there was no question but that it was a better performance. He moves with ease through a large repertory starting with Mozart (in the last few years he has played and recorded a group of Mozart concertos he had never previously touched), proceeding through middle-period Beethoven (he does not play the last five sonatas) and the entire 19th century, and ending up with the impressionists, modern Spanish music, and even such later figures as Villa-Lobos and Szymanowski. His particular composer, though, is Chopin, and as a Chopinist, he is unparalleled today.

He loves what he is doing, and communicates his love to the

audience. The audience reciprocates. Until recently, Rubinstein played over a hundred dates a year. When he was sixty-four years old he felt impelled to give a concerto cycle in New York, playing seventeen concertos in five concerts spread over twelve days. That was nothing compared with his feat in 1961, when he gave ten Carnegie Hall concerts in one season.

Like most major pianists, he has played all over the world. Next October he will visit Russia. The only country he has avoided is Germany. He has not played there since World War I, when he was appalled by the atrocities in Belgium. His dislike of Germany was not improved in 1939 and thereafter. He had "an enormous family" in Poland. "All were killed by Hitler," he simply says. To interviewers he has said, many times, that there are two countries where he has not played—Tibet, because it is too high, and Germany, because it is too low. Otherwise, he plays everywhere, continually, and thrives on it.

"I rest while I am on tour," he says. "I lead a lazy life which most people call tremendously busy. I don't even practice any more. But I am writing my autobiography. I promised it to my good friend Alfred Knopf twenty-one years ago. He advanced me $250 and would not take it back. Last summer I really started working on it. Up to that point I had gotten only to the age of ten."

Rubinstein's statement about not practicing brings a polite, disbelieving smile to most musicians' faces. Pianists, on the whole, practice from five to seven hours a day, 365 days a year. They are compulsive about it. But Rubinstein is telling the truth. His wife, Aniela—everybody calls her Nela—goes through tortures at all of his concerts. She comes from a musical family (her father was an important conductor in Poland) and she has been around pianists all her life. Rubinstein's method drives her out of her mind.

"Artur terrifies me," she says. "And after all these years!" (They were married in 1932.) "He will not work too long on a piece because he is afraid it will lose spontaneity, become stale. And you must remember that he has a wonderful memory and is a *very* experienced musician. After all, he has been playing the same pieces for many years. So the day before the concert he will perhaps run through certain sections of a piece that might give him trouble. Then, the afternoon of a concert, he will play through the whole program, fast, to make sure it is in his fingers.

"On the way to the concert, in the taxi, Artur will complain bitterly. He will say that his fingers are spaghetti, that he will have memory lapses, that he will disgrace himself, that he will never play again. He reduces me to absolute jelly. I understand, but when I sit in my box I die a thousand deaths. Then he comes out and plays the first measures and I know everything is going to be all right."

Backstage, before his concerts, Rubinstein does not appear nervous. Walter Hupfer, who was his tuner for many years, says that he is relaxed and very normal. "He doesn't look worried," Hupfer says. "He knows his instrument and his audience. He doesn't go in for a flashy, fast piano like so many young pianists do. He likes a smooth, mellow instrument with normal action —not stiff, not light."

Hupfer also traveled with Horowitz, and he admires both pianists no end. "Horowitz is like Babe Ruth hitting a home run. Rubinstein is more like Gehrig, played every day, always dependable, get what I mean?"

Steve Borell, who currently is Rubinstein's tuner now that Hupfer has retired from Steinway, also says that Rubinstein demands a smooth, mellow piano that is even in tone and regulation. "And believe me, he knows pianos. For a solo concert he tunes to 440-A, on the sharp side. If he is nervous before a concert, it is not the slightest bit evident." Borell, talking about Rubinstein a few weeks ago, came up with a perfect capsule evaluation of the pianist: "He has contentment and health of mind, and his happiness reflects in his playing."

Rubinstein nevertheless admits to butterflies before he walks out. "Fear before each concert is the price I pay for my superb life." His nervousness immediately dissipates when he strikes the first note. "There are two kinds of shakes. One kind is necessary, to get you into the blessed state of nervous preparation. You can't become inspired without it." The other kind is "the paralyzing kind. If you have that, the only advice I can give you is, don't play in public."

By now Rubinstein has been interviewed to the point where he is in the public domain. Even nonmusical readers know most of the stories about him—about his penchant for the good life, his impeccable taste in wines and cigars, his love of good food, his fine collection of impressionistic paintings (Vuillard is the specialty of the house), his happy-go-lucky life before his marriage, his linguistic ability (perfect in eight languages), his high standing as a raconteur.

When Rubinstein tells a story he really throws himself into it. He acts it out. His face gets wrinkled and shriveled when he is imitating an old man; he simpers when describing a young lady; he climbs on a chair and beats time when telling an anecdote about a conductor. Gregor Piatigorsky, his good friend (it was Piatigorsky who said: "Who is the only musician who has a cello tone like mine? Rubinstein!"), is also one of the great raconteurs, and when the two of them are in a room, the tempo mounts to a hysterical point where perhaps Truth slinks from the room, abashed.

"I was at a party," a friend has said. "Piatigorsky told a story about being in a room with three queens. He shot a look at Rubinstein. Damned if Rubinstein didn't immediately come up with a story about an experience he once had with *four* queens in a *bedroom*. Grisha threw up his hands. 'That one I can't top, Artur,' he said."

Through the years Rubinstein has been telling interviewers about his early life, insisting that he was a talented but sloppy pianist who played more wrong notes than correct ones. He stresses the boulevardier-playboy aspects of his life.

"Looking back at it," he will say, "I was tremendously musical. And I was an avant-gardist. I played all the new music. But I neglected the piano as a virtuoso instrument." Rubinstein's one teacher, Heinrich Barth in Berlin, was a conservative who forbade his pupils to listen to Wagner. Rubinstein moonlighted, learning *Tristan* and *Meistersinger* by heart and also, horror of horrors, the earsplitting monstrosities of Richard Strauss. "I made a career of playing *Salome* in the salons," Rubinstein says. He also investigated the music of Prokofiev, Debussy, Ravel, Stravinsky, Milhaud and the other modernists of the period. But music was the least of it.

"I hung around artists and writers. I had many love affairs. After all, this was Paris. I did not like musicians particularly. All they would talk about was 'Who is the best manager?' and 'How much money did you make on your last tour?' No, I was satisfied to be an unfinished pianist who played with dash. Musicians were irritated and pianists were fur-r-r-ious, but the public loved it."

Statements like this make Mrs. Rubinstein angry. "Why does Artur want to make this kind of propaganda for himself?" she wants to know. "He *never* was a sloppy pianist. He *always* had a great technique. I was interested enough to look up the reviews of Artur's first two American tours, in 1906 and 1919. He got very good reviews and was accepted as one of the most talented pianists. Nobody called him a dilettante."

But the fact remains that Rubinstein never made a big impression in the United States and he left in the mid-nineteen-twenties vowing never to return. He started to make records in the early nineteen-thirties, and if nothing else, those records give the lie to Rubinstein's oft-repeated statement that he did not settle down to work until 1932. His recordings of the Tchaikovsky B flat minor Piano Concerto and the four Chopin scherzos are landmarks in the history of the phonograph; and technically they are flawless. Anybody who could manipulate the keyboard with such style, fluency and accuracy—this was long before LP days, when so many pianists are creations of the recording technicians—had to be one of the great pianists. And, furthermore, he had to be one of the great pianists for some time. A style and technique like that did not develop overnight.

Rubinstein's recordings began to interest the American public. "And," says Rubinstein, "Josef Lhévinne and other great pianists began making tremendous verbal propaganda about me." The day came when Sol Hurok, whose instinct for a personality that can combine great art with equally great gobs of revenue approaches the sublime, approached Rubinstein in London and invited him To Be Presented by Sol Hurok.

Rubinstein was honest about it. He told Hurok that he had never had an American success and that he, Hurok, would lose his shirt. "I can borrow another shirt," said Hurok. They shook hands. Hurok proved to be right. The American public went wild when Rubinstein returned in 1937, and the love affair between them has continued to grow.

Not only in America is Rubinstein idolized. When he returned to Poland a few years ago, it was cause for national rejoicing. Many foreign governments have paid tribute to Rubinstein. A few weeks ago a friend ran into him in the photographic studios of R.C.A. Victor. Rubinstein was resplendent. He was about to have his picture taken, and he was dressed in white tie and tails. He also was wearing some of his decorations. Across his shirt front was a red sash. Dangling from his neck was an order suspended from a ribbon. On his right breast was an order the size of a healthy cabbage. Over his left breast was a row of medals. Rubinstein ticked them off: Alfonso el Sabio, from Spain; Commander of the Legion of Honor ("personally presented to me by de Gaulle"); Commander of Arts and Letters from Chile; decorations from Belgium, Italy, Portugal, Poland.

For once in his life Rubinstein looked sheepish. "My children ordered me here," he said. "They wanted at least one picture of me with my decorations." Then he brightened. "There was this great pianist, Alfred Reisenauer," he said. "Reisenauer was a pupil of Liszt. Once he played at one of the German duchies. Swabia or something like that. When the concert was over, an equerry approached him backstage. Would he prefer a fee of a thousand marks, or the Order of the Purple Pig or whatever? Reisenauer asked: 'How much is the medal worth?' The equerry said twenty-five marks. 'All right,' said Reisenauer, 'I'll take the medal and 975 marks.'"

Rubinstein never has gone into it, and perhaps he has not analyzed it, but one reason he never made a great impression in America before 1937 was that previously he had been ahead of his time. Today Rubinstein is called a Romantic pianist, but he is not one, not if Romanticism is measured by the big pianists of the last century—pianists like Paderewski, Moriz Rosenthal, Vladimir de Pachmann and the other headliners. In an age when the big pianists took (in Rubinstein's own phrase) a slow swan dive into the keyboard, changing tempos and rhythms at will, mooning over emotional messages, constantly arpeggiating chords, changing the notes and striking the left hand before the right (this was supposed to be expressive), Rubinstein's direct and uncomplicated style was bound to leave audiences somewhat perplexed.

It would appear that Rubinstein was Rubinstein from the very beginning. He was influenced as a youth by Ferruccio Busoni, who in so many respects founded the modern school of piano playing. Busoni's probing attitude toward music, his strong intellectualism and his determination to purge interpretation of all excrescences that were called "tradition" left a strong mark on Rubinstein. So did Josef Hofmann's clear, direct style. Hofmann was considered a cold pianist at the turn of the century, and so was Rubinstein, who played Chopin without the mannerisms and affectations of the nineteenth-century Romanticists.

What young Rubinstein did, and what Rubinstein today has done, was to take the best of the old and the new. From the old he adopted a Romantic temperament, though without Romantic excess. From the old, too, he took the emphasis on tone that has never left him. From the new school he took textual fidelity, regularity of meter, and a horror of Romantic excess. What resulted was an amalgam: a pianist who had sentiment without sentimentality, high-tempered nervousness without neurosis, scholarship without pedanticism. An urbane man with eternal *joie de vivre*, his character is reflected in his playing. His interpretations are healthy, virile, sane, poetic. And they must have been the same in the nineteen-twenties.

By the nineteen-thirties, styles of piano playing were creeping up to Rubinstein's. The age of Romanticism was almost over. Gone were nearly all of the great Liszt and Leschetizky pupils. New concepts had come in: concepts of fidelity to the printed note (a concept that never, never concerned the Romantic musician); concepts that put more stress on Classic restraint than on Romantic flamboyance; concepts that concerned new theories about style. All of a sudden a handful of pianists were hailed as representatives of the new style: Rubinstein, Artur Schnabel, Myra Hess. They, of course, had been playing in the new style years before it had been discovered.

But styles eternally change. Rubinstein today is called—mistakenly—a Romanticist. And he is—in relation to the younger pianists, just as he was a Classicist in relation to the older ones. Today's new style is represented by the young spit-and-polish pianists, who never hit a wrong note, who come to music with the utmost dedication, and who all tend to sound alike. Rubinstein does not like this kind of junior executive, gray-flannel playing so common today.

"On stage," he says, "I will take a chance. There has to be an element of daring in great music-making. These younger ones, they are too cautious. They take the music out of their pockets instead of their hearts. And they know little about pedaling or tone production."

Rubinstein himself does not know how to explain the way he produces his tone—the tone that is the envy of all pianists. Part of his tonal genius is physical luck, the way he is built. Rubinstein is fortunate in his physical makeup. His hands do not look particularly large, but in reality they are enormous. His little finger is longer than the middle finger of most normal humans and his long thumb extends downward at an obtuse angle. That, plus the immense breadth of his palm, enables him to stretch a twelfth—C to G. Most pianists feel lucky if they can comfortably take a tenth. And Rubinstein's fingers are well padded at the tips. He has a perfect piano hand. But ask him how he produces his effects, and all he can do is go to the piano and illustrate. His wife thinks the secret is in Rubinstein's hand formation and his inner ear.

Rubinstein shows no signs of letting up. He still is a man of extraordinary vitality who gives the impression of bounding around when he is sitting still.

"I will play as long as I can," he says, "and I only hope my friends will tell me when I cannot." He has a great fear that he will continue to play without knowing when he has passed his prime. That day seems to be well in the future. Rubinstein has even stepped up his recording commitments. As it is, he has recorded more than any pianist in history except, possibly, Alfred Cortot.

"Why," says George Marek, head of R.C.A. Victor, "we have

just signed Rubinstein to a new eight-year contract. Rubinstein wants to record, this year alone, a couple of Mozart concertos, five or six standard concertos and two very unstandard ones— the Rubinstein D minor and the Rimsky-Korsakov. Then he has ideas for several Chopin discs and a lot of Liszt. Not bad, eh?'' Rubinstein through the years has been Victor's best-selling pianist, and the coming year should see his total of LP discs go over three million.

The Rubinsteins and their children divide their time between their houses in Paris (in the Square du Bois de Boulogne) and New York (upper Park Avenue). The children are Eva, thirty, married and living in Connecticut; Paul, twenty-nine, who works for R.C.A. Victor; Alina, nineteen, and John, seventeen. None is, or wants to be, a professional musician. "But John," says Rubinstein, "has a wonderful ear and knows scores better than most conductors." All of the children were educated in the United States.

"That was my job," says Mrs. Rubinstein. "When the children were young, I divided my time between them and Artur fifty-fifty. Artur was made to be a bachelor and not a father. I decided that the children must have a house and not live in hotel lobbies. I was very strict about that. Little by little, Artur became a father. There never were any problems, because contrary to what you might think, he never was away from his children too long. Think of business people. They see their children only on weekends. With Artur he was home all day when not on tour. And then there were long summers when he and the children were together all the time. So we had a perfect family life. Really the children saw him more than most children see their father."

It was Eva who took the leading role in one of the most famous Rubinstein stories. He came home from a tour and she rushed into his arms. "Play for me, daddy," she asked. Rubinstein, touched, sat at the piano. He was determined to play for her as he never in his life had played for anybody. He brought his hands up. "No, daddy," said Eva. "Not the piano. The phonograph."

JAN. 26, 1964

*My own pantheon of Romantic pianists has five gods: Josef
Hofmann, Sergei Rachmaninoff, Benno Moiseiwitsch, Josef
Lhévinne and Ignaz Friedman. Rachmaninoff and Hofmann
shared the apex. They complemented each other. Rachmaninoff
was steady, Hofmann mercurial; Rachmaninoff was the great
etcher, Hofmann the colorist. Two more colossal pianists never
existed. And they admired and loved each other. I interviewed
Hofmann during the war, in 1943, and he was still all broken
up about his friend's death. Henry Pleasants, when he was a
music critic in Philadelphia, once asked Rachmaninoff who the
great living pianists were besides himself. Rachmaninoff
thought a bit. "Well, there's Hofmann," he said, "and me," and
then he closed his lips.*

Did Rachmaninoff Collaborate with God?

TODAY IS the one hundredth anniversary of Rachmaninoff's
birth, and celebrations are in order. Many people will indeed
celebrate; the man left some of the favorite pieces of the twentieth century. The trouble is that, as far as his reputation is
concerned, those pieces—the C minor Piano Concerto, the C
sharp minor Prelude, the G minor Prelude—were and are too
popular.

Rachmaninoff is still very much played, because pianists cannot live without some of his music, and audiences adore it. But
his reputation in intellectual circles is nil. Some years ago this
column pointed out the ridiculous, British-upper-class capsule
estimate of Rachmaninoff in Grove's Dictionary. Unfortunately
it is a view still all too prevalent. Can you imagine, say, Pierre
Boulez devoting a season at the Philharmonic to a retrospective
of Rachmaninoff? That has as much chance of happening as the
earth reversing its spin, the sun going nova, and President Nixon
waiving executive privilege and ordering John W. Dean to tell
all he knows about Watergate.

There is no point talking much about Rachmaninoff's music. It is a constant; it fell into place many years back, has more than held its level, and will remain as it is no matter what changes of taste the future will bring. Rather it is of Rachmaninoff the musician in general and the pianist in particular of whom I would like to speak. For he had one of the more remarkable minds in musical history, and he was one of the greatest pianists who ever lived, and people are apt to forget just what he represented.

There are not too many available recordings of him as a pianist. There are many, for instance, of his great contemporary, Josef Hofmann. For Hofmann often played over the air, and collectors recorded his work from 1935 on, even though he himself did not make a commercial studio recording after about 1925. An extraordinary amount of Hofmann material has turned up in recent years. Of Rachmaninoff, virtually nothing. For he refused, on general principle, to appear on the radio. He was not going to go on a Sunday Philharmonic broadcast and play for X-numbers of people for nothing. When Rachmaninoff played with the Philharmonic, it was on Thursday, Friday and Saturday—but never on Sunday.

And most of his records—he made quite a few for Victor from 1924 almost to his death in 1943—are largely of his own music and are hard to locate. There were a few LP transfers of his playing that are now mostly out of print. Thus, a generation has grown up unfamiliar with the infallible hands that could create such beauty at the keyboard. (But this fall things will be different. R.C.A. will be bringing out a 15-disc release of all the Rachmaninoff recordings.)

He had it from the beginning, as all great pianists do. Rachmaninoff was the pride of the conservatory, the coming man. It was not only that he was such a phenomenal pianist. He could do everything—compose, conduct, sight-read, transpose. His memory was not only all-encompassing; it was actually frightening. He could hear a piece of music—a symphony, say —and play it back not only the next day but the next year. He had the kind of musical mind that immediately absorbs sound impressions or sight impressions. From ear and eye to brain and fingers was an instantaneous process.

His teacher at the Moscow Conservatory, Siloti, would give him a long and demanding piece to learn, and Rachmaninoff would memorize it virtually overnight. His classmate, the pianist and teacher Alexander Goldenweiser, vouches for the fact that Siloti assigned Rachmaninoff the Brahms-Handel Variations, and two days later Rachmaninoff played it "with complete artistic finish." Goldenweiser was baffled. "Whatever composition was ever mentioned—piano, orchestral, operatic or other—by a classical or contemporary composer, if Rachmaninoff had at any time heard it, and most of all, if he had liked it, he played it as if it were a work he had studied thoroughly."

When Rachmaninoff left Russia for good after the Revolution, he had his choice of careers. Several American orchestras, the Boston Symphony among them, asked him to take over as conductor. He was a marvelous conductor, as anybody who has heard his recording of his Third Symphony knows; his conducting had the same rhythmic vitality, precision and aristocracy as his piano playing. But he elected to concentrate on the piano, and to compose on the side. That meant he had to work up a repertory. He knew everything, of course, but he had not done serious concert playing for a long time, except in his own concertos, and he had to spend a bit of time getting his fingers loose again. When he started concertizing there was nobody like him. Only Hofmann was big enough to look him in the eye. Rachmaninoff always said that Hofmann was the greatest pianist of the day. Hofmann always said that Rachmaninoff was.

Fortunate are we who heard his recitals. Rachmaninoff would come out, stiff and severe, never smiling, his hair cropped as close as a convict's. With terrible dignity he would seat himself and wait for the audience to quiet. He played quietly, with a minimum of physical exertion, brooding over the keys. From his fingers came an indescribable tone: warm despite cautious use of the pedals, reaching into every corner of the hall, capable of infinite modulation. Not even Lhévinne had this kind of superclarity; not even Hofmann had this controlled precision.

Many believe that his playing was a bit puritanical, that he was one of the objectivists. False. He took plenty of liberties with the music, confident of his own taste. Hofmann was supposed to be the Romantic, but Hofmann, in truth, was much more the Classicist. For Rachmaninoff, unlike Hofmann, had no hesitation about altering notes and even harmonies, though he did this with unusual tact. (This is an oversimplification. Hofmann too, like every pianist coming from the nineteenth century, occasionally touched up the music, but he did so much less than Rachmaninoff.)

When Rachmaninoff played, it was a unity. Everything was perfectly planned, perfectly proportioned. Melodies were outlined with radiant authority; counterbalancing inner voices were brought out in chamber-music style. And those marvelous fingers were incapable of striking a wrong note. In an age of spectacular technicians, Rachmaninoff was peerless. Complicated figurations—and his own piano music abounds in them —suddenly unraveled themselves in crystalline purity. The playing was at all times elegant. But it had inevitability rather than spontaneity. Rachmaninoff never gave the impression that he was doing something on the spur of the moment. His interpretations sounded as though they had been worked out in collaboration with God—the final statement of a work, to be played eternally this way and no other.

Does this sound flowery? But Rachmaninoff was that kind of pianist, and when you walked out of one of his recitals it was with the feeling that his conception was final. With Hofmann, you knew that the next time it would be different. Hofmann was the most spontaneous of pianists. With Rachmaninoff, you felt that it would be the same next year, and the years after that.

Hofmann deteriorated near the end. Rachmaninoff played as strongly before his death as he ever did. The last time I heard him, in 1940 or 1941, there was no deterioration in his split-second responses, or the way he was able to get over the keys, or the patrician mind that was applied to the music. It is a good memory to have.

APRIL 1, 1973

All great musicians are dedicated, but even more than most of them Rudolf Serkin has spent his long life living, breathing and thinking about music. His influence has been powerful. As a teacher he has had many of the world's most promising young-sters pass through his hands. As the guru of the Marlboro Festival, which attracts the finest young musicians from everywhere, he has trained a whole generation of brilliant tal-ents in chamber music. I should have spent much more time in this article on Serkin's influence. It could be that the current interest of young pianists in chamber music is largely due to Rudolf Serkin, and that is something new in the scheme of things. Certainly most of the virtuosos who were coming up thirty and forty years ago spent very little time with chamber music.

Rudolf Serkin:
In Pursuit of an Ideal

Two RELATED events: on Wednesday, Rudolf Serkin's recital in Carnegie Hall will celebrate the fortieth anniversary of his debut there; and Young Audiences, Inc., will be starting the celebration of its twenty-fifth anniversary. The relation? Rudolf Serkin, himself an educator, has been greatly interested in Young Audiences through the years. Currently he is a vice president on the board of directors and also a member of the national advisory committee. His Carnegie Hall concert this week is a benefit for Young Audiences.

Young Audiences may well be the biggest musical agency in the United States. It is an organization dedicated to bringing music, dance and theater to school children. Under its wing are about 1,500 artists who appear in about 300 ensembles that give some 11,000 annual programs free of charge to the kids. All this is accomplished on a budget not much more than $1.5 million annually. Funding comes from individuals, government, foundations, corporations, schools and PTA's. Young Audiences is

not proud. It will accept money from you and me in its determination to expose children to the best in music.

For his Young Audiences benefit concert Serkin will be playing Mendelssohn's Prelude and Fugue in E minor, the twenty-
four Chopin Preludes and Beethoven's *Hammerklavier* Sonata.
Although Chopin is not a composer normally associated with
Serkin, he does return to the etudes and preludes from time to
time. The rest of the program is echt-Serkin. Of all the great
pianists, Serkin probably has reduced his concert repertory to
the fewest number of pieces. His idea of a great program is an
evening of the last three Beethoven sonatas.

Of course he knows the entire literature as well as anybody.
He also can come up with surprises. He has in the past played,
and also recorded, such unusual items as the Reger F minor
Concerto, the Mendelssohn D minor, the Bartók First, the
Strauss *Burleske*. He likes Reger, and only a few seasons back
played the monumental "Bach" Variations of that composer. He
also likes Schumann, and in the past has given us wonderful
performances of the *Carnaval* and *Abegg* Variations, in addition
to the Konzertstück (Op. 92) for piano and orchestra.

But over a 40-year span, he has remained faithful primarily to
Beethoven and Schubert—at least, in his recital programs. Year
after year he has been content to come to New York with a
relative handful of works. He keeps discovering new things in
them and wants to share those discoveries. So far there have
been no complaints. Serkin has remained one of the most popular of pianists, and today occupies much the place that Artur
Schnabel occupied forty years ago.

Serkin, like Schnabel, represents the Austro-German tradition. There is, however, a great deal of difference between these
two pianists. Serkin's playing has a kind of tension, a nervous
push, missing from Schnabel's more relaxed performances.
This kind of nervousness extends to platform manners. Where
Schnabel sat quietly before the keyboard, Serkin twitches,
attacks, jerks up and down. He has a much more kinesthetic
involvement with music than did his distinguished predecessor.

He is also a stronger technician than Schnabel was—or, at
least, the Schnabel of the last fifteen years before the public.

Pianists who studied with Schnabel say that he really had the entire repertory, Liszt included, at his disposal, but that he did relatively little practicing and never worried much about wrong notes. Schnabel's playing could be peppered with mistakes and memory lapses, even in his recordings. He recorded in pre-tape days, but he could have done those four-and-a-half-minutes sides over and over again until he got them straight. He didn't. The finale of Op. 101 remains little short of a disaster; and how he messed up the octaves in the first movement of the Brahms D minor Concerto recording! Apparently Schnabel could not have cared less. He was after a certain effect, and damn the wrong notes or messed passages.

Serkin, of course, is infinitely more accurate. He has a very big technique, and he is constantly working at it. Friends say that he always has been bothered by the thick fingers of his hands, and he works twice as hard as other pianists to bring those clumsy fingers under control. But it is an article of faith among piano teachers and pedagogues that a nice, fat, thick hand makes a better sound than the long-fingered "artistic" hand; and it is true that Serkin can make a gorgeous sound. It is a sound especially suited for chamber music. Serkin's piano always seems to melt into the ensemble. Naturally he has a marvelous ear, and that always helps.

He is an intellectual pianist—even with the rich sound he produces, even with his frequent Romanticisms—and is accepted by pianists the world over as such. He is a strong personality, and he has the reputation of knowing everything and also of being able to explain everything, which is a different matter entirely. At the Marlboro Festival, with which Serkin has been associated for so many years, all kinds of music are played, and all kinds of problems come up. The musicians faced with those problems talk them over. Then they end up with "Let's ask Rudi." Rudi always seems to have an answer that satisfies everybody.

No pianist has ever succeeded in winning *everybody* over, and Serkin's playing, though universally respected, is not to everybody's taste. Some consider it pedantic. Some would like to see less emotional reserve. Some connoisseurs, especially the Romantic bugs, simply cannot see what all the fuss is about. They respond to tempo fluctuation, and are bored with Serkin's tightly-controlled metrics. But most of us will continue to respond to the nobility of Serkin's mind, to the large-scale scope of his conceptions, to the singular honesty of his musical approach, and to the security of his piano playing proper. From the beginning, Serkin has never hit a note that was esthetically false. He has always had an ideal, and has spent his life in pursuit of it.

JAN. 21, 1976

Had I had more space, I would have gone into other aspects of Hofmann's playing, including his remarkable shift in style in the early 1930's. Before then he had played with extraordinary clarity (there never was a mechanism like his, not even Godowsky's), relatively little pedal and very strict metrics. All pianistic problems were solved in an insultingly easy fashion. There also was the feeling of a tightly reined-in titanic energy. In the 1930's that energy was fully released. It was as if Hofmann had suddenly decided to let himself go. This phase of his playing terribly disturbs some old-maid critics. Not professional pianists, though. Some years ago, during an interview with a pianist, I mentioned that a performance of Hofmann in the Chopin F minor Concerto was available on records. It so happened that this pianist was going to play the F minor in a few weeks, and he begged me to play it for him. I took him home, put the record on, and he couldn't believe what he was hearing. When it was over, he gave me a resigned look. "With this technique, with this rhythm, with this kind of sound in your ears," he said, "how can any of us have a chance?"

Josef Hofmann: The Greatest Pianist of His Time

THE ROMANTIC MUSIC FESTIVAL in Indianapolis starts its ninth season on Tuesday, and for six days Frank Cooper and his merry men will have a lot of fun with forgotten nineteenth-century repertory. To give an idea: on the opening program, Jorge Bolet and the Indianapolis Symphony will be heard in piano concertos by Hummel and Sgambati, while the orchestra on its own will play music by Chadwick and Schelling. Now *that's* the Romantic revival—which, incidentally, Cooper (who teaches piano at Butler University in Indianapolis) launched nine years ago. His Romantic Music Festival was the first of its kind.

Tucked away on one program is a short piece—the *Polonaise Américaine* by Josef Hofmann. Three things about that work: it brings back the name of a pianist who, many think, was the greatest of his time; it reminds us that this year is the one hundredth anniversary of Hofmann's birth (he was born on Jan. 20, 1876); and the Indianapolis audience will be hearing in the *Polonaise Américaine* the work of a ten-year-old prodigy.

Reports about young Hofmann had been circulating in America, but when the ten-year-old pianist made his American debut at the Metropolitan Opera nobody was prepared for the combination of incredible pianistic skill and musical maturity from so tiny a body. Naturally Josef was compared to Mozart and Mendelssohn, and as a performer he might have been in their class. As a composer he ended up a salonist, like so many important nineteenth-century pianists. He turned out a large number of graceful, effective piano pieces, many under the *nom de plume* of Michael Dvorsky. His compositions have not made him immortal. But those who heard his piano playing can never forget the man's aristocracy, flowing line, sensuous sound, brilliant technique and, above all, feeling of spontaneity. Hofmann, somehow, made every other pianist sound thick. His colleagues knew it. Among professional pianists he was acknowledged a miracle.

This is not hearsay. The International Piano Archives, headed by Gregor Benko, is dedicated to the memory of Josef Hofmann, and has collected hundreds of letters and statements from pianists about their idol. Thanks to the Archives, too, the playing of Hofmann in his best years can be heard. Hofmann's recording career was curious. He was the first musician of importance ever to record. Edison was so won over by the ten-year-old Hofmann that he had the child brought to his laboratory late in 1887. Josef sat on his lap while playing the piano and made several piano cylinders. Those have been lost. Later he made more cylinders for Edison, which conceivably still could be tucked away somewhere in Menlo Park.

Then, in 1904, Hofmann started his commercial series of records. He cut some sides in Berlin. After 1911 he made acoustic records in the United States for Columbia and Brunswick. For some reason he stopped recording in 1924, just before the advent of electrical recording. He is on record as saying that the sound did not do him justice. Fortunately for all of us, collectors who had home equipment started taking his playing off the air after 1935 or so. What with one thing and another, the International Piano Archives has had access to (and has released) Hofmann in a handful of concertos, one solo program that he gave at Casimir Hall, some test pressings and other odds and ends.

Hofmann's playing on these recordings is not to everybody's taste. There is general agreement that as a technician he was pretty much in a class by himself. But there are those who are disturbed by his freedom. That kind of listener prefers the early Hofmann recordings, which are incredibly flawless digitally and are rather reined-in emotionally, to the later ones. The later recordings they call "cynical" and representative of the "bad" side of Romanticism.

But those of us who admire Hofmann's playing insist that no pianist of his time—and for all we know, of any time—had a greater power to vitalize Romantic music. Hofmann understood the rhetoric better than anybody. Listen to the way he plays the Larghetto of Chopin's F minor Concerto—the purity of the line, the coruscating functional embellishments in the right hand, the pacings, the way he shapes the declamations of the middle section over the orchestral tremolo, the control of dynamics that allows him to taper down to an all-passion-spent phrase before getting back to the opening section.

Yet such authorities as the late Chopin expert Arthur Hedley, in England, were disturbed by Hofmann's playing in this very concerto. Hedley thought it anarchic. Perhaps the trouble was that Hofmann's conception was so different from everybody else's that it sounded too much like a new work. The conception was different only in phrasing and dynamics. Hofmann seldom fooled around with the notes—much less, incidentally, than his best friend, Rachmaninoff. (Rachmaninoff told everybody that the greatest pianist in the world was Hofmann. Hofmann went around telling everybody that the greatest pianist in the world was Rachmaninoff.) If you follow this performance of the Chopin F minor with the score, you will find very little disagreement between Hofmann and the printed note. But the elegance and originality of the playing make the familiar music sound almost like a different concerto.

Hofmann died in 1957. He was not a happy man toward the end, and he had a drinking problem. He was at his height from 1925 to 1940. One of the great thrills of concert going was to watch his entrance from the wings: that jaunty little man, exerting a palpable aura (my God! a pupil of *Anton Rubinstein!*), striding briskly to the piano, seating himself, and noodling a few chords before beginning. Hofmann, like others of his generation, would often modulate between pieces. (You can actually hear Hofmann do it on one of his recordings.) Once in a while Hofmann could be guilty of unusual behavior. At one concert, while storming through Chopin's F minor Fantasy, he abruptly stopped and left the stage. General heart failure from the audience. A technician came out and replaced a pedal rod. Hofmann returned, and did not start the Fantasy over. He resumed exactly where he had left off. Strange.

In 1937 Hofmann gave a Golden Jubilee at the Metropolitan Opera. With the Curtis student orchestra conducted by Fritz Reiner (Hofmann was then the head of the Curtis Institute of

Music), Hofmann played the Rubinstein D minor Concerto and then his own *Chromaticon* for piano and orchestra. Then he played solos. Hofmann arranged for a private recording of the entire concert. Around 1955, Columbia Records brought out a disc containing the solo portion of the concert. I reviewed it, mentioning also the two works for piano and orchestra, and giving short shrift to the *Chromaticon*. A week or so after the review appeared, my phone rang.

"How nice of you to remember Hofmann's playing," the lady's voice said. "We were so pleased. It is so good to know we are not forgotten." And so on for five minutes.

"Who is this?" I managed to get in, finally.

"Why, Betty Hofmann."

"Where are you phoning from?"

"Los Angeles."

Betty Hofmann, Josef's wife, finally got around to the bone she wanted to pick with me.

"Why didn't you like the *Chromaticon?*" she wanted to know. She thereupon spent ten minutes giving me an analysis. It used all twelve notes of the scale. It was highly advanced for its day. It was a masterpiece of piano writing. It was this and that.

"Yes, yes, ma'am," I weakly kept on saying.

After a half hour of this, Mrs. Hofmann hung up, well satisfied with her day's work. Ten minutes later my phone rang.

"This is Betty Hofmann again. I just wanted to tell you that I phoned Josef in Long Beach, and he told me to call you right back and tell you he agrees with you. The *Chromaticon* is really a terrible piece of music."

APRIL 18, 1976

There are those who maintain that they can tell the difference between a male and a female pianist. I never could, and won-

dered how listeners would react if put to the test. So I prepared a tape that I tried out on three audiences. Then I wrote a Sunday piece about it.

A number of radio stations centered in on the article, preparing their own tapes—not confined to piano—and having a competition. A copy of one tape was sent to me. I flunked it resoundingly. As closely as I can figure out, I worked on the male chauvinist principle that the better performance had to come from a man. KUSC-FM in Los Angeles broadcast an hour-long tape of thirty pieces in its First National Classical Music Sex Quiz. The winner, Ellis Kerschenbaum of Torrance, California, correctly identified the sex of twenty-six out of the thirty. I decided to write an article on the First National Classical Music Sex Quiz, and got Mr. Kerschenbaum on the phone. What was his secret?

"I think," said Mr. Kerschenbaum, "that on the whole men are more neurotic than women. I was listening for that. . . . You might say I was listening for the craziness. Men are a little crazier than women. Some of it was guesswork. I'd be afraid to try it again."

I asked him how much he knew about women.

"I have girl friends," he said, "but I don't consider myself an expert on women."

How Sex Plays a Role at the Piano

Here's where I get into trouble. This article is going to be about the sexes and piano playing: namely, is there any difference, perhaps a matter of sex, when a man and a woman play the same piece of music? Is there such a thing as a "man's" piece of music? Or are such questions merely a reflection of male chauvinism?

It started several years ago in Palm Beach. I was on a panel in a discussion of piano playing, along with several young men and women, all professional pianists. Somewhere along I said something about the Rachmaninoff Piano Concerto No. 3 being a man's work because of its wide stretches, its massive sonorities and the demands for real endurance it poses.

Whereupon a young lady on the stage rose in wrath. She was a very talented young lady, and also a most articulate one. She said it was the most nonsensical thing she ever heard. She said that she could play the Rachmaninoff D minor as well as any man, and that nobody could tell the difference between her playing and male playing. She said that my remarks typified the very thing most females were fighting, and that it would be a better world if certain critics woke up to basic facts of life. She left no doubt about the identity of the critic she was attacking.

All of a sudden she was put to the test. It was suggested that she and a male pianist on the panel play the same piece, behind a closed curtain, and leave it to the audience to decide if there were any distinguishing characteristics. The men on stage looked the other way, but one of them was persuaded—bulldozed might be the better word—to offer his services in this epochal experiment. A Schumann piece was decided upon between the two pianists, and backstage they went. After they finished, an audience poll was taken. Lo and behold! The overwhelming majority of the audience guessed correctly, identifying the sex of the performers.

There were indeed identifying characteristics, and it had nothing to do with the quality of the respective playing. One performance was clear and direct. The other was more highly inflected, full of delicately applied rubatos and variations in the musical line. For what it means, most everybody who was listening concluded that the inflected performance was female. And it was.

But it started me thinking. What if I made up a tape putting back-to-back performances of the same piece played by a major female and a major male pianist? Could anybody really tell the difference? So when I returned home I did prepare a tape. It was a highly unscientific selection, without controls of any kind. I did try to match up periods, and I flipped a coin to determine which artist should play first. I did not look for a woman "who plays like a man." I took the records as they came.

Here is what I ended up with: the Beethoven-Liszt *Turkish* March played by Samaroff and Rachmaninoff; Chopin's C-sharp minor Mazurka (Op. 41, No. 1) played by Rubinstein and Reisenberg; the last section of Liszt's Twelfth *Hungarian* Rhapsody, played by Levitzki and Bachauer; the last section of Chopin's B minor Scherzo played by Horowitz and Darré (one of the determining points here was that both use interlocking octaves in the final unison scale passage); the Strauss-Gieseking *Ständchen* played by Gieseking and Novaes; the Brahms B minor Capriccio played by Hess and Bauer; the Chopin E flat Etude (Op. 10, No. 11) played by Renard and Lhévinne; and the last part of the Chopin E minor Concerto played by Bela Davidovich and Josef Hofmann. Davidovich, who many believe is the finest Soviet woman pianist, has been allowed to leave her country for good and will be making her American debut next season.

I tried the tape out on three audiences. One, numbering about 150, was at the Turtle Bay Music School. The audience there consisted of music lovers and a heavy sprinkling of professionals. The second audience consisted of seven graduate students (three women among them) at the Manhattan School of Music. Six of those seven were skilled pianists, some of whom have plenty of professional experience. The third demonstration was given at the library in Shelter Island, N.Y.—about 110 people, nearly all non-professionals.

The resulting tabulations were fascinating. If any general conclusions can be drawn, it is that the more professional the listener is, the more he or she finds it impossible to determine the sex of an artist. There were, of course, some pianists the professionals immediately guessed. At the first chords of the Chopin Scherzo, there was a gasp of recognition. No one but Horowitz plays so brilliantly voiced a piano, and no one has his particular kind of sonority. The vote here at the Manhattan School was 7 to 0; everybody knew that the first pianist (Horowitz) was a male. Similarly, about 98 percent guessed correctly at Turtle Bay. But in Shelter Island only about 40 percent came up with an accurate response.

As between Davidovich and Hofmann, all three audiences guessed correctly: 7 to 0 at Manhattan, about 75 percent at Shelter Island, about 85 percent at Turtle Bay. It was not a matter of physical strength, for Davidovich, a powerful pianist, got just as much volume as Hofmann did, and maybe more. But apparently the tigerish quality of Hofmann's playing made its point, and few in any of the three audiences had any doubts about who was the man, who the woman.

In a few other places there seemed to be unanimity. In the *Turkish* March played by Samaroff and Rachmaninoff, 90 per cent at Turtle Bay guessed who was the male and 70 per cent at Shelter Island. But at Manhattan, half the class was wrong. In the Chopin Mazurka (Rubinstein and Reisenberg), about 60 per cent at Turtle Bay guessed correctly, 70 per cent at Shelter Island, but only half of those at Manhattan. Between Levitzki and Bachauer in the Twelfth Rhapsody, 70 per cent at Turtle Bay correctly guessed that the first performance was by a man, about 50 per cent at Shelter Island, and five out of six (with one abstention) at Manhattan. There was a surprise (for this poll-taker) in the Gieseking-Novaes *Ständchen*. Who could miss the feminine, elegant, aristocratic, singing quality of Guiomar Novaes? But at Turtle Bay, 85 per cent thought she was the man. At Manhattan the listeners were split right down the middle. It was only in Shelter Island that the correct identities were guessed. Overwhelmingly—about 95 per cent—the Shelter Island audience selected the second performance as played by a woman. Incidentally, the Shelter Island and Turtle Bay audiences voted, also overwhelmingly, in favor of the Novaes as a performance (and in this opinion they were right; Novaes plays circles around Gieseking). But the young professionals at Manhattan again were split in their ideas about the actual performance.

The Brahms B minor Capriccio on the face of it seemed a hard one to guess. Both pianists were British, both reflected much the same culture and philosophical approach to music, and the two performances were very similar. At Turtle Bay there was a 50-50 split in opinion. Yet what was there in the playing to make five out of six voting students at Manhattan detect Hess unhesitatingly, and about 80 per cent of the Shelter Island audience?

Half of the Manhattan kids guessed wrong about Renard-Lhévinne, but here was the Turtle Bay group deciding correctly, with an 85 percent response, that the first performance, that of

Renard, did come from the hands of a woman. And, as noted above, the great majority in the three audiences had no trouble deciding correctly that the second performance of the Chopin E minor Concerto was masculine.

There was one other aspect to the questioning. Before voting on male-female, the audiences were asked which of the two performances they preferred. Here the votes also were very interesting. In the *Turkish* March, all three audiences preferred Samaroff over Rachmaninoff. Rubinstein in the Chopin Mazurka was preferred over Reisenberg at Manhattan, but not at Turtle Bay or Shelter Island. Bachauer was preferred over Levitzki in the Liszt at Manhattan and Shelter Island, but not at Turtle Bay. Horowitz was preferred to Darré at Manhattan and Turtle Bay, but at Shelter Island about 80 per cent liked the lady better. Novaes swept the field at Manhattan and Turtle Bay. For some reason, about 95 per cent at Shelter Island preferred Bauer to Hess in the Brahms, but at Turtle Bay and Manhattan opinion was almost evenly split. The Manhattan kids voted unanimously for the Hofmann interpretation of the Chopin E minor over that of Davidovich, yet in Shelter Island there was a 50–50 vote, and in Turtle Bay 55 per cent preferred Davidovich.

Admittedly this was a hit-and-miss survey, done on the spur of the moment, and anything but scientific. But there was an indication that there is indeed a difference between a male and female approach to a piece. Even with some inconclusive results, there were too many cases where the audiences unerringly hit on the correct sex of the performer. But I wonder how I would score on an equivalent kind of tape that I prepared. One of the Manhattan kids threw a tape at me. It contained, among other things, a male-female performance of a Scriabin etude. There was no doubt about the quality of the playing; one pianist was much superior.

But I guessed wrong about the sex of the player. If there were any identifying sexual characteristics, I for one did not hear or intuit any.

MAY 29, 1979

ors

today? I
ks. They
of the or-

Just as there was talk about my "feud" with Rudolf Bing, so there was talk about a Schonberg-Bernstein feud. But, as with Mr. Bing, I do not know Mr. Bernstein well enough to feud with him. I have been in his company only twice—once for a Times *magazine piece, once for* Harper's. *Like everybody else, I have tremendous respect for Mr. Bernstein's talent, but soon after he took over the Philharmonic, I came to the conclusion that his ego got in the way of his music, and that the self-indulgence he was displaying had no rightful place in a great metropolitan orchestra. Perhaps I was too harsh in this article, but I thought strong measures were needed. Of course it made no difference. A musician with the charisma and skill of a Bernstein can laugh at any critic.*

Bernstein and the Aura of Show Business

THE STATISTICIANS of the New York Philharmonic report that this afternoon will be the 6,456th concert of the orchestra. It also is the concert that concludes the 1961–62 season, and it is a significant break. Next season, on September 23, the New York Philharmonic will hold housewarming ceremonies at its new hall in Lincoln Center. And so goodby to Carnegie Hall, where the Philharmonic has held forth since 1891, and where Mengelberg, Toscanini, Barbirolli, Walter, Rodzinski, Mitropoulos and the others guided the destinies of the orchestra.

But, of course, the new Philharmonic Hall at best can be only

355

the icing on the cake: a most gorgeous, ninety-foot-high icing, to be sure. The important thing is not the building but what goes on inside the building. The tendency to equate accomplishment with glamour is nothing new; but ringing down the ages also come warnings that a book is not to be judged by its cover. And one hopes that the dazzling facade of Philharmonic Hall will not be the equivalent of a cover that surrounds an empyrean of emptiness.

One not only hopes; one desperately hopes. For there has not been too much of recent Philharmonic activity that gives one much hope for the future. Indeed, the most positive step in the right direction was an announcement for the 1963–64 season. At that time the present musical director, Leonard Bernstein, will share the podium with two guests—George Szell and Josef Krips. This means that in the near future the weekly activities of the orchestra will not be disfigured by the bi-monthly procession of incoming and outgoing conductors. And as Mr. Szell and Mr. Krips are disciplinarians, they perhaps will keep the orchestra in shape during Mr. Bernstein's long absences.

There is no need now to go into the question of Mr. Bernstein's musical strengths and weaknesses. All musicians are strong in some aspects of their art, weak in others; and Mr. Bernstein, who is not anywhere near so protean as some of his admirers would indicate, is no exception. Indeed, the future Bernstein-Krips-Szell troika cannot but lead to positive results, for each will complement the other: Mr. Bernstein in the post-Strauss repertory, Mr. Krips in the Romantic Viennese and German works, Mr. Szell in Haydn, Mozart, the Central European composers of past and present.

But in the meantime there remain other specific problems, and most of them center directly on Mr. Bernstein himself. Under his regime the Philharmonic has not developed into an orchestra with the pride, the esprit de corps and the actual accomplishment that should be its right. Some of this can be traced to the fact of Mr. Bernstein's long disappearances. He conducts the first six weeks and the last six, and in between that time the orchestra has no direction in which to aim. No sooner does it get used to one guest conductor than another comes in.

No wonder some of the men are leaning back in their seats. Next season Mr. Bernstein will take on another two weeks. This is not exactly a big deal.

And equally disturbing is the aura of show business that has settled over Philharmonic activities. To take a minor but nevertheless irritating point: those opening and closing slogans for the Bernstein series. This year it was "The Gallic Approach" for the first five weeks, and "The Middle-Europe Tradition" for the last six. To give an idea of how synthetic these labels are, Nadia Boulanger was the one who really conducted a Gallic program, but as it fell outside of the Bernstein series it was unlabelled.

There is, of course, nothing wrong in a conductor building his programs around a theme. He should; and, on the whole, Mr. Bernstein's programs are an improvement over those of his immediate predecessors. But those slogans are artificial and they are pretentious; and they also are as annoying as television commercials with a hard sell (Yes, Franck and Berlioz rinse clean! They SATISFY your white-urge! Yes, Franck and Berlioz rinse clean! They SATISFY your white-urge! Yes . . .).

What they reflect is a music-appreciation philosophy that should have nothing to do with the Philharmonic. It should be the task of a conductor to conduct, and any educational benefits should be peripheral. But what we have been getting, in effect, are Young People's Concerts for Old People. This was all the more true when Mr. Bernstein was lecturing his Thursday evening preview audiences. Apparently he does almost no talking any more.

But he did at least on one occasion this season, and it illustrated the cult of personality in a rather shuddering fashion. That was the week when Glenn Gould played the Brahms D minor Concerto, and when Mr. Bernstein made his now-famous speech telling the audience that he disagreed with Mr. Gould's interpretation and washed his hands of it.

Now, the fact that Mr. Gould was temperamentally and technically unequipped to play the concerto is beside the point at issue. The real point is that Mr. Bernstein made the speech, an act that suggests he has not as yet thought through his responsibilities toward music and toward the Philharmonic subscri-

bers. Rehearsal time is when the thing should have been ironed
out. If Mr. Bernstein so disagreed with Mr. Gould's performance,
he had two courses to follow. He could have become conve-
niently ill and withdrawn. Or, had he acted as a strong conductor should have acted, he would have imposed his will on the
soloist. (Whether or not he could have dismissed the soloist is a
tricky legal point that, says a Philharmonic official, has never
come up. Up to now, conductor and soloist have always managed to iron out their difficulties without public apology and
breast-beating.) In any case, it is the conductor who is in charge,
and the responsibility for the music-making is ultimately the
conductor's.

But to make the speech and go on with a performance he must
have known was a travesty was unprofessional and immature,
and does not say much for Mr. Bernstein's musical integrity.
And that, it would appear, is the major point. It was not the
performance itself but the music director's attitude that suddenly became symbolic of one of the things that ails the Philharmonic. Weakness begets weakness; and, one dare observe,
cheapness begets cheapness. Until the Philharmonic again gets
fired with the thrill of making music, with bigness and excitement, under a conductor who can push the musicians to the
supreme effort, the Philharmonic will remain merely a good
orchestra and not a great one; and the conductor will remain,
well, not Maestro Bernstein, but merely Lenny, the Peter Pan of
music.

MAY 20, 1962

*It was an exciting week in Carnegie Hall when Herbert von
Karajan and Georg Solti conducted their great orchestras cheek
by jowl. It offered a chance to compare, directly, one major
conductor with another. Karajan is probably the greatest living*

technician, and I wish I could respond more positively to his work. I find him reminding me of a precious object in a museum: Look But Don't Touch. Solti, on the other hand, is all passion. Many young critics cannot stand his work, which they consider hysterically overstressed. I have never found it so, however, and I respond more to Solti's passionate involvement than to Karajan's urbane aloofness.

Karajan Is Apollo, Solti Is Dionysus

IN EUROPE nobody is going to put up much of an argument against the proposition that Herbert von Karajan is the world's pre-eminent conductor. Especially in Germany and Austria the man is an untouchable—the criterion to which all conductors must aspire. But in England and America, Karajan is greeted with more reservation. Indeed, Karajan's recently concluded series in Carnegie Hall with the Berlin Philharmonic did not evoke a rapturous press. Quite the contrary. There were comments about Karajan's coolness and objectivity, and the feeling was that Karajan was too concerned with the outward rather than the inner aspects of music, ending up with perfect but lifeless interpretations.

The conductor New York has taken to its heart in recent years in Georg Solti, who had been conducting the Chicago Symphony in Carnegie Hall just before the Karajan appearances. Two more dissimilar conductors cannot be imagined. In every aspect they represent opposite poles of music-making, and they are in many ways to this age what Toscanini and Furtwängler were two generations back. Toscanini was the literalist, Furtwängler the Romantic. Toscanini preferred steady tempos and refused to read things into music. Furtwängler represented the Wagner-Bülow school of tempo fluctuation, and his concerts could be metaphysical events.

Today, Karajan in many ways is representative of the Toscanini approach, but with some significant differences. Karajan, an objectivist, stands quietly before the orchestra, his hands molding the phrases in smooth legato lines. A short, slim, unusually good-looking man with an impeccably groomed head of gray hair, he is by far the most immobile of the great virtuoso conductors. For him there is no podium choreography. An air of ultra-efficiency permeates his work, and his interpretations have the kind of reserve that he himself as a man is reputed to have. Jascha Heifetz used to have much the same kind of platform approach, and he too was constantly accused of being "cold" and too objective.

Karajan is the complete technician. He works hard for polish —polish in execution, polish in interpretation. He is an organizer who strives for balance and proportion; he is a literalist who insists on every note being played accurately; there are no technical secrets that he has not mastered. Every piece he conducts comes through lucidly. But there are other conductors with these skills, and they have not made such a phenomenal career. For Karajan has one other thing to an incredible degree, and that is glamour. He makes a powerful impact on audiences. If the critics did not love him this last trip, the audiences certainly did.

Solti, too, has this kind of audience impact, and he gets it in an entirely different way. Karajan always is the aristocrat. Solti is the least graceful conductor since Dimitri Mitropoulos. His motions are jittery; his whole body is in motion; his shoulders as well as his hands are responding to the rhythm; his beat is a series of jabs, and he looks as though he is shadow-boxing. But he too gets sensational results. If audiences respond so strongly to the Karajan glamour and perfect musical grooming, they also respond in equal measure to Solti's red-hot involvement with the music, to his fervency, intensity and big vision.

The Karajan orchestral sound is silvery. Solti's is molten gold. In his way, Solti is as much the perfectionist as Karajan, and there have been occasional complaints that in his search for the ultimate in orchestral technique Solti too is over-concerned with the outward aspects of music. He has in the past conducted some standard symphonies with what seem to many an undue interest in pure technique rather than a total immersion into the meaning of the score. Those complaints have lessened in recent years. Solti appears now to have arrived at full maturity, and he brings to his music an awesome combination of ear, mind and heart.

He is much more a colorist than Karajan, and there is much more rhythmic drive to his conducting. Karajan has an intellectual view toward music, and conducts with tight emotional control. Solti goes for the grand line and the big effect. In music of a non-Romantic nature, of course, Solti reins in. Those who heard his performances of *Le Nozze di Figaro* last September with the Paris Opéra will never forget the transparency he got into the orchestra. That, and the rhythmic momentum. Solti never makes a rhythmic mistake. The pulse is ever-present, and there are none of the accented upbeats or mashed-potato thickness heard in the work of less-gifted conductors. Karajan's rhythm, incidentally, is equally infallible, but more delicate. He does not favor Solti's kind of push.

Both have conducted the Verdi Requiem in New York. The other week Karajan, in his Carnegie Hall series, led a performance that was all proportion, elegance, planning. Everything was directly, intelligently and handsomely presented, and the music came out in an aristocratic manner. When Solti conducted the Requiem last year, his ideas were altogether different. Tempos were faster, dynamic extremes were more fully exploited, and the approach was decidedly dramatic, not to say operatic. Both conductors exercised ultimate control over their forces, but the Solti manner gave the idea of personal involvement, whereas Karajan did seem a little aloof.

Much the same is true in their respective recordings of Wagner's *Ring* cycle. Karajan's approach is under strict control. This is almost a chamber-music Wagner. Karajan seems to play down deliberately, determined that the singers should be clearly heard. The result is a *Ring* with amazing lightness of orchestral texture. It is a conception that was not altogether admired when Karajan conducted *Die Walküre* some years ago at the Metropolitan Opera. But nobody could deny the expertise of the conducting itself.

Solti's ideas about the *Ring* had the orchestra playing a much more prominent part. Where Karajan deliberately played down, Solti went in for color and passion. Solti's interpretation certainly was more vital. It also was more traditional. Karajan's cooler colors and refusal to plunge himself into the Wagnerian mythos were all but revolutionary. This was modern Wagner with a vengeance. Most old-line Wagnerians, this writer included, responded more to Solti, whose *Ring* was monumental in conception. Solti is Dionysus. Karajan is Apollo. The music world needs both kinds of conductors, if only as an antidote to each other.

Nov. 28, 1976

From most New York Philharmonic subscribers there was a sigh of relief when Pierre Boulez left the orchestra. The man's lack of communication had to sink him in the long run. Philharmonic officials stoutly defended him in public, but reliable reports have it that nobody was happier than the front office when Mr. Boulez went to Paris for good. In many respects Mr. Boulez was curiously naive when he came to New York. He acted as though nobody had ever heard of Berg or Webern, composers who had been regularly played since Dimitri Mitropoulos conducted the Philharmonic, and he acted as though the city was a cultural wasteland. Many professionals resented his attitude.

Summing Up the Boulez New York Era

LAST NIGHT Pierre Boulez conducted the last of the 1976–77 subscription concerts of the New York Philharmonic at Avery

Fisher Hall. When he put down his baton, he not only concluded the season. He ended his six-year tenure as music director of the orchestra. Off he goes to Paris, where he will start work as director of the Institut de Recherche et de Coordination Acoustique/ Musique. He leaves New York quietly, and has said that he will give no interviews. He has made but one comment: "I go because something else is there to be done and for no other reason." Translation: "I am leaving on my own volition, not because I have been fired."

When Boulez was appointed, it was a big surprise. He was not even a dark horse, and his name had not been mentioned among the candidates in the sweepstakes to succeed Leonard Bernstein. The announcement was received with a certain amount of shock. It was known that Boulez had conducted Wagner at Bayreuth, had done a great deal of work with the BBC Orchestra, and was taken very seriously as a conductor by British and Continental critics. On the other hand, he had come to conducting late in his career, did not have a large repertory, and was noted primarily for one thing as a conductor: his transcendent ability to make sense out of avant-garde music going back to the members of the Second Viennese School, Bartók, Stravinsky and thence to the latest moderns.

After the initial shock, there was a feeling that maybe the Philharmonic had made a good choice. Boulez "could bring the orchestra into the twentieth century." He could revitalize the Philharmonic audiences and bring in a younger contingent. He could give the orchestra itself a new viewpoint. True, his appointment was not happily received by many American composers, who sent a joint letter to the press condemning the choice. Boulez, they said, had no sympathy with current American music and had gone out of his way to deride it.

They had a point. Boulez in his youth had been a hothead, apt to shoot off his mouth in conversation and in print. As the leader of the serial avant-garde after the war, as a believer in the imperative of the Webern school of composition, he was apt to dismiss everything else. Webern was the only true god, and even Arnold Schoenberg failed to come up to expectations. "Schoenberg is dead," trumpeted Boulez in a famous article. Nobody can be more intolerant than the leader of a movement, and no wonder many American composers regarded him with suspicion.

So he came. And he certainly tried. There was a revolution in program-making. Gone were the Beethoven, Brahms, Tchaikovsky symphonies. Gone were the familiar concertos. In their stead came music of the twentieth century, virtually unknown works of Liszt and Haydn, a spattering of world premières. Boulez introduced the series known as Prospective Encounters, informal events where he conducted new music by Americans, discussing it with the composers before an audience. He started the Rug Concerts, equally informal, where kids lounged on the floor listening to a predominantly contemporary repertory. He had special festivals: one built around Ives, another around Schubert, a third in which all of the Mahler symphonies were presented. In 1975 he also gave a nine-day festival of contemporary music of the last twenty-five years. Another innovation was the Informal Evenings, where Boulez illustrated and discussed certain problematic music with the audience.

After a season or two it was possible to take the measure of Boulez as a conductor. Certainly he was different from other conductors. Where most of his colleagues approached avant-garde music gingerly and conducted it tightly, carefully, often uncomprehendingly, Boulez revelled in it. An objectivist, a musician interested much more in structure than in emotion, he nevertheless brought to the music he liked an amazing freedom and personality. In short, he conducted avant-garde music Romantically.

On the other hand, where nearly all conductors approach Romantic music with freedom and color, Boulez here was tight and restrained. He had absolutely no feeling for it, and when he attempted a Schumann symphony, the results could be catastrophic. At first he knew little about performance practice in Baroque or pre-Beethoven music but, conscientious musician that he is, he went to experts and learned something about balances and ornamentation in that repertory.

Yet the man could always be capable of surprises. He conducted Berlioz beautifully; and every once in a while was capable of a stunning performance of music that, on the surface of things, was not in his sympathies.

But it is the totality of a man, and not isolated happenings, that complete the picture. As the seasons passed, the total picture emerged. Boulez was a didact. Inspiration meant little to him. He was a very private man, and that extended to his music-making. Often his concerts were disconcerting. There was no evidence that most music *meant* anything to him. There was no joy, no feeling of personality. That flopping right-hand beat from the wrist did not inspire the orchestra to any great flights of imagination or nuance. Going to one of his concerts was like taking a pill. It was good for you, but not an event you looked forward to with great anticipation.

In any case, the Philharmonic did not suffer at the box office. During Boulez's tenure, average ticket sales were at 97 percent of capacity, and during last season, concerts were 99 percent sold out. Which does not mean that audiences were uniformly happy. From the beginning there was continued resistance to the new music that Boulez played. Boulez and all modern composers believe—they *must* believe—that if audiences are exposed enough to the new music, they will begin to respond to it.

That did not happen. Whether because of Boulez's lack of charisma, or because the music really may not have been very good, there often was audible protest from the customers. The natives grew restless and would indignantly stomp up the aisles. Nor was there any sign of the new young audience that the Philharmonic may originally have hoped to reap. Not at the subscription concerts, at least. The kids did turn out for the Rug Concerts and had a wonderful time.

During all this, what did the orchestra itself think?

Here we get into orchestral psychology. The members of major orchestras never think very highly of conductors, unless they are long dead. Anything musicians say about conductors has to be taken with great suspicion. But even with that in mind, it is clear that Boulez in his six years has not won the orchestra over.

The older members of the Philharmonic, who have played under Bruno Walter, George Szell, Pierre Monteux and other giants of the past, and never let you forget it, almost uniformly hold Boulez in contempt. "You have no idea how many times

we bailed him out," one of them says. "Aside from his specialties, he simply does not know the repertory."

Young members of the orchestra are not as derogatory, but
neither are they very enthusiastic. "He is not a free soul," says
one, "but he does have a systematic way of conducting that can
be relied upon. His beat is clear. You might say too clear. He
conducts the way a mechanic might look at an engine. He is not
very touched by music. His relationship with us is on the reserved side, and he is not the kind of conductor to give the boys
a target. It's all very nice machinery. But it's not the essence of
music."

Says another: "There definitely has been growth. Boulez was
very tight at the beginning, emotionless and straight. Each year
he got more uninhibited. Now he is looser, and he even occasionally takes a ritard. Compared with what he used to be at
first, he is free. I'll say this for him: he never came in unprepared. And as a person he was nice to work with. He has been
fair, a gentleman. The best thing about these last six years is
that he taught us to play contemporary music. We are a better
orchestra for it. But outside of his contemporary repertory, he
beats time and not music. I feel there is some sensitivity in him,
but he tries to hide it. His view of the job is to educate the
public. When we heard that Mehta was coming in, there was a
sigh of relief. We want a leader, an inspiration from the podium.
From Boulez we never got it. He's not a performer. He can't
communicate. Nothing *happens.*"

One of the men in the orchestra closest to Boulez through the
years—a musician who really admires him—discounts the prevalent view of the conductor from within the orchestra. "The
guys will gripe about anybody who's there. Some absolutely hate
him. But I admire him for many things, and I'm sorry to see him
go. Next season's programs make Bruckner look modern. Boulez
is a real musician, a great score reader and he can really sight-
read. Don't underestimate his musicianship in the basics. He's
a perplexing man. I know him so well, and I don't know him at
all. His mind works in a funny way. He's not a performer. He
resists being a performer, and he will never 'act' out a score the
way Lenny used to. He doesn't even shape a score. Very seldom

does he appear to be moved by music. I think he's afraid of revealing himself through his performances."

This friend of Boulez has probably put his finger right on the problem. It is not so much that the Boulez repertory is one-sided, and it is true that in recent years he has relaxed a bit. But music-making does involve some kind of transmission from performer to audience, and with Boulez there is virtually no transmission. Those who know him say he can be warm and charming, but on the podium he is a cold, methodical and even forbidding figure. There may be something admirable in his refusal to play the game, as it were; to avoid podium mannerism, keep himself outside of the music and act merely as a transmitter. But what comes out is, alas, so neutral that at times one gets the feeling that an invisible man is conducting the orchestra.

Chances are that we will not be seeing much of Boulez in the future. The Philharmonic release states that he is expected to return to the orchestra as a guest. But he is not down for any appearances next season. Philharmonic management says that Boulez has indicated he will be too busy in Paris, but hastens to add that he will be welcome any time he expresses a desire to return. Boulez himself has made no public statement. He retires as enigmatic a person as he was when he arrived.

A dedicated musician, the inscrutable Boulez has worked hard in his six years as music director of the New York Philharmonic. He has exposed his public to a new kind of repertory, in old music as well as new, and has done his best to create a favorable ambience for the music he so fervently believes in. Nobody can conduct certain phases of twentieth-century music as well as Boulez can, and he leaves behind him definitive performances in that area. In retrospect, though, that is not enough for the conductor of a major symphony orchestra. A broader musical culture is needed. Boulez would have been ideal as a specialist in charge of part of the season. As music director over a six-year period, however, his weaknesses usurped his strengths. There were too many gaps—gaps in technique, emotional gaps. That fatal reserve had to tell in the long run. There were wonderful moments during those six years, but Boulez on the whole failed to capture the imagination of his audiences and, even worse, of his players.

MAY 15, 1977

In 1961, in Bucharest, I spent some time with Sir John Barbirolli. He was a judge in the first Enesco Competition and I was covering it for the Times. *We were at the same hotel. Around midnight Sir John, who never seemed to need any sleep, would turn up, get a bottle of brandy, and discuss the day's doings. He could put away half a bottle without showing any effects. A vital, enthusiastic man, he never spoke about himself unless asked. I asked. He was full of rich stories—sometimes scatological—about many of the great people of the musical world. George Szell, whom I would fleetingly run into from time to time, was much more reserved and wrapped up in himself. I once had to interview him for a Toscanini project, and his reaction was peculiar. Obviously he had a love-hate relationship with Toscanini, and he couched some reservations in very careful terms. He had an all-encompassing memory, and I doubt if there was anything in the standard literature—piano, chamber, symphony, opera, song—that he could not write down complete to the last expression mark. I am sorry I never saw him when he was relaxed. They say that his performance of* Till Eulenspiegel *as a piano solo, with special effects from his cufflinks, was something to send you home talking to yourself.*

Barbirolli and Szell: Almost Opposing Paths to Parnassus

WITHIN THE space of two days, two great conductors died—Sir John Barbirolli, and then George Szell. Both had been active until a short time ago, and there was no hint that they would be taken from us. Szell was seventy-three, but he was trim, athletic-looking and energetic. He always took good care of himself, and seldom did illness of any kind force him to cancel a concert. Barbirolli, who was seventy years old when he died, always was more the bon vivant than Szell, but he too appeared to be a bounding indestructible.

Both conductors were masters, and no two could have been more different. They took almost opposing paths to their Parnassus. Szell was of the Toscanini school—a precisionist, an authoritarian, a demanding taskmaster, a musician greatly interested in the details that went to support a musical structure. Barbirolli was a more inspirational type of conductor, one who never worried very much if details were obscured as long as the spirit of the music was conveyed. Where Szell represented Classic restraint, Barbirolli was very much the extroverted Romanticist. Where Szell maintained a taut line and a tight ship, Barbirolli was relaxed and easygoing in his interpretations, though without ever losing emotional discipline. Barbirolli was a Romantic, true, but never a self-indulgent one.

New York got the chance to estimate Barbirolli in 1937 when he, almost unknown, was chosen to succeed Arturo Toscanini as head of the New York Philharmonic. Much has been written about that episode, and some have concluded that Barbirolli returned to England as an out-and-out failure. This was not the case. The young conductor, then thirty-seven, made it apparent from the beginning that he had certain decided assets—drive, ebullience, a natural and uncomplicated way of making music. He was especially impressive as a Brahms conductor, and one well remembers the ardor and bigness of spirit with which he addressed himself to the D major Symphony.

But there was no denying the fact that under his leadership the New York Philharmonic lost the tight ensemble that Toscanini had given it. Precision conducting was never Barbirolli's strength; he represented something entirely different. Even had he wanted to attempt a Toscanini-like approach he could not have succeeded. He was too inexperienced at that stage of his career, and could not impose his will upon the temperamental virtuosos of the Philharmonic. So after his contract was up he went back to England, to take over the Hallé Orchestra. For many years he did not return to the United States. Word drifted over about the good work he was doing in Manchester, about how enormously Barbirolli had developed as man and musician. There also were phonograph records to admire. But to most Americans Barbirolli was forgotten.

In the meantime Szell began to assume great importance in the American musical scene, especially after he took over the Cleveland Orchestra. His conducting was not to everybody's liking. Nobody disputed his command over an orchestra, or his immense knowledge, or his integrity. Yet to some listeners there was something cold about his interpretations, something forbidding and devoid of humanity. Szell was accused of pedanticism, of sterility, of ignoring the big line in favor of detail. His admirers, however—and they far outnumbered his detractors—kept insisting that not since Toscanini had there been a conductor of such drive, clarity and bigness.

And, indeed, Toscanini and Szell had much in common. There are two main lines in conducting. One stemming from Wagner and Hans von Bülow, and extending through such twentieth-century conductors as Wilhelm Furtwängler, is highly Romantic and personal, marked by constant fluctuation of tempo and broad expressive devices. The other, from Mendelssohn through Weingartner, Richard Strauss and Toscanini, is of a much more objective nature. Romantic excrescences are purged, and the idea is to let the notes themselves do the interpreting, the conductor acting as organizer. Conductors of this school do not look for "meaning." They present the notes, organizing them into structures. Typical of this attitude was Toscanini's comment about the first movement of the Beethoven *Eroica* Symphony. "Some say Napoleon," snorted Toscanini. "Some say Hitler, some Mussolini. Bah! For me it is only allegro con brio."

Szell would have agreed. Like Toscanini, he felt it was his job as a conductor to see to it that everything in a score was heard, that steady rhythm was kept, that ensemble was as perfect as human fingers, lips and brains could manage. All that done, the interpretation would take care of itself.

But there is more to it than that, and it is the mysterious X factor that separates the good technician from the great interpreter. No musician, no matter how "objective" he is, no matter how literally he approaches the printed note, can keep his own personality divorced from his music-making. One is a function of the other. Szell had a strong, even arrogant, personality, and he also had a patrician musical mind, and everything he was reflected itself in his conducting. It was sinewy and powerful conducting, with the kind of logic that creates an architectonic structure rather than a series of episodes.

It followed that Szell, with his kind of logic, his severe approach, his feeling for structure, would be most successful in music where the formal aspects are important. His specialty was music of the German and Austrian composers. Sometimes he conducted French music, and it was all in place, every detail burnished, but a subtle quality in this literature eluded him. His work here lacked charm. Curiously, though, he had an affinity for Verdi. His blazing performance of the *Manzoni* Requiem gave the lie to those who accused Szell of being a calculating machine. Not since Toscanini had there been a performance of equivalent passion coupled to sheer control.

Barbirolli returned to the United States as conductor of the Houston Symphony and then as guest conductor of other groups. He had developed into one of the world's greatest conductors. And his repertory was all-inclusive. Szell, for instance, knew everything, but he avoided great blocks of the repertory. Barbirolli programmed everything—the German school, Elgar and Delius, Debussy and Ravel, Tchaikovsky and the other Russians, and he even started a series of Italian operas on records. If he did not have Szell's absolute precision, he had more charm, and there was a wonderfully genial spirit to his conducting.

And it was big, vital conducting. There were no idiosyncrasies. It was music-making that went along in a sturdy, healthy, colorful manner, with a large amount of Romanticism in it. Few conductors were so successful with the nineteenth-century masterpieces. Barbirolli, without ever indulging himself or sounding affected, instinctively knew when to slow up or speed, when to introduce variation of line and rhythm. His conducting fell midway between the ultra-Romanticism of a Furtwängler and the objectivity of a Toscanini. Just as there was a great deal of Toscanini in Szell, so there was a great deal of Sir Thomas Beecham in Barbirolli. He and Beecham both had an urbane, civilized attitude toward music, reflected in interpretations of controlled freedom in which the players were given plenty of leeway. Szell, one felt, approached his players as though they were potential criminals. Barbirolli approached them as colleagues, without ever losing his authority over them.

The world of music will miss both: the authoritarian, profound George Szell, he of the perfect ear and flawless technique, the master of rhythms, balances and textures, the creator of structures in sound; and the more mercurial Sir John Barbirolli, the warm-hearted, genial Romantic, he of the big line, the delicate color shades, the man as much of emotion as of logic. As interpreters, Szell and Barbirolli were far apart, but both were true to their ideal. In their own way they illuminated for us, incandescently, the meaning of the notes that great men put on paper.

Aug. 9, 1970

PART IX

Miscellany

*Arion made fishes follow him, which, as common ex-
perience evinceth, are much affected with musick. All
singing birds are much pleased with it, especially
Nightingales, if we may believe* Calcaginus; *and bees
amongst the rest, though they be flying away, when
they hear any tingling sound, will tarry behind.* Harts,
Hinds, Horses, Dogs, Bears, *are exceedingly delighted
with it,* Scal. exer. 302. Elephants, Agrippa *adds,* lib. 2.
cap. 24 *and in* Lydia *in the midst of a lake there be
certain floating islands (if ye will believe it), that after
musick will dance.*

—Robert Burton

This was the first piece I wrote for the Times *Sunday magazine. Lester Markel, then the Sunday editor, wanted a profile of Minnie Guggenheimer and asked Howard Taubman to write it. Mr. Taubman was tied up and suggested me. The article wrote itself. Mrs. Guggenheimer was one of the most colorful ladies of New York, and it was necessary only to quote her. Only a few years later, the Lewisohn Stadium concerts faded away. It was by then an anachronism, but for decades it had provided the best of music for New Yorkers who had no other musical outlet during the summer.*

The Summer Concerts of Minnie Guggenheimer

MRS. CHARLES S. GUGGENHEIMER, known to the world at large as Minnie, is an energetic grandmother, seventy-five years old, who almost single-handedly founded the summer concerts at Lewisohn Stadium in 1918 (she was not a grandmother then), still runs them almost singlehanded, smokes about fifty cigarettes a day, wears absurd little hats, drinks Scotch on the rocks for her health, bears a striking resemblance in looks and voice to the late Josephine Hull and has the speech habits of Casey Stengel out of Mrs. Malaprop. Her most remarkable encounter with the anfractuosities of the English language occurred several summers ago, when she strode before the microphone at Lewisohn Stadium and proceeded to read off future programs for her children. (Anybody who pays cash to get into the Stadium is one

375

of her children.) "And tomorrow night," she announced, "we will present one of the greatest names in music—Ezio Pinza Bass." The audience responded with a yell of pure rapture, at which Minnie beamed before realizing that something was wrong. "Oh, no, that can't be right," she said. "That's the name of a fish. I guess it's Ezio Pinza, bass."

Her second most publicized episode came when a titled personage, about to be introduced to the audience, got lost and started to wander into the wings. "Here, Prince! Here, Prince!" yelled Minnie, chasing after him. There also was the time when she was talking about the president of City College. "I don't know what I'd do without him," she told the audience. Evil-minded listeners burst into laughter. "Of course, I don't know what I'd do with him, either," hastily added Minnie.

She likes to talk to her summer audiences, and the older music critics have pointed out that she likes it more and more every year. Her entrance before the microphone, with a cheery "Hello, everyone," has become one of New York's most cherished summer sounds. When a few days go by and she has not appeared on stage, some of the Stadium regulars feel cheated. "We want Minnie!" they chant, and the cry is taken up, resounding from Amsterdam Avenue to the Hudson River.

Some of her addresses have developed into autobiographical dissertations. At the opening concert of the 1956 season she told her listeners that every kind of attraction except a prizefight had been lined up. She announced that this was going to be her thirty-ninth season. She let it be known that she would soon be seventy-five years old and hoped everybody would keep her age a secret. She then proceeded to read off some coming attractions. At other times, she has been known to talk about her children —her own children, not the Stadium audiences—or she may ask 15,000 people a question and then demand they answer one by one. Once she asked the audience to find her a place to live because her building was coming down.

She still, after some forty years of coaching, pronounces the name of a certain Russian composer with a bovine accent: TchaiKOWsky. She used to talk about TchaiKOWsky's Con-*ser*to in B flat minor; now, however, she uses the more orthodox pronunciation of con*chair*to. Seated in her West Fifty-seventh Street office, rattling away to Mrs. Bertha Cohen, her secretary, she may go on like this, in pure Stengelese:

"Next season we must program that wonderful conchairto, the one with a tune, you know, and that nice young pianist, the one from the country. Yes, and that conductor, Markoff, we must use him because he's a local boy." From this, Mrs. Cohen knows that Minnie is referring to Rachmaninoff's C minor Piano Concerto, to Jesús María Sanromá (he's a country boy because he used to appear at the Berkshire Festival), and to Igor Markevitch, a Russian-born maestro who is anything but a local boy. "I have an awful time trying to remember names," says Minnie, somewhat unnecessarily.

Stadium Concerts enters its fortieth season tomorrow and continues through August 3. Minnie's worries about the season are much the same as they were in 1918: (1) money and (2) the weather. Each season the concert series runs into a sizable deficit. And each season, just as regularly as leaves do sprout, birds head north and ball-players south, come newspaper articles hailing the work of Mrs. Charles S. Guggenheimer and asking the New York public to contribute to the cause.

Minnie got into the line of work when, in 1918, she was approached to help raise money for a two-week series of concerts for service men. She was more than successful, though up to then, as she says, the only important thing she had ever done was to have babies. The two-week series in 1918 went very well. "I loved it," says Minnie. "It sort of got under my skin. It was such a joy to see the people coming in. Also, it's the best thing for juvenile delinquency."

These days the budget of the six-week, thirty-concert season runs to some $250,000. The ninety-four-piece New York Philharmonic-Symphony eats heavily into this sum. Soloists nick out another healthy segment. Paid newspaper ads come to $30,000 or so. Minnie has a list of 4,000 people who can be depended on for donations in sums ranging from a dollar to ten thousand dollars. Generally, she personally raises around $75,000. For the last few years the city has helped, buying up to $25,000 worth of tickets, which are dispersed among schools.

She has been known to buttonhole total strangers and ask them to contribute. She has a system for spotting a rich woman (she herself is not wealthy, though she is in comfortable circumstances). "Pearls!" she says. "If she is wearing pearls she has money." But Minnie indignantly adds that reports of indiscriminate begging on her part are a gross canard. "First," she says, "I strike up an acquaintance with them. If we meet at a restaurant or at the theatre I ask them how they are and talk with them for a while, and warm them up." Then she lowers the boom, sometimes with gratifying results. "I sort of have a feeling," she modestly says.

After money, the weather. A rainy season means a bad deficit. Renata Tebaldi, the popular Italian soprano, has been engaged for Thursday evening, June 27. Lewisohn Stadium has long been sold out for the event. But Tebaldi has only that Thursday open, and if the concert is rained out, bang goes about $18,000 at the box office. It wouldn't be so bad if Tebaldi could appear at another time during the season, but as matters stand, that $18,000 would have to be refunded, a process that would grieve Minnie beyond human belief.

"I'm sweating it out," she says. "But if I worried too much about it I'd be three-quarters crazy instead of one-quarter crazy. Anyway, I know for sure that there will be stars and a full moon. I'll arrange it."

She is a great arranger. Sometimes her powers verge on the supernatural. At the annual Gershwin concert in 1954 the clouds started to pile up just at concert time. Minnie sorrowfully came on stage. "Hello, everybody," she cried out, as she always does; and "Hello, Minnie," everybody chorused back, as they always do. "I think," said Minnie, "that we'll have to postpone the concert." About 18,000 voices yelled "No!" in protest; Gershwin night is always a sellout. "Listen, you," said Minnie. "I just came from the north, and there were raindrops as big as apples. If that thing"—pointing to a big, threatening cloud— "meets that thing"—pointing to another black monster—"look out!"

She asked the audience if, despite her warning, it wanted to stay. The audience definitely did. "O.K.," said Minnie, "but we have had so much rain the Stadium is busted. Will you all promise to come back every other night?" Cheers, applause, and the concert went on. After fifteen minutes or so, the clouds crept away. Backstage, Minnie was worried. "They'll think I'm a witch," she said.

One problem that did not come up back in 1918 has to do with airplanes. Minnie has dark suspicions about airline pilots. She thinks that they all love music and sweep low over the Stadium to listen, invariably and unerringly picking out the pianissimo sections of whatever symphony happens to be on the program. After some caustic comments from the music critics about airplanes versus the Brahms Second, the Great Airplane Controversy started.

Minnie wrote to Washington. She got all kinds of legal advice. She threatened to mount antiaircraft guns and personally send off their message. She raised Cain with the Civil Aeronautics Administration. She had lengthy conferences with Admiral Charles E. Rosendahl of the National Air Transport Command. After the smoke cleared, the N.A.T.C., the C.A.A. and the Federal Government retired in some confusion, promising to have pilots re-route their path to and from La Guardia Airport during Stadium hours. Occasionally planes come around, still, but not nearly with the profusion of yore. Some of the veteran ushers think that they are afraid to.

She describes her own musical likes as wide-ranged. "I like all kinds of music. I love jazz and I love what's the stuff that Belafonte does?—calypso. Thanks. And I like Brahms, and I like TchaiKOWsky and Beethoven. I don't care too much for Mozart and Haydn. But what I like or don't like has nothing to do with the Stadium season. It's up to the artist and what I think the public likes." By now, after forty years, Minnie has a very shrewd idea of what the public will support and what it won't.

She also has to deal directly with the tough-minded negotiators of the various musical unions. Much of this she does on the telephone. When telephone talks break down she appears in person. On the telephone, no matter with whom she is talking, her voice goes up to eighty decibels or so, assuming the timbre and resonance of a mezzo-soprano in the Matzenauer tradition.

When she is talking with union men, another twenty decibels can be added. "The unions play havoc with me," she cries. "They *absolutely* wear me down."

Minnie may not know it, but the feeling is reciprocated. She wears down the unions, and they go to battle stations when she heaves into view. "She's indomitable, indefatigable, and she comes storming in like mad," says an official of Local 802, American Federation of Musicians. "She's a sharp bargainer. And can she be stubborn! She's always crying that she hasn't got enough money. Then she really gets excitable. We get the same speech every time she comes in." But she gets along famously with Al Manuti, president of Local 802. They respect each other and are the most beloved of enemies. "Minnie's all right," says Mr. Manuti. "A nice lady. We need more like her, and I hope she'll be around for years to come."

The American Guild of Musical Artists gets the same kind of treatment from Minnie. "She operates in a very individual way," says an A.G.M.A. member. "Little details, such as having contracts signed and other such things—she bridles at them. To her this is small stuff. It's hard to argue with her. First of all, she's a lady, and a grand lady. The problem is to get her to calm down and listen, after which she's O.K."

This A.G.M.A. man is very admiring of her technique, and perhaps even a little bitter about it. "She'll tear our hearts out," he says. "She comes in crying that she's an old lady, that nobody cares for her, that this is her last season, that she'll have to quit because our demands are impossible. I tell you, by the time she's through some of us want to rush down and take up a collection for the Stadium. But we gotta protect our artists so we argue with her. Eventually everything works out."

After a tussle with the unions, with temperamental musicians, with a hogsheadful of mail and importunate telephoners, with press agents and managers, with people who have money to give and won't give, the day can become very tiring for Minnie, and she admits it. "I go home and look at the television. I adore the television and I don't care if it's no good," she says.

Minnie's husband, a prominent attorney, died in 1954. (They were married in 1903.) Her home life and her relations with her children today are full and satisfactory. "I have two children and a daughter-in-law, and a dog, and I love them all alike, and two grandsons." The dog is a poodle, "and the most adorable dog in the world. I think he has fleas. He bit me the other day. I had the happiest married life of anybody. I could almost write a book about why."

Minnie leans forward and imparts the knowledge of seventy-five years of experience. "Women," she says, "must make a fuss over their husbands."

JUNE 23, 1957

Anybody as flamboyant as Sol Hurok was constantly written about, much to the gratification of Mr. Hurok. He was an interesting man—not very well educated, but a visionary with a great deal of charm and a sharp business sense. He also had a great deal of dignity. He needed his name publicized; but, unlike some managers and agents, he never curried favor from critics and journalists. He had a genuine aura, and he did things in a grand way. He might have had his less agreeable side, as those who worked for him can vouch, but he was an authentic force in the American culture of his time, and when he died there was no successor. He was the last of his breed.

Presenting Sol Hurok, Impresario

WHEN GALINA ULANOVA and her husband were ushered by Sol Hurok into the midtown hotel at which the Bolshoi Ballet is staying, they gazed upon a three-room suite. They peeked into a refrigerator that was stocked with caviar, champagne and other necessities for the sustenance of a *prima ballerina assoluta.* On a table was a new electric percolator; next to it an unopened tin of coffee. Ulanova loves coffee. Flowers were all over the place. And in one room was a specially constructed ballet *barre,* complete with full-length mirrors.

"So, my dear," said Hurok, "you can practice here if you wish."

Ulanova was floored. Word of this touch of grandeur began to get around town. A man in the concert business summed it up. "That," he said, "is the difference between an impresario and a manager."

Managers tend to be anonymous business men. Impresarios, and there are few of them left, are the flamboyant medicine men of the artistic world. Diaghilev was one. Duveen was one. Hurok is one. They do things in a big way, automatically taking care that the doings get into all the best papers and columns. They are constantly in the public eye. They are gamblers by instinct, salesmen by necessity, persuaders *par excellence,* and they move in a breathless flourish that creates a breeze heavy enough to tilt an aircraft carrier.

When Hurok, enormous horn-rimmed glasses over his owl-like eyes, pushes his plump frontage into the Pavillon in New York, the Savoy in London or Lapérouse in Paris, headwaiters and flunkies converge like a school of perch around a particularly succulent bait. Hurok gets what Ludwig Bemelmans calls the ten-dollar headwaiters' bow (as against the one-dollar one), and this is the deepest one of all, reserved ordinarily for royalty and important Hollywood figures. Champagne promptly begins to flow, waiters break into a trot and the chef takes particular pains with his châteaubriand. When Hurok walks along Fifty-seventh Street, black felt hat rakishly aslant on his head, silver-topped cane abobbing, it is less a walk than a procession, in the regal sense of the word. Even his Russian accent has the appropriate touch of the exotic.

When he gives a party, it's a real party, not a canapé and Scotch-and-soda affair. Immediately after the curtain went down on the Bolshoi's first night at the Metropolitan Opera, over two hundred formally dressed ladies and gentlemen repaired as

Hurok's guests to the St. Regis Roof, taken over by Hurok for the night. There they goggled at the entire Bolshoi contingent and various notables; drank champagne; ate pirozhki, caviar, beef Stroganoff, chicken Hurok (sliced chicken with white sauce over a bed of rice and noodles), and danced to an eleven-piece orchestra. It was a nice party, and it must have cost Hurok over $15,000.

Hurok gives parties like this partly for business reasons. But people close to him think that business is the least of it.

"He has a great need to justify himself," says a man who has known him for a generation. "The way he fulfills himself is in doing things big and getting his name in print. He needs a feeling of recognition. That's why he overtips and throws his money around, though in some respects he can be a penny-pincher. He unconsciously remembers the old days, when things were precarious. But always he has wanted to be the *grand seigneur*, and in a curious way he has succeeded."

Hurok does not disdain money, but he says that other things are more important. "To be a real impresario, first of all you have to love the things you do," he said the other day. "How much do you love this attraction or that personality? How much do you owe the American public? Those are the important things. The money you think about later."

That last sentence may make some rival managers choke over their coffee, but key members of the Hurok office swear it is true. They insist that Hurok has managed attractions that he knew would lose money but went on nevertheless because he thought they needed support—and there always was the off-chance that they eventually would get around to turning a buck or so.

However, Hurok has managed to survive his philanthropy and come out very well indeed. In the last few years his attractions have grossed well over $5,000,000, thanks to such box-office wows as the Moiseyev Ballet, the Sadler's Wells, the Scots Guards and the Old Vic, not to mention individual musicians of repute like Rubinstein, Stern, Peters, Anderson and Gilels. And the Bolshoi Ballet could well be the biggest box-office draw in the history of the entertainment business.

In investing $100,000 of his own money and committing him-

self to expenses amounting to an additional $350,000, Hurok
has taken a gamble in bringing over the Bolshoi. But while in
show business all gambles are even, some gambles are more
even than others. Nobody in his right mind, for example, would
turn down a chance to invest in a Rodgers and Hammerstein
show, sight unseen. The Bolshoi Ballet appears to be a similar
blue-chip investment, and nobody in the business is losing any
sleep worrying about Hurok's dropping money over it. In fact,
the feeling is one of downright jealousy.

Even though the nut of the American run—the amount Hurok
has to take in if he is to break even—is an enormous $170,000
weekly, and even though the reviews of the opening night were
less than ecstatic, the Hurok organization had so drummed up
the Bolshoi that the entire Met run was virtually sold out in
advance. The rest of the American tour will probably play to
standees also. Which means that, barring something cataclysmic, the Hurok account will once more be enriched.

Up to now, Hurok has had huge success with his imported
attractions, the outstanding case in point being the gross of
$1,600,000 made by the Moiseyev Dancers. How much of this
sum Hurok retained is a business secret but, after all expenses
were paid out, the remaining sum, it is safe to say, made Hurok
content.

The current visit of the Bolshoi is not something that just
happened. Since 1924 Hurok has been dying to get a Russian
ballet company to these shores. At that time he almost closed a
deal with the Leningrad Ballet. It fell through at the last moment. In 1927, 1929, 1930 and 1931 he reopened negotiations.
Not exactly a bashful type, he loudly banged on closed doors and
entered into negotiations with such unapproachables as Maxim
Litvinov.

In the meantime, lacking a Russian ballet company, Hurok
had to make do with such substitutes as Chaliapin, Pavlova, the
German Opera Company, the Russian Opera Company, the Ballet Russe de Monte Carlo, Anderson, Escudero, Shan-kar and
Ballet Theatre.

Hurok has been associated with top attractions since his first
major managerial ventures. This was during World War I (he had

come to America from Russia in 1905 at the age of 17 and ped-
dled pots and pans, among other things, before flirting with the
muse of music) when he took over the Hippodrome in New
York and began presenting the likes of Elman, Ruffo, Tetrazzini,
Chaliapin and Schumann-Heink at a two-dollar top. He came to
the conviction that the public would respond to quality.

But how to tell quality, especially in untried talent? Hurok
operates partly on hunches, on his gambling instincts. "He
smells a good attraction," one competitor says resignedly. "Besides, he's the most imaginative concert manager of the last
half-century."

Anybody who has worked with Hurok concedes that he is a
gambler (and, like all gamblers, he has gone broke more than
once). Not musically trained himself, he somehow knows, however, what will appeal to the man in the street. This may be
because he himself is the man in the street, who doesn't know
much about music but knows what he likes.

Hurok demands one thing of a musician or an attraction: projection. He looks for that indefinable something that comes
right over the footlights and hits the audience in the solar
plexus. When he wandered into a concert hall in Paris, quite by
accident, and heard an unknown contralto named Marian Anderson, he felt chills dance up and down his spine, and his hands
got wet. She projected.

His management of Anderson is a typical example of the way
he works. Anderson's American manager was only too happy to
release her from her contract. Hurok snapped her up, and a hand-
shake was all he and she needed. He saw her through her successful Town Hall debut. Before the ink was dry on the
newsprint that carried her reviews, he had booked her for a pair
of Carnegie Hall concerts a few weeks later. This procedure was
unusual enough to make the music world agog about the new
sensation. Naturally, a heavy tour was easy to book after that.

Years later he was to repeat the formula with Victoria de los
Angeles. The Spanish soprano did not get a rave review from the
leading New York critics, but Hurok was unperturbed. Damn
the torpedoes and full speed ahead, he said in effect, and immediately booked another New York concert. Most managers

would have shaken their heads and muttered something about a bad New York press. De los Angeles was in divine voice for her second concert, and from that point she was established here.

Hurok himself was in divine form for that particular concert. There are those who seriously say that Hurok in the back of the hall can spark an audience to sheer hysteria by the timing, timbre and percussive splendor of his hand-clapping.

When applause threatens to fade away, two or three Hurok taradiddles can set it off in a frenzy again. At the de los Angeles concert he rushed, in the rear of Carnegie Hall, from one side to the other, clapping here and clapping there, with an occasional "Brava!" inserted in a loud, though not particularly mellifluous, voice.

That is part of being an impresario. Another part is application. Hurok is not a very complicated man. He lives for his work; he is the first one in his office and the last one to leave.

"When the other managers are out playing golf or something," says a man in the business, "Mr. Hurok is on Fifty-seventh Street making plans."

Hurok is considered a shrewd but ethical business man. He can drive a hard bargain, but all agree that once a contract is made he sticks with it.

If there is one thing that Hurok knows above all, it is the value of publicity. He is extremely unhappy when his name does not appear in print with regularity, and it is he who takes top billing over his artists with the legend "S. HUROK PRESENTS." Publicity is the life blood of anybody in the managerial business, and Hurok throughout the years has gotten enough to supply transfusions to an entire army division.

"Hurok," one competitor says, "wouldn't mind sleeping on a park bench if he knew he'd be in the papers as the man who brought music to the masses. It's his drive."

He is keenly aware when the homage is not rendered. Last year he attended the kinescope of Marian Anderson's tour of the Far East. When she sang spirituals to the throng at the Gandhi Memorial, Hurok, who has his sentimental side, broke down and started to cry. The kinescope made such an overwhelming impression on him that he went back twice again, and each time he came out of the viewing room with tears rolling down his face. Somebody commented on how wonderful the kinescope was. "Yes," sobbed Hurok, "and they didn't even mention my name!"

APRIL 26, 1959

Chess has always been one of my passions, and I have even written a book about it (Grandmasters of Chess). *I also covered the Spassky-Fischer match in Reykjavik for the* Times *in 1972, all two-plus months of it, and it was a fabulous assignment. Word has gotten around that I am a very strong player. The truth is that I talk a much better game than I play, but I think I have an understanding of the beauty and the mystery of chess, and I see a close parallel with music in it. Many musicians, by the way, have been strong players. Perhaps the most powerful were Prokofiev and David Oistrakh, both of master strength. Among music critics of my acquaintance, Irving Lowens (formerly of the* Washington Star *and now the second in command at the Peabody Institute) and John Dwyer of the* Buffalo Evening News *play a strong, clean game.*

Pawns, Rooks and Notes

STARTING WEDNESDAY, the eyes of America—well, some eyes —will be focused on Curaçao, in the Netherlands West Indies, where once again America and Russia will touch in conflict. It is not an orbital mission, nor is it a musical competition. But the Brooklyn-born Bobby Fischer and the Hungarian-born Pal Benko, now resident in this city, will meet, over the chessboard, the best that the Russians have to offer; and the winner of this

Candidates Tournament will meet Mikhail Botwinnik to play for the world's championship.

And what may chess have to do with the hemidemisemiquavers that normally concern this department? Nothing specifically: no more than painting, literature or the abstractions of pure mathematics. The arts are a complex that, basically, have to do with the esthetic phenomena. Each is different, but each also is, in the Platonic sense, the same. And chess is an art, in that it deals with the materials and processes of creation, and evokes an esthetic response. The more one gets into this ancient game (but it should not really be called a game; it is sheer intellect, tempered with imagination, in which there is no element of chance) the more its parallels with the other arts, and especially the art of music, become clear. Chess writers never for a moment let their readers forget it. How many times has Paul Morphy, the first great American player, been referred to as "the Mozart of chess"?

And there is good reason for it. Chess, like music, has had its Wunderkinder. Morphy, José Capablanca, Samuel Reshevsky, Bobby Fischer—by the time they were ten years old, just high enough so that their eyes were about on a level with the chessboard, they were delighting and amazing onlookers with the beauty and clarity of their combinations, the precision of their style, the instinctive profundity of their moves. It was pure instinct, just as it was with the ten-year-old Mozart or Mendelssohn, for no child, however gifted, can have the experience that maturity brings.

Later on, of course, the Mozarts, Mendelssohns and Capablancas develop their prevailing styles. For every style in music there is a corresponding one in chess. One speaks of Capablanca's Classicism and Alekhine's Romanticism, Reti's hypermodernism and Reshevsky's eclecticism.

But the parallels between chess and music go much deeper. Both are arts of combination, working from the basic material of the thirty-two pieces and the twelve notes of the chromatic scale. There is the material: what can be done with it? To people without a special gift in this direction, the materials lead to ineptness and banality. To those who at least have studied the problems, the materials can be handled logically, though without any individuality. But to those who have genius, the materials can be molded, deftly and inevitably, into creations that bear the mark of the maker and are not to be duplicated by anybody else. Then we get into art. For one of the characteristics of art is its uniqueness. No piece of art—the Mozart G minor Symphony, the Marshall-Levitzky game at Breslau, 1912, Cézanne's card players—can ever be duplicated, perhaps not even by its creator. It can be copied, but that is another thing.

It is rather amusing that in both chess and music the cry has been raised, within recent years, that the end has come. All is technique, memory, intellectualism; there is no more emotion or heart left; oh, for the good old days of Alekhine (Wagner), Capablanca (Ravel) and Anderssen (Liszt). But then, inevitably, come along composers who demonstrate that the twelve notes are not worked out, and chess players who prove that the game, with all of its contemporary stress on pure technique, can yield warmth and excitement. Certainly Bobby Fischer has as good a technique as anybody around. But his game has never slipped into dryness and academism. Quite the contrary.

Fischer is an attacking player. He will take chances and he loves to mix it up. He can see beautiful combinations that literally modulate in a Schubertian sense. One moment, Schubert is in this key, the next in another, but always with logic rather than caprice. Fischer goes about it much the same way; and so, incidentally, do all chess players with Romantic leanings.

It is true that Romantic chess, like Romantic music, is a little out of fashion. As an art, chess also follows the dictates of the age, and always has. In the European Classic revival of the late eighteenth century, the great player was Philidor, a Neoclassicist. The Romantic age had its Anderssens and Birds as well as its Liszts and Schumanns: all of them dashing, spectacular, full of new ideas and bubbling over with exuberance. As the Romantic age spent itself, there emerged a Brahms and a Wilhelm Steinitz. When the Cubists were throwing notions of painting upside down, and when Schoenberg was writing such unorthodox scores as *Pierrot Lunaire*, there also was emerging a new school of chess, headed by Richard Reti, in which all established notions about opening theory were cast away. And today, as in many of the other arts, the trend is towards a cut-and-dried eclecticism, in which memory and pure technique are more important than daring and imagination.

Thus every age produces its own notions about art, and chess is no exception. The great chess player is closely allied to the great composer. He composes over the chess board, creating a new work every time he plays. On him are beating the forces of the age, which have to be modified by his own genius and imagination. He develops his pieces as the composer develops his notes, and the aim in both cases is to produce a work that has originality, validity, logic and beauty. The result is, of course, self-expression (an expert can easily distinguish between a game by Euwe, say, and one by Alekhine) in the most creative sense of the word.

The great chess player does not arrive at his eminence by accident, and he has subjected himself to much the same kind of discipline that the great composer has. In both arts you start at the age of ten or before, and have made some kind of a mark on the international scene by the time you are twenty. You get there by constant practice and study; by memorizing scores and doing exercises; by trying your own creative flights; by evolving a style and sticking to it; by having faith in your talent that amounts to egomania. But none of this will do any good unless you have genius, else you will be a competent craftsman and nothing more. Yes; the composer and the grandmaster are adjacent spokes in the same wheel.

APRIL 29, 1962

The relation between words and music has always been a difficult subject for me to define. I always have been more tone

conscious than word conscious in lied or opera, tending to listen to songs and arias as music and completely ignoring the
words. Some years after writing this article I found something
in the writings of Arnold Schoenberg that paralleled my own
experience. Schoenberg wrote that he had been hearing and
loving the Schubert songs for decades without ever knowing
what the words were about. But when he finally got around to
reading the poems, "it became clear to me that I had gained
absolutely nothing for the understanding of the songs themselves, since the poems did not make it necessary for me to
change my conception of the musical interpretation in the
slightest degree. On the contrary, it appeared that, without
knowing the poem, I had grasped the content, the real content,
even more profoundly than if I had clung to the surface of the
mere thoughts expressed in words."

Music Over Words

WHAT IS a song? Is it a fusion of words and music? Are the
words less important than the music? Does music detract from
the words? Is it true that weak poems are best material for the
art song? Can there be such a thing as a perfect song?

These eternal questions are discussed by Philip L. Miller in
the introduction to his *The Ring of Words*, a recently published
anthology of song texts (and an indispensable reference book
that will supply at-hand translations of the best-known songs of
the literature).

By definition, a song is a fusion of words and music. But, as
Mr. Miller points out, there are two schools of thought as to the
importance of poetry in song: "To some authorities, who remind
us that poetry contains its own music, any attempt to combine
the two arts is pure lily-gilding."

Mr. Miller quotes Jacques Barzun's opinion that "as a general
rule, the text of the best songs and operas is inferior in kind to
the musical setting. A great poem is complete in itself and needs
no additions from another art. Great music is complete in itself,

and only a disagreeable overlap of intentions can result from its being harnessed to great literature."

Mr. Miller concedes that poetry of great intellectual depth or involved symbolism is not too likely to be translated successfully into song, "for song is essentially a lyrical art form." But that does not mean great lyric poetry is not susceptible of musical setting. Goethe certainly was a major poet, and Schubert set fifty-nine of his poems, including such masterpieces as *Gretchen am Spinnrade, Der Musensohn, Heidenröslein* and *Rastlose Liebe.* Hugo Wolf, who had a fine taste for poetry, went to Goethe, Mörike and Eichendorff, among others, for his inspiration. Baudelaire and Verlaine figure prominently in the songs of such composers as Fauré and Debussy—and so on. A quick look at the song literature reveals that many of the greatest songs are set to the greatest poetry.

But, still, does that necessarily mean that the words are co-equal with the music? Or are the words merely a necessary prop upon which to hang the music? We all know, of course, that the best song composers take infinite pains with their settings, trying to capture the meter of the words, trying to invent melodies and harmonies that will enhance, explain and sometimes even illustrate the poetry. Yet it appears to me (and here Mr. Miller and I part company) that nevertheless the music remains more important.

For no amount of great poetry can insure a great song, but a skillful composer can take an inferior poem and make a great song of it. Schumann's *Frauenliebe und Leben* is a case of the triumph of musical genius over wretched poetry. It is the music and the music alone that determines whether or not a song will live. And if Hugo Wolf, with all his literary taste and compositional technique, had not been possessed of an incomparably lyric melodic sense, his music would not have lived.

In any case, music is an objective phenomenon, in that it stands complete in itself and cannot describe anything. It can suggest moods, and that is another matter. But it cannot describe. Those who see pictures when they hear music are simply not hearing music. Time and time again, psychologists have tested listeners with music that is supposed to describe some-

thing: *Don Quixote's* sheep sequence, Debussy's *La Mer* and so
on. A thousand listeners (at least, those who are not already
conditioned by knowing the music in advance) will report a
thousand different pictures. Music is an abstract art.

And thus those who will take a great song and say "My! how
wonderfully the composer is describing the forest!" or the lake,
or a flower, or the sea, are probably not only missing the whole
point of the music but are reasoning after the fact.

For instance, take Schubert's *Gretchen am Spinnrade*. It is set
to Goethe's poem in *Faust,* in which Gretchen, at her spinning
wheel, muses about her love for the missing Faust. *"Meine Ruh
ist hin,/Mein Herz ist schwer . . ."* "My peace is gone,/my heart
is heavy . . ." To these words Schubert composed for the piano
accompaniment a whirling figure obviously supposed to suggest
a spinning wheel. And everybody who listens to the song says:
"How inevitable! How apt, that accompaniment! What a stroke
of genius!"

But suppose that, to the very same accompaniment and vocal
line, Schubert had used instead of the Goethe poem, one by a
poet we shall call Heinrich Schlüssschloss. This great poem is
called *Am Meer,* or *By the Sea,* and its first four lines are as
follows:

> *The sea doth finger*
> *The pebbl'd shore,*
> *Going back and forth*
> *Like a swinging door.*

Now, the *Gretchen am Spinnrade* accompaniment could just
as well represent the ebb and flow of the waves as a spinning
wheel. Those figurations are figurations of back-and-forth movement. Thus, had Schubert used the Schlüssschloss poem, three
generations of listeners and commentators would have been saying: "How inevitable! How apt, that accompaniment! What a
stroke of genius!" And they all would have "seen" waves instead
of a spinning wheel.

There may, however, be an entirely different set of circumstances to consider. All of us hear differently and approach

music in different ways. Some are most responsive to the purely
tonal element of music, and are apt to disregard anything else.
At an opera, this type of listener will often completely forget
about the stage action and concentrate on the musical development, the thematic structure, and so on. Others are much more
responsive to the literary side of vocal music, and will look for
the synthesis of the two.

The same goes for composers. Some, like Wolf, are highly
conscious of literary values and the prosody of the poem they
are setting. Others, like Stravinsky, are much more apt to let
musical considerations take complete precedence over prosodi-
cal considerations. In that case, if the musical line conflicts with
the line of the poem, it is the poem that is going to give way and
not the music.

Benjamin Britten, for instance, is supposed to be a master of
prosody. Yet as often as not he lets the course of the music
determine the accentuation of the word, and not vice versa. In
the recent *War Requiem* are settings like "WHAT passING
BELLS" instead of "WHAT PASSing BELLS" or "What PASSing
bells." Or Britten will do something like "my FAther" immediately followed by "my faTHER." It seems obvious that he has
determined the musical line first, and the words have to fit as
best they can. And some of the metrical groupings Britten uses
have little in common with the prosody of the Wilfred Owen
poems. None of this, though, may be of any great importance in
the long run. The *War Requiem* (or any other words-and-music
combination) is going to live or die not by its prosody but by the
amount of *musical* genius inherent in it.

Sept. 8, 1963

*In the agony of trying to stop smoking (an ordeal that lasted
about three weeks before I was up to two packs again), I seized*

upon my troubles for a Sunday piece. Has anybody compiled an LP disc of songs and other music devoted to tobacco? There is a very large amount of material.

Withdrawal Symptoms

LIFE HAS not been the same since the publication of that last report on smoking. The *Times* is filled with miserable wretches who have forsworn buying cigarettes (but who are continuing to snaffle them when the demands of the flesh grow too strong). Pipes are sprouting like smokestacks on the Pittsburgh skyline. The men's room, normally a place where one could hear all the gossip, has now as its sole topic of conversation: withdrawal symptoms. Everybody talks about withdrawal symptoms as formerly they spoke of the new pool stenographer, or the latest whimsies of the city editor.

My own withdrawal symptom, aside from describing my withdrawal symptoms, has been to look up everything I can find about tobacco and music. There is a consolation in it. One can immerse himself in the weed without actually partaking. How comforting it is to inhale vicariously with the poet in "Wits Recreations" (1640):

> *Things which are common common men do use,*
> *The better sort do common things refuse:*
> *Yet Countries-cloth-breech, & Court-velvet-hose,*
> *Puffe both alike Tobacco through the Nose.*

Proving that even in precigarette days inhalation was the norm. There are many old references to the habit, and many songs were written about it. Charles van der Borren, in the July 1932 issue of the *Musical Quarterly*, wrote an article named "Tobacco and Coffee in Music," coming up with several Elizabethan pieces of music and then moving to the Continent. He notes that smoking was introduced to Holland by the English, around 1620, and one result was the "Toebaks-lied," a famous

Dutch song: *"Isser iemant uyt Oost Indien gekomen, die wat woet! Heeft hyniet van den toeback vernonen?"* Meaning, "Has anybody come from the East Indies who knows anything? Has he not heard of tobacco?" Van der Borren says that this poem was set to a French court air that goes back to 1613. There are quite a few stanzas.

The learned van der Borren discusses tobacco music in France and Germany, and of course mentions Wolf-Ferrari's opera *The Secret of Susanne*. Susanne's secret, as we all know except her husband, is cigarette smoking. Wolf-Ferrari's is the only opera based on such a subject. But the seventeenth century is full of musical tributes to tobacco. One of the most famous is cited by van der Borren. He found it in the 1719 edition of the famous British collection, *Pills to Purge Melancholy*. It is a song with quite a lovely melody, and it has many stanzas, the first of which is:

> *Tobacco is but an Indian weed,*
> *Grows green in the Morn,*
> *   cut down at Eve;*
> *It shows our decay,*
> *We are but Clay,*
> *Think of this and take Tobacco.*

Van der Borren does not go into the history of this poem. It far predates *Pills to Purge Melancholy*, and Norman Ault, the Elizabethan specialist, claimed that it originally was written before 1568. If so, that would put it before the first prose mention of tobacco in the English language—1577, when John Frampton translated from the Spanish a work by Nicholas Monardes. An early variant of "The Indian Weed" begins:

> *The Indian Weed withered quite,*
> *Greene at Morne cut downe at night*
> *Shewes our decay, all flesh is hay;*
> *Thus thinke, then drinke Tobacco.*

In addition to songs, there were catches and glees about tobacco. In the Drexel Collection of the New York Public Library are three volumes of *The Catch Club,* an early eighteenth-century publication that contains catches by Blow, Purcell and other famous English composers. Several are by the less-known Henry Aldrich, in his day (1647–1710) an important architect and scholar. Aldrich must have liked the good life. He wrote one song entitled "A Catch upon Small Beer," and another "A Catch on Tobacco, Sung by 4 Men While smoking their Pipes." The catch starts with "Good, good indeed, the Herb's good weed." Later, most pathetically, "But then to the learned say we again,/ if life's a smoak as they maintain,/if life's a Vapour without doubt,/when a Man does dye,/they shou'd not cry,/that his Glass is run, but his Pipe is out."

The eccentric Captain Tobias Hume wrote a tobacco song in his *Musicall Humours* of 1605. He died mad, an end that may or may not have had to do with his smoking. Another Stuart composer, Thomas Ravenscroft, made a musical reference to tobacco in *A Briefe Discourse* in 1614. And one of the greatest of the madrigal composers, Thomas Weelkes, celebrated tobacco in his *Ayres Or Phantasticke Spirites* of 1608. The author of the lyrics is unknown. Most probably none of the madrigal and ayre composers except Thomas Campion wrote his own lyrics. The Weelkes air has four stanzas, and one of them is most amusing:

> *Fill the pipe once more,*
> *My brains dance trenchmore.*
> >*It is heady,*
> >*I am giddy.*
> >*Head and brains,*
> >*Back and reins,*
> >*Joints and veins*
> >*From all pains*
> >*It doth well purge and*
> >>*make clean.*

A trenchmore is an old English country dance of boisterous nature. Weelkes really must have liked to smoke. In 1618, a minor playwright named Barten Holiday published a work named *Technogamia or The Marriage of the Arts.* In it is a song named "Tobacco's a musician." It is a solo by Phlegmaticao,

who enters with "his hat beset round about with tobacco pipes."
Each of the seven stanzas starts with "Tobacco is." And so to-
bacco is a musician, a lawyer, a physician, a traveler, a critic, an
Ignis fatuus and a whiffler. But it seems that this song was writ-
ten by Weelkes and much later inserted into the Holiday play.
Not many years ago it turned up in a 1609 set of part books in
Weelkes's handwriting. Want to know why tobacco is a musi-
cian? Well, according to Weelkes,

> It descends in a close,
> Through the organ of the nose.

a close being a final cadence. Or why is tobacco a lawyer? Sings
Phlegmaticao, in a joke that must have paralyzed the ground-
lings:

> Tobacco is a lawyer,
> His pipes do love long cases:
> When our brain it enters,
> Our feet do make indentures.

But let's not continue in this vein. The topic, as the report
assures us, is not for joking, and tobacco's not for burning. They
knew this three hundred years ago. Witness the two-line epi-
gram in "Wits Recreations":

> Tobacco is a weed of so
>   great power
> That it (like earth) doth
>   all it feeds, devour.

JAN. 26, 1964

Has the subject of the provenance of the songs in Shakespeare's plays received much attention from recent scholars? I have not kept up with work in the field; my Shakespearean studies stopped in graduate school in 1938, and millions of words have since been written about him. I have never had the time to see if my idea about the Shakespeare song lyrics has been investigated. Every instinct, based on some knowledge of Shakespeare's style, shrieks to me that many of the song texts attributed to him could not have been his.

The Man of Avon and the Music of His Time

SHAKESPEARE'S FOUR-HUNDREDTH birthday is hard upon us, and the occasion is sure to foster another googol of commentary about the greatest virtuoso with words any language has produced. There even has been an article, in a new publication named *Chessworld*, about Shakespeare as a chess player. Working from a painting by Karel van Mander, which is dated about 1603 and is supposed to show Shakespeare at play with Ben Jonson, Paul Leith has reconstructed the position on the board and has come to the conclusion that poor Ben is probably in a mating net. But, Mr. Leith says, the position is ambiguous and perhaps was intended as a symbolic game.

Which leads us (though how, I don't know) to Shakespeare and music. And there we are on firmer ground. Shakespeare's plays have some five hundred passages dealing with music; in addition many of the plays call for musical interludes—songs, and the like. Hundreds of studies about Shakespeare and music have been written. The general facts are clear enough. Shakespeare obviously loved music—as, indeed, most Elizabethans did. It was a very sophisticated musical age. Shakespeare knew music not as a professional but as an intelligent amateur. He had picked up something about musical theory, and that was to be expected. The theaters of his day, after all, employed musicians, and Shakespeare would have been in direct contact with them. Occasionally Shakespeare makes the kind of mistake all non-professionals make. Thus:

> *Thou, trumpet, there's my purse.*
> *Now crack thy lungs and split thy brazen pipe.*
> *Blow, villain, till thy spher'd bias cheek*
> *Outswell the colic of puff'd Aquilon.*
> *Come, stretch thy chest, and let thy eyes spout blood.*

From this comes a hemorrhage, not trumpet playing.

But on the whole Shakespeare's musical imagery is quite accurate. The chances are that he was on friendly terms with some of the best musicians of the day, and the best musicians in England at the time were among the best in the world. Shakespeare lived for a while in the parish of St. Helen's in Bishopsgate Ward. It was a parish in which also lived John Bull, the famous organist, composer and virginals player; Giles Farnaby, the composer of delicate instrumental music; John Wilbye, one of the greatest of the madrigalists; the Bassano family of musicians; and the well-known Thomas Morley, composer, theoretician, instrumentalist and author.

London was a small town, and it is inconceivable that Shakespeare would not have known his immediate neighbors. The intellectuals flocked together then, as they do now; anybody with Shakespeare's obvious crush on music would have sought the company of the great Morley or Bull. In Morley's case, supposition rests on a firm basis. For Morley's *First Book of Ayres* (1600) contains a musical setting of a song from *As You Like It*. This is "It was a lover and his lass," and the presence of the song in the *First Book* raises some very puzzling problems.

When was the play written? Most scholars put it in the summer of 1600 (E. K. Chambers did), though a few say late in 1599. Was the Morley song used in the play? Or was it a setting that came later? If it was used for the play, can we be sure that it was Shakespeare who wrote the words? (The eminent authority E. H. Fellowes flatly said that Shakespeare did not; he believed that the poem predated Morley and Shakespeare.) If it can be proved that Shakespeare did not write the words, then what

about the authenticity of all the other songs in the Shakespeare canon?

Perhaps we will never know the answer. In the preface to his volume of songs, Morley wrote that they were made "this vacation time." Scholars have looked into that statement and come to the conclusion that vacation time for Morley would have been between June 29 and Sept. 29, for at that time the Chapel Royal (with which Morley was connected) was not in operation. Thus, if Morley's statement is to be taken at face value, "It was a lover and his lass" would have been composed the summer 1600, just the time that *As You Like It* was first being formed.

Several possibilities suggest themselves. One sc thought believes that the play preceded the music. Mc would merely have used a lyric available to anybo theory is that the song was a joint composition wrote the words, handed them to Morley, who for the play and then had it published in his *Fi*

But it is not impossible that Shakespeare h do with the words. He wanted a song at play. He calls on Morley and asks for so Morley finds some poetry—either an o up by a friend—and sets it to music own book.

The subject is one that calls fo tigation than has been made to sional who, unlike Ben Jons posterity. He was a practica lutely no proof that he wr song he could have turn tration if needed—to ten minutes of mus sure to get those d course, it could h well be that Sh But it is far f

*I*N A
ning,
town.
violin.
divari or
A few wil
agnini or
will beg, bo
a New York
exposed and
scalp crew cut
But is it an o
Gesù is so mu
better at all? No

A few years after this article was written I was on a panel listening to Aaron Rosand playing, in turn, six violins. Three of the instruments were Cremonese, three were modern. I forget the names of all the panelists, but the veteran critic Irving Kolodin was one, as were the violinist Joseph Fuchs, the recording engineer Thomas Frost, and the musicologist Boris Schwarz, himself a string player. We were not supposed to talk to one another, we sat far apart, and an accountant on stage was tabulating our votes. I knew that in previous tests of this kind, professional string players had failed to tell the difference between new and old violins. I also knew, while Rosand was playing, that my ears kept insisting two of the instruments were magnificent. The jury's decision turned out to be similar to mine. The instrument that received the most votes was a Guarneri, followed by a Bergonzi. I had voted the Bergonzi over the Guarneri, but both were superb Cremonese instruments. In third place was the Strad, followed by the three modern instruments. To my ears, and clearly to the ears of the jury, the difference between the old and new violins was staggering.

Violins, Then and Now

veek or so the 1964–65 music season will be off and run-
nd one of the by-products will be violinists coming to
lmost every one of them will be bearing an old Italian
he fortunate ones will be playing instruments by Stra-
Guarneri. Some will have specimens by Nicolò Amati.
exult in noble violins by Bergonzi, Gagliano, Guad-
e Saló. Those who do not have an old Italian violin
row or steal one. Any debut violinist who steps on
stage without a product from Cremona will feel as
aked as one of the Beatle boys with a down-to-the

en and shut case that a Strad or a Guarnerius del
h better than a good modern instrument? Or
too much work has been done on the physics

of violins, and the work that has been done suggests that a good deal of myth surrounds Cremonese fiddles. Of course there are many imponderables, and science is not so exact when it comes to imponderables. Some decades ago Jeans (or was it Eddington?) wrote that a piano key made the same sound when depressed by the finger of a Paderewski or the tip of an umbrella. That started a hullaballoo, and all experienced pianists rightly laughed. Piano tone is a combination of many factors, and what Jeans (or Eddington) should have written was that the finger of a Paderewski was able to duplicate the sound made by the tip of an umbrella.

Similarly violin sound is a combination of many subtle factors. Obviously some violinists have greater ability than others to generate tone. It is equally obvious that a $50,000 Strad is a better instrument than a pawn-shop $35 special. But can the Strad be duplicated today? Can scientists make vernier measurements, duplicate every bulge and thickness, and come up with a facsimile?

Apparently yes, and apparently no. Some researches indicate that when a group of listeners, even trained ones, *think* they are hearing a Strad, they find the instrument perfect, even though it is a copy. Jascha Heifetz once played a concert using a modern instrument and nobody knew the difference. The Curtis String Quartet made blindfold tests, alternating new and old instruments. Again nobody could tell the difference. Thus the late Frederick A. Saunders, professor emeritus of physics at Harvard (and also a charter member of the Catgut Acoustical Society) came to the conclusion that "The possibility [is] that the difference in quality between excellent old violins and the best new ones is negligibly small. . . . Is it any longer true that no modern instrument can be as good as a Strad?"

The Catgut Acoustical Society is a group devoted to violin acoustics, and its membership consists of physicists, engineers, mathematicians and string players. They meet periodically and happily discuss plate vibrations, varnish, damping factors, tap tones, air resonance, and the special properties of the slip-stick action of the bowed string. Many of their members, including Carleen Maley Hutchins, John C. Schelling, Robert Fryxell and

Alvin S. Hopping, have published definitive work on the problems.

Take varnish. It is an article of faith in most violin circles that the varnish of an old instrument is one of the critical factors in its worth. Thus E. Herron-Allen, in his article on Stradivari in the most recent Grove's, writes that "in the classification of the relative importance of the various factors required to make a perfect violin, material and dimensions are subservient to varnish, and it was in the application of this that Stradivari surpassed his contemporaries." Herron-Allen goes on to state that the secret of the Cremonese varnish, lost today, was common property of makers of the time, "who compounded it from the materials used by the great painters of the epoch." He laments that the quick-drying varnishes of modern times sounded the death-knell of the "brilliant, tender, transparent varnish of the Cremona school."

But, wrote Dr. Saunders, response curves of untreated violins compared with response curves of varnished violins show little difference. He came to the conclusion that the effect of varnish was a negligible factor. He also concluded that—contrary to the opinion of most violinists—no instrument, old or new, can generate an even tone. All instruments "peak," that is, they are louder on certain notes than others. When this was demonstrated to a panel of violinists, they claimed that the testing meters were faulty.

The age of a violin, too (say the scientists), is an uncertain factor in its worth. But it may be that the effects of long-continued vibration seem to be definite and sometimes beneficial. Dr. Saunders cited the case of the "Messiah" Strad in the Oxford Museum. This instrument, in perfect condition, is seldom played, and those who have tried it say privately that it is not as good as other Strads. One interesting speculation of Dr. Saunders concerned the purfling, the thin strips grooved and glued into the front and back plates. After years of playing, the glue finally cracks, thus creating a vibrating plate with very thin edges. Perhaps this makes the difference.

Mrs. Hutchins, who makes her own instruments, pleads for an extension of the violin family. In Renaissance times, the viol family could cover the entire range of pitch represented by the piano keyboard. "On the other hand, the violin family leaves substantial gaps in coverage." But she would be the first to admit that the Cremonese violin makers had some secrets. "We really ought to learn how to make consistently better instruments than the old masters did. If that challenge cannot be fulfilled, we should at the very least find out the reasons for our limitations."

But, one wonders, can those reasons ever be scientifically determined? Aside from subtle psychological considerations, it is a fact that every great violinist from Paganini (who played a Guarnerius) has preferred a Cremonese instrument. Whether the secret is size, or varnish, or material, or age, or ease of playing, or quality of tone, or a combination of all of these, there does seem to be a secret—even if the scientists say that each individual factor seems to be of negligible importance.

And so, this season as in all previous seasons, those unfortunate violinists who do not own a Cremonese instrument are still going to beg, borrow or steal. The chances are, too, that no instrument maker would turn down the secret of Stradivari's lost varnish formula. It was inscribed on the fly leaf of the family bible, but his descendant Girolamo destroyed it, though (says Grove's) "he kept a copy of it which he carefully preserved for any future members of the family who might adopt the profession of their illustrious ancestor."

SEPT. 6, 1964

As a former Baker Street Irregular and as one who as a child committed the Sherlock Holmes stories virtually to memory, it was inevitable that I would do some serious, scholarly writing about my hero. In an article for the Baker Street Journal I proved conclusively that Sherlock Holmes impersonated Harry Nelson Pillsbury in the great Hastings 1895 chess tournament, won by the unknown Pillsbury. And in this Sunday piece I can say with all modesty that I have once and for all settled the awkward questions of Holmes and the violin and the identity of "Tra-la-la-lira-lira-lay." Most students of the problem went astray by taking the first "tra" as a downbeat. But once "tra-la" is considered as an upbeat, with the first accent coming on the "la" in "tra-la-LA," the syllables fit perfectly into the Chopin song.

Elementary, My Dear Watson

THANKS TO *Baker Street,* Sherlock Holmes is very much in the news these days. But for more reasons than one it was just as well that he did not make the trip to New York to attend the opening of the musical. A man of 111 years of age (Holmes was born in 1854) can not be expected to stand the rigors of New York in the winter, and all the excitement attendant upon a Broadway musical show in which he is the hero.

Anyway, the present status of Holmes is a bit of a mystery. Nobody has seen him lately. The late Christopher Morley is said to have paid him a visit in 1955. But Morley never did speak much about it, and rumors, ugly rumors, arose that Holmes was senile. This is hard to believe. Dr. Charles Goodman of New York, who made a set of false teeth for Holmes about thirty years ago, said at the time that Holmes would outlive the choppers. A good deal, incidentally, can be derived about Holmes's present facial characteristics from those teeth, and if you don't believe that, consult the photograph of Dr. Goodman's fine work in the May 1, 1944, issue of *Life* magazine.

It is of Holmes and the violin that we would speak, for in *Baker Street* Fritz Weaver compounds an error that has bothered and confused scholars ever since *A Study in Scarlet* appeared in 1887. There are two pertinent extracts to be quoted, both from *A Study in Scarlet.* Dr. Watson is talking about Holmes's violin playing: "Leaning back in his arm-chair of an evening, he would close his eyes and scrape carelessly at the fiddle which was thrown across his knee." The other extract is quoted by Dr. Watson as Holmes is on his way to a concert given by Norman-Neruda. "Her attack and her bowing are splendid. What's that little thing of Chopin's she plays so magnificently: 'Tra-la-la-lira-lira-lay.' "

Let's look at the facts. We know that Holmes was musical. He was fond of Sarasate, Offenbach, Paganini, the de Reszke brothers, Meyerbeer, Wagner, Mendelssohn. He could discuss learnedly Cremonese violins, and he actually owned a Stradivarius. All this is mentioned in the canon. Even more significant is the fact that Holmes was an expert on early music. His privately printed monograph on "The Polyphonic Motets of Lassus" (if only one could examine a copy!) was "said by experts to be the last word on the subject."

Now, would a man so knowledgeable about music throw a violin across his knees and scrape at it? That is what Weaver and all others do. But observe carefully: *Dr. Watson never said that Holmes threw a violin across his knees.* The word Dr. Watson used was "fiddle." It so happens that the fiddle family is a large and very old one. In Renaissance times there were all kinds of gamba instruments, many of which were played in the lap or across the knees. Of course, Holmes played the violin, and played it as all violinists do. But the man who knew all about Lassus would also have a variety of old instruments in his flat at 221B Baker Street.

The chances are that Holmes was playing a vielle. The vielle is described by Karl Geiringer in his history of musical instruments (Oxford University Press, 1945) as a 5-peg instrument that was a precursor of the violin. Another name for the vielle, says Dr. Geiringer, was "fiedel," which of course means "fiddle." Let's, for goodness sake, give Dr. Watson credit for being accurate. He said "fiddle," and he meant "fiddle"; and he was dead right. And if anybody today wants to see a vielle in action, go to one of the concerts of the New York Pro Musica. He will see an instrument, somewhat resembling a quarter-sized violin. It is too short for an adult to play it under the chin. The Pro Musica man puts it across his knees, as Holmes did. So much for the experts.

That "Tra-la-la-lira-lira-lay" business has put musicians into an even greater flap. What could have been that piece of Chopin's played by Wilma Norman-Neruda (a great violinist of the time, described as The Lady Paganini; her second husband was Sir Charles Hallé, the famous pianist and conductor)? Guy Warrack has suggested the F minor Nocturne. Ernest B. Zeisler makes a claim for the E minor Waltz. James Montgomery has come up with the Etude in E. Paul Clarkson has said that Dr. Watson was mistaken, and that the composer was Handel. Eric Thiman plumps for the Mazurka in E flat minor, Winifred Christie for the *Winter Wind* Etude (of all things!), and William Smith as recently as 1963 suggests the C minor Polonaise.

Many of the above suggestions can immediately be discarded as not exactly fitting the tra-las Holmes was humming. The others, too, can be discarded. What we must look for is something to fit the mood of Holmes, who was leaning back in the cab while "he carolled away like a lark." Thus it has to be a happy piece, not one in a minor key. It has to be short. It has to be something that would adapt itself to the violin. It should be mentioned that every violinist of Holmes's time was making arrangements of Chopin melodies, and the practice is not yet dead. Even singers got into the act. Did not the great Sigrid Onegin take the lead from Trilby and adapt the A flat Impromptu? She even recorded it, on Victor 1373.

It so happens that the answer is easy. The only piece in the Chopin canon that is in a major key and meets all the additional requirements is the first of the Polish songs—the one named *Zyczenie*, better known as *The Maiden's Wish* (see illustration). In the Liszt arrangement for solo piano it was one of the most popular short pieces of the century, and it was recorded by all the great pianists—Hofmann, Rachmaninoff, Godowsky, everybody. It still is played. It makes a wonderful violin encore, and Norman-Neruda's arrangement (presumably it was her own) would have had an expert like Holmes in ecstasy. The fact that it is no longer in existence need not bother us. All violinists made their own arrangements for their own use, never bothering to publish most of them.

Thus Holmes and Watson stand vindicated. No longer will we need studies like that of Herbert Starr in the *Baker Street Journal* (New Series, Vol. 13, No. 1, 1963). So puzzled is Starr by that across-the-knee business that he seriously suggests that Holmes had a prehensile foot with an opposable big toe. This worried Starr no end, because it led to "only the logical and profoundly distressing conclusion that Sherlock Holmes was a chimpanzee." No, don't worry, Mr. Starr. Take it easy, Mr. Warrack. Relax, Jacques Barzun, Rolfe Boswell and the others who have been so concerned about the subject. Just take the Sacred Writings as they are. Dr. Watson was not as bad a reporter, nor was he as unmusical, as some later doubters and men of little faith would have us believe.

TRA LA   LA LI- RA LI- RA   LAY

MARCH 7, 1965

If anything, matters have deteriorated since this outburst was written for the Times *magazine in 1966. Now even straight plays are being miked. Amplification for Broadway musicals is appallingly crude, with "singers" bobbing in and out of microphone range, with sound emanating from speakers at the sides of the theater rather than from off the stage, with engineers riding gain until the eardrums start to bleed. And nobody seems to mind! I still maintain that New York drama critics are letting Broadway get away with murder. Up to now, thank goodness, neither the Metropolitan Opera nor the New York City Opera use amplification, except for special effects. At least, I don't think they do. I also believe that if they did, I would be the first to be tipped off.*

Phantom of the Opera

Now it's grand opera that is beginning to be faced with the kind of musical and ethical problem to which other forms of the lyric theater have already surrendered. Voices seem to be getting smaller, and opera houses—especially in America—are getting bigger. The bigger the house, the worse the acoustics. The worse the acoustics, the more trouble singers have being heard—particularly as our age does not produce the clarion, trumpetlike singers who thrilled audiences during the Golden Age. For this scarcity of big voices various explanations have been offered: dieting, the jet plane, the hurry-hurry of modern life. None is particularly convincing. Children, after all, are still being made much as they always were, and there have been no great changes in the physiological structure of vocal cords that medical science can see.

But there is a way to make small voices into big ones. Amplification does the trick, as Broadway discovered quite a few years ago. Any pipsqueak voice, bolstered by huge amplifiers and speakers and the caressing touch of a monitoring audio engineer, could emerge with the force of a Melchior rolled into a Francesco Tamagno. (Somebody once said of Tamagno—paraphrasing Heine's remark about the pianist Dreyschock—that when he sang in Milan he could be heard in Rome, if the wind was in the right direction.)

Apparently the idea of amplification does not bother many people. Quite the contrary. They insist on it, and want to know what all the fuss is about when somebody objects. Isn't it better, they say, to have a thousand Tamagnos than no Tamagno at all?

Sure. And by the same token, isn't it better to have a thousand students pass an examination by cheating than have nobody at all pass it honestly?

For that basically is what amplification is: cheating. It substitutes an illusion for the real thing. It passes something off as your own that is not your own; something as genuine that is not genuine, as many have discovered after hearing singers on records and then hearing them in the flesh. About twenty years ago the first records by Ferruccio Tagliavini were issued in America. Opera buffs went wild. Here was a tenor with the suavity and sheen of Gigli and the power of Lauri-Volpi. Those fortissimo high notes! Everybody turned out for his Metropolitan Opera debut. Well, the suavity and sheen were there, all right—when the voice could be heard. Tagliavini produced a very small sound. It might have sounded big in the Teatro del Fenice. In the enormous reaches of the Metropolitan Opera it was faint and far-off. On the records, the engineers had given Tagliavini an assist. What we heard on those records was not really Tagliavini.

Nearly all present-day records, of course, are as much the product of the audio engineer as of the artist. But it is not only on LP discs that amplified sound is encountered. It accompanies us everywhere—in theaters and movie houses, in bars and restaurants, in airplanes and automobiles, on the streets and in buses (via transistor radios), on television, in hotel lobbies and even elevators. Virtually all this sound is bad. Distorted, tinny, generally overloud, it assails the ears day in and day out. Inevitably, the ear ends up without discrimination, accepting bad sound as the norm.

About the last refuge of beautiful sound in its pure estate is the concert hall and opera house. Up to now the important opera houses of the world have been free from any hint of amplification for the singing voice. Hence the great fuss last November at the New York State Theater during the run of the Metropolitan Opera National Company. At the first performance, questions were raised by some critics about the quality of the singing and the acoustics of the theater. But after a few performances it was noted that the company seemed to be settling in. The singers appeared to be more comfortable, and they were easier to hear. Then the roof fell in.

Amplification!

Most people could not have cared less, but among the professionals, and among those who have any love and respect for the singing voice, the word went around like a cry of plague in a medieval village. People began to run in various directions, whispering the dread word. It was learned that, after the first few performances, the singers of the National Company were enjoying a little electronic boost for two productions from the control engineer in the rear of the hall. Not much of a boost, officials of the company made haste to say. (Just a little bit pregnant.)

There was consternation in various quarters. The purists—and there did not, alas, seem to be very many—reacted as though in the presence of Original Sin. Winthrop Sargeant, of *The New Yorker*, wrote a statement retracting his nice words about the singers: "This knowledge," he wrote, "puts my account, a week ago, of this performance [of *Susannah*] in question—especially my enthusiasm for the vocal power of . . . the leading lady. Microphones in opera houses make criticism impossible."

Risë Stevens, co-manager of the National Company, sprang like a tigress to the defense of her cubs. The fault, she indicated, was not with the singers but with the hall. But Julius Rudel, manager of the New York City Opera (which takes possession of the State Theater this month) was not entirely displeased with the turn of events. He might even, it was rumored, have been amused. There was nothing wrong with the hall, he said loftily to the press, that *his* singers could not handle; in effect, let him whose foot was the right size wear the shoe.

There were those who asked why nobody had noticed the amplification, and by extension, what was wrong with using it if nobody noticed. (If the tree falls when nobody is around to see it, has the tree fallen?) A few music critics, somewhat red-faced, began to wonder if they could believe their ears any more.

But the New York State Theater was merely doing what the Broadway musical theater had been doing for years, only doing it much better. No musical these days is mounted without full amplification. But on Broadway, producers rent the amplifying equipment (never a satisfactory audio procedure), whereas the amplification system in such new theaters as the State is an integral part of the house. When expertly used, nobody knows it is in operation.

On this point the sound experts are unanimous. Ernest Peters, who helps along the singers at the Winter Garden; Joseph Linsky, the electronics maestro at the New York State Theater; Saki Ouri of Masque Sound; Steve Temmer of Gotham Audio; Irving W. Wood, chief engineer of Sound Systems—all these specialists say that no ear, no matter how golden, no matter how acute and experienced, can tell if a really well-designed amplification system is reinforcing the original sound source. "The object," says Rodney Brabson of Sound Systems, "is that the audience should *not* know."

About two years ago a visitor wandered into an orchestra rehearsal at the Royal Festival Hall in London. The Festival Hall was then notorious for its bleak-sounding acoustics: little bass, a short reverberation period, everything clear but cold. Pretty much as Philharmonic Hall originally was, in fact. The visitor listened and could not believe his ears. He rushed to a telephone and roused the hall's manager, T. E. Bean. "What have you done? What happened? The hall sounds *good!* Is there an electronic pickup?" (This though the visitor could see neither microphones nor speakers.) There was a long pause.

"Come to my office. tomorrow morning, if you can," said Bean finally.

"Oh?" said the visitor. "Electronics?"

"Well . . ." said Bean.

It turned out that the Festival Hall had just installed a system called "assisted resonance." The men with their formulas and slide rules had miscalculated when the hall was being built. Things turned out a mess, and the only way to correct the inferior acoustics, it was decided (with more formulas and slide rules), was to raise the roof 12 feet or so.

This was a prospect not cheerfully to be faced. In fact, it was insupportable. So the electronic engineers were called in. They did this and that with several hundred resonators n the ceiling, each resonator tuned to a specific low frequency, each with a little microphone and speaker.

The system worked fine. Nobody—least of all the musicians

and the London music critics—was aware of what was happening while assisted resonance was being tried out on them. But what about the ethics and esthetics involved? Could the listener be sure of getting the actual sound as produced from the stage?

By all means, said Bean. You can look on assisted resonance as being as much a permanent fixture of the hall as the "clouds" in Philharmonic Hall, he said. We have no engineer "riding gain," and musical values come first, he said. There is utterly no falsification, and the resonators will do no more or less than the ordinary reflecting surfaces of any hall, he said.

And so the visitor walked away, a confused man. On the one hand, there was no argument with success. The damn thing really worked. On the other hand, where did this sort of precedent lead to? For, *pace* Mr. Bean, was there not a kind of morality involved? Was there any assurance that the next system would be as honest? Or the one after that? Or the one still after that? All ending up—twenty years hence, thirty years hence— with completely electronic halls in which live sound has ceased to be?

For one thing does lead to another. As a matter of fact, the August, 1965, issue of the magazine *Radio-Electronics* has a discussion of assisted resonance in which it is stated that the system in the Royal Festival Hall is going to be revised. Each loudspeaker will in future take care of two frequencies instead of one, and a number of larger, 20-watt amplifiers will be introduced. (Just a little bit *more* pregnant.)

The New York State Theater, which uses a completely different kind of system from the Festival Hall, is a case in point. Here an engineer does ride gain—that is, he monitors what is coming off the stage and helps singers along with his fifteen 175-watt amplifiers, his columns of sound alongside the proscenium (six loudspeakers in each column), his footlight mikes, hidden mikes and (perhaps) body mikes.

From the very beginning, the New York State Theater has had its acoustic problems. It was not designed as an opera house. "We never dreamed there would be opera here," says Philip Johnson, the architect. "The *Lear* catastrophe was predictable." He was referring to the hassle in May, 1964, when Peter Brook, co-director of the Royal Shakespeare Company, called the acoustics "appalling." Voices, Brook claimed, simply would not come off the stage.

Vilhelm Lassen Jordan of Copenhagen was the acoustic engineer of the theater. In the April, 1965, issue of the *Journal of the Audio Engineering Society,* he wrote: "The only officially stated purpose of the New York State Theater was ballet. However, use as a theater for musical comedy and for operetta was also envisioned. . . . The effects of the general shape on the acoustics are mainly good since the side walls and side balcony facia give plenty of useful reflections. One point, however, remains doubtful, and this is the balance between orchestra and singers."

Jordan goes on to say that at an early stage the idea of a sound canopy was discussed, but this would have destroyed the concept of the architect. Thus it was decided to abandon this idea and instead to install "an elaborate sound system." Naturally. For music, looks are of course much more important than sound.

It is indeed an elaborate sound system that the New York State Theater has, and it is good. It fulfills the ideal of the electronic maestros: to do the job without anybody's knowing it is in use. Thus, in the New York City Ballet's *Nutcracker,* the chorus of voices does not come from live throats backstage; it comes from impulses on a tape run by Joe Linsky. In the National Company's *Cinderella* and *Susannah,* the voices were monitored by Linsky and sent back in a reinforced state, with nobody the wiser.

Technically speaking, this is heaven compared with what goes on in the Broadway houses. Esthetically speaking, though, it is hell. For how is the audience to know what is reality and what is illusion? On Broadway there is no illusion. All sound is obviously, dreadfully, fearsomely monitored and amplified. The results can be—and generally are—excruciating. Sound is loud, brassy, ear-splitting to the point of pain. Everywhere in the house, everything tends to sound the same, with the subtle timbre of a jukebox.

That audiences will accept the frequent glaring musical distortions on Broadway indicates a kind of aural atrophy. In this respect, the drama critics have been letting Broadway get away with murder. They should know better, and yet they continue to write about "singers" when they might just as well be discussing a tape recording. Musicians know this. Milton Greene, who conducts *Fiddler on the Roof,* says that he hates amplification. It is an "artificiality"; it is "dishonest." But he shrugs his shoulders. "Many singers," he says, "can't even hit two rows over the footlights."

"We strive for subtlety," says Ernest Peters at the Winter Garden, where *Funny Girl* is running. "But it can't always be achieved. When people in the back row pay their money and complain they can't hear, we have to turn it up."

Peters, who has been in audio all of his life, has developed into a bit of a philosopher. "Audiences have lost the art of listening," he says. "For years Broadway managed to get along without sound systems. Actors and singers projected more, and audiences listened carefully. Now, today's singers don't have to worry about projecting their voices. Even in straight dramatic shows they're starting to use mikes. Today in the theater the audience's aural perceptiveness has dropped way down."

Peters presides over seven footlight mikes and an overhead mike, all feeding into speakers above the proscenium and others in the auditorium. Each microphone can be individually controlled and singers individually tracked during a performance. In addition there was the body mike (bosom mike, wireless mike, contact mike—it is variously named) used by Barbra Streisand. This works in the 30-50 megacycle band and, as Streisand was the star (she recently left the show), Peters had to pay particular attention to her.

"She has a couple of high notes I have to monitor very carefully," he said during the last week of her run. "Don't forget, she's on stage all but twenty minutes. With eight shows a week she would be voiceless without amplification."

Peters, whose fingers played over the console the way Rubinstein fingers the piano, said that he monitored Streisand even in her dressing room. He told of the famous entertainer who forgot to turn off her body mike when she was off-stage, bearing it with her to the ladies' room, and . . . Now all microphones are fed into a central control.

"For a while," Peters said, "we tried to keep the system off for Streisand when she had dialogue, using amplification just for her songs. This went on for a month, then Jule Styne stopped it. The transition from off-mike to songs, he said, was too noticeable."

Streisand's fame comes primarily from her ability to belt out a song. But can she? Does anybody who has been thrilled by her dynamism in *Funny Girl* really know? It may be that she could carry to the reaches of Yankee Stadium in a thunderstorm with her unassisted vocal cords. Or it may be that she is not able to project three rows into the Winter Garden without her mike and her man upstairs riding gain. She may be a real singer, or she may be merely a microphone baby. Until she steps out without one, the way Ethel Merman used to do, it is legitimate to raise the question.

The way things are today, one wonders what on earth singers on Broadway did before amplification. It already takes long memories to remember. If nothing else, singers those days were taught to sing, to project their voices. "My voice always stayed fine," Merman says. "I was never sick, never tired." Ever since *Oklahoma!*, though, there has been a complete shift in casting emphasis.

Producers no longer look for singers. Plot lines are too important in today's musicals. As a result, producers look for actors who can sing. If they encounter a great combination of singing and acting, wonderful. That's gravy. But acting and good looks are more important than singing (even in grand opera, where the superdreadnoughts of yore are no longer welcome), and producers settle for actors who may be vocally untrained to the point where they can barely carry a tune. Or literally can't.

Rex Harrison is an example: While his non-singing in *My Fair Lady* was more musical than that of a great many professional singers, it merely cements the point. Today's leading roles in musicals are as often as not taken by boys and girls who are as much a product of the electronic age as any nightclub singer, who would freeze into impotence without his electronic crutch. Has any psychiatrist made a study of the way these people fondle and clutch their microphones? Freud—and Kinsey, too—might have been vastly interested.

Not only have the singers' technique and projection largely disappeared with electronics. Along with that, the public's ear has become dull and thickened. Small wonder, considering the stresses to which it has been subjected.

"People just don't care," says Saki Ouri of Masque Sound. "They are dulled by overexposure, Muzak and so on. In this country people want to hear things loud. They are conditioned by jukebox sound, or by hi-fi sound. You know the old joke. Hi-fi buff walks into Carnegie Hall the first time. He walks out in ten minutes. 'Not enough bass,' he says. If the public goes along, why shouldn't the producers? You know, I have to laugh. Today everybody says they don't like mikes—and everybody uses them. Believe me, it's an irreversible trend."

Most experts agree that it is indeed an irreversible trend, and one that is likely to invade opera houses before long. But the experts do not believe that this is necessarily a bad thing. "It enhances a performance," says one. "In any house only a small area has an ideal sound, and the rest of the audience has to be helped. Isn't that only fair?"

"Sure it's irreversible," says another. "Take the new Metropolitan Opera. That house is awfully big. Who is going to be able to sing in it? I predict that within five years the Met will be using some sort of sound reinforcement system. It won't mean a thing to the great voices there, but it sure as hell will help the weaker voices. And, mister, neither you nor I nor anybody else except those in the know will realize it's being used."

This comment is typical. Informed opinion insists the day is not far off when architectural acoustics will be supplanted by electronic acoustics. In America, where the economics of music dictate immense houses for opera, electronic acoustics (say the professors) is inevitable.

But even in Europe, where opera houses seldom go over 2,000 seats, the trend may also be irreversible. All European opera houses are now being built with complete electronic facilities. The Vienna Staatsoper and the new Festspielhaus in Salzburg have an awesomely full and complicated electronic setup. These sound systems are built in, and can be used for assisted resonance or actual stage pickup if desired.

At present, the Vienna management insists, amplification is used only for "special effects," such as in *Salome*, where the sound system is used to give Jochanaan's voice a hollow effect when he sings from the cistern. But in the new Warsaw Opera, which opened last fall, the director has openly admitted that a super-stereo system to amplify singers' voices was available. Questions were raised after the opening performances. It seems that the voices sounded the same no matter whether they were in the foreground or background. The director apologized and said that things would be put right "with added experience in the new house."

Yes; and that also means the death of singing as we know it. It means every man a Caruso or Tamagno, every woman a Ponselle or Flagstad. Microphones today have become so small and so efficient (we have all read with horror about the bugging that afflicts our society) that audio engineers can isolate any specific performer on stage and ride gain for the benefit of that single fortunate singer, if need be. Singing will then be meaningless, and critical standards will be meaningless. The whole idea should be fought—for the sake of music, for the sake of singing, for the sake of art, for the sake of the future.

FEB. 6, 1966

Searching around for a Sunday piece, weeping and desperate, I remembered some trivia I had encountered the previous week. Jiggery-pokery came out, and I have done worse. I got some mail on this article, berating me for using the music column of the Times *for such puerility.*

Jiggery-Pokery, Musical Jokery

GAMES PEOPLE play. In the February 23 issue of the *Manchester Guardian Weekly* can be found a snappy series of letters revolving around, of all things, the *Soldiers' Chorus* from Gounod's *Faust*. Seems that a reader named Justin G. Brady tormented himself for years humming the words "Our tomcat swallowed a load of bricks" to that popular tune. But that was as far as he remembered. "Our tomcat swallowed a load of bricks, tum, tum, tum, dada daDA daDA." He cried for help. "Can I appeal to your readers to put me out of my misery?"

Sure enough, Margaret Tapp sprang to the aid of Mr. Brady, who presumably can now rest his mind. The Tapp version is:

> *Our tomcat swallowed a load of bricks,*
> *I think he only did it for kicks.*
> *Now he's in such a helluva fix*
> *He cannot stand up,*
> *He cannot stand up,*
> *For the weight*
> *Of his tum.*

But Miss Tapp was not the only reader who supplied words to the *Soldiers' Chorus.* W. D. McNeil came up with a pathetic ditty that starts out: "O, Matilda, look a your Uncle Jim/He's in the bathtub learning how to swim . . ." E. D. Organ writes that he saw a touring company do *Faust* in a Welsh valley town. "The *Soldiers' Chorus* was greatly corrupted by a squad of non-descript conscripts who marched on right and off left, doubled round the backdrop and swelled their numbers to a platoon by repeating the performance several times." What these non-descript conscripts sang, Organ reports, was "Beer, boys and [deleted] the Band of Hope."

The trouble is that there arises an overwhelming temptation at trying the hand at this sort of thing. Like:

We have to listen to Gounod's "Fause"
At the new Meter-o-politan Hause.
We've heard it many a time before,
And we'll hear it again,
And again and again,
And again,
And again.

But it's a dangerous game. Crazy jingles have a habit of sticking in the head, and music can be ruined by them. Some years ago the late Leopold Mannes was talking to me about the Chopin C major Rondo, and he broke into laughter. What was funny? Well, Leopold said, the second subject, the one in A minor, has some built-in words that all old-time pianists used to sing: *"Oi, oi es tut mir weh."* We laughed together, but the damn thing stuck, and I can't ever hear the C major Rondo without giggling when the A minor theme comes along. And what about Walter Damrosch?

Damrosch had a music appreciation hour that was piped into the New York public school system, and those of a certain generation have not ever been able to forget it. Friday mornings we were assembled and marched to the auditorium, and presently The Voice would resound. "My dear children . . ." Damrosch had the idea of implanting great melodies in children's heads by writing words to the tunes and having us sing along. Goodness knows how many years the cause of music appreciation was set back, or how many potential music-lovers were permanently maimed. To this very day there are those of us who cannot listen to the Schubert *Unfinished* without hearing the words:

This is
The symphon-ee,
That Schubert wrote
And never fi-nished.

Or, in the second movement of the Beethoven Fifth:

Sound the trum-pet and drum,
For our he-ro has come

He has come,
He has come,
He has COME . . .

Or, especially unforgettable, to the march movement of the
Tchaikovsky *Pathétique:*

I want to go to Par-ISS,
A-and play with the mi-dinettes.

We sang this lustily, not knowing a midinette from a middy or
a biddy. And, confound it, the words still rattle in my head when
I hear the *Pathétique.* It also occurs to me that Uncle Walter
was a little daring in his advice to impressionable children. Go
to Paris and play with midinettes, indeed!

Turn we now to jiggery-pokery. Anthony Hecht and John Hol-
lander have come out with a little book of poems reviewed a few
weeks ago by *Time.* As *Time* explains the ground rules, the
poems all begin "with a double-dactyl nonsense line, such as
'higgledy-piggledy' or 'jiggery-pokery.' Thereafter comes a famous name—also double dactyllic—followed by another double
dactyl and a line of four beats. Then it begins all over again,
ending, like all jokes, with a punch line. To make things more
sporting, somewhere along the way is a double-dactyllic line of
one word." *Time* gives several examples. A nice one is:

Higgledy-piggledy
Benjamin Harrison,
Twenty-third President
Was, and, as such,
Served between Clevelands, and
Save for this trivial
Idiosyncracy,
Didn't do much.

Lovely. Fascinating. Let's try a few, warming up with:

Higgledy-piggledy
Sergei Rachmaninoff

Sat at the concert grand
Much like a mouse,
Playing his Beethoven
Superpianistically,
Also his Schumann, and
Counting the house.

Ludwig van Beethoven is a perfect double dactyl:

Higgledy-piggledy
Ludwig van Beethoven
Wrote out his symphonies,
Trios and süch.
He did not give them a-
Way to the publishers.
Himmelsgrössmachtige!
He asked for müch.

A pun they want? All right, since it's part of the game:

Higgledy-piggledy
Heifetz and Menuhin
Bowed to the audience
Upside down. Now
Twisting, now fluttering
Contortionistically,
Add they still yet one more
String to their bow.

Once started, it's hard to stop. But the night doth grow long,
ditto ditto my song. One more, and we'll call it quits:

Rickety-rackety
Boulez and Stockhausen
(Serial exponents)
Know all the tricks.
Opium tone-rows they
Inhale with joyousness,
Dodecaphonically
Getting their kicks.

MARCH 26, 1967

Not long after taking the job, I started to write Christmas pieces, at the appropriate time of the year, of course. It became a tradition with me, like my annual New Year's compilation of oddball musical events of the previous year. The Christmas pieces continued through 1975. At that time all Times *critics were asked to write pieces covering the previous twelve months of their specialty. The* Times *was very big on trend pieces. I missed writing the Christmas articles; I had a great deal of fun with them, and they* were *a bit different. Many of them involved pleasant research. But for the following one, George Lang did the research.*

What Would Bach Have Had for Christmas?

GEORGE LANG is a vice president of Restaurant Associates and director of The Four Seasons restaurant in New York. Food is not only his profession. It is his hobby, and it colors his life the way the violin colors the life of Heifetz. He is an old friend of mine, and a couple of months ago I spent an evening with him discussing *Wein, Weib und Gesang.* The conversation veered around to food, as it always does with George, and I asked him about food in Bach's day. What would Bach have had for Christmas dinner? George said that there was surprisingly little material on German cuisine in the eighteenth century. He reeled off a Christmas dinner menu for Bach and his family, and then said that he would look more closely into it.

Last month I got a letter from George. "I didn't realize what I was getting into before I started my research," he wrote. "As you know, gastronomy today means French gastronomy, and all other countries' achievements—if any—are more or less ignored. In addition to this, most of the upper-class and aristocratic cuisine in Europe was heavily influenced by the French, and whether you go to the court of Frederick the Great or to the one of the Russian Czar you'll find the menus written in French.

"I didn't, however, give up that easily, and I narrowed down the period to the years 1708–20, during which J.S.B. lived happily with his wife, Maria Barbara, and from 1721 with his second wife Anna Magdalena. So much for the time. I also narrowed down the geographical area to Thuringia, Saxony and the surrounding areas. The German baroque era more or less formulated and crystalized the style of dining, menu structure, cooking methods, etc. This allows us to take any recipe or menu from, say, 1700–1800, and be quite sure of staying within the realm of probability and authenticity. About 1680 was the time when matching fork, knife and spoon became fashionable for the first time, and the two-pronged fork became three-pronged." There was much more along this line in the letter, plus an invitation to come to his house for a Christmas dinner that would approximate, as closely as possible, a dinner that Johann Sebastian Bach would have had before him on that day in the year, say, 1740.

Nobody in his right mind turns down an invitation for dinner from George Lang. We got there last Sunday at 3 P.M. "It's a late start," said George, when we sat down. "Christmas dinner in Bach's day would have started around noon." He went on to say that he had prepared a meal that, he thought, was honestly representative of Leipzig in the 1740's. There would, however, be a few anachronisms. "We will start with sturgeon from the Rhine. That's all right. But I am serving champagne with it, Louis Roederer, Cristal, 1962. Dom Perignon, who perfected the champagne process in France, died in 1715. It is not likely that Bach would have tasted French champagne. He would have used one of the various sparkling wines known from the Middle Ages. I say 'maybe.' It is possible, though not likely, that one of Bach's patrons would have given him a present of champagne."

We asked George where he had done his research.

"I have a good library," he said. "Then I went to the Forty-second Street Library. My daughter helped me there." His daughter, sixteen years old, nodded demurely. "I checked with a friend in the German consulate in New York and the German embassy in Washington. Restaurant Associates has a good library. At The Four Seasons there is a German captain and a German pastry chef. Both are specialists on old German food.

"Christmas dinners in Germany in Bach's time, I found, had to have a soup. Perhaps beef bouillon. Perhaps cabbage or lentil. There was always a cold plate—Westphalian ham, sausage, things like that. There would have been a fish dish, or maybe a seafood salad with beets, apples, herring, boiled beef cubes in mayonnaise sauce. Always there was goose or gosling. There might be game. I found one menu with venison. My wife and I cooked the dinner. Hope you like it."

We sat down after sturgeon and champagne in the living room. There was, first, bouillon with winter vegetables. The bouillon was served clear, with a whole wheat roll on the side. "All bread in Bach's day was made of whole wheat," George explained. After the bouillon—rich but delicate—was eaten, the vegetables were put on the same plate. Leeks and parsnips boiled in a heavy beef stock are marvelous. So is beef marrow eaten from a bone cut down the middle.

Next came a plate with slices of Westphalian ham and Thuringian sausage, accompanied by a Forster Jesuitengarden 1966. "Bach may not have known this very vineyard," said George, "but he would have drunk a Riesling very much like it." Lucky Bach. This Riesling was the essence of grape. The boiled beef which followed had three varieties—flanken, brisket and oxtail boned in one piece and stuffed (the stuffing being chopped beef, cracked wheat, marrow and leeks). "This stuffed beef is a tour de force," said George. "If Anna Magdalena was skillful enough, she could have done it." With the boiled beef was a baked apple stuffed with wild cherries.

The salad had Bibb lettuce and a delicate dressing. "This is a little anachronistic," said George. "The lettuce is close to Bach's lettuce, but in his day they liked a wilted salad, and they used a lot of sugar and white vinegar. We're being a little fancy, too, on the goose. Bach's family would have had a whole one set before them. We will have just slices off the breast." The goose was accompanied by a puree of chestnuts.

Two varieties of cheese followed. One was a German Tilsit. "The other," said George, "is a cooked cheese, Kochkäse, made by a German family in Wisconsin. Bach would have recognized this taste." With the cheese there came coffee, cookies and a Dresden stollen. A stollen is the classic German Christmas cake, basically a yeast coffee cake with raisins, lemon and orange rind and other flavors. "We may be just a little off here," said George. "In the old times the stollen was served at brunch on Christmas Day. What we are having is a Christmas Eve dinner. I found this stollen recipe in a German book of the early 1800's. It was a household book, with instructions for the butler —how to set a table, how to cook this and that, and so on."

The stollen was not as sweet as the ones you get around New York. It had a firm consistency and was utterly delicious.

"Let's finish off in the living room," said George. Engorged, near death but happy, we managed to push ourselves away from the table and stagger inside. There we sprawled on a couch. There was talk, there was music from the Lang family, and George himself picked up the fiddle, which he plays on a professional level.

He poured some wine into a glass. "Look at the date," he said. We looked, and gasped. It was a bottle of Verdelho Madeira, and on the label the year was given—1748.

"That does not mean this was bottled in 1748," George said. "It wasn't. It was bottled according to the Solera system. A little bit from each year, 1748 to the present, is in this bottle. But if this bottle says 1748, that means that some of the contents of the 1748 cask are here. Bach was alive then. He died two years later. He could have drunk this very vintage. I'm not saying he did. The odds are against it. But he could have. He liked wine. Remember the thing he wrote about wine to his cousin? Look it up when you get home."

We looked it up. In 1748 Bach's cousin, Johann Elias, sent him as a gift a cask of wine. It was damaged and arrived almost two-thirds empty. Bach, acknowledging the gift, lamented mightily. "It is a pity that even the least drop of this noble gift of God should have been spilled." Then the thrifty Bach asked his cousin not to send any more. "For since the carriage charges cost 16 groschen, the delivery man 2 groschen, the customs inspector 2 groschen, the inland duty 5 groschen 3 pfennig and the general duty 3 groschen, my honored cousin can judge for himself that each quart costs me almost 5 groschen, which for a present is really too expensive."

Dec. 22, 1968

It's too bad that William Henry Fry's Santa Claus *Symphony has not been recorded. Bad as it is—ineffably bad as it is—it is a valid example of pre-Civil War Americana, and it tells a great deal (directly and indirectly) about the Zeitgeist of the time. The funny, spirited journalistic battle between Fry and Willis is marvelous reading. In the article I cite Fry's* Leonora *as being the first American opera. Here we get into a hazy musicological area. Stage works called "operas" were being given in the colonies long before the Revolution. But those were ballad operas, inspired by the progenitor of them all—John Gay's* Beggar's Opera *of 1728. To avoid a hassle, let's call* Leonora *the first American* grand *opera. I may be safe there.*

The Story of Santa— and His Awful Symphony

It's the season, and what better time to talk about Santa Claus? The great work by William Henry Fry, that is: "*Santa Claus*—A Christmas Symphony." It had its world première in New York on Christmas Eve of 1853, performed by the Jullien Orchestra (then touring the country), and it is safe to say that it was unique. No American composer had ever composed such a work. None other ever has. Who would tangle with the strains of the *Santa Claus* Symphony? What immortal hand or eye could match its fearful symmetry?

It is a program symphony. First we hear, on the trumpet, announcements of the Savior's coming birth. Then, in the composer's own words, "This is followed by some soft music, the first violins having a volant trill, accompanied variously by the other stringed instruments in a singing strain, while the Flute, Clarionet, Hautboy and Bassoon fly seraph-like through different regions of musical space." After this "artistico-historical introduction," the music comes to earth, with families meeting at Christmas time. But what is this? A "tumultuous run through several octaves" describes a snowstorm. It temporarily recedes, and everybody goes to sleep to the melody of the Lord's Prayer and "the simple lullaby, 'Rock-a-by baby on the tree top.'" All is snug inside.

But outside, the storm rages. In the storm is caught a Perishing Traveler. His "woe and wail" is entrusted to the double bass. As the voice of the Perishing Traveler "ceases in cold death," chimes strike midnight. Suddenly the bassoon takes the melody. Santa Claus is coming. Why the bassoon? It is the "most quaint" of all orchestral instruments. Santa Claus bassoons in to the accompaniment of sleigh bells and cracking whips. He flies down the chimney on the flute, "while harp-like notes on the Violins show the click of the toys as they are thrown into the stockings of the happy little sleepers." The entire orchestra bursts into "Adeste Fideles," which betokens the break of day. "We are now introduced to the happy household. Knockings awaken the little sleepers with cries of 'Get up! Get up! Get up!' imitated on the Horn; and so roused the children rush with joy and seize their toys, and the orchestra now plays 'Little Bo-peep' on toy-trumpets, drums, and so forth. A strain from the Introduction of the Symphony leads to the 'Adeste Fideles' ('Hither, ye Faithful') Hymn, with grand chorus and orchestra, which concludes the piece." You can read the entire program in William Treat Upton's biography of Fry (Crowell, 1954).

William Henry Fry, the political writer and music critic of the *New York Tribune,* was a composer who not many years before his *Santa Claus* had composed the first American opera, *Leonora.* The serious, bearded, irascible Fry spent a good deal of time on *Santa Claus,* and when it was finished he was satisfied.

Jullien performed it, to great plaudits, and Fry settled back to read his reviews. He got many. But the one that bothered him appeared in the *New York Musical World and Times*, edited by Richard Storrs Willis. The entire review took a paragraph or so. Willis rather contemptuously dismissed the *Santa Claus* Symphony as "an extravaganza."

Fry brooded, but not for long. He took pen in hand and wrote an open letter to Willis. What a letter! It ran some forty pages and about six thousand words, and it appeared in the *Herald* on January 10, 1854.

Fry had no illusions about his symphony. He knew it was a masterpiece. An extravaganza, indeed! "I claim for *Santa Claus* that it is the longest unique symphony ever written." Fry stated flatly that *Santa Claus* ranked in value and magnitude with Meyerbeer's *Prophète*. The symphony was written "so as to double the resources and sonority of the orchestra, compared with classical models—and your journal despatches it with a dozen lines." That rankled. And, demanded Fry, what's wrong with inserting humor into music? Shakespeare had humor even in his tragedies. One of the troubles with Beethoven and Mozart, Fry said, was that there was no humor in their music, "Beethoven being incapable of gaiety and Mozart destitute of comedy." Dear Fry.

He continued his defense with the longest sentence ever penned by an American newspaperman, and this entire article would not suffice to contain it. At least he had confidence in himself. In a subsequent letter to *Dwight's Journal of Music*, he discussed his innovations, both in *Santa Claus* and *Leonora*, and modestly stated that while they may not have been as exciting as Wagner's innovations, "they will be found to have worked a revolution in the lyrical and musico-dramatic capabilities of the English Grand Operatic Stage, having achieved what for one hundred years English critics have pronounced impossible."

Willis was not going to take Fry's January 10th communique lying down, and a week or so later published an answer. He had read the argument with stunned surprise. "Now, my dear Fry, I consider any man who honestly entertains (as I honestly think you do) such truly pleasant opinions of himself as are herein

Upstairs, then, to the research music library, and the first stop was the *Oxford Book of Carols.* Two versions of the carol are given. Number 11 lists the tune as "God Rest You Merry, Gentlemen." But Number 12 has "God Rest You Merry Gentlemen." No comma at all. Oxford has a footnote: " 'God Rest You Merry' means 'God Keep You Merry,' but the comma after 'merry' is generally misplaced." This I take to mean that Oxford frowns upon "God Rest You, Merry Gentlemen," though the sentence is ambiguous and capable of the opposite interpretation. Shame on you, Oxford. Continues Oxford: "There is a version in the Roxburghe Ballads, V. III, c. 1770. The second version, No. 12, we have reprinted from a broadside printed by J. and C. Evans, Long-lane, London. . . . In this case we have reproduced the spelling and punctuation." Number 12 is the one without any comma.

The research division of the music library did not have the Roxburghe Ballads. But tucked away in various collections, notably the Drexel, were early printed editions of carols. For instance, there is *A Little Book of Christmas Carols,* edited by Edward F. Rimbault. This dates from the mid-nineteenth century. Here the version is "God Rest You, Merry Gentlemen." A later Rimbault collection, however, gives the title in the index as "God Rest You Merry Gentlemen," with no comma at all. An early nineteenth-century edition of carols, a pamphlet named *Christmas and Christmas Carols,* has "God Rest You, Merry Gentlemen." Another, named *Carols, Ancient and Modern,* also puts the comma after "you." Can it be that the earlier one goes back, the more prevalent is "God Rest You, Merry Gentlemen"?

But no. One of the earliest publications of its kind is *Christmas Carols, Ancient and Modern,* edited by William Sandys (London, 1833). This one has, on page 102, "God Rest You Merry, Gentlemen." Yet, in an appendix where words and music to some of the carols are given, it appears as "God Rest You Merry Gentlemen," without any comma at all. The music itself, incidentally, is of no help. There are no phrase marks indicating the caesura.

The main reading room of the Public Library brought pay dirt in the form of the Roxburghe Ballads themselves. But first I

contained, a fortunate fellow. If anything can make a man happy in this world, it is just such self-convictions as these." Willis demolished Fry's arguments, point by point, calling Fry "a splendid frigate at sea without a helm." On February 8th, Fry came right back, demolishing Willis's rebuttal in a few thousand choice words. Back bounced Willis.

In the meantime, everybody was getting into the act. *Dwight's Journal of Music* published the correspondence, and Dwight himself had a few words to say. The New York Philharmonic, which had been attacked by Fry as never having played an American work since its founding in 1842, wrote a letter saying yes, we have played American works, and appended the list. George F. Bristow, the composer, supported Fry, demanding to know how American composers could exist if their music was despised. The level-headed Dwight wrote a piece calling the controversy ridiculous, pointing out that it was the public that eventually decided the fate of a work of art, and that if the music of Fry or Bristow had any validity, it would live.

But the *Santa Claus* Symphony did not live. It was soon forgotten, along with the controversy, and not until December 6, 1958, was it resurrected by Howard Shanet and the Columbia University Orchestra. Most of the music, one reluctantly must say, is awful. But there are a few sections that definitely anticipate Charles Ives, and are almost reminiscent of the Ives Second Symphony. Then there is that ineffable solo on the double bass, depicting the Perishing Traveler. It would make an Egyptian mummy get up and cry, so plangent is the melodic sweep. Yes, there is something very, very American about the *Santa Claus* Symphony, even if it is the worst piece of symphonic music ever written. So bad is it that it turns out charming: vintage Americana, reflecting an innocent and naive age, a musical Grandma Moses in 1853.

The *Santa Claus* Symphony is all that. But what darker meaning does it have? What is the significance of one line in the description that William Henry Fry appended to the music? For *Dwight's Journal of Music* on December 31, 1853, carried a brief note about the première and called *Santa Claus* a children's symphony. Fry, whose eagle eye never missed a comment about himself or his music, immediately penned a correction to Dwight, which was published in the January 7, 1854, edition. *Santa Claus* is not a work for children, Fry indignantly stated. In this work he, the composer, was trying to achieve, among other things, an oratorio style; and to relate the accents of the English language to music; and to prove that "Rock-a-by baby on the tree top" could, if poetically handled, be as sublime as the Madonna and Child; and to connect the music of nature with the tragedy of human life; and to paint the sublimest music in the world, "that of the Deity singing the monody of the passing world in the winter's wind"; and to paint the songs of the stars and the fluttering ecstasies of hovering angels; and "to paint the change from starlight to sunlight by poetical analogies and mathematical facts"; and, in short, to create a work designed to be of religious and romantic character.

All this is in *Santa Claus,* said Fry. But tucked away in this objective account of the work's wonders is another line, one that gives pause. Not only did Fry want to do this and that in his *Santa Claus* Symphony; in addition he wrote that he wanted to "show all the sexual peculiarities of the orchestra."

The *sexual* peculiarities? *All* of them?

I think we'd better hear this work again.

DEC. 20, 1970

This is my personal favorite of all the Christmas pieces I wrote. I have been in London several times since then but have somehow managed to forget my vow to visit the British Museum and examine the original broadside sheet of "God rest you . . ."

God Rest You, Wanderin
Comma

THIS IS going to be about a comma, and I dare say it is t important bit of musicological research since the inve: the clef. But it has amused me for a week or so, and I a to pass it on to you.

The other week I was thinking about a Christmas p this column, and was leafing through William Chappell *lar Music of the Olden Time.* This important book w lished in 1859 (it has been reprinted in two paperback by Dover), and my eye stopped at Volume II, p. 752. (here is writing about Christmas carols, and he pauses to "God Rest You, Merry Gentlemen."

The title looked wrong to me, and in a moment I rem why. Everybody knows that the correct punctuation Rest You Merry, Gentlemen." But here is Chappell, t that the words of this best-known and best-loved of a were first printed on a broadsheet in the Roxburghe C (III, 452), and that two altogether different tunes exis words. One of those tunes, in E minor, we all know; tl in E flat, is less modal, less interesting and is seldom he

Chappell prints both tunes, with the words. In both, l the comma after "you." But if Chappell indeed was from the original Roxburghe manuscript, whence a comma after "merry"?

A trip to the library was indicated. First stop was the ing music library in the stacks at the library-museum at Center. There must be over a hundred editions of car All are modern editions, and all gave the text as "God l Merry, Gentlemen." So did standard references. The m tal *Granger's Index to Poetry* gave the first line as "C You Merry, Gentlemen." But a glance at Granger's cita the authenticity of the line indicated that all of the sour modern.

looked at A. H. Bullen's *Carols and Poems* (1886) and was utterly confused. The table of contents listed "God Rest You, Merry Gentlemen." The poem, on page 40, had "God Rest You Merry, Gentlemen." Bullen supplied a footnote: "The comma, by a curious oversight, has been misplaced. It should stand before, not after, the word 'merry.' " Then why did Bullen, a great expert in old poetry and one of the foremost scholars of the period, allow the comma after "merry" in his book? And what is his authority for the footnote?

I eagerly awaited the arrival of the Roxburghe Ballads, which perhaps would solve all problems once and for all. While mentally pushing the page boys and muttering to myself, "Let nothing you dismay," I looked up Roxburghe in the Dictionary of National Biography. There it can be learned that John Ker, third Duke of Roxburghe, was one of the great bibliophiles of his time (1740–1804). He collected broadside ballads, adding to the great collection originally formed by Robert Harley, Earl of Oxford. In 1812, after Roxburghe's death, the collection was auctioned. Most of it is now in the British Museum.

Things you anxiously await always take the longest to arrive, but presently all seven volumes of Roxburghe reprints were delivered to me. These books were published one by one starting in the early 1880's. The first three volumes were edited by Chappell, the rest by J. (for Joseph) Woodfall Ebsworth, M.A., Cantab., F.S.A. Vol. VII, published in 1893, contained the carol in question. In the preface, Ebsworth mentions a group of carols he is reprinting, including "God Rest You, Merry Gentlemen." Note the placement of the comma. On page 775 there it is: "Carol I —On Christmas Day—To its own tune of 'Tidings of Comfort and Joy.' " And what do we see? "God rest you, merry Gentlemen." There is an exclamation point after "Gentlemen," but let's not get into *that*.

That should take care of the problem. But does it? Scholars of the day were notoriously inaccurate. I will believe nothing until I see the actual broadside sheet in the British Museum. It would not surprise me if the original had no punctuation at all. Anyway, if J. Woodfall Ebsworth, M.A., Cantab., F.S.A., has indeed transcribed the carol accurately, the comma after "merry" is a later addition, for no earlier text than the Roxburghe has ever turned up. So, God rest you, merry gentlemen, in this Christmas season, and that's the way I'm going to consider the carol until better evidence comes along.

DEC. 26, 1971

The only reason this column is in the book is the last paragraph. It was written well before the discovery of the famous "accidental" 18½-minute erasure on the June 20, 1972 White House tape.

How to Manipulate a Musician—or Even a Politician

NEARLY EVERYBODY in the country is tape conscious these days, thanks to an invention that was developed in Germany in the early 1940's. Almost immediately, it was realized that the tape machine was a versatile tool. With it any sound could instantly be recorded, played back, erased, dubbed in, manipulated, even falsified if one's inclinations ran in that direction. Those early machines, incidentally, were not necessarily tape machines. There were experiments with spools of wire, and some of those hit the market. But wire proved nowhere near as versatile as tape. Splicing was difficult. And often there were backlashes, resulting in tangles of wire that you wouldn't believe.

Recording companies pounced on tape recording. It was the greatest breakthrough since the invention of electrical recording in 1925. But there were side effects. Many soon began to wonder how honest tape recording was. Did a finished product, often the result of splice after splice, really give a true idea of the artist? What relation did the additions of engineers—reverberation effects, superimposed dynamics and so on—have to the real thing? Was not an LP record, and later a stereo record, an artificial product that had nothing to do with music as actually practiced by professionals in the concert halls and opera houses? The purists raised all the issues and more. The technologists, headed by John Culshaw of Decca in England, proclaimed defiantly that recordings were things-in-themselves and, in effect, should be treated as a new art form.

It was not always thus. Before tape recordings, the disc was musically honest, in that it was not susceptible to tampering. If a musician did not like the way a playback sounded, he would have to replay it in its entirety until it came out to his satisfaction. There simply was no way to alter anything on wax, or, later, acetate. As such, a Caruso, Rachmaninoff or Fats Waller record is a trustworthy statement.

There was, however, one area of recording in which all kinds of tricks could be practiced. Piano rolls could be doctored at will—and they were. The International Piano Library owns a Paderewski roll with the plaintive notation in the pianist's own hand: "Please fix." And fix they did. Technicians would lay out the roll, cover up holes and punch new ones according to specific calibrations, and make uneven scales or sloppy passage work sound inhumanly perfect. One important pianist once reminisced about some piano rolls he made around 1920. He heard the playback and was appalled; it was full of wrong notes. Not to worry, said the technicians. Come back next week. Next week the pianist heard flawless playing. "My God! I sounded like Hofmann," he said. Did he allow the improved version to be released under his own name? "Of course," he chuckled.

With the arrival of the tape machine, the record industry began to amass its own set of horror stories. Recordings began to be issued that were entirely unrepresentative of the artists whose names appeared on the label. One of the most famous stories concerns a fairly well known pianist engaged to record a pair of concertos. Artur Rodzinski was engaged to conduct the orchestra. At the first session it was clear that the pianist was not up to the demands of the music. He made mistake after mistake, broke down again and again. Each time the engineers would come rushing out. "Don't worry. We'll fix it."

And so, after a completed concerto that was a composite of hundreds of splices, all concerned went to the playback room to hear the results. It was a lovely performance. The pianist leaned back, enjoying every moment of it. Finally he looked at Rodzinski and said: "Not bad, eh?" Rodzinski looked down at him.

"It's beautiful," he said. "Don't you wish you could play like that?"

Some artists actually resisted the determination of the recording engineers to supply a superhumanly perfect product. Emil Gilels was one. During his first American tour, about fifteen years ago, he paused in Chicago to record the Tchaikovsky B flat minor with Reiner. During the taping he hit a clinker, and the section was redone and spliced in. When he heard the playback, Gilels was disturbed. True, he said, the "improved" version was more accurate, but it did not have the flow of the section with the wrong note. He insisted that the original be used. The wrong note was less important to him than the sweep and continuity of the phrase. And the recording was issued as he wanted, clinker and all.

Many musicians pay lip service to this philosophy, saying that they would rather have a technically flawed passage with spirit rather than a perfect but spiritless one on their recordings. But what they say and what they do can be, as with the Watergate witnesses, two different things. One violinist some years back told a reporter that he, the violinist, was disgusted with recording technology. When *he* made a recording, he said, it was the real thing. No splices, no interference with the continuity. Bravo. Several weeks later the reporter ran into the violinist's recording engineer, and there was a discussion about him. "That s.o.b.," said the engineer, "gives us more trouble than any musician we have under contract. Every second note is spliced in."

But there are those who frankly admit that they make full use of what tapes have to offer. There is a veteran pianist who sees nothing wrong in splicing a note or two. He talks about the difficulties of the old days; how, when recording a very difficult piece, it might take weeks before a single side came out correctly. "You don't want to go down in history represented by a record that has technical mistakes on it," says this pianist, who is very proud of his technique. So he would play the same piece ten, fifteen, perhaps thirty times. But at the thirtieth run-through the result, while note-perfect, completely lacked spirit. "So what's wrong," he says, "in splicing one correct note into a master tape?"

As time went on, there developed an interesting spinoff. Transistors came into being, equipment became miniaturized, and a new industry came into being—pirated performances. Entrepreneurs would go to important concerts with tiny tape recorders hidden on their person. Some of these recorders were capable of astonishing fidelity. These men would tape the concert, repair to their friendly neighborhood pirate, and, literally, the very next day it was possible to purchase tapes of the concert at the underground boutique. Perhaps all this was against the law, but it was impossible for the concert halls and opera houses to search everybody coming in. One underground operator reported that the morning after the recital of a famous artist he had a choice of five different tapes of the event. He chose the one with the best sound, ran off a few dozen reels for sale and was in business.

What can be done with music can also be done with voice, as the Watergate investigators are discovering. Samuel Dash, chief counsel to the Senate's Special Watergate Committee, however, has known this all along, and is coauthor of a book on the subject. He taped a sample political speech and then edited it so that its meaning was reversed. According to Dash, it was impossible to detect the tampering. According to other authorities, extemporaneous speech is far more difficult to edit than music. It can be done, but a staff of trained operators and technicians would be necessary. If, for instance, somebody in authority decided to do some hanky-panky with the White House tapes, so many operatives would have to be used that the secret would be impossible to keep; and, at the end, there would be no guarantee that experts could not detect a doctored tape. Of course, as with any tape, there is always the possibility that, purely by accident, of course, somebody may push the ERASE button . . .

AUG. 12, 1973

In the early fall of 1973 I accompanied the Philadelphia Orchestra to China, and we all felt like Marco Polo when we disembarked at the Peking Airport. Very few Americans had visited China since the revolution. The Philadelphia Orchestra was the first American symphonic group ever to play there. The major reason for my visit was the inability of The New York Times *to open a bureau in the People's Republic. No American could get a visa as long as the United States recognized Taiwan. Thus when I was invited by the Philadelphia Orchestra, the* Times *jumped at the chance. I ended up writing two pieces a day during the ten days of the visit. The* Times *could not get enough copy and kept asking me for more. That was no great problem. With so many new impressions, it was easy to write, and I also had something like twenty hours on my side because of the time change. Ergo, no deadline problems. I phoned all my stories to the recording room in New York; it was much easier than Telex. A few months after the visit, there was a shift in ideology, and Schubert and Beethoven were both cited as running dogs of capitalistic imperialism.*

Will a Hundred Composers Bloom?

THE CONDUCTOR of the Central Philharmonic Society in Peking is a tall, portly, extroverted, fifty-six-year-old musician named Li Teh Lun. He was the host and principal speaker at a party that the musicians of the Central Philharmonic gave for the musicians of the Philadelphia Orchestra a week ago yesterday. It was a lovely afternoon of fraternization, and it also threw light on certain doctrinal procedures of the People's Republic of China. And it demonstrated that conductors anywhere in the world are more or less equivalent in matters of confidence and ego.

Li is nothing if not confident. He came up as a cellist and music teacher, switching to conducting in his twenties. The State sent him to the Moscow Conservatory for a four-year course in conducting. "No use," grinned Li, who speaks a bit of English. He said that conductors cannot be taught, they have to have it from the beginning. Chinese normally do not show anger, they are much too civilized for that. But through Li's affable veneer, it was clear that he was seething at a remark made by a British journalist last March after the visit of the London Philharmonic to China. The critic said that Li and the players of the Central Philharmonic could play Chinese music well enough but had no idea at all of Western music. That was one reason Li was anxious to have Eugene Ormandy and the Philadelphia Orchestra players listen to him and his orchestra in the Beethoven Fifth. And so, after a speech welcoming his visitors, Li gazed upon his captive audience and mounted the podium to demonstrate "his" Beethoven Fifth.

He started with immense vigor, but also with a triplet in the opening three notes, losing the two-four meter. The performance had plenty of fire. It also was a bit rough. Li was trying too hard, perhaps. And one could guess the nervousness of players and conductor, performing in front of the virtuoso Philadelphia Orchestra and its virtuoso conductor.

After the first movement, Li asked Ormandy to carry on. "The Boss," as the Philadelphia players call their conductor, shed coat and tie—Peking is having one of the hottest spells in memory —and took the Central Philharmonic through the slow movement. This was a lesson in sheer technique and professionalism. Ormandy had the predominantly youthful players of the Central Philharmonic going through hoops for him. He is, of course, vastly more experienced than Li, and infinitely more familiar with the score. What he did was pace the players, asking for more tone, more breadth, fuller bowing, steadier rhythm. All this without once stopping. By giving the players plenty of air space to punctuate phrasing, Ormandy had them playing almost like a major ensemble.

Li listened inscrutably. Later on he had a few comments to make. "The men are more used to my beat," he said. "It took them a little time to get used to Ormandy's." Yes, he said, he had a lot to learn from Ormandy. "But I haven't learned it yet." A statement that perhaps can be taken several ways.

There was a world première at this demonstration concert of the Central Philharmonic. It was Wu Tsu Chiang's *Moon Reflected in Two Fountains*, for string orchestra. This was a sweet —indeed, oversweet—piece that had an oriental-sounding melody superimposed over harmony tonics, dominants and subdominants. "Why this kind of music?" somebody asked Li. Wouldn't you think that Oriental melody, with its own kind of scale and intervallic structure, would need its own kind of harmony and not conventional western harmony? Shouldn't the intervals of the melody dictate a different kind of harmony?

Suddenly doctrine reared up. Westerners are apt to forget that Chinese culture as well as Chinese life is governed by Mao thought. It was as far back as 1942, in his talk at the Yenan Forum on literature and art, that Mao Tse-Tung laid down a doctrine that has been cultural law ever since.

Mao followed a Marxist-Leninist line that claimed art is a servant of the State. Literature and art, said Mao, must "fit well into the revolutionary machine as a component part." Art should serve the people. "We must popularize only what is needed and can be readily accepted by the workers, peasants and soldiers themselves." The purpose of art is to extol "the revolutionary struggle of the masses." The audience is not an elite, it is the workers, soldiers and peasants of the Revolution.

Before the Cultural Revolution of 1966, some Western music was played. But after 1966, thanks largely to the influence of Mme. Mao, the repertory was narrowed down to a point where there were only eight or nine approved works in the entire musical repertory. That is literally true. Today there are signs that restrictions are being eased a tiny bit. The very fact that the Central Philharmonic had Beethoven's Fifth on its stands was a significant indication, and the piece by Wu was still another.

But during even the worst throes of the Cultural Revolution, the few approved works were anything but authentic Chinese. It is true that they used pentatonic-sounding melodies here and there, and the orchestrations did have a few old Chinese instruments. But the music sounded like Khachaturian, vintage 1950, and that is not strange, considering that most talented Chinese musicians were sent to the Soviet Union—primarily Moscow and Leningrad—for study.

For this there was still another reason involving Mao thought. At the Yenan Forum he had said that proletarian music did not necessarily have to divorce itself from the best of the past and the best that foreign countries had to offer. "We should take over the rich legacy and the good traditions in literature and art that have been handed down from past ages in China and foreign countries, but the aim must still be to serve the masses of the people." Mme. Mao was insistent on reinforcing this doctrine, and composers today are still faced with it. Wu said that his new work was an attempt to fuse the styles of East and West. "We want to learn and absorb from the West," he said, "but we also want to develop our own music."

Li agreed. He said that at present Chinese music could not be too complicated. If it were, it would not be understood by the masses. "Later on, perhaps, we shall find our own language. Right now we are looking for the way." He said that much Chinese music currently being composed was frankly experimental. It had to fulfill the conditions of Mao thought, and there was much discussion about how to go about that. "We wish to express our life and aspirations in music. We have the task of educating and uniting the people." Which is good Maoist doctrine, and also good Leninism.

If any of this sounds familiar, one has only to think of Soviet doctrine about the arts. Cultural Maoism and the Zhdanov ideology of 1948 lie side by side, in the same bed and covered by the same Leninist blanket. But look what has happened to

Russian music. Perhaps the Chinese will find a way out of the impasse, but if they do it will take many years and an unprecedented change in the approved ideology.

SEPT. 23, 1973

The afternoon after this piece was published, I found a telephone message on my desk. Call Admiral Hyman Rickover. I called the number, identified myself and the Admiral got on the phone. "Oh, yes," he growled. "Damn good piece on elitism, that," and hung up. Then I started worrying. Did he get the central point of my argument, or was he thinking in terms of the Ubermensch? *I still don't know. Elitism can be a dangerous and two-edged term. Yet, as I say, all of the great thoughts of man in any field are almost by definition elitist, even if they come from somebody as wretched as François Villon, as mean and venomous a racist as Richard Wagner, as humble as Anton Bruckner. Elitism of the mind is one of the few things of enduring value in the world.*

Elitism, in the Arts, Is Good

WE'VE BEEN hearing quite a bit about elitism these days, much of it stemming from the Washington offices of Senator Claiborne Pell. The National Endowment for the Humanities, he indicates, has been wasting its money supporting intellectuals in projects that do not benefit most of the people. Senator Pell would like a broader base of operations, with moneys disbursed to state arts groups. Already he has the new heads of the National Endowment for the Humanities and the National Endowment of the Arts running scared. Each has promised no letdown in quality, but they disavow "elitism" and murmur comforting phrases in the direction of the important senator.

This may be good politics, and the yahoos in America will applaud. But it could be death for the health of the arts in this country. Intellectual activity, of which the arts is one manifestation, is and always has been elitist. Demagogues and yahoos do not like this; they would like to drag us down to their own level. We live, after all, in democratic America, where all men are created equal. But surely the Founding Fathers did not expect that phrase to be taken literally. They meant that all men are created entitled to equal rights, which is a different proposition entirely.

For all men are not created equal, and the Founding Fathers, a group of elitists themselves, knew this perfectly well. If all men were created equal, all of us would be Newtons, Einsteins, Beethovens or Rembrandts. Genius is a rare commodity, and the percentage of geniuses who add something permanent to human knowledge and the enhancement of life is rarer still. The few men and women in history who have managed to do this are mankind's true elitists, probably our only ones. Through them, and them only, we progress. Through them, and them only, we are capable of growth.

The arts always have been an elitist manifestation. Great art always has been the product of a mind working alone, thinking as no previous mind has done, arriving at concepts that through the centuries still amaze and startle. The great creators work on a rarefied, elite level, and those of us less gifted can only stand off in awe and—yes—worship. All we can do is aspire to enter, as closely as we can, into the mind of the creator, trying to identify with his body of work, hanging onto him when he makes those quantum jumps. It is a humbling and at the same time ennobling process; the mind of genius is never easy to enter, but the rewards are infinite if one devotes the time and effort.

It is a lifetime process, and not many are willing to make that effort. Just as there are relatively few geniuses at any time, so there are relatively few appreciators in the best sense of the word. On its highest level the appreciation of art is as elitist as the creation of art. Those listening to a Beethoven symphony, content merely to let the music wash over them, are operating at a very low level. It is necessary, for the music to mean something more than a collection of pleasant sounds, to know something about the composer, his place in history, the place of a particular work in his total output, the place of the total output in relation to the music of the time, the technique of composition, the technique of performance. So many things; and so few of us come near a full understanding.

Thus, there is a positive danger in the attitude that disparages the intellectual elite. Elitism of the intellect should be a term of praise rather than disparagement. But the word itself is an unfortunate one that has too many bad associations. There is a tendency, when the word "elite" is mentioned, automatically to equate it with a moneyed elite, or an elite that comes only from birth or high political position. That washes off into the intellectual elite, making any form of elitism "bad" or "undemocratic."

We cannot afford to let such ideas take over. If the Government is going to try to foster some kind of healthy ambience for the arts and for scholarship in America—as it has been doing now for some ten years—it should not play politics. On the contrary, it should redouble its efforts to help the so-called "elitist" organizations, for from them much of the important work comes. Indeed, it could be argued that in the arts (forgetting science and humanities for the moment) it is more important to help the big established institutions—the symphony orchestras and opera houses, the repertory drama and ballet companies— than the individual creator.

Major creative talents have a way of finding their own level, but in our economic system the organizations that bring art to those who want it are hard pressed by inflation, rising costs and the like. Many of them are actually in imminent danger of going out of business. Nowadays their major efforts are more concerned with mere existence rather than artistic policy. An organization like the Metropolitan Opera, faced with an ever-increasing deficit, finds its economic woes impinging on its repertory; it simply cannot take a chance with operas that will not consistently draw a 90-plus audience percentage.

It is not only the Metropolitan Opera. Cultural organizations throughout the country are faced with much the same problem. And yet there are those who would take large amounts of government money and spend it on such idiotic projects as programs for street dancing or semi-amateur theatricals or some kind of boondoggle that will delight the heart of *nykulturny* local politicians. All it does is expose audiences to bad art; and if it be said that audiences at all times have been exposed to bad art, there still seems no compelling reason why *our* money should go to foster it.

What is needed is a thorough examination of our priorities. If, for instance, we want to create a culturally literate American audience, we have to look at the inadequacies of the education of American children, who by and large grow up culturally deprived. Children have to be exposed to the arts as a natural process of life. That means constant exposure. It does absolutely no good to send a group of children to a museum once a year or to some kind of condescending "youth concert." Listening to music or looking at a painting demands as much knowledge and concentrated effort as any of the three R's. Money on the local, state and Federal levels must be diverted into long-range and consistently applied cultural programs for the young if they are going to grow up with any feeling for the arts. Only a few of the lucky ones get it at home.

Similarly, if we want any kind of cultural sophistication among the adult population, we must fund the service organizations. One desirable program would be a series of concerts (symphony, chamber, whatever) on the very highest level and at much lower ticket prices. The great orchestras and important opera houses of the country should be devoting at least some of their season to nonsubscription performances at, say, a three-dollar top, those events funded by Government money. That, perhaps, might even take the horror off the word "elitism." This kind of project might conceivably be more important than giving money to tenth-rate creators for works of art that will die as soon as they are born. In any case, if there is a climate in which the arts can flourish, the creators will benefit thereby, and the important ones will flourish, too. So will the interpreters of art.

But we will never arrive at that point if art is diffused into a vague mass medium without standards. Nor will we arrive at that point if attacks are made against the only things that really count: the important creators (the elitists, if you will) and the important organizations that bring the work of the creators of past and present to the public under the most favorable conditions. Without them there is nothing.

FEB. 5, 1978

Envoi

Many such things, much more could I say,
But that for provender my cattle stay,
The sun declines, and I must needs away.
                              —Juvenal

I am not given much to self-analysis, but as I look back on it all, I think I can explain the low profile I have maintained through the years. Subconsciously, I think, I did not want to rock the boat—*my* boat. Suppose the editors of *The New York Times* suddenly realized that they were paying me for so pleasant a pursuit as going to concerts and writing about them? It should have operated the other way around. *I* should have been paying *them*. This was no real job; at least, through the years, I was never conscious of working. The hours spent in preparation, in reading and studying, were not work. They were a pleasure. Perhaps if the editors and the world at large realized it, something terrible would happen. I would be a millipede exposed to the sun, facing certain death. So I quietly went my way, bowing three times to the East every morning for my good luck.

What has it added up to, this happy life of daily reviews and Sunday pieces? I don't exactly know. Maybe I have helped some music lovers broaden their frame of reference. Maybe I have helped launch a career or two. Maybe I have had some influence

in helping performers break away from sterile literalism. Maybe
I have been partly responsible for the Romantic revival. Maybe
I have acted as a corrective against the modern music lobby
during the wild postwar days of international serialism. Maybe
I have written some pieces that have amused or entertained my
readers. Maybe the occasional performer has taken one or two
of my words to heart. Maybe, in my discussions of certain es-
teemed musical figures, I was correct in pointing out that the
emperor had no clothes. All I can say for certainty is that I have
had a wonderful life, happily doing the thing I love best to do,
and doing it for what is generally conceded to be the greatest
newspaper in the world.

New York
August 11, 1980

Index